JOYCE’S LOVE STORIES

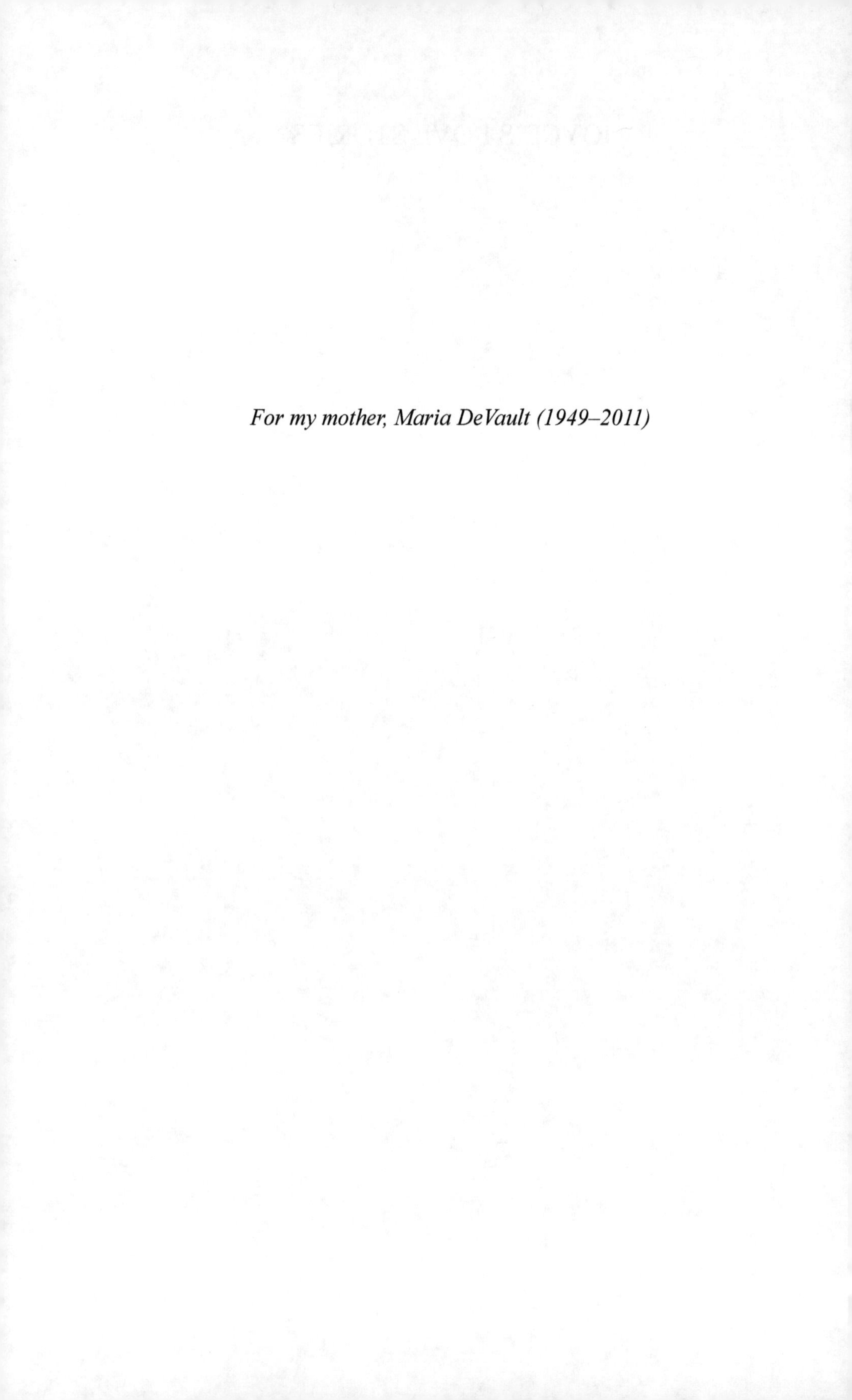

For my mother, Maria DeVault (1949–2011)

Joyce's Love Stories

CHRISTOPHER DEVAULT
Mount Mercy University, USA

LONDON AND NEW YORK

First published 2013 by Ashgate Publishing

2 Park Square, Milton Park, Abingdon, Oxon OX14 4RN
711 Third Avenue, New York, NY 10017, USA

Routledge is an imprint of the Taylor & Francis Group, an informa business

First issued in paperback 2016

British Library Cataloguing in Publication Data
DeVault, Christopher.
Joyce's love stories.
1. Joyce, James, 1882–1941 – Criticism and interpretation. 2. Love in literature. 3. Narcissism in literature.
I. Title
823.9'12-dc23

The Library of Congress has cataloged the printed edition as follows:
DeVault, Christopher.
Joyce's Love Stories / by Christopher DeVault.
pages cm
Includes bibliographical references and index.
ISBN 978-1-4094-4276-9 (hardcover: alk. paper)
1. Joyce, James, 1882–1941—Criticism and interpretation. 2. Love in literature. I. Title.
PR6019.O9Z52965 2013
823'.912—dc23

2012044682

ISBN 978-1-4094-4276-9 (hbk)
ISBN 978-1-138-25046-8 (pbk)

Contents

Acknowledgements

I cannot begin to thank Patrick A. McCarthy for his support throughout the completion of *Joyce's Love Stories*, particularly his patience in reading multiple drafts of every chapter and his invaluable suggestions about developing and revising the book manuscript. I would also like to thank Zack Bowen, Margot Norris, John Paul Russo, and Tim Watson for their insightful comments about each draft of the project and for their support throughout the entire process.

I was also fortunate to receive institutional support from Mount Mercy University, who granted me two summer scholarship stipends to revise the manuscript into a publishable book. I am grateful to Mount Mercy for its generous support of my work.

Chapter 1 on "A Painful Case" was originally published as an article, "Love and Socialism in 'A Painful Case': A Buberian Reading," in the Spring 2010 edition of *College Literature* (37.2). I would like to thank *College Literature* for allowing me to reproduce this essay in *Joyce's Love Stories*, and I also wish to thank my anonymous reader at *College Literature*, whose comments about the essay significantly helped me strengthen my analysis of "A Painful Case" for the project.

I am indebted to my editor at Ashgate, Ann Donahue, for her support of my book and for her helpful assistance throughout the publication process. I am also grateful to my anonymous reader at Ashgate, whose indispensable suggestions substantially helped me refine significant parts of my argument.

Finally, I would like to thank my family for their love and support throughout my academic career. I especially want to thank my wife Ann for her encouragement, patience, and optimism during the writing and publication of my book, and I am eternally indebted to my mother Maria, whose lifetime of love and sacrifice is the source of whatever success has come my way.

List of Abbreviations

D	*Dubliners*. New York: Penguin Books, 1992. Print.
E	*Exiles*. New York: Viking Press, 1961. Print.
FW	*Finnegans Wake*. New York: Penguin Books, 1999. Print.
G	*Giacomo Joyce*. London: Faber and Faber, 1968. Print.
JJ	Richard Ellmann. *James Joyce: New and Revised Edition*. Oxford: Oxford University Press, 1982. Print.
LI	*Letters of James Joyce*. Volume 1. Ed. Stuart Gilbert. New York: Viking Press, 1957. Print.
LII	*Letters of James Joyce*. Volume 2. Ed. Richard Ellmann. New York: Viking Press, 1966. Print.
P	*A Portrait of the Artist as a Young Man*. New York: Penguin Books, 1992. Print.
SH	*Stephen Hero*. Ed. Theodore Spencer. New York: New Directions Books, 1944. Print.
U	*Ulysses*. Ed. Hans Walter Gabler. New York: Vintage Books, 1986. Print.

Passages from *Ulysses* are identified by episode and line number. Quotations from *Finnegans Wake* are referenced by page number and line number.

Introduction

At the end of *A Portrait of the Artist as a Young Man*, a departing Stephen Dedalus recalls his mother's "pray[er] … that I may learn in my own life and away from home and friends what the heart is and what it feels." Stephen, now fully committed to his individual aesthetics, chooses instead to "encounter for the millionth time the reality of experience and to forge in the smithy of my soul the uncreated conscience of my race" (*P* 275–6). *Ulysses* may demonstrate Stephen's failure to accomplish these goals, but his author succeeds in "forg[ing]" this Irish "conscience" largely because James Joyce recognizes the importance of May Dedalus's "pray[er]" in fulfilling her son's prophetic calling. Indeed, Joyce frequently ties the efficacy of his characters' social and political pursuits to their knowledge of "what the heart is and what it feels," as their capacity to love directly determines their ability to interact productively within Ireland. While the majority of his protagonists can neither love nor engage their community effectively, Joyce's depiction of Leopold Bloom compellingly shows how the affection that pervades personal relationships can empathetically guide social encounters and challenge the paralysis he attributes to everyday Dublin. By highlighting this intersection between the "heart" and the "smithy of [one's] soul," we see a love ethic emerge that extends throughout the Joycean oeuvre and promotes a loving model of civic dialogue over what Joyce called the "old pap of racial hatred" (*LII* 167).

This love ethic has largely been ignored by the scholarly literature on Joyce's works because his amorous episodes are not usually taken at face value, and with good reason. Given his observations that "it seems to me that a lot of this talk about love is nonsense" (*LII* 192) and "when I hear the word 'love' I feel like puking" (qtd in *JJ* 631fn), to assert the existence of a love ethic within his works seems to taint them with an incongruous and misguided sentimentality. Joyce's criticism of the "lying drivel about pure men and pure women and spiritual love and love for ever" is legendary, as his characterization of these romantic invocations as "blatant lying in the face of the truth" ties such advocacies of love to the conventional sexual morality against which his literature mounts a direct assault (*LII* 191–2).[1] For this reason, most scholarly analysis on love and Joyce has either qualified amorous representations as ironic gestures or reserved an earnest advocacy of love for the later writings of an older and more mature author.[2] Although some scholars

[1] Mary Colum similarly notes Joyce's "sinister way of commenting on that emotion called romantic love. 'What they call love,' he would say argumentatively, 'is merely a temptation of nature in one's youth'" (398).

[2] For example, Richard Brown argues that "for Joyce … love was by no means such a positive term," using Stephen Daedalus's interactions with Emma Clery in *Stephen Hero* to assert that "for Joyce … romance, both in the mythologizing of the Byronic poet lover (*SH* 37) and in Emma's chaste holding back (*SH* 215), is a 'burgher' or bourgeois notion" (31). John Gordon describes readings of "love's adequacy" as the "key" to *Ulysses* as

have sought to highlight the amorous significance of Joyce's writing, their analyses are mostly limited to *Ulysses*, arguing that Hans Walter Gabler's restoration of the infamous "love" passage in the "Scylla and Charybdis" chapter compels us to recognize that "the theme of love … pervade[s]" Joyce's landmark text (Ellmann "Big Word" par. 12).[3] Given the widespread dismissal of love in Joyce and the limited scope of the challenges to that dismissal, my desire to locate an earnest, ethical endorsement of love throughout the Joycean oeuvre might seem like a naïve, unproductive examination of nonexistent romance initiated by one of "the kind of people who want 'love' to be the answer to everything" (Goldman 18).

While this hesitation is certainly understandable and the justification is persuasive, I believe that we should resist Joyce's suggestion that "it is useless to talk about this any further" (*LII* 192). Instead, to understand the role that love plays in Joyce's works, we should look at the context for his repulsion towards romance to determine the specific foundations of his objections. When we undertake this analysis, we see that Joyce's "sinister … comment[ary]" on "romantic love" is primarily driven by his rejection of the Catholic marriage sacrament instead of the idea of love itself.[4] Indeed, the November 13, 1906 letter to his brother Stanislaus that is the source of most of his amatory quips[5] is largely an attack on the conventional sexual morality of Catholic Ireland, as the "lying drivel about pure men and pure women and spiritual love and love for ever" primarily describes the sexual "purity" of Francis Skeffington and his contemporaries, and the main

"similarly dubious, due to Stephen's history and the word's debasement in the adult world" ("Love" 243). Even Richard Ellmann, perhaps the most prominent advocate of love in Joyce's works, recognizes that the author "never uses the word 'love' without tension … In his personal life, he was also chary of it" ("Crux" 29).

[3] Richard K. Cross's analysis of Joyce and Malcolm Lowry similarly contends, "That [*Ulysses* and *Under the Volcano*] hinge on the issue of love, broadly construed, can scarcely be doubted" (64). Ruth Bauerle also notes that "the central position of love shown here does add, however, to my own personal belief that Joyce's Ulysses is as Luciano Pavarotti once remarked on television of opera, 'all about love'" ("Love" 817).

[4] Joyce's religious rejection of marriage is well-documented. Stanislaus Joyce describes the "cold scorn" that Joyce "poured" on the "sexual morality" behind marriage, writing that "to make the heavy burden of marriage the exorbitant price of coition was, in his view, to sow the seeds of discord, while at the same time it debased what might be a franker and freer relationship between men and women" (155). Maria Jolas also notes that "in the case of Joyce and Nora … Joyce was against marriage. That was an intellectual attitude of his" (qtd in Dillon 46).

[5] In my analysis of love, I make a distinction between the terms "amatory," which the Oxford English Dictionary defines as "Of or pertaining to a lover, to love-making, or to sexual love generally" (380), and "amorous," which it defines as "Loving, affectionate, devoted, ardent" (410). I use "amatory" to describe the abstract, physical longings of narcissistic desire at the heart of Joyce's condemnation of love (i.e., the "amatory freedom" and "amatory aesthetics" I attribute to Stephen Dedalus), whereas I use "amorous" to describe the reciprocal affirmation of otherness advocated by Martin Buber and found in Joyce's characterizations of Leopold and Molly Bloom.

reason Joyce gives for "a lot of this talk about love [being] nonsense" concerns the domestic instability of the traditional Irish Catholic marriage.[6] When we take this into account, it becomes harder to view Joyce's skepticism as a totalizing rejection of love, as the anti-marital foundations for his most notorious barbs force us to qualify his objections and consider his reactions to forms of love that were not tied exclusively to the sacrament.

Additionally, the suffocating sentimentality that pervades traditional expressions of love and marriage serves as a significant impetus for Joyce's amatory "nausea." This revulsion is clearly evident in Joyce's characterization of "love for ever" as "blatant lying in the face of the truth," and Stanislaus's observation that Joyce abandoned love poetry because he could not play the sentimentalist demonstrates his rejection of maudlin romantic schlock. ("My brother was beginning to realize that he was not made of the proper stuff to be a lover, because he was not a sentimentalist" [151].)[7] Also, when we note that Joyce's "contempt for sentimentality was in great part instinctive aversion to what he regarded as a clownish idealization of lust—a remnant, this, of earlier piety" (S. Joyce 153–4), we see that sentimental romance and marriage are not simply two forms of love that Joyce rejected. Rather, Joyce's derision of sentimentality is shown to be another component of his assault on Catholicism, as he equates the "clownish idealization of lust" with the pious sexual morality that he famously castigates as "lying drivel." Joyce may "feel like puking" over the thought of romance, but the sentiment that compels his nausea is limited to a conception of "true love" that primarily validates the moral teachings of the Catholic church, not a totalizing rejection of all forms of love.

Moreover, even if contextualizing Joyce's objections fails to convince us that he did not dismiss all forms of love, the author's committed familial affection complicates our ability to justify this dismissal. Joyce clearly refused religious notions of romantic piety, but his lifelong devotion to Nora Barnacle makes it difficult to attribute a totalizing rejection of love to the author. Critics frequently cite the author's "You ask me why I don't love you" letter to Nora as evidence of his hesitancy towards speaking the language of love (*LII* 55), but as we examine Joyce's subsequent correspondence with Nora, we witness his growing comfort with articulating his amorous passion for her. Joyce may qualify his feelings for Nora in that famous September 19, 1904 letter ("You ask me why I don't love you but surely you must believe I am very fond of you and if to desire to possess a person wholly, to admire and honour that person deeply, and to see to secure that person's happiness in every way is to 'love' then perhaps my affection for

---

[6] This critique of Catholic marriage is also the context of the quotations from *Stephen Hero* that Brown cites to support his contention that "for Joyce, as we have seen already, love was by no means such a positive term."

[7] Ellmann also notes that a primary reason why Joyce was skeptical towards love was that "no one knew better than he how quickly a mention of it could become sentimental" ("Crux" 29).

you is a kind of love" [*LII* 55]), but only a few days later he would tell J.F. Byrne that "there's not another girl in the world I could ever love as I do Nora" (148), and he would admit to Stanislaus in a February 7, 1905 letter that "I admire her and I love her and I trust her" (*LII* 80). Additionally, when we note that Joyce remained emotionally devoted to her throughout their thirty-six years together, we see Joyce's enduring love for Nora even if he had intellectual misgivings about the language.[8] Thus, although Joyce may criticize sentimental depictions of romantic purity, his personal and professional lives rest upon a continued affirmation of Nora that demonstrates a passion more authentic than the sappy love stories that he derided.

Therefore, before we can examine the earnestness of Joycean love, we should step back and ask ourselves what form of love we are dealing with. If love refers simply to the eternal pledge of devotion under the Catholic marriage sacrament, then the Joycean critique of love has merit. However, if we expand our definition to encompass the affirmation of a beloved other, then Joyce's antagonistic attitude becomes less clear. Indeed, Janine Utell's *James Joyce and the Revolt of Love* has recently posited the legitimacy of a Joycean love ethic, arguing that "marriage – and its dark margin, adultery – becomes a site … for grappling with, confronting, facing, and ultimately recognizing the other." Her Levinasian examination of marriage "from *Exiles* and *Giacomo Joyce* to *Ulysses* and *Finnegans Wake*" compellingly demonstrates that "adultery in Joyce's texts highlights the impossibility of complete oneness, while also highlighting the ethical necessity of acknowledging that impossibility," which transforms marriage into "the crucible in which Joyce formulates a conception of ethical love" (2). Utell has thus initiated a shift away from the traditional dismissals of love in Joyce's works and laid the groundwork for the amorous analyses of the Joycean oeuvre that are needed to grasp its full ethical and political potential.

Joyce's Love Stories aims to develop this consideration of Joyce's love ethic by reading his works with respect to Martin Buber's interpretation of love as the "affirmation of *otherness*" (M. Friedman *Life* 79). In so doing, I argue that we should expand our understanding of Joycean love to consider the everyday amorous relationships between individuals that extend beyond marital or sexual desire. While this study will certainly consider romantic relationships as a key component of Joyce's love ethic, recognizing that Joyce's treatment of love also examines the ethical responsibilities of individuals, artists, and citizens reveals that amorous sentiment is neither derided by Joyce nor solely confined to his later works, but is present as early as *Dubliners* and spreads throughout the Joycean oeuvre. To undertake this investigation better enables us to witness the full extent of the author's love ethic, highlighting the true love of others over the narcissistic desire of the self and enabling a more dialogic form of socio-political interaction that embraces the compassion and solidarity needed for progressive politics.

[8] "His life showed that he was capable of loving one woman, and as long as I knew him he took no kind of real interest, least of all emotional or intellectual interest, in any other" (S. Joyce 153).

The Vital Acknowledgement of Many-Faced Otherness

Buber's writings are the perfect starting point for this investigation because they promote reciprocal, equal relations between individuals as necessary to affirm otherness in the face of alienation and discrimination. To highlight this reciprocity, Buber isolates two conflicting forms of human relationships: I-You[9] ("the world of relation") and I-It ("the world of experience") (*Thou* 56). Whereas the I-You relationship focuses on the mutual acceptance of the two individuals involved, the I-It relationship emerges from the subject's perception of their partner as either an object for examination or a mirror to reflect their own grandeur:

> The I of the basic word I-You is different from that of the basic word I-It. The I of the basic word I-It appears as an ego and becomes conscious of itself as a subject (of experience and use). The I of the basic word I-You appears as a person and becomes conscious of itself as subjectivity (without any dependent genitive). Egos appear by setting themselves apart from other egos. Persons appear by entering into relation with other persons. (*Thou* 111–2)

This distinction foregrounds the I's relationship with the other as the foundation for authentic existence. Even though Buber acknowledges that the I-It world is necessary for human life (since the subject needs to make use of objects to ensure their physical survival), a primary reliance on I-It relationships is problematic because it fails to perceive the other as anything other than an object of inquiry or a means to an end. While the subject of the I-You relationship turns to and affirms the other with their entire being, the subject of the I-It relationship turns away from and imposes barriers between themselves and their counterpart. This distant lens of perception reduces the other to a disposable commodity and denies both parties access to meaningful, reciprocal interaction within their particular social realm, thus alienating the participants from each other and from their surroundings. As Buber argues, "Without It a human being cannot live. But whoever lives only with that is not human" (*Thou* 85).

This distinction between I-You and I-It lays the groundwork for Buber's advocacy of genuine dialogue between individuals. Similar to his distinctions between the two "basic word[s]," Buber distinguishes between dialogue, in which two individuals turn towards and affirm each other with their whole being, and monologue, in which individuals' obsession with their own survival prevents them from confirming others as unique from themselves. He argues:

> To be aware of a man, therefore, means in particular to perceive his wholeness as a person determined by the spirit; it means to perceive the dynamic centre which stamps his every utterance, action, and attitude with the recognizable sign of uniqueness. Such an awareness is impossible, however, if and so long as the other is the separated object of my contemplation or even observation, for this

9 Buber actually characterized the I-You relationship as I-Thou, but the edition of *I and Thou* used for this study translates "Ich-Du" as "I-You," so that translation will be used.

> wholeness and its centre do not let themselves be known to contemplation or observation. It is only possible when I step into an elemental relation with the other, that is, when he becomes present to me. (*Knowledge* 70)

Buber thus argues that the foundation of "genuine conversation, and therefore every actual fulfillment of relation between men" is the "acceptance of otherness," that subjects can recognize and affirm others as unique and complete people even when they acknowledge disagreements or conflicts between them (*Knowledge* 59). In contrast to monologists (who either reject those who think differently than they do or reshape their difference into a confirmation of themselves), dialogists "affirm the person [they] struggle with," resisting the temptation to transform others into reflections of themselves and instead "confirm[ing them] as creature and as creation" (*Knowledge* 69). The performance of the I-You relationship through genuine dialogue thus provides a practical method for authentic interaction among individuals, a form of everyday social communication in which "the elemental otherness of the other [is] not merely noted as the necessary starting point, but is affirmed from the one being to the other" (*Knowledge* 59).

The ethical benefits of Buber's dialogism are most evident and persuasive in his reflections on love and desire. In this realm, the struggle between I-You and I-It manifests itself through a conflict between the love of others and a narcissistic desire that Buber dismisses as "the lover's delight in the possibilities of his own person" (*Man* 5). According to him, "Love does not cling to an I, as if the You were merely its 'content' or object; it is between I and You. Whoever does not know this, know this with his being, does not know love" (*Thou* 66). In contrast to the narcissistic "kingdom of the lame-winged Eros," full of "mirrors and mirroring,"[10] in authentic amorous encounters, "there is no mirroring. For there I, the lover, turn to this other human being, the beloved, in his otherness, his independence, his self-reality, and turn to him with all the power of intention of my own heart … I do not assimilate into my own soul that which lives and faces me, I vow it faithfully to myself and myself to it" (*Man* 29). This comparison foregrounds the recognition of the loved one's being and a confirmation of their otherness as a precondition for true love. In contrast to the narcissistic tendency to use the love object as a mirror to reflect the lover's grandeur, love entails the "responsibility of an I for a You," a "vow" that establishes an equal, reciprocal connection between two people based upon "the equality of all lovers" (*Thou* 66). Love is thus shown to be a vital form

---

[10] Gilya Gerda Schmidt explicitly articulates Buber's rejection of narcissism, identifying the "narcissistic personality" as "the major impediment to the formation of the type of personality and community he envisioned" and labeling this "self-interest" as "nauseating because it bore no consideration for anything but one's own concerns, with no thought for the needs of the community" (68). Jeffrey Rubin, while not referring to Buber specifically, similarly recognizes that "love does not live when we conceive of the other narcissistically," contending that "relating to others in terms of what the person does or does not offer the self inhibits mutuality. Extreme self-investment can render the other invisible" (52).

of dialogism, as the affirmation of the beloved's otherness establishes a mutual bond not between a lover and their love object, but between two equal lovers who confirm each other with their entire hearts. Buber may not conclude that dialogism and love are synonymous, but he rejects "love without dialogic, without real outgoing to the other, reaching to the other, and companying with the other," branding this narcissistic "love remaining with itself" as "Lucifer" (*Man* 21).

However, the implications of this amorous dialogism are not limited to the specific relationships between individuals. In fact, Buber argues that the affirmation of the beloved's unique being that arises from this dialogue enables its participants to embrace otherness on a broader scale, which carries with it progressive political possibilities:

> I wish his otherness to exist, because I wish his particular being to exist. That is the basic principle of marriage and from this basis it leads, if it is real marriage, to insight into the right and the legitimacy of otherness and to that vital acknowledgment of many-faced otherness—even in the contradiction and conflict with it—from which dealings with the body politic receive their religious ethos. (*Man* 61)[11]

Thus, the acceptance of the loved one's otherness translates into a general acceptance of otherness that can undo the socio-political boundaries that alienate individuals from each other. By allowing the affirmation of others to shape our social interactions, the dialogic nature of true love transforms the body politic into Buber's idea of "community," which he defines as the "genuine living together of men of similar or of complementary natures but of differing minds" and the "overcoming of *otherness* in living unity" (*Pointing* 102). In contrast to the enforced conformity of the crowd, the "living unity" of the community enables difference to flourish among socio-political agents who constantly "affirm the [people they] struggle with," which makes the loving embrace of otherness the vital foundation for this civic dialogue.

Additionally, love is essential to promote Buber's community because the intensity of such relationships opens up the socio-political arena to an engagement with otherness that is more akin to affirmation than mere tolerance. Buber argues:

> The question is not one of exercising 'tolerance,' but of making present the roots of community and its ramifications ... It is not a question of a formal apparent understanding on a minimal basis, but of an awareness from the other side of

[11] One could argue that Joyce would reject this endorsement of love because it uses marriage as the central metaphor by which love transcends the personal realm. However, not only do Joyce's strongest endorsements of love emerge from the Bloom and Earwicker/Plurabelle marriages, but my readings of Joyce's love stories will also argue that the affirmation of otherness plays a vital role in the success of both the relationships and the socio-political interactions of his lovers. Thus, even though he explicitly rejects the sacrament of marriage, Joyce frequently affirms what Buber refers to as the "basic principle of marriage."

> the other's real relation to the truth. What is called for is not 'neutrality' but solidarity, a living answering for one another—and mutuality, living reciprocity. (*Pointing* 102)

Because the lover's "wish" for their beloved's "entire being to exist" constitutes an aggressive affirmation of otherness, the "vital acknowledgement of many-faced otherness" enabled by that "wish" provides the best opportunity for individuals within a given social arena to look past their political differences and forge the "solidarity" and "living reciprocity" that comprise Buber's community. Bell hooks confirms this potential for solidarity by noting love's ability to overcome the fear of difference that upholds authoritarian political structures:

> Fear is the primary force upholding structures of domination. It promotes the desire for separation, the desire not to be known. When we are taught that safety lies always with sameness, then difference, of any kind, will appear as a threat. When we choose to love we choose to move against fear—against alienation and separation. The choice to love is a choice to connect—to find ourselves in the other. (93)

Rather than promoting sameness and labeling difference as a threat to the body politic, love's endorsement of otherness compels individuals to relate to others not as ciphers or threats, but as legitimate political subjects, which dissolves the foundations of "structures of domination" and paves the way for more positive political engagement. In contrast to the "alienation and separation" of autocratic structures, a socio-political community shaped by love fosters compassion, solidarity, and "living reciprocity" between its members, replacing the alienation of repressive social systems with a more inclusive, accommodating method of civic interaction.

While the socio-political goals of this amorous dialogism may seem lofty, Buber's community is not a utopian fantasy. In fact, Buber rejects the notion that "his insistence on the power of relation to give meaning and direction to our lives" relegates him to the role of a "romantic optimist" (Moore 220), insisting that a dialogic engagement with otherness is a practically productive manner of improving everyday interactions between others.[12] Specifically, Buber's insistence on the temporality and impermanence of the I-You relationship demonstrates his refusal to advocate a fantastic, sentimental endorsement of true love as the

---

[12] Moore continues by emphasizing Buber's insistence that this charge of "romantic optimis[m]" is "quite false, for he never asserted that we can overcome our disharmony, the twofoldness of our attitude toward the world, simply through our own 'good will.' 'I am a realistic meliorist; for I mean and say that human life approaches its fulfillment, its redemption, in the measure that the I-Thou relation becomes strong in it'" (220). Laurence J. Silberstein similarly contends that "Buber eschewed all messianic hopes and identified himself as a meliorist. Acknowledging that we can never achieve an ideal society free from alienation, he insisted on a gradualist strategy in which we work toward creating greater opportunities for genuine dialogue and community" (185).

guaranteed solution to the world's evils. Whereas Joyce rejected the "lying drivel" concerning "love for ever," Buber insists that such a state of amorous permanence is impossible, as the potential always exists for a You to regress into an It:

> Even love cannot persist in direct relation; it endures, but only in the alternation of actuality and latency. The human being who but now was unique and devoid of qualities, not at hand but only present, not experienceable, only touchable, has again become a He or She, an aggregate of qualities, a quantum with a shape. Now I can again abstract from him the color of his hair, of his speech, of his graciousness; but as long as I can do that he is my You no longer and not yet again. (*Thou* 68–9)

However, even though the I-You relation formed by an amorous encounter will inevitably fade away, the lover's ability to affirm their beloved's otherness is still valuable because "whatever has thus been changed into It and frozen into a thing among things is still endowed with the meaning and the destiny to change back ever again" (*Thou* 90). Because of this fluctuating nature of human relation, it is more important for lovers to maintain the capability to enter into amorous dialogues than it is for them to aspire to an ideal, perfect union since the continued ability to affirm the otherness of potential loved ones better prepares them to interact productively with the others they encounter.[13] Regardless of the outcome of specific relationships, the compassion and solidarity that occurs through loving dialogues allow "genuine communication" to be "actualized through the everyday relationships and occupations in which we are engaged" (Silberstein 179–80), enabling those who lovingly reach out to the other to "act, help, heal, educate, raise, [and] redeem" (*Thou* 66).

The Pale Passionless Beauty of a Pearl

Although Joyce explicitly derides the sentimental fantasy of true love, Buber's pragmatic endorsement of amorous dialogue provides an exemplary framework to read Joyce's writings, as the conflict between love and narcissism is a critical site for his critical examination of paralytic Dublin. Indeed, Buber's fascination "with the turbid, the repressed, the pedestrian, with toil and dull contraryness" complements Joyce's focus on the everyday, and his advocacy of dialogue as a means to counteract the "dully-tempered disagreeableness, obstinacy, and contraryness in which the man, whom I pluck at random out of the tumult, is living" coincides with the attempts by Joyce's characters to escape their stultifying situations (*Man* 36). Also, Joyce frequently highlights the need for reciprocal love, either through his early cautionary tales that highlight the pitfalls of rejecting otherness or through

[13] Maurice Freidman argues that "It would be a mistake to understand the 'ought' that arises out of this ethic to mean that one ought every moment to be in an I-Thou relationship, as if that were an ideal to aim for. The 'ought' that is asked of one is the *quantum satis* – what one is capable of at any moment" (*Eternal* 76).

the redemptive potential of Leopold and Molly Bloom's turn towards each other and the perpetual renegotiation of narcissism into dialogue in *Finnegans Wake*. This not only puts Joyce at odds with theorists like Jean Paul Sartre,[14] Simone de Beauvoir,[15] and Emmanuel Levinas,[16] who critique the viability of reciprocal love, but it also places him in line with Buber's advocacy of such reciprocal affirmations as the precondition of genuine dialogue. Thus, when we read Joyce's love stories as endorsing dialogic alternatives to everyday paralysis, we uncover the relationship between personal and socio-political love in his works that is at the foundation of Buber's construction of community, enabling us to see how the preoccupation with self-promotion inhibits the ability of Joyce's characters either to transcend their isolated existences or to reshape Ireland productively. For that reason, although Joyce would consider it "a mistake for you to imagine that my political opinions are those of a universal lover" in a May 1905 letter to Stanislaus (*LII* 89), his oeuvre elucidates the individual and political implications of the amorous choices his characters make, demonstrating how the capacity to love and affirm otherness is essential to improve the Dublin body politic.

In fact, when we evaluate Joyce's outlook on love with respect to his relationship with Nora, we see that his affection for her echoes Buber's call to turn lovingly towards the other. I have already noted that Joyce's relationship with Nora rendered him more comfortable with speaking the language of love, but his descriptions of the viability of their relationship also rely on I-You rhetoric that champions the reality of their amorous situation over an idealized romantic bliss. This is especially true in Joyce's August 21, 1909 letter to Nora, written four years after his dismissal of the "politic[s]" of "universal [love]" to Stanislaus and three years after his derision of the "lying drivel" of "love for ever." Here, his renewed affection for Nora after wrongly suspecting her of an affair with Vincent Cosgrave establishes a contrast between poetic and actual love that reveals the vitality of

---

[14] Sartre's view that humans are alienated from each other and view others as objects leads him to critique reciprocal love as "involv[ing a] self-defeating mutuality" that "must therefore involve an insurmountable contradiction within its very structure" since it derives from "an outgrowth of conflict and the mutual desire to possess other subjectivities" (Singer 296; 292).

[15] De Beauvoir's gendered reading of love similarly argues that the "reciprocity" of what she calls "'authentic love'" is "not possible today, because woman is not free economically and therefore she will be dependent on a man and hence at his mercy" (Leighton 79). She argues that "'The supreme goal of human love … is identification with the loved one,'" which causes the lover to be consumed by her beloved since her desire for his regard encourages her to sacrifice her identity to him to the point where "'when she questions herself, it is his reply she tries to hear'" (De Beauvoir qtd. in Leighton 78).

[16] Levinas's depiction of the self's infinite obligation to the Other precludes reciprocal love since the relationship between self and other is inherently asymmetrical, and thus reciprocal encounters would risk consuming the other into the self's reflection. While Levinas portrays "'Agape in terms of responsibility for the other,'" he privileges love that is "'originally without reciprocity, which would risk compromising its gratuitousness or grace or unconditional charity'" (qtd. in Beals 34).

their relationship. Initially, Joyce contemplates Nora's reaction to *Chamber Music*, noting that "when I wrote [those verses] I was a strange lonely boy, walking about by myself at night and thinking that some day a girl would love me" (*LII* 236–7). This description of young Joyce echoes Stephen's romantic quest for a fictitious, ideal Mercedes in the second chapter of *Portrait*, especially considering that his description of this hypothetical beloved as "a girl fashioned into a curious grave beauty by the culture of generations before her" represents the ideal muse of his youth as a hodgepodge of romantic and poetic clichés (*LII* 237). Thus, his subsequent recognition that "I never could speak to the girls I used to meet at houses" signifies his acknowledgment of the futility of chasing such romantic symbols (*LII* 237), as the attempts by young Joyce to "meet in the real world the unsubstantial image which his soul so constantly beheld" (*P* 67) lead him to girls that inevitably fall short of his ideal.

By contrast, Joyce recognizes that his love for Nora is based on a more realistic affection than the romantic musings of his youth. He explicitly acknowledges that "you were not in a sense the girl for whom I had dreamed and written the verses you find now so enchanting" (*LII* 237), and his subsequent declaration of affection for Nora reveals the extent to which their relationship overwhelms the amatory idealism that preceded it: "But then I saw that the beauty of your soul outshone that of my verses. There was something in you higher than anything I had put into them" (*LII* 237). This comparison between youthful and mature romance demonstrates Joyce's preference for an authentic affirmation of his beloved over the self-indulgent quests of his past. By noting that "there was something … higher" in Nora than in the muse that inspired *Chamber Music*, Joyce demonstrates both the vibrancy of his confirmation of his partner and the artificiality of the romantic archetypes that comprised his poetic longings (especially considering that this comparison immediately follows his recognition of his youthful muse's "fashion[ing] by the "culture of generations before her"). Thus, when Joyce proclaims that *Chamber Music* "holds the desire of my youth and you, darling, were the fulfillment of that desire" (*LII* 237), he shows how the maintenance of real-world love outweighs the pursuit of abstract ideals, as his juxtaposition of Nora's disparity with his youthful love objects with her role as the "fulfillment of [his] desire" promotes a practical foundation for his realization of their love.

This comparison between real-world love and abstract desire continues in Joyce's subsequent distinction between opals and pearls. As he continues to extol the vitality of his love for Nora, Joyce contrasts his youthful and present-day romances through the difference between pearls and opals, which allows him to promote the emotional power of the present over the passionless abstraction of the past:

> Do you know what a pearl is and what an opal is? My soul when you came sauntering to me first through those sweet summer evenings was beautiful but with the pale passionless beauty of a pearl. Your love has passed through me and now I feel my mind something like an opal, that is, full of strange uncertain hues and colours, of warm lights and quick shadows and of broken music. (*LII* 237)

This passage confirms Joyce's preference for the emotional warmth of real-world attachments over the hollow ardency of romantic idealism. The "pale passionless beauty of a pearl" represents the empty nature of a life spent chasing after fictitious love objects, as the desire to make the real world fit an abstract notion of ideal love and beauty necessarily robs that experience of any romantic energy. His description of his first meeting with Nora counteracts this "pale passionless beauty" because the spontaneity of their encounter forces him to relate to his future partner not as the next candidate for his ideal muse, but as an actual person whose warmth and love fill him with "strange uncertain hues and colours, [with] warm lights and quick shadows and [with] broken music." The fact that these "hues and colours" are "strange" and "uncertain" shows that Joyce's love for Nora emerges out of his affirmation of her otherness rather than her ability to fit his romantic ideal since his inability to classify the sensations that her affection instills in him shows his inability to explain his passion for his partner through a preconceived lens of ideal beauty. This both emphasizes the incongruence between his real-life love for Nora and the abstract, sentimental longings of his youth and demonstrates the authenticity of their relationship because Joyce enters into direct relation with Nora rather than classifying or explaining his love through the I-It world of experience. In that sense, Nora truly does become the "fulfillment of [his] desire," as the "love" that "passes through [him]" throughout their relationship unites Joyce and Nora in a mutual affirmation of otherness that brightens the "pale passionless beauty" of his past.

Joyce's adoration of Nora thus demonstrates that his characterization of "spiritual love" as "blatant lying in the face of the truth" is not a blanket rejection of love. To attribute such a totalizing refusal to Joyce ignores the evolution of his amorous feelings, as evidenced by his lifelong devotion to Nora and his understanding that his affection for her is based on an affirmation of her specific person that transcends the abstract romantic discourses of his youth. When we read Joyce's attitudes towards love with respect to Buber, we find that the author's romantic nausea is not provoked by all forms of love, but rather by the sentimental proclamations of abstract desire that he finds in his contemporaries' hollow platitudes, a narcissistic assimilation of otherness into preconceived notions of sexual morality that explicitly evokes Buber's "kingdom of the lame-winged Eros." In that sense, Joyce's devotion to Nora demonstrates Buber's contention that the potential for loving dialogue exists in our everyday interactions, as his ardent confirmation of her being establishes a real-world "inclusive Eros" that replaces the "passionless" nature of his Dublin existence with the mutual vibrancy of true love.

The Word Known to All Men

In an October 25, 1909 letter to Nora, Joyce writes that "I *know* and *feel* that if I am to write anything fine or noble in the future I shall do so only by listening at the doors of your heart" (*LII* 254). Taking this into account, it is unsurprising that a central conflict for many of Joyce's protagonists is their pursuit of love, as these characters frequently tie their personal and social happiness to their ability to attain the adoration that they desire. For an author who "feels like puking" at the thought of love, he writes about the subject extensively, and his narratives frequently demonstrate the futility of romantic passion that is not grounded in the affirmation of one's beloved. Indeed, when we acknowledge that Joyce's "fine" and "noble" works are brought about by "listening at the doors of [Nora's] heart" and that his post-1909 lovers would wrestle with the productivity of their amorous quests in an increasingly more nuanced manner than the narcissists of *Dubliners*, we see the extent to which the conflict between true love and narcissistic desire pervades the Joycean oeuvre, and the way that Joyce resolves this conflict articulates a consistent love ethic that demonstrates the ability of authentic expressions of love to counteract the alienation of everyday Dublin.

The most famous textual example of this conflict occurs in the notorious "love" passage in "Scylla and Charybdis." By reinserting this fragment into Stephen's Shakespeare lecture, Gabler provides us with the most direct comparison between love and narcissism in Joyce's works, as Stephen's meditation on Thomas Aquinas's *Summa Contra Gentiles* highlights the disparity between these competing desires and the implications of this conflict: "Do you know what you are talking about? Love, yes. Word known to all men. *Amor vero aliquid alicui nonum vult unde et ea quae concupiscimus*..." (*U* 9.429–30). Given that the Gabler text has become the standard edition of *Ulysses*, it does not accomplish much to rehash the arguments concerning his reinserting this passage at this time since my study is not dependent upon its legitimacy. Nor is it necessary to determine whether "love" is the definitive "word known to all men" since the comparison of love and narcissism would still exist within the Joycean oeuvre if the "word" were conclusively revealed to be "death,"[17] "yes,"[18] or any other alternative solution. What should call our attention to this passage is not simply Stephen's reference to "love" as the "word known to all men," but the fragments of the *Summa* that follow it.

Don Gifford and Robert J. Seidman translate these Aquinas passages to read:

> For if we understand or rejoice, it follows that we are referred somehow to some object: whereas LOVE WILLS SOMETHING TO SOMEONE, since we are said to love that to which we WILL SOME GOOD, in a way foresaid. Hence WHEN WE WANT A THING, we are said simply and properly to DESIRE IT, and not to love it, but rather to love ourselves for whom we want it. (221)[19]

---

[17] Richard J. Finneran argues that "despite the host of distinguished critics who have argued that 'the word known to all men' is love ... it seems clear that death must be the answer" (574).

[18] Cheryl Fox contends that "examining the ways in which 'love' and 'yes' are treated throughout the novel reveals the inappropriateness of 'love' as the word known to all men and the 'rightwiseness' of 'yes'" (799).

[19] Capitalization is Gifford and Seidman's and refers to the Aquinas fragments that Stephen utters in *Ulysses*.

This passage highlights the disparity between the love of self and the love of others that is at the heart of Buber's amorous writings. Whereas the willing of something for the good of another person is brought about by the lover's affection for that person, the desire for "thing[s]" is not brought about by any particular feelings for the object itself, but rather by its ability to advance the lover's personal goals.[20] That Aquinas distinguishes between the "love" of others and the "desire" for objects demonstrates the incompleteness of the latter yearning since whatever is being pursued (be it object or person) is emptied of its specific essence and relegated to a disposable commodity to fulfill one's narcissistic pursuit.[21] The Aquinas portions of the "love" passage thus become explicit textual examples of the conflict between narcissistic monologue and loving dialogue that pervades Joyce's writings, establishing an ethical framework to evaluate not simply *Ulysses*, but the author's oeuvre as a whole.

The power of the "Scylla" restoration as an indictment of narcissism is even more compelling considering that Joyce has Stephen articulate this comparison. As I will argue in later chapters, Stephen's pursuit of love throughout *Portrait*, *Stephen Hero*, and *Ulysses* is the embodiment of narcissistic desire, as his search for a love object whose adoration will provide him with artistic inspiration inhibits his ability to forge loving connections through his everyday interactions with others. It is thus significant that Stephen is the character who pursues the "word known to all men" throughout *Ulysses,* for his desire to find the real-world love object who will ease his loneliness by speaking the "word" to him echoes his quest to "meet in the real world the unsubstantial image which his soul so

---

20 Gifford and Seidman similarly read this passage as establishing the contrast between love and narcissism, writing that "Aquinas is distinguishing between 'True love [which] requires one to will another's good' and self love, which wills another's good primarily as conducive to one's own good" (221). Ellmann also notes that "Aquinas is distinguishing between love, which as he says in the first six words, 'genuinely wishes another's good,' and, in the next five, a selfish desire to secure our own pleasure 'on account of which we desire these things,' meaning lovelessly and for our own good, not another's" ("Preface" xii).

21 Jean Kimball reads the *Summa* fragments differently, arguing that Aquinas does not offer a comparison of love and narcissism. To her, "when he goes on to make a hierarchical distinction between amor amicitiae as the primary sense of love and amor concupiscentiae as the secondary sense, this distinction is between the love of someone and the love of something, not between the love of the other and the love of self, as it appears to be in the definition that he quotes from Aristotle" ("Death" 146). However, given that the "love of someone" could involve self-love as well as the love of others and that the "love of something" could encompass people as well as objects, the Aquinas passage could still be read as denigrating narcissism because self-love commodifies the love object by conceiving of them simply in terms of utility (especially considering that amatory narcissism is grounded in Buber's I-It relationship). In that case, the question becomes whether the beloved is treated as the "direct … object" of "amor amicitiae" or the "indirect object" of "amor concupiscentiae," a distinction that evokes the conflict between true love and narcissistic desire even if it is not explicitly mentioned in the *Summa.*

constantly beheld" that Joyce earlier dismissed as an empty, abstract endeavor. For that reason, when Stephen contemplates the Aquinas passage, we cannot help but associate those definitions of love with narcissistic desire because Stephen uses those *Summa* fragments to reassure himself of the legitimacy of his pursuit of the "word known to all men." Thus, the narcissism of Stephen's meditations manifests itself not only through the Aquinas passage, but through the manner in which that passage is deployed, which transforms these aspects of Stephen's lecture into the self-serving "contrapost" to both "Bloom's definition of love" and his loving interactions with others throughout Bloomsday (Gabler 17).

The narcissistic motivations behind Stephen's musings also help to explain the fragmented presentation of the Aquinas passage. As many have noted, Stephen pieces together individual words from the *Summa* to put forth an unintelligible presentation of Aquinas's amorous comparison. While some argue that the fragmented nature of this meditation prevents us from engaging the conflict between love and narcissism satisfactorily, the incompleteness of Stephen's thoughts actually amplifies the validity of this comparison. Even though Stephen's muddled Latin essentially says that "love wills something to someone" and that "when we want some good, we desire it," we cannot evaluate the Aquinas fragments without simultaneously recalling the portions that have been excluded (especially considering that Stephen's presentation of it ends with an ellipsis). Given that Stephen is using Aquinas's definitions of love to validate his search for the "word known to all men," to note that his justification for the pursuit is based on bits and pieces of Aquinas cobbled together shows how the young artist self-servingly reshapes the *Summa*'s comparison of love and narcissism into an abstract quotation that misses the point of the passage. Not only does this incompleteness highlight the self-absorbed and incomplete nature of Stephen's pursuit of the "word known to all men," but his inability to use this pursuit to persuade the audience of his lecture demonstrates the inevitable failure of the undertaking, as his abstract validation of ideal love falls short of improving his real-world situation.

This hollow nature of Stephen's undertaking is highlighted further by his interpretation of love as a "word known to all men." Regardless of whether love is a "truth universally acknowledged," Stephen certainly portrays it in this manner, representing love as a static emotion that is understood by everyone. This intellectual understanding of love inevitably falls short of fulfilling his desires for two reasons. First, by limiting its existence to a mere "word" instead of an actual relationship, it relegates Stephen's pursuit to an abstract form of love, which mitigates its real-world, emotional resonance.[22] Second, by defining love as a "word" that is "known," it confines amatory attachments to the I-It world of inquiry instead of the I-You world of relation, and the fact that this "word" is

---

[22] Henke argues that "Joyce might be suggesting, as well, that 'love' may simply be a 'word' and not a reality to the young, inexperienced and misogynist artist who 'knows' this ubiquitous monosyllable as a textual surface, a sign on the white field of a desiring consciousness, but not as a palpable and concrete experience" ("Reconstructing" 90).

"known" by "all men" arrests the vibrancy of amorous encounters in a totalizing definition of a universal experience. This static understanding of love prevents Stephen from recognizing and affirming the otherness of his potential love objects, which renders him incapable of either attaining the specific affection he desires or using love to advance his art. The "Scylla" restorations thus provide an explicit articulation of the comparison between love and narcissism not simply through the words that are quoted, but through the motivations of the speaker, and Stephen's failure to use the passage to advance his goals demonstrates how the obsession with self-advancement is ultimately self-defeating.

The legitimacy of the "love" passage's restoration may never be resolved satisfactorily, but such a resolution is not necessary to discover the prominence of love in Joyce's works. Even if Gabler never reinserted this passage into "Scylla," the disparate manners in which Stephen and Bloom seek the love they desire would still establish the comparison between narcissistic monologue and amorous dialogue at the heart of Buber's writings. This conflict plays itself out not just in *Ulysses*, but throughout the Joycean oeuvre, as the pursuit of love becomes a popular method for Joyce's characters to escape the humdrum nature of paralytic Dublin. However, the majority of these protagonists succumb to narcissistic desire by pursuing abstract symbols of ideal love whose attainment would mirror their self-worth, but whose inherent fictitiousness inevitably frustrates their quests. As we witness the downfalls of James Duffy, Gabriel Conroy, Stephen Dedalus, and Richard Rowan, we appreciate the dialogic acceptance of otherness behind Leopold and Molly Bloom's affection for each other and the perpetual renegotiation of love and narcissism in the scenes that cycle through the *Wakean* dreamer's subconscious, which enables Joyce's depictions of their relationship to demonstrate the personal and socio-political benefits of true love. Joyce may primarily portray narcissistic protagonists who fall short of escape and exile, but it is ultimately the lover who is able to survive productively in Dublin, and a Buberian investigation of Joycean love enables us to look past the threat of sentimental nausea to see how the capability to love can improve even the most paralytic of social conditions.

Chapter 1
Love and Socialism in "A Painful Case"

In "The Open Closet in *Dubliners*: James Duffy's Painful Case," Roberta Jackson challenges the narcissistic characterization of James Joyce's protagonist that has assumed the level of critical commonplace in *Dubliners* scholarship. Contextualizing the story within "the homophobic climate that existed in late-Victorian and Edwardian Britain" (88), Jackson contends that the traditional reading of "Duffy's isolation" as "a neurotic symptom in a man unable to give or receive love" relies on an assumption of his heterosexuality that is challenged throughout "A Painful Case" (90). Rather than reading him as a solipsistic loner who "denie[s] life and happiness" to Emily Sinico (*D* 113), she argues that "Duffy is trapped," that "his neuroticism arises from his necessary isolation and his need to distance himself from the homophobia of the patriarchy (90). By taking up Eve Kosofsky Sedgwick's suggestion that her queering of Henry James's "The Beast in the Jungle" would "work just as well—even better—for Joyce," Jackson highlights a potentially damning limitation of the narcissistic reading of Duffy (83):

> Sedgwick's observations on the limitations and rigidities of Jamesian criticism also apply to nearly all the criticism on "A Painful Case." She … not[es] that the "easy assumption (by James, the society, and the critics) that sexuality and heterosexuality are always exactly translatable into one another is, obviously, homophobic. Importantly, too, it is deeply heterophobic: it denies the very possibility of *difference* in desires, in objects." (86)

Jackson thus implicates traditional criticisms of "A Painful Case" in what Joseph Valente calls the "compulsory heterosexuality" of Joyce scholarship (1), perpetuating the primacy of heteronormativity by assuming Duffy's rejection of Mrs Sinico to be the refusal of a mutual, reciprocal sexual attraction. However, while she effectively highlights the dangers of automatically castigating Duffy as egotistical, Jackson's totalizing rejection of such narcissistic analyses precludes an ethical evaluation of his treatment of Mrs Sinico, which ignores her significance to the text and limits the critical potential of Joyce's story.

Margot Norris offers a similar examination of Duffy's sexuality; however, she does not completely disqualify consideration of his narcissism. Instead, her reading bolsters both Valente's characterization of Joyce criticism in general and Jackson's assessment of "A Painful Case" scholarship, while imposing an ethical demand upon future inhabitants of this critical path:

> In "A Painful Case" the discourse that constitutes "the closet" is the one that resolutely interprets Duffy's refusal of heterosexual love as volitional in specific registers of ethical culpability coded as egotism, narcissism, solipsism, and

> coldness. An ethical leap is required to imagine that Duffy's "hunger-strike against desire" (as Earl Ingersoll suggestively calls it [126]) could be prompted by a criminalized, prosecutable, and therefore frustrated and perhaps repressed desire for a same-sex object. This possibility does not readily *occur* to either the narrator or the reader, and it is this *not-occurring* that is precisely the epistemologically closeting gesture. (*Suspicious* 170)

Norris's reading accomplishes more than simply putting forth an analysis of Joyce's story that portrays Duffy as possibly homosexual; by focusing on the potential of this reading to occur to the reader and the critic, she constructs an ethical gateway around "A Painful Case" that forces scholars to reexamine their assumptions about the story's sexual politics before they can offer judgments of its characters.[1] Given the growing consideration of the role heterosexism may play in Duffy's alienation, Norris challenges readers to "take ethical responsibility for now imagining the thoughts and feelings of the possibly homosexual man" and critiques the insistence on "resolutely interpret[ing]" him narcissistically as risking "ethical incrimination in 'the epistemology of the closet'" (167;170). Thus, it is essential to determine whether the narcissistic reading of "A Painful Case" is inextricably complicit in an "epistemologically closeting gesture" or if it is possible to expose the ethically problematic nature of Duffy's actions even if they are brought about by societal repression.

Reading "A Painful Case" under a Buberian rubric of love enables a narcissistic interpretation of Duffy that does not perpetuate "the closet" because it compels us to evaluate his reactions to Mrs Sinico's otherness rather than the viability of a sexual relationship between them. Jackson's and Norris's interrogations are primarily compelling because the critical literature they question represents Duffy's and Mrs Sinico's interactions erotically, which necessarily foregrounds assumptions of his heterosexuality. Specifically, their focus on Duffy's aphorism that "love between man and man is impossible because there must not be sexual intercourse and friendship between man and woman is impossible because there must be sexual intercourse" complicates these scholarly attempts to rebuke his rejection of Mrs Sinico (*D* 108), inviting us instead to "imagine a homosexual Duffy ... consigned to a life without interlocution or dialogic possibility" (Norris *Suspicious* 168). Reading "A Painful Case" with respect to Buber provides an alternative to this "double-bind created for gay men" (Jackson 90) because his characterization of love as an "affirmation of *otherness*" enables Duffy to achieve dialogue without compromising his sexuality. For this reason, Duffy would not have to repress his sexuality to love Mrs Sinico because Buber's definition

---

[1] Colleen Lamos provides a compelling reading of Duffy that satisfies this ethical dilemma, arguing that "for Duffy, the foreclosure of same-sex love coincides with the foreclosure of other-sex love; he disavows *both* homosexuality and heterosexuality" (66). By contrast, I argue that what Duffy refuses is empathy or compassion of any kind, which transcends issues of sexual orientation and influences his interactions with others in both the personal and political realms.

imposes no sexual restrictions. Thus, by framing his rejection of Mrs Sinico in terms of empathy as well as sexual desire, we uncover a "neurotic" narcissism that springs from a homosexual Duffy's "necessary isolation" from the "homophobia of the patriarchy," which enables us to evaluate his actions even after we take Norris's "ethical leap."

Additionally, undertaking this examination reclaims Mrs Sinico's place in the text. Whereas narcissistic readings emphasize Duffy's desire for recognition and relegate Emily Sinico to the mirror of his self-image, queer readings prioritize Duffy's sexual alienation over his treatment of Mrs Sinico and reduce her to a "[stand-]in for the canonical critics who do not consider other possibilities for his behavior." (Jackson 92). Not only do these Duffy-centric interpretations reenact her erasure from the text, but in their rush to either excoriate or exonerate Duffy, they ignore Mrs Sinico's role as another lover in "A Painful Case" who is dismissed and alienated by her society. Mrs Sinico may not suffer the explicit persecution a homosexual Duffy would face, but Joyce similarly depicts her as "obliged to live utterly without interlocution or dialogic possibility," which makes her compassion and empathy throughout the text a striking contrast to Duffy's self-exile. Not only does she treat Duffy with kindness, but her encouragement that he "let his nature open to the full" constitutes a loving embrace that could counteract the personal and societal alienation of both characters (*D* 106). In fact, when we consider the political content of their conversations, Mrs Sinico's "almost maternal solicitude" becomes an invitation for Duffy to develop more productive relations not just with her, but with his fellow Dubliners (*D* 106), which makes his refusal of her a simultaneous rejection of his sociopolitical future. For this reason, retrieving Mrs Sinico's place in the text is essential for a productive evaluation of the continued ethical responsibilities of those who suffer societal alienation, and reading "A Painful Case" with respect to Buber's "vital acknowledgment of many-faced otherness" allows us to discover how the inability to negotiate the text's conflict between love and narcissism carries both personal and political consequences.

The Pupil's Deliberate Swoon

Joyce's depictions of narcissistic desire in *Dubliners* are a critical method by which he writes his "chapter in the moral history of my country." Not only do these love stories highlight Dublin as the "centre of paralysis" (*LII* 134), but their protagonists frequently perform what Buber calls "say[ing] You and mean[ing] It" (*Thou* 85), pursuing connections with loved ones not because they desire to form a passionate attachment to them, but because such connections enable them to escape their paralyzing lives. For example, the "Araby" narrator associates his fascination with Mangan's sister with the humdrum descriptions of his neighborhood to such an extent that the chivalric quest he undertakes in her name becomes synonymous with escape. In so doing, his worship reduces her to "little more than the shadow of a dream" (Henke *Desire* 19), as his adoration of her "brown figure" and his depiction of her "image" as a "chalice" he "b[ears]" amidst a "throng of foes" subordinates her specific essence to an ideal romance whose unattainability is confirmed throughout the story (*D* 22; 23). While he characterizes her name as a "summons to all my foolish blood" (*D* 22), his failure to forge a romantic bond with Mangan's sister beyond his adoration of her name reduces his isolated esteem to a "surrogate ... for an actual relationship with a girl" (Brandabur 51). Indeed, not only is their only conversation compromised by awkwardness, but even when he pledges to attend Araby to purchase something for her, her "image" is then replaced by "the syllables of the word *Araby*" that "cast an Eastern enchantment over me" (*D* 24), at which point Mangan's sister disappears from the story. For that reason, even though the narrator "[sees] myself as a creature driven and derided by vanity" after his failed trip to Araby, that recognition provides no room for any substantive feelings for Mangan's sister. Instead, the epiphany concludes his symbolic transition away from her, replacing the exotic representation of Araby that was provoked by their conversation with an "anguish[ed] and ang[ry]" reflection of himself (*D* 28).

Similarly, Eveline Hill characterizes her desire to marry Frank as part of her overall desire to leave Ireland. By contrasting the respectability of her marriage in Argentina with her mother's marital suffering, Eveline transforms her engagement into a way to avoid the abuse that Joyce isolates as the inevitable result of Irish marriages throughout *Dubliners*.[2] Her resolution to flee this fate reveals her preference for security over love in her feelings for Frank: "Frank would save her. He would give her life, perhaps love, too. But she wanted to live. Why should she be unhappy? She had a right to happiness" (*D* 33). Eveline's need to escape her mother's fate is certainly understandable and the implications that she is potentially threatened by her father's abuse makes her more a victim of paralysis than she is a paralyzer, but her use of Frank to facilitate her escape demonstrates her use of their relationship to invoke her "right to happiness," which reduces Frank to "the invisible vehicle for bestowing respectful treatment on her" (Norris *Suspicious* 62). This use of Frank as a means to an end culminates in her inability to board the night boat at the story's conclusion, an inaction that is significant not only for its embodiment of paralysis, but also for its confirmation of Eveline's misrecognition of Frank. Indeed, her inability to affirm Frank as they are about to depart culminates in her "clutch[ing] the iron [railing] in frenzy," replacing her resolution that "Frank would save her" with her newfound fear that "he would drown her" (*D* 33; 34). This confirms that her personal security has always been the foundation of her affection for Frank; thus, when she ceases to believe that he will provide her this escape, she becomes incapable of affirming or even acknowledging his presence. Thus, the concluding observation that her "eyes gave him no sign of love or farewell or recognition" shows that the romance developed throughout the text is constructed on a tenuous, narcissistic foundation (*D* 34), and

---

[2] This domestic violence is also the context for Joyce's assertion that "a lot of this talk about love is nonsense" in his 1906 letter to Stanislaus, in which he specifically references "Counterparts" as an example of his criticism (*LII* 192).

Eveline's inability to follow through on her quest for escape both dissolves the symbolic love created by that quest and prevents her from evading her mother's paralyzing fate.

Thus, the narcissism of the collection's love stories becomes a vital element of Joyce's critique of Irish paralysis, as he not only depicts doomed Dubliners who are incapable of escaping their hopeless conditions, but he also highlights their inability to love and affirm others as a central reason why their attempts to improve their lives are inevitably self-defeating. This approach is developed in a more pernicious fashion in "A Painful Case," as Duffy's attempts to evade the persecution of a heterosexist Dublin also undercut his ability to forge the bonds with sympathetic others needed to reverse his repressed existence. As many critics have noted, Joyce represents Duffy as the epitome of Irish paralysis, a person so obsessed with his mental cohesion that he is incapable of any interaction with others.[3] Joyce initially notes that Duffy "lived in Chapelizod because he wished to live as far as possible from the city of which he was a citizen," an observation whose reference to citizenship signifies a rejection not simply of Dublin, but of its Dubliners (*D* 103). While Jackson reads this self-exile as evidence of his "desire to resist the power of the patriarchy" (91), it also provides two examples of the narcissism that springs from that desire. First, his exile prevents him from interacting with anyone different from himself. Indeed, Joyce depicts Duffy as a man with "neither companions nor friends, church nor creed" (*D* 105), a person whose "[abhorrence]" of "anything which betokened physical or mental disorder" prevents him from affirming otherness (*D* 103). Second, his self-banishment compels him to reflect solely on his own condition, as Joyce notes that Duffy "lived at a little distance from his body, regarding his own acts with doubtful side-glances" and "had an odd autobiographical habit which led him to compose in his mind from time to time a short sentence about himself containing a subject in the third person and a predicate in the past tense" (*D* 104). Jackson highlights these tendencies as indicative of "someone always under surveillance" (91), but they also show how Duffy's mindset "turns on a tautological self-relation, which excludes the uplifting impact of others, since it merely repeats in the third person understandings achieved in the first one" (Doherty 103). While the repressive instruments of societal heterosexism make this mindset understandable, Duffy's "tautological self-relation" instinctively compels him to subordinate the concerns of others to his own, demonstrating the inherent narcissism that emerges from his sexual repression.

---

[3] For example, Dominic Manganiello argues that Duffy falls prey to an "egoism [that], when it becomes solipsistic, is harmful, a deprivation of life" (79). Trevor L. Williams notes that Duffy is "one of those characters who (like Eveline and Maria at the opposite end of the social scale) is prevented even from speaking, so thoroughly deprived is he of authentic subjectivity" (98). Finally, Gerald Doherty contends that "Duffy's verbal asceticism … point[s] to a disavowal of all sociopolitical contracts. He rejects exactly those group identifications though finding the "ego ideal" also means joining the larger community" (103).

Duffy's isolation is temporarily set aside upon meeting Emily Sinico at a concert in the Rotunda. To Joyce, Mrs Sinico is not simply a potential love object since she suffers from an amorous repression similar to the alienation Jackson and Norris attribute to Duffy. While her desires are certainly not subject to the policing a homosexual Duffy would face, Joyce describes her as another Dubliner whose life is characterized by isolation and loneliness. Noting that her husband "had dismissed his wife so sincerely from his gallery of pleasures that he did not suspect that anyone else would take an interest in her" (*D* 106), Joyce portrays Mrs Sinico as a compassionate person earnestly seeking reciprocated affection, but he denies her an outlet for her amorous longings, ending her lonely existence in a "death" attributable to the "sudden failure of the heart's action" (*D* 110). Even though her love may be legally sanctioned by the Dublin patriarchy, Mrs Sinico joins James Duffy as the story's "outcast[s] from life's feast" (*D* 113), as she "symptomatizes the fate of desire whose prospects for fulfillment have been blocked" (Doherty 100).

However, while Mrs Sinico may share an analogous amorous isolation to Duffy, her attitude towards others is substantially different. This distinction is important to our ethical evaluation of the characters since it enables us to discern a more compassionate reaction to social isolation than Duffy's "neurotic" narcissism. Initially, Mrs Sinico's reaction to the concert articulates an accommodating method of social interaction within a dismissive society that contrasts to Duffy's self-exile:

> One evening he found himself sitting beside two ladies in the Rotunda. The house, thinly peopled and silent, gave distressing prophecy of failure. The lady who sat next him looked round at the deserted house once or twice and then said: — What a pity there is such a poor house to-night! It's so hard on people to have to sing to empty benches. (*D* 105)

Mrs Sinico's initial impulse is to feel sorry for the performers that "have to sing to empty benches," which displays her ability to empathize with others in similarly distressed conditions.[4] On the other hand, Duffy's perception of the low attendance as a "distressing prophecy of failure" demonstrates how his "odd autobiographical habit" affects his everyday perceptions, as he characterizes the situation as primarily a disappointing end to his evening. He may take Mrs Sinico's remark as "an invitation to talk," but the account of that conversation mentions nothing

---

[4] Suzanne Katz Hyman recognizes that "whereas Duffy's attitude towards people is to shut himself off from them, Mrs. Sinico's is one of active sympathy. She responds emotionally, and it is not surprising that her first sentence ends in an exclamation mark" (113–4). David G. Wright also argues that "Emily Sinico seems one of the most empathetic characters in *Dubliners*, perhaps a potential Gretta Conroy. The only thing we ever hear her say is her statement of regret at the low turnout for a concert" (110). I will only add that while this "regret" may be the only explicit statement uttered by Emily Sinico, the narration of her later conversations with Duffy provides another opportunity for us to hear her thoughts and opinions. As I will argue later, her suggestion that Duffy share his ideas with her and others further supports Hyman's and Wright's descriptions of her as empathetic.

about the people with whom she has just sympathized (*D* 105). In fact, while Duffy accepts Mrs Sinico's "invitation," his perceptions of that exchange exclude whatever dialogue occurred, focusing on her appearance instead of her words. By responding to Mrs Sinico's lament with reflections that shut out her voice, Duffy changes the subject from the concert's low attendance to his impression of his new acquaintance, confirming his inability to acknowledge her empathetic remark. Their disparate reactions to the same situation provides the first comparison of the competing forms of love in "A Painful Case"—while both mourn the concert's low turnout, only Emily Sinico shows herself capable of an empathetic embrace, which by comparison reveals Duffy's reaction to be the first textual example of his being "ever alert to greet a redeeming instinct in others, but often disappointed" (*D* 104).

Duffy's thoughts during this conversation strengthen the comparison of their different perspectives. As Duffy tries to "fix her permanently in his memory," he perceives that the initially "defiant note" of Mrs Sinico's gaze becomes "confused" by a "deliberate swoon of the pupil into the iris, revealing for an instant a temperament of great sensibility" (*D* 105). Not only does this observation indicate his preference for constructing a mental image of Mrs Sinico instead of conversing with her, but his perception of her "swoon[ing]" gaze illustrates that Duffy initially is intrigued not by Mrs Sinico's intelligence or air of "defian[ce]," but rather by the potential for him to gain her esteem and devotion. This interest is certainly understandable in a person who has been rejected by a repressive Dublin, but Duffy's focus on the excitement in Mrs Sinico's gaze rather than the content of her remarks demonstrates the self-absorption that springs from this societal repression, and this desire to secure Mrs Sinico's esteem rather than to "affirm" her "as creature and creation" will influence his future interactions with her.

Duffy's subsequent encounters with Mrs Sinico magnify his interest in attaining her devotion. During these interactions, he "len[ds] her books" and "provide[s] her with ideas" in an attempt to "entangle his thoughts with hers" (*D* 106). This observation is important not only because it demonstrates how Duffy reshapes Mrs Sinico into his mirror image, but also because it simultaneously recognizes her willingness to heed his ideas. While the specifics of Duffy's attempts to "share his intellectual life with her" make the enterprise seem one-sided, Mrs Sinico's eagerness to "[listen] to all" transforms Duffy's intellectual monologue into a dialogic encounter (*D* 106). This representation of Duffy as orator and Mrs Sinico as listener provides further evidence of the difference in the two lovers' approaches towards others, as the latter's thoughtful attention enables her to transcend her role as Duffy's sounding board and demonstrates the ability of one lonely Dubliner to affirm and encourage the otherness of another. The combination of her attention and her "[urging] him to let his nature open to the full" enables Joyce to show how Mrs Sinico's empathy could transform Duffy's "li[fe] at a little distance from his body" into a dialogic connection with another that could counteract his alienation. Thus, Emily Sinico's "invitation to talk" becomes an invitation of openness that provides the possibility for two societal outcasts to develop a loving bond with each other that could undo their melancholic situations.

However, Duffy is incapable of accepting this invitation. Instead of seizing the opportunity for dialogue, Duffy transforms Mrs Sinico into his "confessor," enabling their subsequent conversations to remain one-sided and dominated by his intellectual musings.[5] Essentially, Duffy responds to Mrs Sinico's invitation by denying her the ability to speak, reshaping her attention into another mechanism for him to carry out his "odd autobiographical habit." His climactic depictions of their union demonstrate the narcissistic underpinnings of his involvement with her: "This union exalted him, wore away the rough edges of his character, emotionalised his mental life. Sometimes he caught himself listening to the sound of his own voice. He thought that in her eyes he would ascend to an angelical stature" (*D* 107). Rather than returning Mrs Sinico's gaze, Duffy has instead refashioned her image to serve as a reflection of his own greatness, revealing his preference for "emotionalis[ing] his mental life" over connecting emotionally to another human being. This gesture is understandable given that this may be the first affectionate connection a perpetually persecuted Duffy has made in a long time, but rather than developing the reciprocal affirmation needed to shape that connection meaningfully, it instead transforms Mrs Sinico to a mirror instead of a lover and shows how Duffy's narcissistic desire for "ascen[sion]" ironically "excludes the uplifting impact of others."[6] Even if this narcissism emerges from his ostracism from Dublin, Duffy's inability to affirm Mrs Sinico confines his interest in her to Buber's "kingdom of the lame-winged Eros," which reduces any interaction between the characters to Duffy "listening to the sound of his own voice."

This inability to feel affection for Mrs Sinico is further evidenced in Duffy's subsequent reflections on their union. Whereas his previous thoughts were charged with emotional energy, the meditations that immediately follow Duffy's desired exaltation deflate that amorous potential: "As he attached the fervent nature of his

---

[5] Hyman also notes the anonymity of this confessional role by arguing that "the idea of seeing her as confessor is congenial to Duffy. Confession is a purely verbal transaction; it is anonymous and one-sided. There is intimacy combined with impersonality. The confession is a formal, ritualized means of 'opening oneself to the fall' and still feeling safe" (114–5). Thus, while Mrs Sinico offers Duffy the opportunity to share his passions and aspirations, he transforms her into an impersonal, silent priest and robs her of her individual identity, revealing his continued inability and disinterest in recognizing the otherness of the people he encounters.

[6] Critics have long argued that Duffy uses Mrs Sinico's affection to reflect his own greatness. Henke, for example, notes that "Duffy adopts a stance of deliberate obliquity by replicating his own mirror image in Emily's adoring gaze" (*Desire* 35). Raffaella Baccolini also observes that "there is a sense, in fact, that if Mr. Duffy ascends to an angelical stature for Mrs. Sinico, he does so even more for himself; it is Mrs. Sinico's respect for him – or perhaps the very way in which he perceives her – that generates such feeling" (153). Finally, Cynthia Wheatley-Lovoy characterizes Duffy as being "largely immune to the effects of Sinico's otherness. Like Narcissus's pool, she represents to him only a reflector of his own image" (184).

companion more and more closely to him, he heard the strange impersonal voice which he recognized as his own, insisting on the soul's incurable loneliness. We cannot give ourselves, it said: we are our own" (*D* 107). The voice's message that "we cannot give ourselves … we are our own" not only shows that Mrs Sinico's emotional attachment to Duffy will be rejected because it requires a concession that Duffy is incapable of giving; it also reveals the alienation inherent in his interpretation of love and his interactions with others. He can use "the fervent nature of his companion" to strengthen his self-love, but his insistence that he is his own isolated being renders him incapable of returning her devotion.[7] Thus, a homosexual Duffy's insistence on "the soul's incurable loneliness" demonstrates the extent to which societal heterosexism hinders the ability to develop dialogic connections with others, as his "need to distance himself from the homophobia of the patriarchy" precludes him from affirming Mrs Sinico's otherness and foreshadows the dissolution of their relationship.

This dissolution occurs when Mrs Sinico places Duffy's hand on her cheek. While critics have pointed to Duffy's resulting "disillusion[ment]" as evidence of either romantic misinterpretation or adulterous scandal,[8] reading his disgust with respect to the monologic lament that preceded it reveals the narcissistic tendencies behind his rejection. Duffy's observation that "her interpretation of his words disillusioned him" foregrounds the irresolvable conflict between their differing attitudes towards love (*D* 107), forcing him to acknowledge that Mrs Sinico's embrace constituted an invitation for Duffy to reciprocate her "fervent" devotion for him. While he was able to use her affection to improve his self-love, he recoils when asked to return the favor and "break[s] off their intercourse" (*D* 108). It is significant here that Joyce refers to the relationship that Duffy rejects as "intercourse" since it forces a comparison between his dialogues with Mrs Sinico and his later lamentation over the impossibility of love or friendship because of sexual intercourse. By describing Mrs Sinico's invitation of openness as "intercourse," Joyce provides an alternative to Jackson's "double-bind created for gay men" by expanding Duffy's definition of "friendship between man and woman" to enable dialogic "intercourse" to replace the necessity of "sexual intercourse." Nevertheless, Duffy's self-absorption forces him to reject this alternative, as his insistence that "every bond … is a bond to sorrow" (*D* 108)

---

7 Edward Brandabur confirms Duffy's disinterest in reciprocating Mrs Sinico's desire for empathetic dialogue, arguing that "Theirs is a relationship without reciprocity. He does not draw her out, inquire into what she thinks. It is on his part a friendship of use" (78).

8 Patrick Bixby contends that "as soon as Mrs Sinico touches Duffy, she puts an end to their 'intercourse' and brings him face to face with what he identifies as perversion" (117). Bernard Benstock also argues that "Duffy had already answered his question as to why he rejected her love: middle-class propriety had insisted upon it" (*Dubliners* 130). Finally, Brandabur reads Duffy's rejection similarly, noting that "as long as the relationship remains overtly respectable, he can maintain an angelic self-image in what he actually regards as a morally compromising situation; but when this state threatens to become openly immoral, he must stop it" (78).

echoes his earlier isolation of "the soul's incurable loneliness." This refusal demonstrates the relationship between his inability to give himself to Mrs Sinico and the rejection that springs from her desire for reciprocal affection, and it is this inability to "turn to [her] with all the power of intention of [his] own heart" that renders his desire for "love" and "friendship" truly "impossible."

Of course, if one reads Mrs Sinico's outburst as the assertion of heterosexual desire onto a repressed homosexual, then the latter's refusal of that desire is not itself endemic of callous solipsism. Considering that Duffy's desire to "share his intellectual life" with Mrs Sinico likely constitutes the most meaningful relationship that he has experienced in a long time, her placing his hand on her cheek forces him to realize that she did not understand him to the degree that he initially perceived, which is an understandably traumatic epiphany that makes his rejection of her unsurprising. What compels our ethical evaluation of Duffy's narcissism is not simply the rejection of Emily Sinico, but the way that he performs that rejection. He could still refuse Mrs Sinico in a way that acknowledged her imprisonment in a loveless marriage and that empathized with another Dubliner who is forced into perpetual loneliness. Such a reaction would constitute a performance of love for her even as he is turning down her desire for sexual intimacy. Instead, Duffy's rejection demonstrates the extent to which his "desire to resist the power of the patriarchy" compromises his ability to empathize with his former companion. His "disillusion[ment]" over "*her* interpretation of *his* words" projects blame onto Mrs Sinico, not only rejecting her desire for recognition, but demonizing that desire as a revolting sentimental display that precludes him from further "intercourse." Also, when Mrs Sinico begins to fall during their farewell encounter, Duffy, rather than helping her, "[bids] her good-bye quickly and [leaves] her" (*D* 108), mirroring his earlier tendency to refuse alms to beggars and thus treating his former companion as an outcast unworthy of his attention. Especially when we contrast this disgust with Mrs Sinico's empathy, Duffy's inability to see or to treat her as a fellow victim of social alienation confirms his unwavering obsession with his "mental life" and robs him of the compassion needed to transcend his alienation.

This lack of empathy is further supported by Duffy's reaction to the newspaper account of Mrs Sinico's death. Instead of lamenting the loss of a former friend, Duffy deems her death "vulgar" and "commonplace" and calls her "one of the wrecks on which civilisation has been reared" (*D* 111–2). In a gesture that confirms the instinctive self-absorption behind his alienated existence, Duffy casts himself as the primary victim of the tragedy, arguing that Mrs Sinico had "degraded" him by listening to "what he held sacred." This fear of degradation confirms that what Duffy values most is the sanctity of his self-image, as he is willing to cast Mrs Sinico aside and mock her suitability as "his soul's companion" the second her swooning gaze becomes tainted (*D* 111). His concluding dismissal of Mrs Sinico confirms his determination to represent her love as a "degrad[ing]" threat to him: "He remembered her outburst of that night and interpreted it in a harsher sense than he had ever done. He had no difficulty now in approving of the course he had taken" (*D* 112). Duffy thus reinterprets Mrs Sinico's gesture in a "harsher" light to reassure himself that he was right to reject her, another projection of blame that is exacerbated by his conscious acknowledgement that he is strategically denigrating her. Even if sexual persecution has hindered his ability to demonstrate the degree of compassion that Mrs Sinico expresses, his callous dismissal of her character in both life and death cannot escape ethical scrutiny: by prioritizing his potential degradation over Mrs Sinico's suffering, Duffy closes off the openness that she encouraged and erases her from her own tragedy.

However, Duffy's subsequent reflections on his relationship with Mrs Sinico open up the possibility for him to experience compassion. His perceptions that "he thought her hand touched his" (*D* 112) and that "at moments he seemed to feel her voice touch his ear [and] her hand touch his" (*D* 113) establish a posthumous mental connection between Duffy and Mrs Sinico that could provide the opportunity for him to affirm her otherness. For this reason, Suzanne Katz Hyman points to Duffy's increasingly sympathetic characterizations of Mrs Sinico's memory as evidence that "for the first time Duffy allows himself to become aware of love" (118), highlighting a redemptive quality to the story's conclusion.[9] However, while Duffy's thoughts about Mrs Sinico are certainly fonder than his earlier castigations, Joyce's description of his epiphany demonstrates his inability to shake off the narcissism that springs from his social ostracism. Specifically, while Duffy does indeed think about Mrs Sinico in a warmer light towards the end of "A Painful Case," these meditations are expressed through his "tautological self-relation," which undoes their empathetic potential.

Initially, Duffy's preoccupation with the image of Mrs Sinico continues to deny her the empathy she sought in life. The narrator notes that "as he sat there, living over his life with her and evoking alternately the two images in which he now conceived her, he realized that she was dead, that she had ceased to exist, that she had become a memory" (*D* 112). While the medium of memory would necessarily force individuals to relate to departed loved ones as images, Duffy's specific "evoking" of the "two images" he had "conceived" of Mrs Sinico foregrounds that at no point during their relationship had Emily Sinico ever been anything but an image to him. During their initial encounter, her swooning gaze compelled Duffy to represent her as a woman of "great sensibility"; as their friendship became more intimate, Duffy depicted her as his sounding board, his confessor, and the mirror of his grandeur; and when she ultimately met her tragic end, she was reduced to "one of the wrecks on which civilisation has been reared." Thus, when his recollections conjure up her "images," Duffy reveals himself to continue to rely on the symbolic representations of her that he had "fix[ed] … permanently in his

---

[9] John Rickard supports this redemptive characterization of Duffy by contending that "though Duffy's epiphany is excruciating and leaves him alone, he *feels* for the first time, and we are justified in regarding the destruction of 'his moral nature' as a triumph of involuntary memory … If the reader hopes that Mr. Duffy will learn to love and to accept human companionship, that goal is more available at the end of 'A Painful Case' than it was at the beginning" (65).

memory," which reduces his mourning to another exercise of his "mental life" that falls short of affirming her difference and mourning her tragedy.

Additionally, Duffy's preoccupation with his potential demise pushes Mrs Sinico out of her own story. While he finally acknowledges "how lonely her life must have been, sitting night after night alone in that room," her tragedy is immediately assimilated into his recognition that he will have the same fate, that "his life would be lonely too until he, too, died, ceased to exist, became a memory, if anyone remembered him" (*D* 112–3).[10] These lamentations reveal that Duffy's sorrow for Mrs Sinico is triggered not out of any compassion for her specific condition, but rather out of the recognition that by rejecting "his soul's companion," he has guaranteed his own perpetual loneliness by denying himself his most ardent love object. ("One human being had seemed to love him and he had denied her life and happiness" [*D* 113].) Thus, at the moment when Mrs Sinico "seem[s] to be near him in the darkness," Duffy's preoccupation with his impending isolation prevents him from acknowledging that ghostly presence to any substantive degree. In that sense, Duffy's acknowledgement that he has "sentenced her" to a "death of shame" performatively re-enacts that death sentence, as the focus on Duffy's loneliness over Mrs Sinico's erases her from his memory (*D* 113).

This erasure of Mrs Sinico is complete by the story's conclusion, where Duffy hears the engine of a goods train "reiterating the syllables of her name." However, as he continues to grieve over his deplorable future, Duffy begins to "doubt the reality of what memory told him," enabling this last connection with Mrs Sinico to slip from his grasp: "He halted under a tree and allowed the rhythm to die away. He could not feel her near him in the darkness nor her voice touch his ear. He waited for some minutes listening. He could hear nothing: the night was perfectly silent. He listened again: perfectly silent. He felt that he was alone" (*D* 113–4). By "*allow[ing]* the rhythm to die away," Duffy consciously gives up any connection with Mrs Sinico's memory that was created by his reflections on her death, withdrawing back into the solitary existence that characterized Joyce's initial depictions of him.[11] Not only does this tactic cement Duffy's "soul's incurable loneliness," but it also constitutes the second time in "A Painful Case" that Mrs Sinico has been killed by a train because the dying out of her name simultaneously kills off whatever compassionate feelings were generated by Duffy's memory of

[10] Thomas Jackson Rice reads Duffy's lament here as "nothing but self-pity," illustrating that "those Dubliners who can see, such as Mr. Duffy, see only mirror images of themselves. Those who can speak and hear listen only to the sound of their own voices" (45). Henke goes one step further and contends that Duffy "plagiarizes her story and steals her suffering by converting melodrama into high tragedy" (*Desire* 37).

[11] This would run counter to Rickard's reading of the story's conclusion that Duffy's "awakening can be read as one of the few rays of hope or possibility in *Dubliners* – hope that a paralyzed character can break through the habits and behavioral modes that imprison him or her" (65). Duffy "allowing" the memory to slip from his mind signifies his refusal to "break through" the alienation that characterizes his relationship with Dublin, thus dimming the "rays of hope" that Rickard sees as emanating from the story's concluding epiphany.

her. The story thus ends not with the empathetic embrace of a loved one's memory, but rather with a "short sentence about [Duffy] containing a subject in the third person and a predicate in the past tense." This final articulation of Duffy's "odd autobiographical habit" confirms the prevalence of his narcissism throughout the story, which prevents us from dismissing the traditional reading of Joyce's protagonist even after we have "take[n] ethical responsibility for now imagining the thoughts and feelings of the possibly homosexual man." By continuing to hold Duffy up to scrutiny, we see how his societal persecution provokes a narcissistic response that, while not explicitly "deny[ing] life and happiness" to Mrs Sinico, prevents the compassionate love needed for him to transcend his self-affirming mental life "without any communion with others" (*D* 105).

The Hard-Featured Realists

In *Martin Buber's Social and Religious Thought*, Laurence J. Silberstein argues that "to achieve genuine community and to actualize the idea of community, we must create the social conditions that facilitate dialogue – that is, the mutual confirmation of human beings by one another" (180). To demonstrate the importance of this loving dialogue in "actualiz[ing] the idea of community," this section explores the political implications of Duffy's refusal of Emily Sinico. Similar to the previous analysis, it argues that the interactions between Mrs Sinico and Duffy represent a conflict between two different methods of love. However, by reading the political content of their conversations with respect to Buber, we discover that Duffy's inability to affirm Mrs Sinico's otherness is indicative of a larger societal alienation that undermines his socialist aspirations. To that end, our task will be to recognize that the love Emily Sinico offers Duffy is not simply the embrace of an individual other, but rather an opportunity to transform that affirmation of otherness into a broader social dialogue that would enable him to bring about the political change that he desires.

Of course, the sociopolitical implications of *Dubliners*'s love stories are not limited to "A Painful Case." In fact, the collection frequently demonstrates the inverse of Buber's contention that individual affirmations of otherness result in a broader acceptance of "many-faced otherness" (*Man* 61), as the local refusal to acknowledge one's beloved frequently perpetuates a broader refusal to affirm the difference of the other Dubliners whom the characters encounter. I have already noted the personal limitations of the "Araby" narrator's "b[earing]" the "chalice" of his love for Mangan's sister, but it is significant that this grail is "bor[ne]" amidst "a throng of foes" since the narrator specifies the everyday Dubliners he encounters as the "foes" against which this "chalice" protects him. Here, his insistence that "her image accompanied me even in places the most hostile to romance" highlights the boy's antagonistic use of his infatuation with Mangan's sister as armor that shields him from the Dublin environment he disdains (*D* 22), and his growing ambivalence towards his schoolmates as the Araby bazaar draws closer confirms that his obsession with fulfilling his romantic quest magnifies his alienation from his community. Similarly, in "Two Gallants," Corley and Lenehan's self-serving exploitation of a slavey is complemented by a broader conversational monologism that prevents meaningful relationships with others. Not only does Corley continuously use his romantic boastings to drown out Lenehan throughout their conversations, but Lenehan's solitary walk around Dublin while Corley manipulates the slavey similarly excludes the presence of others. Although he acknowledges the people he encounters as he waits for Corley, Lenehan consistently promotes his own reflections on "how pleasant it would be to have a warm fire to sit by and a good dinner to sit down to" over the people around him (*D* 52), as "he found trivial all that was meant to charm him and did not answer the glances which invited him to be bold" (*D* 50). This refusal of the "invit[ations]" and "glances" he comes across mirrors Corley's disinterest in "the speech of his companions" and confirms the broader refusal of others at the heart of both lotharios' self-absorption (*D* 45).

The political implications of this univocality manifest themselves in "A Little Cloud," where Little Chandler's preoccupation with sentimental romance ignores the poverty and exploitation that inspires his poetic exercises. Chandler's poetic rejection of otherness is explicitly demonstrated by his preference for the passion of Byron's poetry over the reality of his marriage to Annie, but his initial awareness that such "a gentle melancholy took possession of him" is brought about by watching the "untidy nurses" and "decrepit old men who drowsed on the benches" outside his office window (*D* 66; 65). However, although he wishes to "give expression" to this "melancholy" in a "book of poems" (*D* 68), that emotional response never translates into any empathy for these impoverished people, but merely becomes a generic "melancholy" to be expressed in the poetry that he wishes to use to make people listen to him. This subordination is exacerbated by Chandler's disdain for the poor people he comes across during these moments of inspiration, as he pledges to "give no thought" to the "horde of grimy children [that] populated the street" and to "[pick] his way deftly through all that minute vermin-like life" (*D* 66). For this reason, when he desires then to "give expression" to these thoughts in a "book of poems," he demonstrates the dismissal of social exploitation inherent in his artistic desire, transforming his art into rejections of otherness that use poverty as inspiration for the "poetic moment" and then discard these objects of inspiration once they have outlived their utility (*D* 68). Thus, Chandler's poetic aspirations consistently highlight the ambivalence towards otherness behind his sentimental romantic ideals, and his subsequent desire to "pipe the Celtic note in lofty purple prose crafted to impress the British intelligentsia" reveals the extent to which the narcissistic pursuit of ideal romance perpetuates the alienation that compelled those pursuits and short-circuits artistic attempts to counteract Ireland's colonial state (Henke *Desire* 29).

By tracing the progression of the amatory quests in *Dubliners* from the personal to the sociopolitical arenas, Joyce shows that the lovers who perceive themselves as victims of Irish paralysis become the instruments of their own victimhood, as their limited obsession with personal liberation prevents the broader affirmation of social otherness needed to transform Dublin into a more vibrant and accommodating body politic. This political narcissism is confirmed by Duffy's foiled socialist ideals in "A Painful Case." Indeed, it is not much of a stretch to depict Duffy as an aspiring revolutionary; certainly Joyce's protagonist sees himself in that manner. His disdainful references to his Dublin citizenship and bank clerkship signify Duffy's ambivalence towards the prevailing socio-economic structures in Ireland, and his refusal to "concede" to the "conventions which regulate the civic life" speaks to a secret desire to undermine those regimes through acts of dissent (such as the fantasized robbing of his bank) (*D* 105).[12] Bernard Benstock reads Duffy along these lines, arguing that this secret desire "implies not only a disregard for the class ethic, but a purposefully thought-out disdain for the validity of that ethic" (*Dubliners* 91). Trevor L. Williams points to Duffy's attendance at Irish Socialist Party meetings as further evidence of these revolutionary aspirations, noting that "this is the only example in *Dubliners* (indeed in the whole of Joyce) of a bourgeois character seeking some kind of alignment with the working class" (99). On the surface, these political aspirations seemingly separate Duffy from *Dubliners*'s other protagonists who either blindly accept their sociopolitical existences or seek merely individual escape, which potentially makes Duffy the type of revolutionary that could cause meaningful change in Dublin.

However, Duffy is unwilling to engage in the substantive interaction with others needed to effectuate that change. His manufactured isolation may separate him from the social structures that exclude him, but by retreating to Chapelizod instead of remaining within the "city of which he was a citizen," Duffy renders himself so far removed from the center of paralysis that his suburban dissent accomplishes nothing. Unlike Bloom, whose outcast status does not preclude him from remaining in the city and interacting with the Dubliners who ostracize him, Duffy resolves to remove himself from Dublin in much the same way that Stephen Daedalus pledges to "subtract [him]self" from the Catholic church in *Stephen Hero* (*SH* 233). Such a "subtract[ion]" may bolster Duffy's self-image as the society-spurning intellectual, but it also reduces any acts of revolt to negative strategies of individual "escape or release from various constraining elements in his environment" that lack the constructive power to produce any meaningful reform, rendering his efforts "superficial and even self-defeating" (Thornton 78).[13]

---

[12] Doherty similarly reads Duffy's desire to rob his bank as a revolutionary aspiration, describing him as the "quintessential nonvertical man, to whom anarchic exploits or adventures (like "rob[bing] his bank") never occur" (103).

[13] Thornton's analysis of negative resistance is articulated within the context of *A Portrait of the Artist as a Young Man*. While he refers specifically to Stephen's desired exile from Ireland, I argue that this criticism of "atomic individualism" applies equally well to Duffy's disdain towards Dublin. Similar to Thornton's characterization of John Blades's reading of Stephen, Duffy's desired method of liberation fails partly because it privileges "freedom from" instead of "freedom to" (Thornton 78–9).

The individual focus of Duffy's political fantasies is also emphasized by his disinterest in helping those in similar or less fortunate situations than himself. Duffy espouses intellectual aspirations towards a socialist ethic, but his refusal to give alms to the beggars he encounters constitutes a curious ambivalence towards people who have been exploited and excluded by the prevailing economic structures in Dublin. Similarly, he attends the meetings of an Irish Socialist Party, but abruptly stops going because he does not want to deal with "hard-featured realists" whose "inordinate" interest in wage issues demonstrates their lack of "an exactitude which was the product of a leisure not within their reach" (*D* 106–7). Not only do these qualified assertions of socialism reveal his revolutionary aspirations to be half-hearted intellectual curiosities, but his refusal to assist those less fortunate than he betrays his reliance on the very class judgments that Benstock characterizes him as disdaining. Duffy's contradictory politics thus provides a compelling microcosm of the ways in which societal persecution of difference is internalized and redeployed at the local level, as Duffy's alienation from Dublin does not prevent him from vilifying and excluding his fellow "outcast[s] from life's feast." Not only does this exclusionary redeployment isolate the contradictory nature of Duffy's politics, it also precludes him from affirming the "many-faced otherness" of the inhabitants of his body politic, which indefinitely prolongs his alienation from Dublin.

Additionally, Duffy's promotion of his intellectual socialism over his colleagues' concerns limits the effectiveness of his political aspirations. Recall that a central component of Buber's politics is that individuals "affirm the person [they] struggle with," that civic actors accept the validity of dissenting viewpoints and engage in reciprocal sociopolitical dialogue even when they "must offer strict opposition to his view about the subject of [their] conversation" (*Knowledge* 69). This affirming dissent ensures that disagreements do not undermine the decisionmaking capabilities of the body politic by promoting a cooperative environment that enables conflict to "be humanly arbitrated and led towards its overcoming" (Buber *Pointing* 238). Duffy's dismissal of the "hard-featured realists" eliminates this cooperation because his refusal to entertain socialist beliefs that counter his intellectual interests compels him to reject one of the few sociopolitical groups that would be receptive to his ideas. Not only does this dismissal deny him the audience and political organization to fulfill his aspirations, but by rejecting the workers' "inordinate" concern with wage issues instead of seeking a compromise that could advance both his academic pursuits and their economic goals, Duffy locks himself into a purely idealist, utopian politics whose effectiveness does not extend beyond his intellectual musings. This limited political interaction may be more comfortable to the alienated Duffy, but his refusal to engage potential allies with diverging viewpoints compromises the real-world attainment of his socialist aspirations and ensures that his revolutionary fantasies will never escape that fantastic realm.

However, Emily Sinico's empathy provides Duffy the opportunity to reevaluate his sociopolitical aspirations. I have already argued that Mrs Sinico's "urg[ing]" for Duffy to "let his nature open to the full" is simultaneously an embrace of empathy towards her newfound companion and an invitation for him to engage in the same openness and compassion. It is also significant that Duffy chooses to respond to Mrs Sinico's invitation of openness by relating his frustrations over the Irish Socialist Party meetings to his newfound "confessor." Thus, when she gives this political conversation the same unwavering attention she gave his intellectual musings and suggests that he "write out his thoughts," Mrs Sinico puts forth more than simply a continuation of her listening silence (*D* 107). By encouraging Duffy to write out his socialist thoughts, she by extension is suggesting that he share those thoughts with others. Especially when we note that this suggestion immediately follows Duffy's articulation of difference between himself and the "hard-featured realists," Mrs Sinico's observation reshapes her invitation of openness in politically productive ways, advising her companion to engage other political subjects regardless of whatever differences potentially draw them apart. This invitation would effectively reverse Duffy's rejection of the working and middle class socialists by providing him the opportunity to supplement their "interest … in the question of wages" with his intellectual "exactitude" (*D* 107), which could pave the way for more effective political cooperation. Thus, not only is Mrs Sinico capable of empathizing with Duffy, but that empathy also enables her to recognize the potential for individuals within a given body politic to put aside their differences and work together in a non-alienating manner. This not only confirms Mrs Sinico as one of Joyce's early proponents of true love and genuine dialogue, but it also transforms the empty paper on Duffy's writing desk into a potential vehicle for entry into the sociopolitical arena from which he has isolated himself.

However, Duffy refuses Emily Sinico's invitation. He recoils at the notion that he should share his ideas, arguing that his audience's lack of sophistication would inevitably render useless this political endeavor: "For what, he asked her, with careful scorn. To compete with phrasemongers, incapable of thinking consecutively for sixty seconds? To submit himself to the criticisms of an obtuse middle class which entrusted its morality to policemen and its fine arts to impresarios?" (*D* 107). The contrast between Mrs Sinico's and Duffy's impressions of this possibility is unsurprising given the conflicting ways in which they respond to others. Whereas Mrs Sinico sees the possibility of cooperation among differing sociopolitical parties, Duffy uses those differences as justifications to refuse association with his counterparts. His characterization of this enterprise as a "compet[ition]" with "phrasemongers" demonstrates his determination to view interactions within the political arena antagonistically, ignoring the possibility of collaboration amongst people with opposing viewpoints. His fear that he would have to "submit himself to the criticisms of an obtuse middle class" also shows his inability to entertain difference, as the possibility that someone could argue against his socialist suggestions is enough for him to avoid undertaking the project altogether. This insistence on competition instead of cooperation reveals that Duffy's interaction with Mrs Sinico has not emboldened him productively, and his continued antagonism pushes him further away from the "overcoming of *otherness* in living unity" that Buber argues is necessary for the effective resolution of social and political conflicts (*Pointing* 102).

In addition, Duffy's use of disparaging labels to characterize his audience strengthens his refusal to "affirm the person [he] struggle[s] with." Not only does he reject the thought of political competition, but the notion that he would have to engage with "phrasemongers" (whose "phrase[s]" presumably do not match his own) is an especially repulsive prospect to him. Also, his sneering characterizations of his audience as an "obtuse middle class" signify not only his unwillingness to work with others who think differently, but also his continued reliance on class demarcations to close himself off from his fellow Dubliners. His mention of "morality" and "fine arts" as evidence of his audience's "obtuse[ness]" bolsters this class snobbery, enhancing the scope of his exclusion to encompass not only those with different political beliefs, but also those with different cultural and social views, regardless of their relevance to his specific argumentation.[14] This guarantees the failure of his political aspirations because by representing anyone who may think differently from him as unworthy of hearing his superior ideas, he continues to deny himself an audience for his politics and foreclose the cooperation needed to contribute to the body politic in any meaningful way. His refusal to engage in the same openness that Mrs Sinico has offered him thus renders him incapable of turning his political fantasies into reality, locking him into negative strategies of exile and escape and a utopian desire for a "social revolution" that "[will not] be likely to strike Dublin for some centuries" (*D* 107).

What is especially significant about Duffy's refusal of Mrs Sinico's suggestion is that the "careful scorn" generated in response to her openness begins the process that shuts her out of the rest of the story. Even though the next paragraph seemingly implies a growing intimacy between the two parties, Mrs Sinico's proposal that Duffy write down his ideas is actually the last thought she expresses in Joyce's story. After he belittles her suggestion, Emily Sinico loses her voice, and the open dialogue that had existed in the previous paragraphs quickly slides back into Duffy's monologic desire to "entangle his thoughts with hers" so as to exalt his "mental life." Mrs Sinico's empathetic embrace may have provided an opportunity for Duffy to engage in both personal and political openness, but his inability to accept the difference that such openness entails compels him to reject that embrace on both levels. This foreshadows his rejection of her passionate display and his more aggravated retreat from Dublin.

The dual nature of this rejection is more apparent when Duffy "return[s] to his even way of life" after rejecting Mrs Sinico (*D* 108). Not only does he further limit the amount of time he spends in the city, but Duffy now "wr[ites] seldom in the sheaf of papers which lay in his desk" (*D* 108), which not only indicates his retreat

---

[14] Doherty agrees with this class-based reading of Duffy's politics, arguing that "Duffy's disavowal of identification with the 'obtuse middle class' reflects the same highbrow contempt for what lies hierarchically below his superior vision – his 'careful scorn' of their ethico-cultural judgements" (103).

from his revolutionary fantasies, but takes on amorous importance considering his political conversations with Mrs Sinico. Given her insistence that he write his political ideas down, to note that the paper on Duffy's desk remained practically blank after his rejection of Emily Sinico constitutes a refusal not simply of her love, but of the sociopolitical interaction and cooperation that comprised her invitation of openness. This refusal is particularly evident considering that the only statement identified on his papers is Duffy's aphorism that "Love between man and man is impossible because there must not be sexual intercourse and friendship between man and woman is impossible because there must be sexual intercourse." While Jackson and Norris persuasively highlight this quotation as evidence of Duffy's homosexual lamentation, reading it in relation to the personal and political refusals that compelled it broadens the scope of that lamentation to encompass an isolation akin to his earlier reference to "the soul's incurable loneliness." Also, when we interpret Duffy's sparse writing as a rejection of Mrs Sinico, Joyce's famous quotation takes on political significance, as Duffy's dismissal of the interpersonal interaction behind "love" and "friendship" echoes his earlier refusal to risk the "criticisms of an obtuse middle class" by "writ[ing] out his thoughts." In both cases, Duffy rejects the potential for communication by arguing that its inevitable failure makes it hopeless to even try to forge such connections. Such logic would be understandable given Duffy's perpetual persecution by the Dublin heteropatriarchy, but it also cements a sociopolitical defeatism that not only guarantees his personal loneliness, but also nullifies his intellectual socialism since "no social revolution" to his liking can "strike Dublin" if he deems it useless to participate in the movement. Thus, by reading his aphorism in relation to the virtually blank pages on which it appears, we see how Duffy's definitive rejection of Mrs Sinico also forces him to abdicate the social relationships needed to fulfill his political aspirations.

Additionally, Duffy's focus on sexual love limits his ability to transcend his alienated state. Even if physical intimacy undermines certain forms of relationships, viewing love as an embrace of otherness would enable Duffy to experience "love" and "friendship" with both individuals and the Dublin body politic because this form of love transcends issues of sexuality. However, in "break[ing] off [his dialogic] intercourse" with Mrs Sinico, Duffy also refuses this broader amorous interpretation that could enable him to negotiate his sociopolitical position within Dublin despite the sexual alienation that he experiences. Instead, his aphorism locks him into a limited sexual love that does nothing to ameliorate his alienated state and encourages him to forgo the political outlet he needs to set his socialist ideas in motion. Duffy's renewed attention to his orderly life thus solidifies his refusal of Dublin through a continued rejection of Mrs Sinico's empathetic embrace.

This continued refusal of personal and social empathy is confirmed by Duffy's castigation of Mrs Sinico after reading the newspaper article. I have already mentioned the disparaging representations that Duffy hurls at his former companion as he blames her for her tragedy, but what gives these representations political significance is his equation of Mrs Sinico with the lower-class individuals whom he deems unworthy of his assistance. Not only does Duffy hold Emily Sinico accountable for her "miserable and malodorous" "vice," but his grouping of her with "the hobbling wretches whom he had seen carrying cans and bottles" to bars directly ties Mrs Sinico to the alms beggars he refused to help at the story's opening" (*D* 111). Especially when we recall Duffy's refusal to assist her during their final meeting, this comparison completes the depersonalization of Emily Sinico that began with his dismissing her invitation of openness. Furthermore, it constitutes his definitive rejection of love and socialism by depicting her as a generic vagrant whose vulgarity renders her unworthy of his affection.

These reflections on Mrs Sinico's tragedy subsequently compel Duffy to visit the public-house on Chapelizod Bridge, where he is thrust into the company of the "working-men" whose interests he spurned at the Irish Socialist Party meetings. In a manner similar to his ambivalence towards writing out his political thoughts, Duffy's vacant gaze at these men "without seeing or hearing them" signifies his continued inability to relate to either the memory of his former companion or the people to whom she encouraged to open himself (*D* 112).[15] This failure to acknowledge the otherness of these bar patrons parallels his subsequent inability to recognize Mrs Sinico's tragedy as distinct from his own loneliness, and because of this, his "allow[ance]" of "the rhythm [of the train] to die away" at the end of "A Painful Case" renders him incapable of feeling her touch or hearing her voice in much the same way as he is incapable of "seeing or hearing" the working-men's concerns. His concluding sense "that he was alone" thus signifies a renewal of both his personal and political exile, as his rejection of Mrs Sinico's memory also rejects her desire for him to empathize and cooperate with his socialist colleagues, preventing him from engaging the Dublin body politic in any productive sense.

****

It is entirely possible that the alienation Duffy experiences is the product of a societal heteronormativity that forces him to repress his sexual identity. If that is indeed the case, then Duffy's exile takes on a more complex ethical significance that Joyce's readers must acknowledge before judging his actions. However, while the persecuted Duffy's resulting ambivalence towards his fellow Dubliners would certainly be understandable, his reaction to Emily Sinico's situation cannot escape ethical scrutiny. Even if Duffy's sexual orientation prevents him from entering into the type of relationship that Mrs Sinico possibly desires, the way that he interacts with and subsequently dismisses her is still complicit in a narcissistic endorsement

[15] Seamus Deane persuasively articulates that "this moment is designed to remind us of Mr. Duffy's earlier political affiliation … Here is the counterexample to the previous instance of etherealizing. Mr. Duffy neither sees nor hears the men and their conversation about money and a gentleman's estate in County Kildare. But all the detail reinforces the contrasts between the physical and the refined, the worker and the intellectual, intellectual and scandal, egoism and love, that the story is elaborating" (24–5).

of love that refashions difference into reflections of the lover's grandeur and rejects what cannot be assimilated. That his narcissism may be shaped by his broader struggles with heterosexism does not undercut the need to examine "A Painful Case" through Buber to pinpoint the ways in which Duffy's resulting egoistic outlook on otherness is ethically and politically problematic. It may not be possible to return to the purely narcissistic reading of Joyce's protagonist, but continuing to challenge the homosexual Duffy's treatment of Mrs Sinico allows us to witness the ways in which societal policing of difference becomes internalized and reenacted on the individual level. Thus, by incorporating a critique of Duffy's narcissism into the queer readings of "A Painful Case," we further ascertain the insidious nature of the Dublin patriarchy, as the victims of sociopolitical persecution perform versions of that very persecution on their fellow Dubliners, failing to recognize that all members of the paralytic body politic are "outcast[s] from life's feast."

In that sense, Emily Sinico provides a way for Duffy to come to grips with his societal isolation, and by extension, she becomes one of Joyce's earliest proponents of love as the affirmation of otherness. In her ability to feel compassion for people she has not met and her recognition of the importance of cooperation despite political difference, Mrs Sinico becomes the embodiment of empathy in *Dubliners*, a person whose loneliness does not prevent her from loving and affirming the others she meets. Even her silence registers louder than Duffy's thoughts, as her unwavering attention towards her new companion and her desire for him to share his ideas with others establish a compassionate invitation of openness whose acceptance could enable both characters to transcend their lonely states. However, Buber demonstrates the necessity of reciprocal affirmation, and Duffy's rejection of Mrs Sinico as one "unfit to live" denies life to both parties. The "painful case" of Sinico and Duffy thus repeats itself throughout *Dubliners*, finding its concluding parallel in Gabriel and Gretta Conroy. Like "A Painful Case," "The Dead" forces us to acknowledge not only the personal consequences of narcissistic desire, but also how that narcissism precludes the cultural and political acceptance of difference that could improve the stultifying conditions of Joyce's Dublin. It is thus necessary for us to move from the unacknowledged music of the Rotunda's empty benches to the *Distant Music* of the Morkans' staircase to recognize the ways in which our awareness and acceptance of otherness determines our relationships with others both living and dead.

Chapter 2
The Strange Friendly Pity of "The Dead"

In "The Geometry of Meaning in *Dubliners*: A Euclidian Approach," Thomas Jackson Rice argues that "unlike Duffy or the boy of 'Araby,' Gabriel [Conroy] appears to progress toward a genuine act of communication and an uncontaminated moment of vision in the conclusion of his story" and "this progress is accompanied by an escape from egoism and a new acuity of perception" (46). This comparison of Duffy to Gabriel is not surprising since critics have frequently tied these two Dubliners together, arguing that they demonstrate a progression in Joyce's characters' attitudes towards others.[1] Whereas Duffy's narcissism prevents him from properly grieving for Emily Sinico, Gabriel is thought to develop an awareness of Gretta's otherness that is both dialogic and transformative at the conclusion of "The Dead," replacing his self-absorption with an acceptance of difference that is encapsulated by "generous tears" and the "snow [that] was general all over Ireland" (*D* 224; 225). However, while Gabriel's concluding thoughts about Gretta are certainly more affectionate than Duffy's rejection of Mrs Sinico, this comparison is insufficient to conclude that he experiences a productive, loving epiphany. When we read his thoughts and actions throughout "The Dead" with respect to Buber, we see Joyce confirm the futility of attempts to replace a stagnant romantic present with projections of an idealized past, and Gabriel's epiphany thus becomes the final evidence in *Dubliners* of the inability of narcissism to shield individuals from the mundanities of everyday Dublin.

However, this is not to say that Gabriel behaves as callously as Duffy. In fact, despite his inherent self-absorption, Gabriel remains a sympathetic protagonist in *Dubliners,* a "well-meaning sentimentalist" whose obsession with bestowing generosity upon others falls short of achieving his desired outcomes (*D* 221). This is what makes his narcissism in "The Dead" so jarring, since one need not be conniving or cruel to subordinate the affirmation of difference to the preoccupation with oneself. "The Dead" thus shows us the egoism of a hospitality divorced from love, that exercises in pity that do not also include the acceptance of otherness are half-hearted sympathetic gestures that fall short of reaching their ethical potential.

---

1 Other examples of this connection include Lucia Boldrini, who notes that "Gabriel's 'indifferent' voice signals the moment when he almost unwillingly gives up his pretense of superiority and prepares to listen to Gretta's story with equanimity rather than in order to judge her, and it can be contrasted with Mr. Duffy's 'strange impersonal voice'" (241); and Cynthia Wheatley-Lovoy, who contends that "In 'A Painful Case,' the monologic self wins the day as Duffy successfully silences the voice of Sinico, but in so doing, he fails to achieve self-reflexivity, while in 'The Dead,' Gabriel's inability to appropriate the female voice leads to a dialogic decentering and successful achievement of the reflexive" (181).

This emptiness also carries with it sociopolitical repercussions, as the inability to embrace difference, even in displays of generosity, can reinscribe the cultural boundaries that compel people of different classes to talk over and dismiss each other.

Admiring and Happy Eyes

In "Joyce's 'The Dead': The Dissolution of the Self and the Police," John Paul Riquelme articulates the traditional reading of "The Dead," which divides the story into three principal encounters that contribute to Gabriel's concluding epiphany:

> A great deal of Gabriel's anxiety in the story concerns his fear of slipping from the pinnacle that he occupies: that is, his fear that others will not see him as he wishes to be seen. His experiences in turn with Lily, with the nationalistic Miss Ivors, and with his wife indicate to Gabriel and to the reader that the views some others hold about him do not in fact conform to his own. The encounters provide perspectives for reassessing his standing and his positions. (125)

This characterization of Joyce's story thus contends that Gabriel's sense of socio-cultural superiority is questioned by his conversational blunders with Lily and Molly Ivors, paving the way for his self-absorption to be fractured conclusively by the revelation of Gretta's relationship with Michael Furey.[2] This explication of the story represents these encounters as parallel to each other, portraying Lily, Miss Ivors, and Gretta as equal participants in the dissolution of a pre-determined cultural identity. Such analysis ignores the role that Gabriel's love for his wife plays in his social and cultural views, as his proud characterizations of Gretta as a reflection of himself signify an ignorance of her otherness that influences his interactions with everybody he encounters. For that reason, Gretta is not simply the final challenge in a series of contestations to her husband's identity, but instead offers the loving alternative to contemporary stagnancy that Gabriel seeks throughout "The Dead," an empathetic embrace whose rejection confirms the inextricable narcissism at the heart of Gabriel's love and hospitality.

Traditionally, analyses of "The Dead" begin with Gabriel's conversation with Lily in the Morkans' pantry; however, since the way that Joyce's protagonist approaches this conversation is influenced by the way he relates to his wife, it is necessary to examine Gabriel's initial interactions with Gretta before analyzing the rest of the story. Indeed, the initial acts of generosity described in "The Dead" are performed by Gabriel towards Gretta, and while his first line of spoken dialogue is delivered to the caretaker's daughter, the subject of his initial statement is his wife, attributing the reason why they are late to the fact that "my wife here takes three

---

[2] Leonard's Lacanian reading of "The Dead" similarly divides up the story. He contends that "a Lacanian plot summary of 'The Dead' would present the story as three attempts by Gabriel Conroy, with three different women, to confirm the fictional unity of his masculine subjectivity" (289).

mortal hours to dress herself" (*D* 176). Vincent Cheng identifies this statement as a "seemingly good-humored comment" that reflects a hospitable paternalism, a "form of infantilization, similar to the affectionate attitude of the British Empire towards its colonies as incorrigible children … who can thus be only properly ruled by the parent empire" (135). In that sense, not only does this condescending comment demonstrate how such colonial infantilization is redeployed by Dubliners onto each other, but having Gabriel utter such a jest about his wife illustrates the direct relationship between his marriage and the social persona he performs throughout the dinner party (especially considering he offers an infantilizing comment about Gretta to a servant whom he subsequently will treat as a child). By incorporating this unflattering depiction of his wife into this small talk, Gabriel indicates the primacy of his obsession with Gretta's well-being in his overall conceptions of generosity, revealing the "good-humored" desire for domination at the foundation of his love for his wife.

This infantilization continues in Gabriel's and Gretta's conversation with Kate and Julia Morkan. After Kate approves of their plans to stay in a hotel after the party, Gabriel jokes, "But as for Gretta there … she'd walk home in the snow if she were let" (*D* 180). This serves as another incorporation of a condescending reference to Gabriel's wife into socially-appropriate conversation, legitimizing a solicitous paternalism whose domineering nature is emphasized by the qualifier "if she were let." In response, Gretta mockingly chastises Gabriel for his obsession with the family's security, noting the "green shades for Tom's eyes at night and making him do the dumb-bells, and forcing Eva to eat the stirabout" as instances where his concern for his family's well-being compels him to force undesirable precautions upon them (*D* 180). Even though his family's safety is at the heart of these actions, Gabriel's determination to impose these precautions upon Gretta and the children despite their objections signifies his obliviousness to difference, as his concern for their care compels him to relate to them not as autonomous individuals, but rather as helpless dependents whose health reflects his familial compassion back onto himself.[3] This reveals Gabriel's inherent obsession with judging what is best for the people he encounters, a well-intentioned but narcissistic display of power that influences the acts of generosity he displays throughout the story.

Gabriel's refusal to acknowledge objections to this generosity is highlighted further by his reactions to Gretta throughout this conversation. As Gretta quips about being forced to wear galoshes in wet weather, she laughs and gives a mock-

---

[3] Riquelme similarly articulates the ways in which it influences his subsequent encounters by arguing, "More than just a judge of what is good for his family, Gabriel is the main arbiter of taste and action in the story, rendering judgments of praise and blame in his thoughts and in his after-dinner speech. He speaks as one of those in his society empowered to maintain order, tradition, and the status quo" ("The Dead" 124–5). I would only add that rather than reading his familial concern as a subset of his overall desire to "maintain order, tradition, and the status quo," Gabriel's preoccupation with "rendering judgments of praise and blame" stem primarily from his love and concern for his family, as this section of the chapter primarily demonstrates.

chastising glance at Gabriel, "whose admiring and happy eyes had been wandering from her dress to her face and hair" (*D* 180). This description of his "admiring and happy eyes" not only foreshadows the lustful desire that consumes his thoughts towards the story's conclusion, but also shows his preference for admiring her appearance over heeding her words. Such a preference signifies Gabriel's impulse to represent Gretta as a symbol of socially-proper wifedom, especially considering that the description of his gaze as "admiring and happy" anticipates his subsequent observation that her refined presence instilled him with pride throughout the party. ("He had felt proud and happy then, happy that she was his, proud of her grace and wifely carriage" [*D* 216].) Thus, Gretta's appearance drowns out her words, and by indicating that his gaze "had been wandering" across her body, Joyce reveals that Gabriel's objectification of Gretta has occurred throughout this conversation, which indicates how this symbolization will play out in the subsequent conversations Gabriel has at the party.

The exchange over Gabriel's obsession with galoshes also demonstrates the sociocultural implications of his familial "solicitude." When Kate and Julia seek further clarification about galoshes, Gretta describes them as "guttapercha things. We both have a pair now. Gabriel says everyone wears them on the continent" (*D* 181). This observation illustrates both the cultural fascination behind Gabriel's obsession with galoshes and the colonial implications of that interest. His suggestion that they own the "guttapercha things" because "everyone wears them on the continent" shows that he deems galoshes to be a status symbol that signifies his socioeconomic prowess. Not only does this continental justification transform Gabriel's concern and generosity into reflections of his social standing, but it also reveals the imperialist logic behind that generosity since the reference to guttapercha explicitly highlights Great Britain's exploitation of India.[4] By incorporating a symbol of colonialism into Gabriel's paternalism, Joyce demonstrates the imperialist potential of the rejection of otherness, as Gabriel's co-option of his family's health for social advancement also justifies Britain's subordination of its colonies' interests for its material gain. Cheng is thus correct that Gabriel's fascination with galoshes ties his patronizing familial concern to his emulation of "a more 'civilized' dominant European culture, whose very cultural superiority and refinement depended on the exploitation of its colonies" (136–7), and this narcissistic motivation behind his performances of generosity influences his gestures of hospitality towards his fellow guests.

The connection between Gabriel's sociopolitical superiority and his generosity is confirmed by his thoughts of his mother. As Gabriel recalls the tenuous nature of her relationship with Gretta, "a shadow passed over his face as he remembered her sullen opposition to his marriage. Some slighting phrases she had used still rankled in his memory; she had once spoken of Gretta as being country cute and that was

[4] Gifford's annotations stress that galoshes were "made of India rubber or the less elastic gutta-percha" and "became fashionable and popular" in Great Britain in the late-nineteenth century (114).

not true of Gretta at all. It was Gretta who had nursed her during all her last long illness in their house at Monkstown" (*D* 187). Although this reflection may signify Gabriel's defense of his wife against the haughty condemnations of his mother, it also vindicates the segregating social structures upon which her disapproval is based. Not only does Gabriel represent Gretta as not being "country cute" instead of disputing the legitimacy of that label, but by following this rebuttal with his observation that Gretta nursed his dying mother, Gabriel rhetorically characterizes that empathy as the reason why his wife is not "country cute." This both solidifies Gabriel's connection between generosity and social standing and confirms his obsession with overshadowing his wife's low birth by elevating her to his socio-cultural level. Rather than represent Gretta's compassion as an affirmation of her otherness, Gabriel rhetorically co-opts that compassion in order to dissolve that otherness, revealing the preoccupation with class differences at the heart of his feelings for his wife. This preoccupation will later compel Gabriel to qualify Molly Ivors's observation that Gretta is from Connacht by clarifying "shortly" that "her people are," implying that their marriage has erased his wife's West Irish origins (*D* 189). Similar to his fascination with galoshes, Gabriel's determination to undo Gretta's "country cute[ness]" betrays his aspiration for a "cultural superiority and refinement" that suppresses "the more primitive, unrestrained, and still uncolonized Irish free spirit allied symbolically to the West of Ireland and Gretta's roots in Galway" (Cheng 137), confirming the denial of otherness that undergirds his generosity throughout the text.

Having established the self-absorption in Gabriel's devotion to his family, we can now turn to his conversations at the Morkans' party to discover how his amatory narcissism influences his social interactions. When we read these conversations with respect to his initial representations of Gretta, we see Gabriel adopting similar strategies of hospitable paternalism that validate his self worth. The temptation then may be to continue to read such similarities as evidence of Gabriel's broader obsession with socio-cultural superiority, to which his devotion to Gretta is merely one of the story's three subsets. However, when analyzing "The Dead" with respect to Buber, we see how Gabriel's misrecognition of his loved one influences his general ignorance of the "many-faced otherness" of his social environment (*Man* 61). In each of these episodes, Gabriel's determination to transform his counterparts into reflections of his hospitality and sophistication compel him to disregard their difference, and the recurring failure of these interactions sets Gabriel up for the amatory frustration that concludes Joyce's story.

Gabriel's interaction with Lily illustrates this connection between his romantic and social encounters. Similar to his reactions to Gretta, Gabriel infantilizes Lily, using his memory of her as a "child [who] used to sit on the lowest step nursing a rag doll" to justify his patronizing comments towards her. Gabriel also interweaves observations about Lily's social status with these infantilizing representations, basing his patronizing attitude towards her on the "three syllables she had given his surname," which reveals a flat accent characteristic of low

Dublin culture. His subsequent combination of her child-like appearance with her "pale … complexion" and "hay-coloured hair" thus construct an image of Lily that is doubly condescending, and his contemplation of her appearance under "the gas in the pantry" signifies Gabriel's temptation to define Lily's existence by her position within the Morkans' house (*D* 177). Similar to Gabriel's portrayal of Gretta as the socially-respectable wife, this characterization of Lily allows him to use stereotypical assumptions about her existence to guide their interaction in a way that comfortably validates his social superiority.

Gabriel's subsequent conversation with Lily continues to categorize her according to his socioeconomic assumptions. Based on the girl's age and social status, he asks "in a friendly tone, do you still go to school?" When she reveals that she has completed her education, Gabriel immediately and "gaily" responds, "O, then … I suppose we'll be going to your wedding one of these fine days with your young man, eh?" (*D* 177). These questions strengthen Gabriel's attempts to symbolize Lily, as his recognition of her potential wedding date arises not from any personal knowledge of her, but rather because marriage is one of the only socioeconomic options still available to a lower-class Irish female who is no longer in school. In that sense, these patronizing questions echo Gabriel's earlier jests about Gretta's unruliness, revealing such polite paternalism to be crucial in validating his self-image. Thus, by asking such questions to a woman that he has symbolically constructed as a lower-class child, Gabriel represents Lily's past, present, and future and redefines her otherness in ways that authenticate his superiority.

However, Lily's response complicates Gabriel's hospitable paternalism. When Gabriel asks if her wedding day is around the corner, Lily answers "with great bitterness" that "the men that is now is only all palaver and what they can get out of you" (*D* 178). This response is shocking to Gabriel not only because it contradicts his assumptions of Lily's future, but also because her bitterness foregrounds their insulting nature. Nevertheless, while "the high colour of his cheeks" does demonstrate his embarrassment over Lily's anger, Gabriel's reaction reveals his continued inability to recognize her otherness. The narration notes that "Gabriel coloured *as if he felt* he had made a mistake" (*D* 178; italics mine), which betrays his opinion that he actually did not make a mistake, and his removal of his galoshes "without looking at her" demonstrates his determination to disassociate himself from Lily the second she ceases to conform to his representation of her. This desire to evade Lily's anger is confirmed by the "Christmas-time" present of the coin, which he places in her hand and escapes before she has the chance to return it (*D* 178). This final gesture illustrates both Gabriel's indifference towards Lily's specific identity and the socioeconomic foundations of his generosity, as the "friendly tone" of his prescripted, patronizing questions finds its counterpart in the monetary gift he provides to evade the girl's response. Thus, rather than accept Lily's "bitterness" as evidence of her otherness, Gabriel covers over that difference with a display of generosity that enables him to continue treating her as the symbolic child he initially constructed, demonstrating that his embarrassment in the pantry has done nothing to change the way he interacts with others.

Gabriel's subsequent encounter with Molly Ivors further perpetuates his socio-cultural anxiety. Similar to Gretta and Lily, Miss Ivors's appearance dominates Gabriel's initial perceptions, compelling him to make assumptions about her sociopolitical identity that predetermines his interactions with her. He represents Miss Ivors as a "frank-mannered talkative young lady," a characterization that combines negative depictions of her outspokenness with an infantilized description of her youth. Bolstered by his subsequent attention to her "freckled face and prominent brown eyes," the Molly Ivors that Gabriel describes seems barely older than Lily, even though she and Gabriel "were friends of many years' standing and their careers had been parallel, first at the University and then as teachers" (*D* 187; 188). This paternalist depiction of Miss Ivors as a "young lady" enables Gabriel to dismiss whatever unpleasant remarks come from her "frank-mannered talkative" manner as evidence of a youthful precociousness. His concluding observation that "she did not wear a low-cut bodice and the large brooch which was fixed in the front of her collar bore on it an Irish device" may demonstrate Gabriel's awareness of their differing national and cultural positions (*D* 187), but by combining this observation with the infantilizing description that preceded it, Gabriel undercuts such difference as evidence of a quaint political enthusiasm that he can legitimately dismiss.

Nevertheless, the dispute that occurs during the dance forces Gabriel to pay more than a passing notice to Molly Ivors's otherness. While admittedly Miss Ivors rudely castigates Gabriel for his ambivalence to an Irish Ireland, she is actually more willing than her partner to accept their differing attitudes. Even though she chides his patronage of the unionist "rag" and calls him a "West Briton" (*D* 188), Miss Ivors acknowledges that "I was only joking" and eagerly concedes that "she liked [his review of Browning's poems] immensely" (*D* 189). By contrast, Gabriel reacts to Molly Ivors's chastisement in a manner similar to Lily's bitter retort, "glanc[ing] right and left nervously" and "avoid[ing] her eyes" (*D* 190) while hiding his consternation under "soft friendly tone[s]" (*D* 189) and "good humour" (*D* 190), which confirms his use of politeness to avoid conversations that don't validate his socio-cultural superiority. When he finally does engage Miss Ivors's nationalist charges, his sudden outburst ("O, to tell you the truth … I'm sick of my own country, sick of it!" [*D* 190]) illustrates the suppression of difference at the heart of his gentility, as his inability to undercut Miss Ivors's rebukes through "good humour[ed]" deflections gives way to a harsh rejection of the foundation of his colleague's otherness. Whereas Miss Ivors could see past their differing attitudes and still compliment his review, Gabriel's agitation prevents him from acting in a similar manner, and the end of the dance enables him to retreat from her as quickly as he escaped Lily.

Gabriel's thoughts after the dance also echo his insecurities after the pantry exchange, where the social superiority that compelled his previous assertions of hospitable paternalism now encourages him to become the party's censor. That Miss Ivors's charges against Gabriel might be valid is irrelevant; what matters is the impropriety of asserting these jests in public and "[trying] to make him ridiculous before people," a social transgression that legitimizes his desire to "banish from his mind all memory of the unpleasant incident" (*D* 191). Echoing the colonial implications of his earlier thoughts of Gretta, Miss Ivors's calling him a West Briton compels Gabriel to deride his colleague through language reminiscent of Britain's rejection of "the more primitive, unrestrained, and still uncolonized Irish free spirit." His labeling of Miss Ivors as a "girl or woman, or whatever she was" recalls his initial characterization of her as a "frank-mannered talkative young lady," only this time her refusal to play the obedient child encourages Gabriel to deny her humanity by classifying her identity as potentially other than "girl or woman" (*D* 191). This dehumanizing classification continues through Gabriel's representation of Molly Ivors's gaze as "staring at him with her rabbit's eyes," as her calling him a West Briton essentially transforms her from a child into an animal (*D* 191). This reveals Gabriel's desire to shut out Miss Ivors's attempts at dialogue, especially considering that his characterization of her eyes as rabbit-like constitutes a refusal of her gaze, mirroring both his earlier "avoid[ance of] her eyes" (*D* 190) and his subsequent condemnation of her "critical quizzing eyes" (*D* 192). Thus, by trying to "banish from his mind all memory" of his exchange with Miss Ivors, Gabriel rejects the otherness displayed by her playful rebukes, and his use of social etiquette to suppress his colleague betrays the colonial potential of his obsession with generosity.

This rejection of Miss Ivors's otherness continues in his preparation for his dinner address. Similar to his earlier agitation, Gabriel attempts to blame Miss Ivors entirely for his present irritation, ignoring her jesting tone to paint her as an initiator of "ill-feeling between them" who "would not be sorry to see him fail in his speech" (*D* 192; 193). Gabriel even rejects her "[praise]" of his Browning review, doubting the sincerity of her compliments and suggesting that she did not have "any life of her own behind all her propagandism" (*D* 192). This rhetorical interrogation is significant not only because it suppresses Miss Ivors's attempts at dialogue by representing her approval of his review as insincere, but also because it signifies Gabriel's refusal to accept her otherness by reducing her qualified rebuke to a generic "propagandism." When read alongside his earlier chastisements of her decorum, the repressive element of Gabriel's hospitable paternalism becomes apparent, as his displeasure over his conversation with Miss Ivors entices him to "banish" her otherness "from his mind."

The height of Gabriel's narcissistic hospitality occurs at the Morkans' dinner table. While Gabriel may seem more generous and sympathetic than Duffy, examining his reactions to the sociopolitical identities of his fellow dinner guests reveals him to display an anxiety towards cultural difference reminiscent of the hostility in "A Painful Case." Gabriel does act more politely towards his fellow Dubliners, but that politeness masks an intolerance towards otherness that inevitably promotes his sophistication over the crude manners of his counterparts. This intolerance is evident during his conversations with Lily and Miss Ivors, but the extent to which Gabriel fails to affirm his fellow guests is demonstrated throughout the construction and performance of his Christmas dinner speech.

Here Joyce demonstrates how the failure to confirm individual otherness impedes broader sociopolitical interactions, as the frustrations Gabriel experiences during the earlier conversations undermine the success of his speech and illustrate his general inability to interact productively within his body politic.

Gabriel's initial thoughts about his speech illustrate this refusal of cultural otherness. As he attempts to recover from his conversation with Lily, he fears that the failure of their interaction will translate into a similar disaster at the dinner table. While his fear that "he had taken up a wrong tone" in his speech seems to acknowledge his culpability for this imagined communicative breakdown (*D* 179), the reasons why the tone of his speech is incorrect prevent this from being a productive breakthrough. His reference to the "indelicate clacking of the men's heels" (*D* 179) echoes Duffy's castigation of the "working-men ... dragging the sawdust over their spits with their heavy boots" in the Chapelizod public-house (*D* 112), as Gabriel blames the audience's lack of proper cultural knowledge for the failure of his address. Thus, by changing the Browning quote to "some quotation that they could recognise from Shakespeare or from the Melodies" (*D* 179), Gabriel's alterations become further evidence of a socially-classifying generosity that bestows kindness on an uncultured group primarily to confirm his sophistication. Rather than envisioning the failure of his speech as an opportunity to affirm the otherness of his fellow guests, Gabriel instead exploits their otherness to explain away that failure and to characterize his revisions as validations of his superiority, demonstrating how the colonial logic that Cheng identifies in his social pretensions pervades his monologic interactions with others.

Additionally, the anxiety over the speech that follows his exchange with Molly Ivors highlights the narcissistic foundations of his address. As Gabriel tries to balance the revisions of his address with his agitation with Miss Ivors, he adds a platitude towards his aunts that will secretly enable him to rebuke his former colleague:

> He would say, alluding to Aunt Kate and Aunt Julia: Ladies and Gentlemen, the generation which is now on the wane among us may have had its faults but for my part I think it had certain qualities of hospitality, of humour, of humanity, which the new and very serious and hypereducated generation that is growing up around us seems to me to lack. (*D* 193)

By identifying the Morkan sisters with the older hospitable generation that is threatened by Miss Ivors's younger "hypereducated" group, Gabriel performs another act of infantilization that essentially transforms him into a benevolent adult teaching "hospitality," "humour," and "humanity" to a precocious youth (even though he belongs to the same generation as Miss Ivors). The social respectability that he plans to endorse in his speech thus becomes merely another power play by which Gabriel can regain the control lost by Miss Ivors's jests, revealing both the exclusionary and hypocritical nature of his generosity.

The hypocrisy of this tactic is also confirmed by his concluding thoughts over these revisions. His self-satisfied "very good: that was one for Miss Ivors" (*D* 193) demonstrates that his praise of the old generation's hospitality is not brought about by any sincere admiration for those qualities, but is solely uttered to score a point against Miss Ivors. His subsequent reference to the aunts whom he ostensibly is praising as "two ignorant old women" (*D* 193) confirms his disinterest in an earnest endorsement of "hospitality," "humour," and "humanity," which forces us to view his performances of generosity and decorum as strategic exclusions of his fellow Dubliners. Gabriel's reworking of his dinner speech thus sets up his dinner-table performance to be the ultimate act of hospitable paternalism, and his determination to defeat his colleague reduces this opportunity to engage productively with his fellow Dubliners into both a rejection of Miss Ivors and the Morkan sisters and a congratulatory address to himself.

The performance of Gabriel's dinner speech confirms the exclusionary nature of this endorsement of generosity. Consistent with his desired alterations following the encounter with Miss Ivors, Gabriel begins his address with the generational argument that he desires to be the retort to her: "I feel more strongly with every recurring year that our country has no tradition which does it so much honour and which it should guard so jealously as that of its hospitality" (*D* 203). Tanja Vesala-Varttala persuasively argues that this collective representation of Irish hospitality "conjures up a firm sense of belonging and togetherness that would counter Miss Ivors's remarks about his being a 'West Briton' (*D* 190)" (41). Indeed, Gabriel's isolation of this hospitality as a national "tradition which does it so much honour" represents the generosity at the heart of his social identity as a collective attribute inherent in all the Irish, and his suggestion that Ireland "should guard" this quality "jealously" represents inhospitable individuals as threats to the nation. Thus, Gabriel fashions what could have been a sincere celebration of Irish hospitality into a weapon to suppress the inhospitable charges of a "frank-mannered talkative young lady," confirming the exclusion of otherness behind Gabriel's hospitality.

This totalizing characterization of hospitable Ireland also ignores the unique identities of his fellow citizens. Whereas previous thoughts about his speech emphasized his audience's difference, Gabriel's oration imposes a rhetorical sameness on not only the dinner table, but on the entire country, enabling him to suppress any distinctions in "grade[s] of culture" by representing everyone as possessing the same generosity that he does. Vesala-Varttala argues that "making the other into a reflection of oneself also has its problems: 'How does one know whether one sees oneself or the other in the mirror of comparison?' (ibid., p. 150). Gabriel imposes sameness onto the group of Dubliners in order to make them serve his own selfish needs" (42). Thus, not only does this tactic enable him to suppress Miss Ivors, but by using his interpretation of hospitality as a marker of authentic Irishness, Gabriel banishes the otherness of his fellow Irish by viewing all Dubliners as reflections of himself, and the continental foundations of his previous assertions of generosity transform this celebration of Irish hospitality into the policing of a "primitive" and "unrestrained" population.

Gabriel's assault on inhospitality strengthens when he recalls the absence of Miss Ivors from the dinner table. As he soaks in the "hearty murmur of assent" to his words that "ran through the table," he remembers that "Miss Ivors was not there and that she had gone away discourteously" (*D* 204). This representation of Miss Ivors's departure as "discourteous" builds confidence in Gabriel and emboldens his condemnation of the "new generation, educated or hypereducated as it is." In a manner more explicit than his earlier construction of this argument, Gabriel represents the "serious and enthusiastic" generation embodied by Miss Ivors as the central threat against which hospitable Ireland should be on guard, noting that such Dubliners "lack those qualities of humanity, of hospitality, of kindly humour which belonged to an older day" (*D* 204). Thus, the infantilization that Gabriel mentally constructed emerges in his dinner speech, and he can use his assumed position as the hospitable patriarch of the older generation to admonish the person whose otherness lies at the heart of his criticism.

Miss Ivors's absence at the dinner table also amplifies the monologic aspects of Gabriel's address. While the "hearty murmur of assent" illustrates that Gabriel's points have their share of support, his determination to use his speech as a coded attack on Miss Ivors excludes that "murmur" because his words are not intended for his fellow guests. Instead, Gabriel desires to castigate his former colleague regardless of her departure, resulting in an odd performance of exclusion aimed at an already absent party. That Gabriel performs the revised speech anyway demonstrates the hollow nature of his affirmation of hospitality because nobody at the dinner table has been let in on the real implications of his oration. This reverses the "generous" nature of Gabriel's earlier amendments to his speech (since he is ultimately uninterested in whether his speech is "above the heads of his hearers" [*D* 179]) and results in him rejecting difference merely for its own sake, transforming his advocacy of "humanity," "hospitality," and "kindly humour" into an empty performance of exclusionary flattery whose audience is solely himself.

Gabriel's concluding remarks confirm the narcissistic nature of his speech. Whereas the first half of his address focused on the exclusion of the "hypereducated" generation epitomized by Miss Ivors, the second half is comprised primarily of flattering characterizations of the Morkan sisters that sharply depart from what we know to be Gabriel's actual attitude towards his aunts. Considering his earlier characterization of his aunts as "two ignorant old women," Gabriel's subsequent celebration of the Morkan sisters as the "Three Graces of the Dublin musical world" becomes an empty flattering gesture instead of an earnest appreciation of their hospitality (*D* 205). Rather than embrace their kindness despite his feelings that they are inferior, Gabriel chooses to reshape their otherness into an elevated symbolic representation that demonstrates his cultural sophistication. Thus, when he bids the table to "drink to their health, wealth, long life, happiness and prosperity," he suppresses the otherness he finds threatening and characteristic of a lower "grade of culture" under a generic banner of "hospitality" (*D* 206).

Gabriel's speech thus concludes an evening that reveals his tendency to reconstruct the otherness of his counterparts into reflections of his generosity and high culture. While the temptation may be to read these encounters as isolated examples of cultural snobbery, reading Gabriel's conversations with respect to his initial thoughts of Gretta reveal another factor behind his behavior. The hospitable paternalism inherent in Gabriel's central relationship becomes amplified on a broader scale throughout the evening, as his determination to transform Gretta's "country cute[ness]" into reflections of his cultural sophistication reveals both the preoccupation with sameness that dominates his interactions with his fellow guests and the colonial implications of such rejections of otherness. The dinner speech may seem to be a success to him, but his inability to embrace his audience's differing social identities confirms his refusal to affirm the "many-faced otherness" that Buber argues is essential to maintain productive social relationships. What we are left with at the party's conclusion is an awareness of the monologic nature of Gabriel's social etiquette, a narcissistic obsession with sameness that ultimately will permeate the "friendly pity" he will display towards his grieving wife at the story's end (*D* 223).

The Face for which Michael Furey Had Braved Death

Towards the middle of his speech, Gabriel states that "our path through life is strewn with many … sad memories: and were we to brood upon them always we could not find the heart to go on bravely with our work among the living" (*D* 205). In a sense, the ecstatic lust that fills Gabriel's mind throughout the second half of "The Dead" constitutes his failure to take his own advice. While his memories of marital bliss are not necessarily sad, Gabriel's thoughts throughout their journey from the Morkan house to the hotel constitute his determination to "linger on the past" (*D* 205), envisioning the joy of his early relationship with Gretta to cover over their present marital stagnation. Such an obsession may entice Gabriel with the possibilities of sexual conquest, but by subordinating his awareness of the present to a remembrance of the past, Gabriel retreats into a narcissistic celebration of his own romantic prowess that creates the misrecognition at the heart of his climactic dialogue with Gretta. What occurs during the story's final exchange constitutes Gabriel's final encounter with the otherness inherent in his relationship with his wife, and the way that he responds to the revelation of Michael Furey will go a long way towards evaluating the epiphany he experiences.

At the party's conclusion, Gabriel finds his wife standing on the Morkans' staircase listening to Bartell D'Arcy sing "The Lass of Aughrim." As he watches Gretta react to the music, Gabriel intellectualizes her emotional state:

> There was grace and mystery in her attitude as if she were a symbol of something. He asked himself what is a woman standing on the stairs in the shadow, listening to distant music, a symbol of. If he were a painter he would paint her in that attitude. Her blue felt hat would show off the bronze of her hair against the darkness and the dark panels of her skirt would show off the light ones. *Distant Music* he would call the picture if he were a painter. (*D* 211)

As before, Gabriel's interpretation of Gretta's reaction to the music relies on material observations that classify her thoughts and emotions according to her physical characteristics. Numerous critics have read this gesture as further evidence of Gabriel's cultural snobbery, subordinating Gretta's specific emotions to a masturbatory mental exercise, and since my reading of this scene coincides with this analysis, I will only offer a few additions.[5] First, the narcissism of Gabriel's gesture is confirmed not by his perception that Gretta is a "symbol of something," but rather by his concession that his wife is *not* a symbol. His observation that the "grace and mystery in her attitude" makes it seem "*as if* she were a symbol" demonstrates that Gabriel is fully conscious that Gretta is not the image that he constructs. This makes Gabriel's decision to symbolize her anyway a deliberately performative gesture that subordinates Gretta's otherness to his intellect, reducing her to an object of inquiry and forgoing the opportunity to forge an authentic connection with her.

Second, the parallels between this artistic rendering of Gretta and their earlier exchange over the galoshes demonstrate the pervasiveness of Gabriel's symbolic attitude towards her. His preoccupation with her "blue felt hat" and the "bronze of her hair" echoes the earlier gaze of his "admiring and happy eyes," which "wander[ed] from her dress to her face and hair" throughout their conversation with the Morkan sisters. Especially considering his earlier determination to present his wife as the opposite of "country cute," this sustained effort to envision Gretta as a symbol of wifely grace signifies Gabriel's desire to supplant her otherness with a characterization of a sophisticated wife that validates his social worth. This symbolic gesture thus reveals the fear of difference in Gabriel's romantic desire, illustrating that the exclusion of otherness that comprised his encounters throughout the dinner party ultimately stem from his struggles to accept the "grace and mystery in [Gretta's] attitude."

Finally, the vague nature of Gabriel's representation foreshadows his misrecognition of Gretta's emotional state. Gabriel's reaction to seeing his wife is not significant simply because he represents her as a symbol, but rather because he recognizes her to be a symbol "of something." His reliance on her physical appearance to signify her emotional state may encapsulate his wife as a symbol, but it is incapable of the understanding needed to embellish that symbol in any

[5] For example, Baccolini describes the scene as "another instance where Joyce's women are denied subjectivity in two ways. First, Gretta's experience is not directly described but is mediated by Gabriel's perception; second, the sight of his wife leads Gabriel to imagine himself as artist and his wife as the model and muse" (155). Henke similarly argues that "Shrouded in grace and mystery, Gretta becomes a model of feminine tranquility, a romantic image of blue and bronze, blurred in a setting of vague nostalgia. Her feelings are framed and appropriated, her passions castrated and erased" (*Desire* 44). Norris also notes that "The very form of Gabriel's gesture toward woman – the rhetorical question ('He asked himself what is a woman ... a symbol of') that proclaims its disinterest in what woman is in favor of parading its own profundity – masks artistic conceit as gyneolatry" (*Suspicious* 219).

significant manner. Thus, Gabriel's inability to articulate comprehensively the symbol that Gretta represents produces an incomplete interpretation that fails to grasp the significance of her emotions. This makes it inevitable that Gabriel misrecognizes the "colour on her cheeks" and the "shining" of "her eyes" as evidence that she feels the desire that festers in him during this encounter, as his determination to construct Gretta into a mirror of his desire only results in an incomplete representation of a generic love object.

The memories stirred by this attitude towards Gretta bolster Gabriel's romantic self-absorption. As the Conroys search for a cab to the hotel, "moments of their secret life together burst like stars upon his memory" (*D* 214), as Gabriel's obsession with the symbolic Gretta compels him to recollect past marital bliss that contrasts with the stagnancy he attributes to their present relationship. Such recollections demonstrate John Rickard's contention that "Gabriel … tries to create a past better than the present in order to avoid facing the present" (69). While Rickard specifically refers to the dinner speech, his reading applies just as well to this situation since Gabriel's desire to live within the warm memories of past romance entices him to ignore the marital rut into which he feels they have fallen. This obfuscation of the present is evidenced further by the "wave of yet more tender joy" that "escape[s] from his heart" as a result of these memories, which encourages Gabriel to "recall to her those moments, to make her forget the years of their dull existence together and remember only their moments of ecstasy" (*D* 215). Not only do such desires contradict Gabriel's earlier warnings against "linger[ing] on the past," they speak to his continued efforts to promote a fantasized romance with a symbolic Gretta over the present relationship he has with her, and his longing to "recall to her those moments" foreshadows his attempts in the hotel room to force Gretta to comply with his fantasy.

The monologic nature of this desire is evidenced further by Gabriel's disinterest in conversing with his colleagues during the cab ride:

> He was glad of its rattling noise as it saved him from conversation. She was looking out of the window and seemed tired. The others spoke only a few words, pointing out some building or street. The horse galloped along wearily under the murky morning sky, dragging his old rattling box after his heels, and Gabriel was again in a cab with her, galloping to catch the boat, galloping to their honeymoon. (*D* 215)

What is significant about this observation is not simply that Gabriel's fantasy dissuades him from interacting with anyone, but that Gretta is included among the list of people with whom Gabriel is "saved" from conversing. The juxtaposition of Gabriel's relief over being "saved … from conversation" and Gretta's "tired" stare "out of the window" demonstrates that the lust generated by Gabriel's misapprehension of her emotion does not encourage him to communicate with her. Instead, he leaves his wife behind and transports back to their honeymoon, eschewing their present-day relationship for further experience of their past romance. This explicit comparison between their past and present romances reveals that the fantasies developed by Gabriel during their journey to the hotel have no place for Gretta to participate, but are instead masturbatory longings for past connubial bliss. Thus, when he uses the desire stirred by these memories to envision a sexual union between them at the hotel, the monologic nature of those memories guarantees that the fantasy he constructs disqualifies any empathetic embrace of her agony, subordinating whatever emotions that were actually stirred by "The Lass of Aughrim" to the generic devotion needed to fulfill Gabriel's desires.

The specific description of Gabriel's sexual fantasy confirms this exclusion of Gretta's otherness. As they head to their hotel room, Gabriel rehearses his anticipated sexual encounter in his mind, and the fantastic description that results demonstrates the inevitable expulsion of Gretta's longings from his desires:

> After the kindling again of so many memories, the first touch of her body, musical and strange and perfumed, sent through him a keen pang of lust. Under cover of her silence he pressed her arm closely to his side; and, as they stood at the hotel door, he felt that they had escaped from their lives and duties, escaped from home and friends and run away together with wild and radiant hearts to a new adventure. (*D* 216)

Once again, Gabriel's "keen pang of lust" is enabled "under cover of [Gretta's] silence." By isolating his wife's "silence" as the catalyst for their "new adventure," Gabriel explicitly reveals that the renewal of marital love he desires to consummate has no place for the emotions Gretta is experiencing. Rather than acknowledge her disturbed mood, Gabriel uses the silence perpetrated by that mood to construct a fantasized encounter in which Gretta will submit to his romantic prowess. Indeed, his subsequent longings to "seize her" (*D* 217) and "crush her body against his" (*D* 218) illustrate his impulse to subordinate her anguish to his lust, confirming the narcissistic desire triggered by and thus inextricably linked to his symbolic perceptions of Gretta.

The resulting disparity between Gabriel's imagined encounter with Gretta and the reality of that experience needs little direct engagement. It is indeed nothing revolutionary to assert that Gabriel's assertions of sexual conquest are supplanted by the primacy of Michael Furey in Gretta's mind. It is also unnecessary to devote substantial analysis to the resulting reconceptualization of class and social hierarchies since most scholars will stipulate that Gabriel's realization that a "boy in the gasworks" could consume his lover's thoughts forces him to reevaluate his socio-cultural assumptions throughout "The Dead" (*D* 221). Instead, what requires our attention at the conclusion to Joyce's story is not the story of Michael Furey itself, but how Gabriel perceives this story to take place and the conflict that emerges between Gabriel's and Gretta's apprehensions of Furey's fate. Doing so enables us to ascertain the ways in which the hospitable paternalism that Gabriel performed at the Morkans' party influences his reactions to his wife's anguish, which clarifies our understanding of both the form of love he expresses at the story's conclusion and the ability of that love to translate into an ethically productive epiphany.

It is generally agreed that at the end of "The Dead," Gabriel enters into a "different kind of communion with [Gretta] than he had anticipated, resulting in his recognition of her otherness" (Rice 47). Indeed, many Joyce scholars argue that the revelation of Michael Furey transforms Gabriel's shallow genteelness into a "strange, friendly pity" for his wife's misery (*D* 223), which compels him to "[reject] both [his] narcissistic and naturalistic selves" (Balsamo 773).[6] However, while Gabriel's attitude towards Gretta may seem softer and more humble at the story's conclusion, the actual affection that he expresses towards her is only further proof of the narcissistic ambivalence towards difference that typifies his generosity throughout the text. In actuality, Gretta comes closest to an empathetic embrace in "The Dead," whereas Gabriel's continued preoccupation with sameness and self-serving sympathy undermines his redemptive potential. To realize this, we must compare Gretta's anguish during this scene to Gabriel's reactions to that anguish to discover the differing attitudes toward otherness at the heart of their contrasting understandings of Michael Furey's tragedy.

Initially, Gabriel ignores the substance of Gretta's remorse by transforming her memories into a romantic competition with Michael Furey. While Benstock argues that Gretta's account of Furey "relegat[es] Gabriel Conroy to the persona of the retroactive cuckold" (*Dubliners* 164–5),[7] the antagonism between the two rival "suitors" is constructed entirely in Gabriel's head. He may feel that "while he had been full of memories of their secret life together, full of tenderness and joy and desire, she had been comparing him in her mind with another," but at no point during Gretta's recollection of Galway does she articulate such a comparison or supplant her love for Gabriel with her anguish for Michael Furey (*D* 221). Rather, Gretta solely laments Furey's tragic death, a compassionate reaction to being reminded about a childhood tragedy that has nothing to do with her marriage. While Gretta's melancholy is brought about by empathizing with Furey's illness and death, Gabriel's "dull anger" is triggered by how this death influences him, isolating their different approaches to otherness in a manner that parallels Mrs Sinico's and Duffy's reactions to the Rotunda concert's failure. This disparity is bolstered by Gabriel's "cool interrogation" of his wife, where his ironic supposition that "you were in love with this Michael Furey" is clarified by Gretta that "I was great with

---

[6] Other critics who read the story's ending redemptively include Harold Mosher Jr., who argues that "the ending does not bring closure but rather openness to Gabriel's westward progress, at least a partial awareness of self, the possibility of an escape from the limits of past routine and of repeated actions and hackneyed language" (64); and Wheatley-Lovoy, who notes that "the imperative mood [of his concluding thoughts] indicates that Gabriel is talking *to himself*, a distinct shift toward the dialogical and a first step toward true reflexivity" (188–9).

[7] Norris goes a step further in reading this scene as Gretta's revenge against Gabriel, arguing that she "takes revenge for a denied trip to Galway by revisiting it spiritually and romantically in a way that displaces her husband forever from the passional center of her life and marginalizes him in his own self-image" (*Suspicious* 217).

him at that time."[8] This reveals that she did not experience the stereotypical love with Furey that Gabriel assumes and that whatever romantic connection that was experienced "at that time" has now worn off (*D* 221). For those reasons, Gretta's tears are not those of lost love, but are rather evidence of her ability to empathize with the emotional and physical deterioration that comprised Michael Furey's death. Gabriel and Gretta are thus talking at cross purposes, and his insistence on projecting a romantic competition where it does not exist demonstrates his inability to understand or affirm either his wife or her former companion.

Gretta's subsequent attempts to envision Michael Furey confirm her empathetic reaction to his otherness. One could argue that if Gabriel is guilty of a narcissistic obsession with the physical appearances of Gretta, Lily, and Miss Ivors, then Gretta's evoking the image of Michael Furey at the conclusion of "The Dead" is complicit in a similar narcissism. However, Gretta's representations of the "expression" in Michael Furey's "big dark eyes" are not designed to assign him a socio-cultural identity or to highlight her sophistication (*D* 220). Rather, her focus on his love for her and his death provides Furey with an identity separate from social categories, and it enables Gretta to empathize with his tragic fate and affirm their emotional connection. Just as Emily Sinico feels compassion towards the singers having to perform to an empty Rotunda, Gretta's lament for Michael Furey is guided by her compassion for his tragedy. ("He died when he was only seventeen. Isn't it a terrible thing to die so young as that?" [*D* 221].) Gretta's characterization of Furey as a person instead of a symbol thus enables her declaration that "I think he died for me" (*D* 221), and her subsequent account of his death bears witness to him in a manner that "confirm[s] him as creature and creation" (Buber *Knowledge* 69), which provides a thoughtful contemplation of a victim of West Irish paralysis.

By contrast, Gabriel's refusal to acknowledge Michael Furey proves his inability to empathize with others. While Gabriel's previous encounters had been initiated by his contemplating the physical appearance of his acquaintances, when he first becomes aware that Gretta's tears are shed for Furey, "Gabriel [is] silent [because] he [does] not wish her to think that he was interested in this delicate boy" (*D* 220). This performed disinterest influences his subsequent responses to Gretta's story, as each of her attempts to envision the departed boy are interrupted by Gabriel's insistence that she continue describing his tragedy. When she pauses to note that "he had a very good voice, poor Michael Furey," Gabriel interrupts her digression with a curt "well; and then?" that forces Gretta to continue recounting his death (*D* 222). Soon after, she notes that "I can see his eyes as well as well!

---

[8] Seamus Deane's footnote in the Penguin *Dubliners* describes this phrase as "slang" that implies that Gretta "got along very well with him to the point where the relationship might well have become serious, though as yet without any great sexual connotation" (*D* 316fn). By contrast, Gifford notes that "the connotation of the word ['great'] is the intimacy of friendship rather than of 'love" (*Joyce* 124). In either case, Gretta is describing a serious emotional bond that does not approach the sentimental attachment that Gabriel assumes, making her anguish in the hotel room more characteristic of empathy than of romantic love.

He was standing at the end of the wall where there was a tree," but she is again cut short by Gabriel's question "And did he go home?" (*D* 223). In each instance, Gretta's attempt to imagine her departed friend is denied by Gabriel's insistence that she carry on with her story, which subsequently prevents him from relating to Michael Furey as anything other than a generic rival for Gretta's affection. Gabriel's refusal to allow Gretta to describe Furey thus becomes an explicit rejection of his otherness.

For that reason, Gabriel's subsequent inability to "apprehend" the "wayward and flickering existence" of Michael Furey does not signify simply his transition away from the social categorization that has comprised his identity, as it is traditionally read (*D* 224). Rather, it simply demonstrates Gabriel's ignorance of Michael Furey's appearance since he never let Gretta describe him. Thus, when he groups the "boy in the gasworks" with the "vast hosts of the dead" that he also evokes, Gabriel transforms his refusal to acknowledge Michael Furey's otherness into a broader inability to grasp the "many-faced otherness" of those who comprise his concluding epiphany (*D* 224). Even if Gabriel rejects his earlier socio-cultural superiority, he is still no closer to an understanding or acceptance of otherness since he replaces social standing with a totalizing death whose inescapability unites all of humanity in a sameness similar to the "hospitality" he endorsed at the dinner table. Gabriel may recognize the fate that unites all beings living and dead, but his refusal to accept Michael Furey or the "vast hosts" he conjures up as anything beyond their inclusion in the body count prevents this epiphany from influencing his future interactions within the Dublin body politic in any productive sense.

Reading Gabriel's attitude towards Michael Furey in dialogue with Gretta's eulogy to her deceased friend thus demonstrates the underlying conflict between their two methods of dealing with otherness. Gretta's attitude throughout the hotel scene shows the empathy at the heart of her interactions with others, revealing her desire to understand and mourn the tragedy of Michael Furey without ever denying her love for Gabriel. Specifically, her remark that Gabriel's lending the sovereign to Freddy Malins proves him to be "a very generous person" and her kiss affirming that generosity both demonstrate that the agony brought about by "The Lass of Aughrim" has not taken the place of her present love for her husband (*D* 219). Unlike Gabriel, Gretta can negotiate the past and the present, and her ability to love the sophisticated Gabriel Conroy and to mourn the "boy in the gasworks" simultaneously reveals the affirmation of difference at the heart of her attitude towards her fellow Dubliners. By contrast, Gabriel's "dull anger" over the revelation of Michael Furey indicates his overall inability to accept others who are not reflections of his grandeur. That his anger gradually gives way to a "strange friendly pity" does not negate the continued refusal of otherness that undergirds that "pity." In fact, while some might argue that Gabriel's concluding epiphany enables him to understand Gretta's situation and affirm her otherness, reading Gabriel's thoughts after she has gone to sleep reveals his mental transformation to be a more benevolent version of the narcissistic preoccupation with sameness and the rejection of difference that he has demonstrated throughout "The Dead."

In her advocacy of a reformed Gabriel, Sonja Bašić draws upon "Gabriel's tender pity for his sleeping wife" as evidence that "his love is presented by Joyce as a good, human (and humanly limited) love" (35). While Gabriel's feelings for Gretta certainly become fonder at the end of "The Dead," his "tender pity" also separates himself from her and calls that love into question. Specifically, Gabriel's meditations on the memory of Michael Furey carry with them a suppression of his present affection for his wife. He initially notes that "it hardly pained him now to think how poor a part he, her husband, had played in her life," which demonstrates both his continued subordination of present responsibilities to past romantic bliss (even though the bliss is not his own this time) and the suppression of his amorous responsibilities to his wife. Also, the symbolic image he constructs of the sleeping Gretta is further alienated from his heart. Gabriel notes that "he watched her while she slept as though he and she had never lived together as man and wife," a gesture that could signify his desire to contemplate Gretta in a new way, but that also entails the suppression of his love for her in order to perform that contemplation. Rather than simply state that he saw Gretta in a different light, Gabriel explicitly represents her as a being other than his wife, which shows how his new-found admiration for Michael Furey's sacrifice compels him to downplay his humdrum perception of his marriage. Thus, when he notes that his image of Gretta "was no longer the face for which Michael Furey had braved death," he preferences the passion encapsulated in the image of the dying boy over the haggard expression of the grieving wife, revealing the "strange friendly pity" spurred by these contemplations to continue to promote past romance over present stagnation (*D* 223).

In addition, Gabriel's characterization of Michael Furey as a romantic paragon undercuts the viability of his epiphany. While his concluding thoughts about the Galway boy are kinder than his previous rejections, these benevolent representations still fail to acknowledge him as anything other than an abstract image, this time as a tragic romantic hero. That Gabriel formulates contradictory generic impressions of Furey at the story's conclusion both highlights the arbitrary nature of his attitudes towards others and nullifies the redemptive potential of his epiphany since his positive impression of the Galway boy still replaces his otherness with a stereotypical romantic identity. In a sense, Gabriel's "strange friendly pity" becomes an intellectual exercise akin to his contemplations of Gretta on the staircase, as his envious admiration of Michael Furey's sacrifice essentially seeks to ascertain what a "young man standing under a dripping tree" is a symbol of (*D* 224). Similar to the monologic ecstasy stirred by *Distant Music*, this symbolic contemplation fills Gabriel with a self-pitying jealousy because he perceives that Michael Furey "pass[ed] boldly into that other world, in the full glory of some passion," whereas Gabriel will "fade and wither dismally with age" (*D* 224). Thus, when Gabriel recognizes that "she who lay beside him had locked in her heart for so many years that image of her lover's eyes when he had told her that he did not wish to live" (*D* 224), he does not convey an empathetic acceptance of either Gretta or Michael Furey; instead, he uses his wife's anguish as evidence that the Galway boy's death has affected Gretta more than Gabriel's love, which continues to reduce her empathetic outburst to a generic longing for lost love and reveals that the only tragedy for which Gabriel can mourn is his own.

This envious representation of Michael Furey's death complicates our ability to read the "generous tears" that subsequently "[fill] Gabriel's eyes" in any empathetic sense (*D* 224). While some critics point to this outburst as the confirmation of Gabriel's epiphany,[9] juxtaposing his "generous tears" with the melancholy envy that produced them precludes us from using this as evidence of a shift away from narcissistic love. Since Gabriel cries primarily because he feels that he has been usurped by Furey, we cannot read his tears as evidence of empathy towards either Gretta or Furey, but must rather recognize them as a sign of Gabriel's continued preoccupation with his self-image. This preoccupation is bolstered by his subsequent concession that "he had never felt like that himself towards any woman but he knew that such a feeling must be love," which may seem to connote the reclamation of his love for Gretta, but is actually a rejection of that love in favor of self-pity (*D* 224). When he proclaims that the passion that compels a person to die outside his lover's window "must be love," Gabriel implies that the romantic bond he shares with Gretta is not love, for "he had never felt" this passion that "must be love." By placing a romantically self-destructive Michael Furey on a pedestal, Gabriel confirms his preference for the passions of the past over the love of the present, transforming what could have been an empathetic breakthrough into another self-absorbed exercise. Similar to Duffy's appropriation of Mrs Sinico's tragedy, Gabriel's "generous tears" use the tragedies of Michael Furey and Gretta Conroy to mourn his "soul's perpetual loneliness" (*D* 107), erasing both Galway characters from their own story and using his envious desire to perform his concluding rejection of otherness.

---

[9] Rice contends that "Gabriel's recognition of this could be considered just as self-pitying as Duffy's final vision of himself 'outcast from life's feast' had Joyce not prefaced it by noting that '*Generous* tears filled Gabriel's eyes' (emphasis mine) and followed it with a significant moment of perception, assisted by the altruistic, generous tears that both blur and create Gabriel's vision" (47–8). Riquelme also argues that "we can read Gabriel's 'generous tears' as linked more with the snow, 'general all over Ireland,' than with his earlier self-interested magnanimity. In this alternative reading, Gabriel is not merely exercising his habit of dominating solicitude again; he has discovered through a heightened sense of mortality his kinship to a group" ("The Dead" 137). In addition to my narcissistic reading of these tears, I would note that even if we interpret "generous" in ethical instead of numerical terms, we cannot divorce this outburst from his earlier performances of "generosity" that were narcissistically guided. Specifically, we must read Gabriel's "generous tears" alongside Gretta's reference to him as a "very generous person" earlier in the scene, specifically recalling that Gabriel brought up lending Malins the sovereign to get Gretta into bed. When we also remember that Gretta's ambivalence compelled Gabriel to condemn "the sottish Mallins and his pound," we realize that Gabriel's performances of "generosity" are always guided by self-interest, which provides a story-specific context for us to read the "generous tears" he sheds at the end of "The Dead" (*D* 218).

This refusal of difference undermines the epiphanous efficacy of the "snow [that] was general all over Ireland" at the story's end (*D* 225). Ellmann interprets this snowfall as Gabriel's recognition of humanity's interconnectedness, noting that "Gabriel is conceding and relinquishing a good deal—his sense of the importance of civilized thinking, of continental tastes, of all those tepid but nice distinctions on which he has prided himself" (*JJ* 249).[10] However, if love requires the empathetic affirmation of the difference within others, then Gabriel's advocacy of death as humanity's equalizer risks covering over that otherness with an all-consuming sameness. Cheng contends that this blanketing can "break down the barriers of difference … into at least a recognition of generosity and sameness, all shades of equal color" (146–7), but to have Gabriel perform this gesture immediately after ignoring Gretta's empathy and Furey's identity risks the erasure of more than discriminatory signs of difference. Rather, it compels the dissolution of all markers of otherness by asserting that humanity's common fate means that everyone is essentially the same, transforming the "sameness" Gabriel advocates here into a self-serving consumption of the other. The snow thus becomes a narcissistic gesture akin to Gabriel's advocacy of "hospitality," "good humour," and "humanity" during his speech, a totalizing endorsement of collectivity that represents "all the living and the dead" as reflections of himself (*D* 225). Gabriel's epiphany of "The Dead" may enable him to understand how death equalizes everyone, but that equalization ultimately prevents him from the acknowledgment and affirmation of otherness that is essential to promote ethically productive relationships. What emerges from Gabriel's "swoon[ing]" acceptance of the "general" snowfall is thus not a renewed love for Gretta or an acceptance of cultural difference, but rather a resigned submission to a solitary "journey westward" spurred primarily by the envious admiration of "a young man standing under a dripping tree" (*D* 225).

****

Riquelme argues that the resolution of "The Dead" constitutes "Gabriel's recognition of his connection to the dead, his recognition—and ours—that 'death' … is the word known to all men and all women" ("The Dead" 136). While this is certainly true, it is also the central problem with Gabriel's epiphany, as his subordination of love to death continues the obsession with sameness and the ambivalence towards difference that characterize his interactions at both the amorous and social levels. His final thoughts before falling asleep may prepare him "to set out on his journey westward," but there is no textual indication that the traveler who awakes the next morning will be closer to empathizing with either Gretta, Michael Furey, or any

---

[10] Earl Ingersoll similarly argues that the snow enables Gabriel to understand "the principle of identification, the power of metaphor allowing him to see his experience as synonymous with those of Michael Furey, his aunts, and all the living who will one day be among the dead" (153).

of the Dubliners whom he has patronized throughout Joyce's story (*D* 225). By reducing his affection for Gretta to a "strange friendly pity," Gabriel denies himself the loving embrace that enables his wife to give life to Michael Furey through her response to "The Lass of Aughrim," choosing instead to affirm an abstract human commonality that sacrifices a vibrant otherness to a stultifying sameness. While his "long[ing]" to bury "the years of their dull existence together and remember only their moments of ecstasy" does precipitate a commitment to this "journey westward," his inability to acknowledge Gretta's anguish as anything other than a refusal of his love guarantees that he will travel alone, ending *Dubliners* with an emotional exile indicative of the self-absorbed attempts of its protagonists to escape the sociopolitical paralysis that grounds the collection.

In that sense, Gabriel's "journey" sets the stage for our next two encounters with Joycean lovers. Like the protagonists in *Dubliners*, Stephen Dedalus and Richard Rowan find themselves trapped within a stultifying Ireland that constrains their free expression, and like Gabriel, both artists will choose the life of the exile over the empathetic embrace of the lover. However, the protagonists of *Portrait* and *Exiles* will be more successful in their escapes, enabling Joyce to examine the efficacy of amatory exile from the perspectives of those who actually fly beyond the geographic borders of Irish paralysis. Nevertheless, Stephen's and Richard's inevitable returns to Ireland reveal this liberation to be temporary, and through their attempts to renegotiate their positions within the city from which they fled, Joyce shows that the refusal to love one's fellow Dubliner inevitably short-circuits the narcissistic lover's escape from everyday Ireland even when they succeed in leaving the country. As we shall discover, the shortest way to Tara is not via Holyhead, but is rather ventured along the streets of Dublin, as the desires for amatory freedom inevitably give way to the embrace of "Love's Old Sweet Song."

Chapter 3
Stephen Dedalus's Marketplace of Love

Towards the conclusion of *Stephen Hero*, Stephen Daedalus tells Cranly that poetry is the exemplary form for the artist to profess amorous desires because "song is the simple rhythmic liberation of an emotion. Love can express itself in part through song" (*SH* 176). However, while Stephen may endorse the ability of poetry to liberate these emotions "in part," he acknowledges the limitations of expressing his specific desires through the antiquated language of the genre. Echoing Joyce's early criticism of the "lying drivel" about "spiritual love and love for ever" (*LII* 191), Stephen argues that it is impossible for the modern lover to pledge eternal devotion to a loved one, and for that reason, he feels it necessary "to express his love a little ironically" (*SH* 174). Given that Daedalus and his *Portrait* counterpart unite such amatory poetry with their efforts to elude the repressive instruments of Catholicism and nationalism, Joyce's attributing to his doppelganger a refusal of love that he had since discarded enables him to reflexively examine the aspiring exile's responsibilities towards his fellow Dubliners and to criticize a desire for individual liberation so totalizing that it cannot accept others who do not share his commitment.

Of course, Stephen Daedalus was not meant to see the light of day and the Stephen Dedalus of *Portrait* undergoes significant changes from Joyce's initial draft. Nevertheless, this episode from *Stephen Hero* is important to our overall consideration of Stephen for two reasons. First, it isolates Stephen's aesthetic preoccupation with love, revealing amatory desire to be a primary catalyst for his art. Not only do his verses "give him pleasure," but the "mature and reasoned emotions" of love provide the inspiration necessary for Stephen to fulfill his artistic calling, which parallels the tram poem and the "Villanelle of the Temptress" Stephen writes for E.C. in *Portrait* and the vampire poem he attempts to write in *Ulysses*. Second, it shows Stephen dismissing eternal love as a "feudal terminology" rendered obsolete by the contingency of the modern lover and endorsing instead an amatory interaction more akin to a form of gift exchange (*SH* 174). To Stephen, "it might be a test of love to see what exchanges it offers … when we love, we give … We give something, a tall hat or a book of music or one's time and labour or one's body, in exchange for love" (*SH* 175). This characterization of amatory exchanges echoes the Aquinas fragments Stephen considers in "Scylla," portraying love as a commodity that the lover gains in exchange for a desirable good or service. From this perspective, Stephen embodies the narcissistic lover by valuing love not as a method to "will some good" to a loved one, but as a "thing" desired by the lover to strengthen a deeper self-love (Gifford and Seidman 221).

This commodification continues in a conversation with Lynch, where Stephen embellishes his marketplace of love. Here Stephen rails against the lover who pledges devotion to a love object through marriage, noting instead that "I like a woman to give herself. I like to receive" (*SH* 202). This distinction between love and freedom becomes the focal point of his meditations on amatory desire: "A human being can exert freedom to produce or to accept, or love to procreate or to satisfy. Love gives and freedom takes" (*SH* 203). While subsequent Stephens do not voice this distinction as explicitly as Joyce's initial version, Stephen's aesthetic agendas throughout Joyce's works are frequently grounded in this delineation between love and freedom that advocates the latter's "acceptance" and fulfillment of individual desires over the former's compassion and sacrifice. Rather than seeking a reciprocal attachment to a loved one, Stephen prefers an amatory freedom that advances the good of his beloved only if it simultaneously promotes his own desires. Thus, even though the Stephen of *Portrait* and *Ulysses* negotiates these conflicts in a more nuanced manner than Stephen Daedalus's blanket narcissism, examining Stephen's amatory longings from initial manuscript through published works reveals the extent to which this subordination of the love object becomes the foundation of Stephen's amatory aesthetics and a driving force behind his departure from Ireland.

In that sense, Stephen's attitude towards love enables Joyce to develop the critique of narcissism that he initiated in *Dubliners*, as his desire to advance his individual agenda through the submission of love objects complements the self-centered escapes of his predecessors. Also, like his *Dubliners* counterparts, Stephen's amatory meditations are largely symbolic. Rather than affirming his loved ones' otherness, Stephen ignores the specific attributes of his lovers, reducing them to either vessels into which he can pour his soul's longings or muses for his artistic ideas. In so doing, Stephen "constructs these women out of the materials of his culture" (Harkness *Voices* 57) in the same way that young Joyce "fashioned" his muse for *Chamber Music* out of the "culture of generations before her," and Joyce's acknowledgement that "the beauty of [Nora's] soul outshone that of my verses" as he composes *Portrait*'s drafts foreshadows the elusiveness of Stephen's love objects and reveals Joyce's critique of the sentimentality behind Stephen's amatory freedom (*LII* 237). Thus, by draining his love objects of their specific essence, Stephen substitutes a "cool scholasticism" for the reciprocal confirmation that Buber argues is needed to maintain meaningful relationships, reducing his pursuits to a "distancing form that abstracts love" (Polhemus 260).

Furthermore, Stephen foregrounds rejection in his amatory pursuits, acting under the assumption that his love will inevitably be unrequited. Even when no outright refusal occurs, the existence of differing viewpoints or qualified love is sufficient for Stephen to assert that his love has been betrayed and to justify his separation from his love object. Not only does this construct a self-fulfilling prophecy where the suspicion of unrequited love entices Stephen to act in ways that destroy his amatory quest, but it also excludes the acceptance of otherness that is necessary for true love because rather than "affirm the person [he] struggle[s] with" (Buber *Knowledge* 69), Stephen views the mere existence of otherness as a rejection of himself. This predominance of rejection and refusal in Stephen's longings exacerbates his own fascination with refusal and limits his artistic options to the point where exile becomes the only alternative available. Thus, though Joyce is certainly sympathetic to the repressive social institutions that compel Stephen's flight, he criticizes the extent to which he enacts his refusal, and evaluating *Stephen Hero* and *Portrait* through Buber's amorous writings enables Joyce to interrogate a rejection of Dublin primarily grounded in the lover's individual "subtract[ion]" from the community (*SH* 233).

The Unsubstantial Image

Stephen's amatory framework begins to take shape in *Portrait*'s second chapter. Similar to Joyce's childhood wanderings around Blackrock, Stephen envisions himself as a modern Edmond Dantes searching for his ideal Mercedes, and Joyce isolates the social significance of this preoccupation with romance by shifting between Stephen's meditations on love and his recognition of his family's deteriorating financial situation. By juxtaposing Stephen's brooding on *The Count of Monte Cristo* with the Dedalus family's perpetual relocation, Joyce illustrates that Stephen uses amatory desire to avoid the despair that permeates his family life. In so doing, Joyce describes Stephen's pursuit of love as the quest to find an ideal love object whose submission will repair his wounded self-image.

Initially, Stephen's idealization of Mercedes demonstrates his preoccupation with characterizing love objects as symbols. Throughout *Portrait*'s second chapter, Stephen's longings are devoted entirely to an ideal projection of Dantes's lover who will rescue him from the paralysis of his surroundings: "As he brooded upon her image, a strange unrest crept into his blood. Sometimes a fever gathered within him and led him to rove alone in the evening along the quiet avenue. The peace of the gardens and the kindly lights in the windows poured a tender influence into his restless heart" (*P* 67). What is striking about this observation is not simply Stephen's fantasized preoccupation with a fictional love object, but that his pursuits of Mercedes isolate him from his environment. While he fashions these romantic quests as havens from his family's financial deterioration, the "fever" the image "gather[s]" in his "restless heart" completely cuts him off from his surroundings, compelling him to "rove alone" in order to quell the "strange unrest" Mercedes instills within him.

The extent to which Stephen's idealized romance alienates him from his fellow Dubliners is evident in his subsequent meditations: "The noise of children at play annoyed him and their silly voices made him feel, even more keenly than he had felt at Clongowes, that he was different from others. He did not want to play. He wanted to meet in the real world the unsubstantial image which his soul so constantly beheld" (*P* 67). This longing establishes a mutual exclusivity between Stephen's everyday life and his amatory desires, pitting the "silly voices" of his fellow children against the "unsubstantial image" of his ideal Mercedes for supremacy over his attention. His observation that he "wanted to meet in the real world the unsubstantial image which his soul so constantly beheld" illustrates his preference for a symbolic encounter over the real-world "play" of his childhood existence, strengthening an idealistic, solitary framework that eschews the social interaction necessary for true love. Rather than accepting and affirming the otherness of his fellow Dubliners, Stephen rejects their "silly voices" and instead affirms the image of an ideal Mercedes whose pursuit and capture will repair his "restless heart."

Also, the specifics of his desired encounter with the "unsubstantial image" of Mercedes enhance the narcissistic nature of his longings. Stephen recognizes the inherent futility of seeking refuge in an imaginary lover, but he does not let that impossibility deter his quest. Instead, he takes comfort in "a premonition" that assures him that "this image would, without any overt act of his, encounter him" (*P* 67). While primarily enabling Stephen to brood on a fictional Mercedes despite the acknowledged impossibility of an actual encounter, the "premonition" also contributes to the development of his amatory narcissism because it subordinates the image of his love object to his prowess as a lover. What is telling about Stephen's premonition is not simply that the "unsubstantial image" will encounter him, but that his Mercedes will find him "without any overt act of his." This qualification illustrates that Stephen's fantasy does not consist of a reciprocal encounter in which Stephen advances the good of his loved one, but rather comprises a monologic encounter in which his loved one submits to his affection. His subsequent meditations on this "premonition" illustrate that his pursuit of Mercedes is desirable not because of any actual love for her, but rather because "in that moment of supreme tenderness he would be transfigured. He would fade into something impalpable under her eyes and then in a moment, he would be transfigured. Weakness and timidity and inexperience would fall from him in that magic moment" (*P* 67). Similar to Duffy's fascination with Emily Sinico, Stephen shapes the image of Mercedes into a mirror that reflects his grandeur and serves as the catalyst to his spiritual awakening. Stephen thus values love not as an end to itself, but rather as a means to a narcissistic end, enacting the subordination of the love object to the lover that will typify the "romantic irony" he endorses in *Stephen Hero*.

This objectification of Stephen's love object is also evident in his choice of Edmond Dantes as an ideal lover. Henke's description of this choice foregrounds its direct relationship to Stephen's narcissism, as his idealism of Dantes "identifies with a man betrayed by his friends and his mistress, unjustly exiled and imprisoned, but eventually able to wreak vengeance on those who failed him" (*Desire* 60). This reveals the prominence of rejection in his amatory meditations and his determination to refuse his love object during their climactic encounter. Stephen's fantasized reenactment of *The Count of Monte Cristo* highlights his desire to conclude his pursuit of Mercedes by rejecting her love:

> In his imagination he lived through a long train of adventures, marvelous as those in the book itself, towards the close of which there appeared an image of himself, grown older and sadder, standing in a moonlight garden with Mercedes

> who had so many years before slighted his love, and with a sadly proud gesture of refusal, saying:
> —Madam, I never eat muscatel grapes. (*P* 65)

By highlighting Mercedes as the ideal love object, Stephen defines a woman who "slighted his love" as his beloved, committing himself to an amatory pursuit in which his feelings will never be completely requited. Stephen thus desires not to be the lover who affirms a loved one, but rather the jilted lover obsessed with revenge. When we read his fascination with Dumas's novel in conjunction with his desired transfiguration, the extent to which Stephen's amatory views necessitate the subordination of his love object becomes apparent. To attain the awakening he seeks, he must find an ideal lover that will submit completely to him. However, by identifying Mercedes as the love object he seeks, Stephen renders inevitable the rejection of his desire, fulfilling his "premonition" by pursuing a real-world Mercedes whose inability to give him unconditional adoration justifies her exclusion. This emphasis on rejection in Stephen's interpretation of love thus illustrates its narcissistic underpinnings and foreshadows the extent to which Stephen will alienate the people around him to obtain the transfiguration he desires.

However, Stephen finds it difficult to fulfill his premonition. While he feels it inevitable that his Mercedes will spur his transfiguration, Stephen cannot shut out the stultifying nature of his surroundings, as the disappointments experienced at the Whitsuntide play and the Cork auction drive him further away from his loved ones. Much like Joyce's inability to "speak to the girls I used to meet at houses" (*LII* 237), a brooding Stephen recognizes "his own futile isolation. He had not gone one step nearer the lives he had sought to approach nor bridged the restless shame and rancour that divided him from mother and brother and sister." However, even though he acknowledges that "his life had grown to be a tissue of subterfuge and falsehood," the "savage desire" for spiritual transfiguration continues to dominate his actions, reducing his everyday interactions to "idle and alien" trivialities (*P* 105). The necessity of achieving "the enormities which he brooded on" thus consumes Stephen, transforming the "fierce longings of his heart" into the "wasting fires of lust" that entice him to accept a prostitute as his Mercedes (*P* 105; 106). The beginning of *Portrait*'s third chapter reveals that whatever awakening that occurred through Stephen's encounter with the prostitute has driven him further away from his fellow Dubliners, replacing the "wasting fires of lust" with "a cold lucid indifference" that "reign[s] in his soul" (*P* 110). His desired transfiguration has thus alienated him from everyone he encounters, requiring him to seek another amatory awakening to repair his wounded self-image.

The opportunity for this second awakening presents itself at the retreat held by the college of the sodality of the Blessed Virgin Mary. It is a critical commonplace to read Father Arnall's hellfire sermon as triggering the shock that compels Stephen to seek salvation through religious devotion. While this assessment is certainly correct, we must also consider the role that love plays in enticing Stephen to repent his sinful ways. Indeed, it is the sermon's juxtaposition of fear and love that appeals to Stephen's romantic sensibilities and ultimately encourages him to repent his lustful past.

Stephen recognizes the need to repent throughout the sermon, but initially his pride holds him back. What finally compels him to repent is the articulation of God's love as the guarantor of a successful confession. Father Arnall concludes by arguing that God's enduring compassion for humanity ensures that even the most mortal sins will be absolved by an earnest repentance:

> [God] is there in the tabernacle burning with love for mankind, ready to comfort the afflicted. Be not afraid. No matter how many or how foul the sins if only you repent of them they will be forgiven you. Let no worldly shame hold you back. God is still the merciful Lord Who wishes not the eternal death of the sinner but rather that he be converted and live. (*P* 145)

By depicting God as a merciful, compassionate deity, Father Arnall presents the love of heaven as the alternative to the terrors of hell, guaranteeing salvation to those who repudiate their sins through confession. His subsequent juxtaposition of God's love with the act of contrition reveals the interconnected nature of repentance and love, and the articulation of this relationship is what finally compels Stephen to "[bow] his head, praying with his heart" (*P* 146). His thoughts before his confession illustrate this determination to replace the "wasting fires of lust" with the heavenly embrace of God's love, pledging that "he would be at one with others and with God. He would love his neighbour. He would love God Who had made and loved him. He would kneel and pray with others and be happy. God would look down on him and on them and would love them all" (*P* 154). This newly-acquired pledge to "love his neighbor" stands in sharp contrast to the "contempt of others" articulated at the chapter's beginning (*P* 113), and Stephen's desire to "be at one with others and with God" signifies his attempts to replace a limited, self-serving desire with an all-encompassing, transcendent love.

However, reading Stephen's musings on God's love in conjunction with his earlier longings reveals the narcissistic underpinnings of this spiritual transfiguration. Father Arnall's juxtaposition of fear and love may have enticed Stephen to repent his transgressions, but it also compels him to seek a self-serving interpretation of heavenly love that embraces God's compassion primarily to save his damned soul. He observes that "everybody in the chapel would know then what a sinner he had been. Let them know. It was true. But God had promised to forgive him if he was sorry. He was sorry" (*P* 155). Stephen's reasoning that "God had promised to forgive him if he was sorry" reveals his repentance to be an early example of his "marketplace of love" since he characterizes the spiritual connection he desires as a give-and-take situation where he offers his confession to purchase God's forgiveness. The repudiation of his lustful desires through spiritual love thus becomes just another opportunity for Stephen to achieve his transfiguration, replacing Mercedes with God in his quest for the ideal love object.

Stephen's observation also reveals his continued alienation from his fellow Dubliners. His flippant "let them know" illustrates his inability to truly "be at one with others," as his pride compels him to separate himself from the others in his position. Even though the other inhabitants of the chapel are seeking the same repentance he desires, Stephen's inability to empathize with their common situations entices him to imagine them spurning his sinfulness, constituting a perceived rejection of his soul's longings that justifies their exclusion. Departing from his earlier pledge to "be one with" and "love his neighbor," this snide response to the possibility of his sins being discovered demonstrates Stephen's continued desire to seek transcendent love while driving a wedge between himself and others.

The narcissism of Stephen's religious devotion continues in his rigorous spiritual performances throughout *Portrait*'s fourth chapter. While Stephen embraces his obligations at the sodality and submits his life to "a rigorous discipline" (*P* 162), his thoughts concerning the necessity of this discipline betray his self-serving intentions:

> His life seemed to have drawn near to eternity; every thought, word and deed, every instance of consciousness could be made to revibrate radiantly in heaven: and at times his sense of such immediate repercussion was so lively that he seemed to feel his soul in devotion pressing like fingers the keyboard of a great cash register and to see the amount of his purchase start forth immediately in heaven, not as a number but as a frail column of incense or as a slender flower. (*P* 160)

Here, the metaphorical cash register reiterates Stephen's perception of God's love as a commodity that can be endlessly purchased through religious performance instead of a transcendent compassion that unites God and humanity in a loving embrace. By equating his "rigorous discipline" with incense and flowers, Stephen illustrates that his spiritual life is primarily an attempt to save himself by adhering to an economic interpretation of religious devotion. Stephen's sacrifice to God's compassion is essentially represented as a prison sentence, and his narrow design to use his "time served" as a ticket to his desired transfiguration constructs a substandard version of the love he seeks.

Unsurprisingly, Stephen's commodification of his religious devotion undermines his ability to attain the transcendent love he desires. While he characterizes the world as "one vast symmetrical expression of God's power and love" (*P* 162), Stephen is incapable of experiencing that love and compassion in his heart. He recognizes the centrality of the "passions of love and hate" in the religious life to which he has pledged himself, but his self-serving commitment to that life makes him "unable to harbour them for any time or to force his lips to utter their names with conviction." Instead of being tied to God and humanity in an all-encompassing love, Stephen's adherence to the "great cash register" only purchases a "brief iniquitous lust" that "slip[s] beyond his grasp leaving his mind lucid and indifferent" (*P* 161). He may feel that his spiritual redemption can be obtained solely through overt spiritual obligations, but his unwillingness to sacrifice his individual desires and to give himself completely to God's compassion merely results in a half-hearted devotion to a transcendent love.

The half-hearted nature of this commitment is evident in Stephen's attitude towards his fellow Christians. His subsequent thoughts demonstrate the incompatibility of his spiritual obligations with compassion towards others:

> To merge his life in the common tide of other lives was harder for him than any fasting or prayer, and it was his constant failure to do this to his own satisfaction which caused his soul at last a sensation of spiritual dryness together with a growth of doubts and scruples. His soul traversed a period of desolation in which the sacraments themselves seemed to have turned into dried up sources. (*P* 164)

Stephen's inability to "be at one [both] with others and with God" demonstrates the inevitable failure of his spiritual transfiguration. While he is willing to interpret Father Arnall's sermon literally by punishing his senses and seeking continual repentance, Stephen's failure to "merge his life" with his fellow Christians betrays the spirit of that sermon because he is unwilling to sacrifice himself meaningfully for others. By refusing to love his neighbor as himself, Stephen adopts instead a hollow form of religious devotion that will fall short of achieving his salvation. This fate is evidenced by the gradual deterioration of the religious discipline to which Stephen submits himself, as his continued rejection of others transforms the sacraments he upholds into "dried up sources," ironically unraveling his encounter with God through each subsequent performance of that encounter. His subsequent musings on his hollow confessions demonstrate this insufficiency, as the sacrament Stephen deems integral to his salvation now perpetuates "restless feelings of guilt" and creates an endless cycle by which "he would confess and repent and be absolved, confess and repent again and be absolved again, fruitlessly" (*P* 166). By subordinating his obligation to love others to his rigorous devotion to a narcissistic reawakening, Stephen denies himself the transcendence that his initial confession made possible.

The inevitable deterioration of that transcendence is evident in Stephen's rejection of "the chill and order" of the Catholic life (*P* 174). He may briefly consider the sodality director's offer and imagine himself to be a priest, but those specific contemplations illustrate the increasingly narcissistic nature of his religious framework:

> How often had he seen himself as a priest wielding calmly and humbly the awful power of which angels and saints stood in reverence! His soul had loved to muse in secret on this desire. He had seen himself, a young and silentmannered priest, entering a confessional swiftly, ascending the altarsteps, incensing, genuflecting, accomplishing the vague acts of the priesthood which pleased him by reason of their semblance of reality and of their distance from it. (*P* 171)

Stephen thus finds the priesthood desirable not because of the position's devotion to God and humanity, but rather because it grants him the "awful power" that would enable him to be revered by angels and saints. By recognizing that he "loved to muse in secret on this desire," Stephen reveals that his religious adoration is not brought about by a humbling compassion, but is rather compelled by a proud desire to obtain a transcendent power over humanity that would compel the adoration of the masses. This observation exacerbates his growing indifference towards Christ's universal commandment, replacing his desire to love his neighbor with a more powerful yearning to compel his neighbors to love him. However, even this transcendent power is ultimately insufficient to entice his acquiescence to a life of endless religious devotion, and his refusal of the director's proposal in order to "be elusive of social or religious orders" constitutes his greatest endorsement of freedom over love (*P* 175), which necessitates the renewal of his amatory quest to discover an alternative to the spiritual compassion he rejects.

The climax of this renewed quest occurs on Dollymount strand. As Simon Dedalus inquires about enrolling his son in the University College of Dublin, Stephen ponders the new intellectual opportunity that potentially awaits him, representing this scholarly path as an escape from the "chill and order" of the religious devotion that he has rejected. In language reminiscent of the premonition concerning Mercedes, Stephen considers these thoughts to be an "elfin prelude" to an unforeseen destiny that will enable him to eschew completely the Catholic Church in favor of the free intellectual life he now considers integral to his transfiguration (*P* 179). His subsequent castigation of the Christian brothers he encounters in Dollymount illustrates the extent to which his rejection of religious love constitutes an uncompromising advocacy of intellectual freedom:

> It was idle for him to move himself to be generous towards them, to tell himself that if he ever came to their gates, stripped of his pride, beaten and in beggar's weeds, that they would be generous towards him, loving him as themselves. Idle and embittering, finally, to argue, against his own dispassionate certitude, that the commandment of love bade us not to love our neighbour as ourselves with the same amount and intensity of love but to love him as ourselves with the same kind of love. (*P* 180)

This rejection of the Christian brothers reveals the narcissistic nature of the intellectual life with which he replaces his religious devotion. His inability to love his neighbor as himself "with the same kind of love" illustrates an inevitable disconnect between himself and others that will typify the transfiguration he desires. His subsequent decision to replace the commitment of the brothers with the unfettered expression of "the artist forging anew in his workshop out of the sluggish matter of the earth a new soaring impalpable imperishable being" thus signifies his desire to cast aside the bonds that compel individuals to sacrifice themselves out of love for each other (*P* 183), ensuring that narcissism will permeate whatever aesthetic persona he constructs.

This aesthetic opportunity is provided by a chance encounter with a girl on the beach "gazing out to sea." Stephen's descriptions of the girl's "fuller and softhued" thighs, "soft and slight" bosom, and "long fair hair" clearly reveal his attraction to her (*P* 185–6). However, while he is obviously enchanted with the girl's beauty, her ability to be assimilated into his symbolic depiction of a sea-bird provides him the most excitement. Henke's observation that Stephen's representation of the girl "sublimates erotic agitation beneath effusions of purple prose" speaks to this preoccupation with symbolic desire (*Desire* 74), as it is his characterization of her bird-like beauty rather than his specific attraction that emboldens his adoration. In this sense, the bird girl loses any explicit significance and Stephen essentially becomes his own love object, as his ability to create symbolic beauty out of the "sluggish matter" of his surroundings generates his most ardent romantic exclamation of the text. By divesting the girl of her unique worth and envisioning her instead as a static representation of ideal beauty, Stephen thus unites his developing aesthetic persona with the amatory narcissism that dominates his reflections, and it is this ability to fulfill the prophecy of his last name through an unfettered expression of desire that compels him to cry "heavenly God" in an "outburst of profane joy" (*P* 186).

However, Stephen's encounter with the bird girl is not as transcendent as he imagines. While he rejoices in his aesthetic apprehension of the woman's symbolic beauty, he ignores the stranger's specific reaction to his gaze that reveals the ultimate futility of his adoration:

> When she felt his presence and the worship of his eyes her eyes turned to him in quiet sufferance of his gaze, without shame or wantonness. Long, long she suffered his gaze and then quietly withdrew her eyes from his and bent them towards the stream, gently stirring the water with her foot hither and thither. The first faint noise of gently moving water broke the silence, low and faint and whispering, faint as the bells of sleep; hither and thither, hither and thither: and a faint flame trembled on her cheek. (*P* 186)

While Stephen foregrounds his adoration of the bird girl as the central epiphany of his quest, the girl's reaction to this adoration reveals the incompleteness of that epiphany and the misrecognition of his love. The observation that the bird girl "quietly suffers his gaze" only to "withdraw her eyes" indicates that the connection initiated by Stephen's apprehension of her symbolic beauty has been terminated by her desire to ignore his lustful stare, articulating an implicit rejection of Stephen's worship that echoes his preoccupation with Mercedes.[1] That his "outburst of profane joy" is uttered in reverence of a love object that casts his presence aside reveals Stephen to have once again constructed a romantic path to

---

[1] Alan W. Friedman similarly notices the detachment inherent in this epiphanous encounter, describing the scene as a "non-occurrence" (71) and writing that "rather than serving as 'the angel of mortal youth and beauty, an envoy from the fair courts of life' who will 'throw open before him in an instant of ecstasy the gates of all the ways of error and glory,' as Stephen would have it, the 'birdgirl,' like Emma on the tram, becomes something he can imaginatively capture and make into what he will so long as no direct contact occurs" (60–1).

a desired re-awakening that contains the rejection of that romance at its heart. This demonstrates that this climactic scene is not an authentic encounter between two lovers, but is rather the fetishization of a love object that suffers and ultimately rejects the encounter, which alienates the lover from the adoration he seeks and foreshadows the inevitable failure of Stephen's desired transfiguration.

This inevitable alienation is evident in Stephen's detachment from his surroundings throughout the episode. Even if the brief connection made with the young woman is sufficient to compel Stephen's artistic calling, the narration of that connection is bookended by observations of his isolation from the others present on Dollymount strand. Stephen's initial contemplation of his prophetic surname is juxtaposed with his recognition that "he was alone. He was unheeded, happy and near to the wild heart of life. He was alone and young and willful and wildhearted, alone amid a waste of wild air and brackish waters and the seaharvest of shells and tangle and veiled grey sunlight and gayclad lightclad figures, of children and girls and voices childish and girlish in the air" (*P* 185). Even though this observation illustrates a present contentment through his "happy" and "willful" heart, the repetition of Stephen being "alone" and "unheeded" dominates this description, illustrating the disconnect between the protagonist and the "gayclad lightclad figures" who fail to recognize his presence. This isolation continues after Stephen's "outburst of profane joy." After he pledges "to live, to err, to fall, to triumph, to recreate life out of life," he recognizes that his epiphany has clouded his awareness of his surroundings (*P* 186). Upon emerging from his internal jubilation, "He halted suddenly and heard his heart in the silence. How far had he walked? What hour is it? There was no human figure near him nor any sound borne to him over the air" (*P* 186–7). Stephen's recognition of this aloneness reveals that his encounter with the bird girl has done nothing to ameliorate his continual isolation from his environment, as the lack of "human figures near him" echoes his "unheeded" presence amidst the other inhabitants of Dollymount strand earlier in the episode. Even if the encounter with the bird girl fulfills Stephen's artistic calling, his epiphanous outbursts are drowned out by the silence that surrounds it, and the fact that *Portrait*'s fourth chapter concludes with this quiet recognition shows that Stephen's rejection of the obligation to love his neighbor in favor of the call "to recreate life out of life" simultaneously abdicates the romantic affirmation he desires and signals the beginning of an isolated and exiled artistic existence.

A Test of Love

This chapter now turns to *Stephen Hero* and the conclusion of *Portrait* to analyze the young poet's rehearsals of his amatory framework in his real life relationships. As the repressive elements of Irish Catholicism and nationalism increasingly constrain his individual freedom, Stephen's desire to find the real-world counterpart to his ideal Mercedes encourages him to relate to the most important people in his life as similar symbolic catalysts for his transfiguration. In his interactions with Emma and Cranly, Stephen ignores the specific characteristics of their affection for him, focusing instead on the ways in which they can be re-presented to either validate or be excluded from his romantic and artistic agendas. Henke's contention that Stephen represents women as "one-dimensional projections of a narcissistic imagination" is thus revealed to transcend gender concerns (*Desire* 50), as his encounters with everybody he esteems sacrifice the specifics of those encounters to the potential for his beloveds to fit within an amatory freedom that is oxymoronically narrow and rigid. The repressive elements of his environment may make his desire for freedom understandable, but the end result is a cycle of rejection and alienation, as the inability of his real-world love objects to measure up to his ideal compels Stephen to refuse their affection and choose exile as the necessary path to aesthetic liberation.

The real-world limitations of Stephen's amatory freedom are demonstrated through his interactions with Emma Clery. In both *Stephen Hero* and *Portrait*, Emma serves as Stephen's primary Mercedes, a young woman whose beauty and attraction to him make her a viable candidate for his artistic muse, but whose religious devotion prevents her from submitting to his narcissistic notions of love. While Stephen may view Emma's Catholic piety as another repressive threat to his liberation, reading her religious acquiescence with respect to Stephen's amatory ethics actually reveals more about the lover than about his beloved. In fact, it is almost impossible to come to a reliable understanding of Emma because every representation of her throughout both texts is controlled by Stephen and filtered through his aesthetic and amatory lenses of perception. Thus, Emma struggles to function in either book as much more than a "metaphorical adjunct to the thoughts of the narrator" (O'Brien 213), and recognizing this enables us to view the encounters between them as opportunities to evaluate the practical efficacy of Stephen's amatory framework.

The incompatibility of Stephen's amatory freedom with his affection for Emma is most evident in *Stephen Hero* and *Portrait*'s fifth chapter. As Stephen begins to prioritize his aesthetic goals over his Dublin obligations, he finds it difficult to love Emma in manners that do not conflict with his desires for freedom and exile. Since the epiphany on Dollymount strand solidified his determination to become the artificer as the alternative to the "chill and order" of Catholicism, it is unsurprising that Stephen attributes the difficulty in maintaining an attachment to Emma to the failure of her image to inspire his art. While he frequently contemplates her beauty, he repeatedly discovers that he is incapable of utilizing that beauty for artistic inspiration because Emma's affection is tied to moral and romantic obligations that oppose his desire to "be elusive of social or religious orders." Since to acquiesce to Emma would call his rejection of Catholicism into question, Stephen forgoes an amorous attachment, attributing the dissolution of those ties to her unworthiness to be his muse and her perceived betrayals of his love. Thus the more he pursues his transfiguration, the more he is compelled to act in manners that render that transfiguration impossible, as his refusal to compromise his amatory freedom inevitably alienates him from Emma.

Initially, Stephen's observations at the Daniel family parties in *Stephen Hero* reveal the relationship between Emma's shifting aesthetic value and his waning affection. Both Joyce and Stephen recognize that "it was not for such [images] that [they] had constructed a theory of art and life and a garland of verse," but whereas Joyce developed a more meaningful attachment to Nora, the Stephen of *Stephen Hero* cannot escape the "vulgarity of [Emma's] manners," equating her cultural inferiority with an inability to "understand him or sympathise with him" (*SH* 158). That he equates this inferiority with her declining sympathy not only shows that he characterizes her "vulgarity" as a rejection of his love, it also betrays the lack of reciprocity in their relationship since his denigrations of her Catholicism signify his refusal to "understand" or "sympathise with" her. Stephen's determination to "be sure of her" may connote an attempt to "understand" Emma (*SH* 158), but he never attempts to "sympathise" with either her principles or her affection, which denies the affirmation of otherness needed to develop their relationship.

This ambivalence is also present in Stephen's method of testing the veracity of Emma's manners. While one could see Stephen's ambivalent characterizations of Emma's Catholicism as an acknowledgement of her otherness, his desire to "be sure of" her prevents that acknowledgment from translating into an affirmation not only because it equates the "vulgarity of her manners" to the constancy of her affection, but also because it necessitates sex to test that constancy. By following his uncertainty with his "longing for a mad night of love" (*SH* 158), Stephen requires Emma to surrender her body to his lustful advances to prove her loyalty. This envisioned test reveals Stephen's desire for amatory mastery because in order to prove her love, Emma would have to betray those religious principles that Stephen considers vulgar and stupid (*SH* 66). Rather than affirming Emma's otherness, Stephen attempts to destroy it, which limits the possible outcomes of his pursuit of Emma to either her consumption or his rejection.

This attempt at amatory mastery renders Emma's rejection of Stephen inevitable, as his desire to eliminate her "vulgarity" is contested by her refusal to submit completely to his longings. This refusal is evident early in *Stephen Hero*, where he acknowledges that "Emma allowed him to see her home several times but she did not seem to have reserved herself for him." Stephen's recognition that "above all things he hated to be compared with others" reveals the extent to which he desires Emma to "[reserve] herself for him," and his observation that "he would have preferred to have been ignominiously left behind" shows his determination both to isolate himself from his counterparts and to dissolve any attachment with Emma should she choose not to share that isolation. That he identifies her "body compact with pleasure" as the main reason why her lack of complete devotion has not driven him away (*SH* 66), when read with his subsequent desire for intercourse to "be sure of her," initiates the narcissistic comparison of love and freedom that his later conversations with Cranly and Lynch expound. In that sense, the acceptance of Emma's body through sex would validate Stephen's amatory freedom, which makes his offer of "a mad night of love" the climactic encounter of his pursuit of her in *Stephen Hero* and the ultimate test of his amatory framework.

Unsurprisingly, Emma rejects this proposition. At first, her "large oval eyes" staring directly at the "disorderly figure beside her" demonstrate her empathy for his struggle through life "without help or sympathy from anyone" (*SH* 197). However, when his monologue shifts from his despair to her "body compact with pleasure," her flushed cheeks and tear-filled eyes signify her transition from sympathy to humiliation, and the removal of her eyes from his gaze and her hands from his grasp reveal the irreparable fracture of their loving connection. Her refusal reveals Stephen to be so obsessed with his liberation from Catholicism that he can neither perceive nor affirm the possibility that Emma does not share his desire for amatory freedom. Therefore, when his proposition is rejected, he reasons that her refusal was not because he insulted her love, but simply because he would not participate in a simonious Catholic marriage. His declaration that "I believe you hear my words and understand me, don't you" is ironic given that his "wondering at [the] cause" of Emma's tears reveal his inability to either hear or understand her (*SH* 198). Stephen's preoccupation with his own desires thus reduces Emma to a generic love object, and the concluding characterization of their relationship as "all but union" signifies their inability to develop a productive, empathetic connection (*SH* 199).

Stephen's rejection of Emma is further evident in his reflections on her refusal. As he considers her justifications for storming away, Stephen rationalizes this outcome by blaming her deceptive adherence to the Catholic Church, revealing his determination to view her reaction as a rejection of his love. Because Emma chooses to advocate religious beliefs that Stephen feels do not "[imply] a more genuine emancipation than his own," he represents her disgust as a "deceptive and cowardly" betrayal of his affection (*SH* 210). This attempt to exclude Emma by depicting her as villainous continues her objectification for two reasons:

First, it attributes Emma's rejection to religion instead of love. Stephen cannot acknowledge that Emma was insulted by his proposal because to do so would invalidate his amatory freedom. Instead, he equivocates that "it is no insult … for a man to ask a woman what I have asked you. You are annoyed at something else not at that" (*SH* 198–9). As he reflects on her refusal in the above passage, that "something else" becomes a "menial fear" to go against the hypocrisy of Catholic marriage that Stephen opposes. By attributing her reaction to a religious "attitude of insincerity or stupidity" (*SH* 210), Stephen maintains the validity of his attitudes towards love by characterizing Emma's humiliation as a religious rejection.

Second, it represents Emma as a symbol. While Stephen does not hesitate to deem Emma a "marsupial," his "anathemising" is not brought about by her specific attitude towards his proposition, but rather stems from the "insincerity" and "stupidity" of "the general attitude of women towards religion" (*SH* 210). Not only does this rebuke demonstrate his unwillingness to entertain beliefs that dissent from his own, but the "general" nature of his condemnation denies Emma's voice even though he ostensibly rejects her because of that voice. Stephen's attitude throughout the proposal thus confirms his unwillingness to "understand" or "sympathise" with her condition, and his determination to use her to attain a passion that does not conflict with his amatory freedom pushes his greatest love away.

Portrait also illustrates that Stephen distances himself from E.C. because of her incompatibility with his endeavors. Joyce may not characterize Stephen's perceptions of E.C. nearly as callously in *Portrait* as he does in *Stephen Hero*, but the role that art plays in his rejection of her is still present in the transition from manuscript to completed text. This relationship is demonstrated during the two poetic endeavors in the fifth chapter. Initially, Stephen's construction of the villanelle uses E.C.'s interest in Father Moran to cast her as his titular siren. As Stephen ponders her interaction with the priest, we cannot help but notice that the exchange contains little if any actual flirting. Father Moran simply expresses optimism that women and the church will come around to the language movement, and E.C.'s participation in this dialogue is limited to the phrase, "And the church, Father Moran?" Still this response is sufficient for Stephen to "leave the room in disdain," arguing that "he had done well not to salute her on the steps of the library. He had done well to leave her to flirt with her priest, to toy with a church which was the scullerymaid of Christendom" (*P* 239). When reading his departure with respect to the conversation that provoked it, we see that E.C. is not being charged with flirting with Father Moran, but rather with an interest in the church that depreciates her value as his love object. Indeed, her rapt attention signifies interest in Nationalist and religious ideas that Stephen has rejected, and thus E.C. is criticized not because her Catholicism is a beguiling ruse, but because it is sincere.

What seems to anger Stephen the most is that E.C. is willing to entertain a discussion with the priest to begin with. This outburst of "rude brutal anger" (*P* 239) parallels *Stephen Hero*'s Stephen's irritation that E.C. "did not seem to have reserved herself for him," especially considering his recognition that she would rather confess her sins to this priest of the "formal rite" than to her "priest of the eternal imagination" (*P* 240). This observation directly ties her hesitancy to submit to Stephen to her suitability as his muse since she would have to act against her faith and sacrifice her "soul's shy nakedness" to Stephen for him to proclaim her loveliness poetically (*P* 240). By having this criticism spur the villanelle's completion, Joyce reveals that it is not E.C.'s duplicitous nature that is demonized in the poem, but rather her refusal to compromise her faith for Stephen. Thus, Stephen may be justified in resisting the "nets" of "religion" for constraining his flight (*P* 220), but his inability to forge a connection with E.C. because she does not share that feeling of entrapment demonstrates his inability to compromise with or affirm the otherness of his love objects and foreshadows his inevitable alienation from E.C.

This alienation is confirmed in a subsequent encounter on the library steps, where Stephen's inability to use E.C. for poetic inspiration encourages him to cut ties with her altogether: "She had passed through the dusk … Darkness was falling. *Darkness falls from the air*. A trembling joy, lambent as a faint light, played like a fairy host around him" (*P* 252–3). Stephen's equation of E.C.'s presence with Thomas Nashe's poetry shows his continued efforts to use her image for artistic purposes. However, when he subsequently uses this poetic description of her to envelop his visions of Covent Garden under a "darkness of desire" (*P* 253), he recognizes that "the images he had summoned gave him no pleasure. They were secret and enflaming but her image was not entangled by them. That was not the way to think of her. It was not even the way in which he thought of her. Could his mind then not trust itself?" (*P* 253). Stephen's assertion that his artistic exercise "gave him no pleasure" reveals that the dissolution of their relationship has provoked an aesthetic ambivalence, replacing his previous outbursts of jubilation with a vague "darkness of desire." His aesthetic exercise is further compromised because he incorrectly remembers the Nashe poetry, that "it was not darkness that fell from the air. It was brightness. *Brightness falls from the air*. He had not even remembered rightly Nash's line. All the images it had awakened were false" (*P* 254). By acknowledging that he has mistaken "brightness" for "darkness," Stephen highlights the futility of his "darkness of desire," as his attempts to use E.C. for artistic inspiration transforms what he had perceived to be "secret and inflaming" images into "lice born of the sweat of cloth" (*P* 254). These characterizations of his creations as "vermin" and "lice" (*P* 254) illustrate that Stephen's mind truly cannot "trust itself," as his refusal to connect emotionally with his muse forces him to evoke a misinterpretation of her image that taints each aesthetic creation it inspires.

Stephen's first thought after recognizing this artistic misapprehension is to reject E.C. as his love object. In rhetoric reminiscent of his rage over Father Moran, Stephen exclaims, "Well then, let her go and be damned to her" (*P* 254). The juxtaposition of this bitter rejection of E.C. with his misapprehension of the Nashe poetry illustrates that when she proves incapable of aiding Stephen's aesthetic endeavors, she becomes an impediment to his amatory freedom and must be cast aside. However, he again cannot represent his exclusion of E.C. as a rejection of her affection because to do so would expose cracks in his narcissistic interpretation of love. Instead, he represents her shunning of him on the steps and her inability to inspire viable art as refusals of his desire, using his subsequent suspicions of a relationship with Cranly to represent her as rejecting him for another person. In this sense, E.C. does become a Mercedes for Stephen, as his continued pursuit of transfiguration is foiled by what he represents as unrequited love, and while his conflicted feelings for E.C. in *Portrait* do not approach the coldness of Stephen Daedalus's scorn in *Stephen Hero*, his resolution to "let her go and be damned to her" similarly provides the "sadly proud gesture of refusal" that will complete this amatory quest.

While Stephen's interactions with Emma indicate his unwillingness to love others who do not share his beliefs, he is willing to make an exception to this prohibition through his friendship with Cranly. Upon first glance, it seems puzzling that the most genuine emotional connection in either *Portrait* or *Stephen Hero* is made between Stephen and a friend whose "submissive deference" to "rabblement and authority" should also exclude him from the artist's affection (*SH* 123). Yet despite cringing at Cranly's religious devotion, Stephen "[feels] hope" when he "[looks] steadily into [Cranly's] pair of bright dark eyes" (*SH* 108; brackets mine) and frequently walks "arm-in-arm" with him (*SH* 125), and Joseph Valente contends that "Cranly increasingly comes to *take over* the place of E.C. as Stephen's object of affection" ("Thrilled" 65). Even *Stephen Hero*'s narrator acknowledges that "it would seem at first somewhat strange and improbable that these two young men should have anything in common" given both their conflicting religious and political attitudes and Stephen's desire to distance himself from anybody who shares such disparate beliefs. However, when we read Stephen's connection to Cranly within his narcissistic framework of amatory freedom, two characteristics of this relationship explain its existence:

First, Stephen characterizes Cranly as submitting to his grandeur. While Emma's Catholic devotion gets in the way of her relationship with Stephen, Cranly seems willing to subordinate his adherence to "rabblement and authority" to maintain his friendship with him. Stephen even acknowledges in *Stephen Hero* that he would normally consider Cranly's religious submission "a real sign of interior corruption had he not daily evidence that Cranly was willing to endanger his own fair name as a member of the Sodality and as a general lay-servant of the Church by association with one who was known to be contaminated" (*SH* 122–3). Cranly's religious devotion thus becomes excusable because his friendship with one of the "contaminated" signifies his willingness to compromise his principles out of affection for Stephen, making him the poet's ideal love object.

Second, their monologic interaction ensures that Stephen does not have to sacrifice himself to maintain the relationship. While Stephen's interactions with others are tainted by their disagreements with him, he primarily feels affection for Cranly because he "seldom or never obtruded his presence upon these monologues. He listened to all, seemed to understand all, and seemed to think it was the duty of his suppositious character to listen [to] and understand. He never refused his ear" (*SH* 124–5). Stephen essentially treats Cranly as an empty vessel into which he can pour "all the tumults and unrests and longings in his soul, day after day and night after night, only to be answered by his friend's listening silence" (*P* 192). These references to Cranly's "listening silence" as a sounding board for Stephen's "longings" thus demonstrate a direct link between Cranly's silence and Stephen's affection, which enables him to be the submissive love object that Stephen desires.

However, this monologic relationship does not last. What begins as Cranly's willingness to listen to Stephen's beliefs gradually becomes a frustration over those longings and a desire to interject his feelings into their exchanges. Whether by voicing his disagreement or by letting his disapproval seep into his "listening silence," Cranly makes his objections to Stephen evident: "If a [conversation] monologue which had set out from a triviality seemed to him likely to run on unduly he would receive it with a silence through which aversion was just discernible and at a lull bring his hammer down brutally on the poor original object. At times Stephen found this ultra-classical habit very unpalatable" (*SH* 125–6). Not only does Joyce's replacement of "conversation" with "monologue" further emphasize the one-sided nature of Stephen's interactions with Cranly, but his description of the latter's attempts to "bring his hammer down" on Stephen's meditations conveys Cranly's frustration and Stephen's anger over his friend's interruptions of his monologues. Indeed, Cranly's intrusions into the conversation reveal his unwillingness to submit completely to Stephen's intellectual desires, and the resulting frustration over these attempts to render their friendship dialogic compels Stephen to lash out at Cranly.

Interestingly, Stephen's reaction to Cranly's frustrated silence is to suspect him of interfering in Stephen's relationship with E.C. When E.C. shuns him on the library steps, Stephen latches on to her greeting Cranly instead of him, noting that "she passed out from the porch of the library and bowed across Stephen in reply to Cranly's greeting. He also? Was there not a slight flush on Cranly's cheek?" While this reaction may seem simply to signify Stephen's jealousy, his subsequent meditations on E.C.'s slight reveal the foundations of his suspicions towards Cranly: "Did that explain his friend's listless silence, his harsh comments, the sudden intrusions of rude speech with which he had shattered so often Stephen's ardent wayward confessions?" (*P* 252). This not only highlights *Portrait* Cranly's similar attempts to render his relationship with Stephen dialogic, but by equating Cranly's "listless silence" and "sudden intrusions of rude speech" with an affair with E.C., Stephen represents Cranly's irritation as a betrayal of his affection. This representation enables Stephen to ignore Cranly's frustration with their monologic relationship, projecting the blame for any strain in their friendship onto Cranly. By characterizing his friend's unfavorable reaction to his monologues as a refusal of his love, Stephen preserves the stability of his "self-centred" framework of amatory freedom and lays the groundwork for the rejection of his friend's affection at the conclusion of *Portrait*'s fifth chapter.

This rejection of Cranly's love culminates in a conversation between the two friends concerning Stephen's deteriorating relationship with his mother. Whereas Stephen fears that submitting to his mother's desire to make his Easter duties would be a dangerous submission to Catholicism, Cranly argues that he should still submit to these duties as a gesture of love to his mother. From this perspective, it is understandable that Stephen reacts negatively to Cranly's advice since he is encouraging him to submit to a religious performance that constrains his freedom; however, Stephen's specific reaction in *Portrait* also demonstrates his annoyance that Cranly's advice contradicts his earlier "intelligent sympathy" and attempts to transform their conversations into dialogues. Ultimately, Stephen views Cranly's advice as a refusal of his love not only because it calls for him to submit to a religious institution that he rejects, but also because it demonstrates Cranly's ability to empathize with others, showing that his heart is not completely reserved for Stephen. His recognition that Cranly "felt then the sufferings of women … and would shield them with a strong and resolute arm and bow his mind to them" reveals that Stephen cannot rely upon his unconditional esteem, but instead must settle for being merely one of the people with whom Cranly can sympathize (*P* 266). The seeds of doubt that were stirred on the library steps thus sprout into a confirmation of Stephen's misrecognition of Cranly, as what initially seemed like a deferent to his beliefs has become capable of tainting Stephen's monologues with the demands for reciprocation from which he seeks to escape.

Cranly's refusal to submit completely to his affection compels Stephen to end their friendship. He resolves, "Away then: it is time to go. A voice spoke softly to Stephen's lonely heart, bidding him go and telling him that his friendship was coming to an end. Yes; he would go. He could not strive against another. He knew his part" (*P* 267). This juxtaposition of Stephen's reflections on Cranly's heart with his determination to leave Dublin demonstrates that Cranly's suggested condescension to the Easter duties constituted a betrayal of his affection, representing the continuance of their friendship as an inevitable "[striving] against another." Additionally, the reference to Stephen's "lonely heart," when read alongside Cranly's ability to empathize with others, reveals Stephen's determination to view his loved one's affection for others as a rejection of himself, representing the refusal to love only him as a betrayal of his affection. The openness of Cranly's heart ultimately becomes his undoing, as his inability to devote himself entirely to Stephen's desires compels the poet to terminate their relationship.

Valente thus correctly argues that "Cranly plays *the* decisive role in motivating Stephen's self-exile" since his characterization of Cranly as an antagonist illustrates the final flaw in his amatory freedom ("Thrilled" 66), as Stephen's commitment to his artistic endeavors blinds him to the most authentic emotional attachment in his life. Indeed Cranly's offer to be Stephen's "noblest and truest friend" (*P* 269) and his despondence to Stephen's determination to "discover the modern of life or of art whereby [his] spirit could express itself in unfettered freedom" (*P* 267) reveal both that his affection for Stephen supersedes any intellectual disagreement and that he would be willing and able to provide the love that Stephen has been pursuing throughout both *Portrait* and *Stephen Hero*. However, in so doing, Cranly also "embodies the most profound danger yet to Stephen's heterosexual self-conception" partly because he "represents the persistence of Stephen's religious sensibility in, and despite, his apostasy" (Valente "Thrilled" 66), and thus their bond would inevitably counter the amatory freedom Stephen feels is necessary to fulfill his desires. Stephen's narcissism thus cannot comprehend the depths of Cranly's affection, misrecognizing his despair as merely "[Cranly's] own loneliness which he feared" and refusing his offer of real-world affection for the renewed desire to chase symbolic love. The fifth chapter's concluding silence signifies the final sundering of Stephen and Cranly's friendship, and Stephen's inability to compromise with his love object ends up completing his alienation from his surroundings and necessitating his departure from Ireland.

****

In the second chapter of *Portrait*, Stephen expresses his frustration with the "hollowsounding voices" of his fellow Dubliners, noting that "he gave them ear only for a time but he was happy only when he was far from them, beyond their call, alone or in the company of phantasmal comrades" (*P* 88–9). This statement echoes Stephen's earlier suppression of the noisy children to pursue a symbolic

Mercedes and illustrates his preference for the symbolic pleasure of fantastic encounters over the humdrum attachments of his everyday life. While Stephen may desire to "meet in the real world the unsubstantial image which his soul so constantly beheld," the inevitable outcome of these pursuits is the rejection of his love object and the resumption of his fantasy. Perhaps Stephen's "desire to press in [his] arms the loveliness which has not yet come into the world" renders this outcome inevitable (*P* 273), as the promise of future "phantasmal" love overwhelms the emotional attachments available to him. In this sense, his desire to use love to enable his freedom from the "nets" that hold him back may be understandable, but his inability to affirm those who think differently from him ensures that every attempt to find his soul's "unsubstantial image" in the "real world" is doomed before it starts, and Stephen's attempts to win the affection of his fellow Dubliners inevitably turn "hollowsounding" and give way to the promise of the future beauty he is destined to create. Thus, an endless cycle of amatory pursuit and rejection plays itself out, and at *Portrait*'s conclusion, Stephen is left with only the ardent devotion to an amatory freedom whose narcissistic underpinnings limit its viability.

Of course, personal love is not the only goal of Stephen's amatory freedom, since his epiphany over the bird girl entices him both to pursue an alienating form of love and to "create proudly out of the freedom and power of his soul, as the great artificer whose name he bore" (*P* 184). For this reason, the amatory freedom that emerges from this climactic scene also carries aesthetic possibilities, and when we continue to examine Stephen's commitment to this framework, we discover that his advocacy of love is not limited to his pursuits of his ideal Mercedes. Rather, the ideals behind his desire for transfiguration pervade his artistic beliefs, compelling him to create an aesthetic system that could validate his quest for freedom even if his personal love stories do not end successfully. As we turn our attention to the artistic sections of *Portrait*, we witness the relationship between Stephen's desire for love and his attempts "to recreate life out of life" (*P* 186), and we see how the narcissism that felled his individual pursuits of romantic submission implicates his amatory aesthetics.

Chapter 4
The Artist's Amatory Aesthetics

While Stephen's desire for freedom undermines his potential romances in *Stephen Hero* and *Portrait*, the attainment of his artistic agenda is ultimately more important to him than the real-world experience of love. Even if he is unsuccessful in easing his loneliness through the affection of his loved ones, Stephen's rehearsals of love assist in the creation of an aesthetic system that is directly influenced by his amatory ideals. His poetry in *Portrait* is influenced by his attraction to E.C. (and finds its complement in his anticipated wreath of romantic verses in *Stephen Hero*), and his climactic epiphany in *Portrait*'s fourth chapter is predicated on a romanticized encounter with a girl whose symbolic beauty unites Stephen's amatory and artistic longings. In that sense, Stephen's desire to "forge in the smithy of [his] soul the uncreated conscience of [his] race" could be seen as the composition of a love poem to Ireland, as the juxtaposition of this desire with his longing "to press in [his] arms the loveliness which has not yet come into the world" transforms his anticipated reclamation of his homeland into an amorous embrace (*P* 273).

For this reason, Dominic Manganiello is correct that Stephen's "egoistic" and "esthetic" desires carry "far-reaching political implications" (78–9). Indeed, Stephen's efforts to create a new Irish conscience provide a potential alternative to the didactic art of his contemporaries, which glorifies Catholicism and nationalism and thus exacerbates Ireland's paralysis. Pericles Lewis thus characterizes Stephen's art as an "act of martyrdom," arguing that "through his writing … Stephen will offer a sacrifice of his own soul to Ireland. Just as this act of martyrdom will save the Irish, however, it will also allow Stephen to achieve unfettered freedom because, in embracing his moral unity with the Irish race, he will reconcile his ethical self with his socially constructed identity" (33). However, while Lewis argues that this aesthetics constitutes an "embrac[e]" of "moral unity" between Stephen and Ireland, Stephen's refusal to compromise with those outside his intellectual framework disqualifies his aesthetics as an "act of martyrdom" and overwhelms the sociopolitical benefits of that embrace. He may argue that he wants to save Ireland by "forg[ing]" this "uncreated conscience," but the only person he is really interested in saving is himself, as his attempts to apprehend ideal beauty promote his amatory freedom over his fellow Dubliners.

Let Us Take a Woman

In *I and Thou*, Buber argues that "the eternal origin of art" is a direct encounter between an artist and "a form that wants to become a work through him" (60). Just as he grounds the ethics of loving relationships in the "responsibility of an I for a You" (*Thou* 66), Buber notes that "if [the artist] commits it and speaks with his being the basic word to the form that appears, then the creative power is released and the word comes into being." For this reason, the artist cannot objectify or dismiss the subject of their work because "whoever commits himself may not hold back part of himself; and the work does not permit me … to seek relaxation in the It-world; it is imperious: if I do not serve it properly, it breaks, or it breaks me" (*Thou* 60–1). Buber thus reveals the ethics of the aesthetic I-You relationship, requiring artists to engage in direct encounters that affirm the otherness of their objects of inspiration. The failure to engage in this artistic affirmation reduces the "form" to a "thing among things" or an "aggregate of qualities," which may enable it to be better "experienced and described" (*Thou* 61), but which also alienates the participants of this aesthetic encounter and drains the art of its "creative power."

This obligation reveals a significant limitation of Stephen's art throughout *Portrait*: just as he uses his love objects to realize his amatory premonition, so too does he utilize the subjects of his poetry as instruments to fulfill his aesthetic calling. This may seem like a reasonable approach and Stephen certainly is not obligated to portray objective reflections of his surroundings, but his resolution "to recreate life out of life" in *Portrait*'s fourth chapter (*P* 186) ties his aesthetics to Buber's "eternal origin of art," which requires him to affirm the "life" he uses for regenerative inspiration. However, rather than engaging the subjects of his art in exclusive, direct encounters, Stephen reduces them to "aggregate[s] of qualities," reshaping his experiences to validate the predetermined objectives of his aesthetics. This tactic may make the fulfillment of these goals easier to accomplish, but it also replicates the central error of his romantic efforts in *Portrait* and *Stephen Hero*. Much as his pursuit of symbolic phantoms alienated him from his loved ones, his quest to uncover preconceived artistic ideals robs those encounters of the exclusiveness needed for them to realize their creative potential, which limits the viability of his amatory aesthetics.

The limitations of Stephen's aesthetics are initially demonstrated in his attempt to write an ode to E.C. in *Portrait*'s second chapter. Given that his artistic struggles mirror his amatory difficulties, it is fitting that one of the earliest subjects of his poetry is one of his first love objects, and this episode enables us to see how Stephen attempts to reshape his romantic failures into validations of his premonition. The reader's introduction to E.C. compellingly represents her as Stephen's ideal Mercedes, as the momentary connection between them at a birthday party transforms his isolation into the "joy of … loneliness" and reshapes the merriment from which he previously had been excluded into a "soothing air." This description of the party mirrors Stephen's amatory premonition since his isolation from the "gay cocked hats and sunbonnets" "danc[ing] and romp[ing] noisily" echoes the annoying play of the Blackrock children with which his pursuit of Mercedes opposes (*P* 71). By juxtaposing these annoyances with E.C.'s glance, Joyce parallels Stephen's fantasies in Blackrock with this actual encounter in Harold's Cross and invites us to anticipate their subsequent tram ride as the climactic encounter between the young man and his Mercedes (*P* 72).

However, while Stephen recognizes these possibilities with E.C. on the tram steps, he is incapable of initiating the contact needed to realize that potential. He acknowledges "a voice within him … asking him would he take her gift to which he had only to stretch out his hand," but his recollection of an encounter with Eileen Vance paralyzes him, reducing him to a "tranquil watcher" of his own love scene (*P* 72–3). The hint of rejection in Eileen's laughter and retreat undermines his ability to initiate a kiss:

> She too wants me to catch hold of her, he thought. That's why she came with me to the tram. I could easily catch hold of her when she comes up to my step: nobody is looking. I could hold her and kiss her. But he did neither: and, when he was sitting alone in the deserted tram, he tore his ticket into shreds and stared gloomily at the corrugated footboard. (*P* 73)

The conclusion of this encounter shows that Stephen's fantasies have left him unprepared to experience an actual connection with a real-world lover. He can imagine pursuing his ideal Mercedes, but by viewing these pursuits as alternatives to real-world connections, he undermines his ability to realize them in his everyday encounters. Indeed, by following his memory of Eileen with the observation that E.C. "too" desires him to kiss her, Stephen reveals that his inability to "take her gift" on the tram is not an isolated misstep, but is rather proof that whenever he finds "in the real world the unsubstantial image which his soul so constantly beheld," he cannot initiate the contact needed to obtain the love he desires. Stephen's earlier insistence that his desired transfiguration occur "without any overt act of his" thus undermines this possibility and reduces Stephen to a "tranquil watcher" rather than an active lover (*P* 67).

The aesthetic implications of Stephen's frustration are evidenced by his attempts to use the tram encounter to compose a poem to E.C. His desire to capture this experience in a Byronic ode demonstrates both his early prioritization of aesthetic gains over amorous affection and his efforts to use his love objects to inspire him to greatness. However, the incompleteness of the encounter translates on the page, and he is ultimately incapable of encapsulating the reality of that experience in an effective poem. Indeed, Stephen's brain "refuse[s] to grapple with the theme" (*P* 73), as his feelings for E.C. are not sufficient in themselves to compel his artistic endeavor. Rather, he can only begin to write after "brooding on the incident" and "[thinking] himself into confidence" (*P* 74). This reliance on "brooding" and "thinking" prevents Stephen from using E.C. for artistic inspiration because it detaches him from the emotional connection needed to actualize that encounter through his poem. By representing Stephen as consciously willing himself to create, Joyce establishes a parallel between his romantic paralysis on the tram and his artistic paralysis at his desk, showing Stephen's aesthetic inspiration to be provided not by his love for E.C., but by his determination to perform the role of the artist.

The vague content of Stephen's art also reveals his failure to forge a meaningful aesthetic connection with E.C. While he is ultimately able to complete his poem, the finished product bears little resemblance to its moment of inspiration. His preference for idealized romance over actual connection realizes itself in his decision to purge from his art the details he considers "common and insignificant." Thus the specifics of their encounter are omitted from his poem, as the "balmy breeze" and the moon's "maiden luster" replace the events on the tram steps, and the multiple expressions of fear, anticipation, and desire during that encounter are reduced to an "undefined sorrow" (*P* 74). In essence, Stephen constructs the first example of the aesthetic stasis he will explain to Lynch in *Portrait*'s fifth chapter, excluding specific details from consideration so as to reach a transcendent, ideal beauty. This exclusion may enable him to complete his ode, but it also reduces his encounter with Emma to a "thing among things" by using only the bits and pieces of their exchange that are most convenient to his objectives, which prevents the direct engagement with his subject needed to unlock his poem's "creative power." Stephen does render a symbolically poignant account of the parting of two lovers, but the incomplete representation of that experience limits his poetic effort to "the performance of a series of clichéd gestures" (A. Friedman 61).

Additionally, the muse of Stephen's ode is mysteriously absent. Not only does "there [remain] no trace of the tram itself nor of the trammen nor of the horses" in his poem, but neither he nor E.C. "appear vividly" in their own encounter (*P* 74). Instead, Stephen recasts both E.C. and himself as generic lovers whose departing kiss provides a jarring contrast to the lack of consummation in the actual encounter. E.C. is reduced to clichéd woman in love, and Stephen's dismissal of their specific actions and desires on the tram as "common and insignificant" demonstrates that the reality of his amatory pursuits means little to his artistic endeavors. This tactic may encourage Stephen to use his poetry to "[redeem] the failed literal kiss into a successful symbolic one" (Froula 208), but the prioritization of ideal romance over his specific emotions undercuts the aesthetic value of that "rede[mption]." Stephen may not be obligated to provide a completely accurate account of the tram episode, but his disinterest in encapsulating E.C.'s specific essence in an ode entitled "To E— C—" shows the extent to which he treats the subjects of his art as commodities instead of subjects for his affirmation. This inability to affirm E.C. in either his experiences or his art thus leaves Stephen with little more than a substandard poem that "statically embalm[s] the experience of romantic epiphany" (Henke *Desire* 62).

While the youthful Stephen struggled to engage in the direct encounters needed to compel his poetic endeavors, his older counterpart consciously shirks this "eternal origin of art." His earlier struggle to express his feelings for E.C. initiated his inability to affirm otherness through his art, but as Stephen develops his uncompromising commitment to amatory freedom, he explicitly subordinates her otherness to his aesthetic objectives, representing her religious beliefs as dangerous submissions to be countered by his aesthetics. This strategy is best expressed in the "Villanelle of the Temptress," where a bitter Stephen casts his love object as a siren that consumes the hearts of her victims. In his presentation of both the composition of the poem and the finished product, Joyce highlights the ways in which Stephen does not "[commit]" or "[speak]" the "basic word" to E.C. "with his being," but rather reduces her affection to an "aggregate of qualities" that either validate or threaten his artistic endeavors. The result of this exercise represents her religious devotion and her interactions with others as evidence of her unsuitability as his love object and muse, and in so doing, exposes holes in both Stephen's narcissism and his amatory aesthetics.

It is easy to compare the villanelle to the tram encounter. In fact, Joyce invites this comparison by having Stephen observe that through the composition of the villanelle, "he had written verses for [E.C.] again after ten years" (*P* 241). However, while these two episodes are similar in many ways, the themes of the resulting poems are drastically different. Whereas the earlier poem used E.C.'s affection for Stephen to represent an ideal love, the villanelle foregrounds rejection and duplicitous desire as its subject. Her "strange wilful heart" may inspire a "rose and ardent light" that compels his artistic creation (*P* 236), but Stephen now finds it impossible to characterize E.C. as an affectionate lover who validates his amatory aesthetics.

Stephen's depiction of E.C. in the villanelle is initiated in the conclusion of the preceding scene. On the library steps, Stephen spots E.C. conversing with friends, and his thoughts turn to bitter rebukes of her interactions with Father Moran. However, Stephen concedes that he may have misread the situation: "And if he had judged her harshly? If her life were a simple rosary of hours, her life simple and strange as a bird's life, gay in the morning, restless all day, tired at sundown? Her heart simple and wilful as a bird's heart?" (*P* 235). Stephen may intend to concede E.C.'s potential virtue, but the wording of this concession still casts her in a negative light. In fact, Stephen's considering the sincerity of E.C.'s devotion re-enacts his pondering the "vulgarity of her manners" in *Stephen Hero*, as the description of her faithful life in *Portrait* as "simple and strange," while overtly conceding that he may have misjudged her, equates her Catholic beliefs with the cultural inferiority with which he charged her in the other text. Thus, even if E.C. is not duplicitously fraternizing with Father Moran, the interaction itself is sufficient to render her unworthy of being either his love object or his muse.

The relationship between E.C.'s faith and her negative portrayal in the villanelle becomes clear through Stephen's subsequent epiphany. While he may deem this "instant of inspiration" as stemming from an "enchantment of the heart," the specifics of that epiphanous "instant" reveal that this "enchantment" should be read ironically (*P* 235):

> An afterglow deepened within his spirit, whence the white flame had passed, deepening to a rose and ardent light. That rose and ardent light was her strange and wilful heart, strange that no man had known or would know, wilful from before the beginning of the world: and lured by that ardent roselike glow the choirs of the seraphim were falling from heaven. (*P* 236)

Stephen may acknowledge a "rose and ardent light" that compels his artistic creation, but that "ardent roselike glow" also serves as an enchantment that compels the virtuous to fall under its submission. Thus, when he equates the temptress to the "lure of the fallen seraphim" and asks if she is "weary of ardent ways," he criticizes an all-consuming passion that entices men to "fall from heaven" to submit to the will of an alluring siren (*P* 236). Even though Stephen does not specify whose "strange wilful heart" is being rebuked, that heart is itself a clear signifier of E.C., whom Stephen had just described as possessing a heart that was "simple and wilful." That her "simple and strange" life and "simple and wilful" heart become the "strange wilful heart" that is the "lure of the fallen seraphim" reveals that Stephen casts E.C. as the temptress of his villanelle because of her adherence to Catholicism. By tying the "lure of the fallen seraphim" to the possibility that her life really was "a simple rosary of hours," *Portrait*'s Stephen agrees with his *Stephen Hero* counterpart that E.C.'s faith precludes her from being the catalyst for his artistic greatness. Stephen thus depicts this "vulgarity of her manners" as a rejection of his love, transforming her "simple and wilful" heart into a siren's song to be rejected by his villanelle.

This representation of E.C. continues in the villanelle's second stanza. As Stephen comes up with the rhymes that will structure his poem, he finds himself still caught within the "roselike glow" that triggered his artistic epiphany. This recognition returns his thoughts to E.C., noting that the glow's rays "burned up the world, consumed the hearts of men and angels: the rays from the rose that was her wilful heart" (*P* 236). Here the representations of E.C.'s affection are more dangerous, as what had previously lured potential lovers from their virtuous path now consumes them completely. This all-consuming characterization of her "wilful heart" finds its place in the second stanza, where Stephen writes, "Your eyes have set man's heart ablaze/And you have had your will of him./Are you not weary of ardent ways?" (*P* 236). This depiction of the temptress, as well as the past-tense observation that she "ha[s] had [her] will of him," enables Stephen to describe E.C.'s "simple and strange life" as a consumption and rejection of his love, ironically reading her refusal to submit completely to his will as a demand that he submit completely to hers. Thus, when he again questions if the temptress is "weary of ardent ways," it qualifies those "ways" as attempts to use Stephen's passion to lure him away from his aesthetic aspirations, serving as a dangerous submission to be avoided. Stephen thus uses E.C. to construct a poetic Mercedes, transforming his heart's most ardent love into a deceitful temptress that he must refuse to maintain the sanctity of his amatory freedom.

Stephen's use of memory in writing the villanelle also shows his ignorance of the "eternal origin of art." After writing the poem's initial stanzas, he recalls his recent interactions with E.C. in a manner similar to his use of the tram memory to compel his ode. However, the memories he conjures up for inspiration this time only foreground their isolation. His recollection of a musical gathering parallels the birthday party by having E.C. interrupt Stephen's social alienation; however, she is now incapable of provoking what he earlier called the "joy of loneliness," and their interaction is drowned out by the meaningless chatter around him. Stephen's recollection of a carnival also compels an amatory response through his descriptions of the "faint glow" of E.C.'s cheek and the "soft merchandise" of her given hand, but that potential is quashed by her labeling Stephen a "great stranger" and by his sarcastic retort that compels her to leave (*P* 238). In neither memory does Stephen turn to and affirm the muse of his villanelle; instead, he latches onto specific markers of E.C.'s agitation to blame her for their discord. In the musical encounter, he notes that E.C. listened to his singing, "or feigned to listen," and the return of the alienating voices upon this qualification ties her half-hearted recognition to his isolation. Similarly, his memory of the carnival is introduced by the observation that "at certain instants her eyes seemed about to trust him but he had waited in vain," signifying a lack of her complete adoration that is emphasized by her "eyes [being] a little averted" throughout the scene (*P* 238). Stephen's obsession with diverted glances and feigned attention thus provides evidence of E.C.'s dismissal of his adoration, and her perceived rejection of his love transforms what was the "flattering, taunting, searching, [and] exciting [of] his heart" at Harold's Cross into a frustrated and "ang[ry] … homage" (*P* 72; 239).

As Stephen begins the second half of his villanelle, his rebukes of E.C.'s "ardent ways" become harsher. In the fourth and fifth stanzas, he articulates the destructive consequences of his temptress's enchantment, highlighting the fourth stanza's "broken cries" and "mournful lays" as evidence of the consumptive nature of her passion and using the fifth stanza's "sacrificing hands" to demonstrate the submission that men must undergo to pay homage to her beauty. However, while this recollection may enable him to finish his poem, his reliance on symbolizing E.C. prevents Stephen from using this poem to promote his amatory aesthetics. Indeed, the "rude brutal anger" stirred by his memories depersonalizes Stephen's temptress by "[breaking] up violently [E.C.'s] fair image" and foregrounding "distorted reflections" of that image. The alluring siren that is criticized towards the end of the villanelle ceases to be simply E.C. and now becomes the "flowergirl in the ragged dress," the "kitchengirl in the next house," and whoever else may be conjured up by his representation of E.C. as the "batlike soul" who serves as a "figure of the womanhood of her country" (*P* 239). Stephen essentially pluralizes the "you" in his interrogation of E.C. and rejects each "batlike soul," transforming his villanelle from a personalized castigation of his love object into a generic critique of all Irish women. Harkness is thus correct that "the reality of E.C. disappears from the poem" (*Voices* 85), and this depersonalization of Stephen's muse drains his villanelle of the passion that inspired its creation, which alienates him from both his love object and Ireland.

However, although Stephen's rage inspires most of the poem, his meditations on the final stanza take on a more thoughtful tone. As he reflects on E.C. possibly showing her family the poem, a wave of remorse for having potentially wronged her envelops Stephen and entices him to write the sixth stanza in a tenderer mood. This compassion represents the first time Stephen has attempted to empathize with E.C. through his poetry, and his subsequent desire for a revitalized union with her makes it seem that a meaningful attachment between them is finally possible. However, he falls short of the loving gesture needed for such an attachment to occur.

Initially, Stephen's desired encounter is imaginary. While Stephen rejects an actual connection with E.C. through his refusal to give her the villanelle, he wonders whether during the creation of that poem, "in the mysterious ways of spiritual life … her soul at those same moments had been conscious of his homage" (*P* 242). This possibility causes him to imagine a scenario in which her knowledge of his adoration enflames her desire and compels an amatory encounter. By rejecting the possibility of a real-world encounter and focusing instead on a fantasized union, Stephen shuts E.C. out of any potential romantic connection, which reduces Stephen's renewed desire to a masturbatory homage to himself. Also, Stephen's description of "her nakedness yield[ing] to him, radiant, warm, odorous and lavishlimbed" demonstrates that his desired encounter with E.C. still requires her to submit her body and soul completely to his dominion. By continuing his desire for authority over E.C., Stephen adopts the "ardent ways" for which he criticized his beloved, effectively representing himself as the temptress of his own villanelle. This action nullifies the empathy that preceded it by replacing his affirmation of E.C. with her consumption, and it guarantees that he will not transform her into his ideal Mercedes since her "vulgarity of manners" will compel her to reject his demands for her submission.

Finally, his focus on E.C.'s gaze solidifies the castigatory tone of the villanelle. Admittedly, Stephen's fantasized encounter could rectify his recalled breaches of their relationship because its description of her eyes "opening to his eyes" would supplant the "feigned attention" and "averted eyes" that earlier convinced him of her betrayal. However, when that imagined gaze is represented in the final stanza, its description solidifies his earlier portrayal of his muse as an alluring siren luring virtuous men to their doom. Stephen's assertion that "still [she] hold[s] our longing gaze/With languorous look and lavish limb," while perhaps intending to signify the renewed gaze that he finds in this imagined encounter, directly recalls the second stanza's accusation that her "eyes have set man's heart ablaze," enabling her to "have … [her] will of him" (*P* 243). By characterizing her gaze in this manner, Stephen eliminates the redemptive aspects of E.C.'s imagined acknowledgement of his adoration and reduces her eyes "opening to his eyes" to another tactic by his poem's temptress to compel her lover's submission. What could have been a compassionate ending that affirmed genuine empathy and love becomes another castigation of E.C.'s perceived duplicity, and Stephen's attempt to express his feelings for her through the villanelle's "homage" weakens with every pencil stroke.

In his description of worthwhile art, Buber argues that the artist "cannot experience nor describe" the subject of his aesthetic encounter; he "can only actualize it" (*Thou* 61). To do so "involves a sacrifice and a risk" since the "exclusiveness" of this encounter demands that "all that but a moment ago floated playfully through one's perspective has to be exterminated" (*Thou* 60). Stephen's poetic endeavors in *Portrait* can be seen as his refusals to undergo this "sacrifice" and "risk," as his desire to "recreate life out of life" compels him to reshape his everyday encounters in manners that validate his ambivalence towards Ireland.

Just as he subordinates his real-world pursuits to his quest for his ideal Mercedes, Stephen is less interested in affirming the otherness of his poetic subjects than he is in re-presenting them to neatly coincide with his aesthetic goals. It is uncertain whether we can completely "[exterminate]" our surroundings to participate in this encounter, and Buber concedes that such connections inevitably regress into the I-It world. However, Stephen's ambivalent attitude towards E.C. in both the tram poem and the villanelle signify his disinterest in such aesthetic affirmations, which explains why he can never effectively encapsulate his feelings for her in a meaningful poem. Thus, Stephen becomes the "tranquil watcher" not only of his love life, but of his artistic calling as well, as his refusal to "confirm" either his love objects or his muses "as creature and creation" unravels both his amatory and his poetic efforts (Buber *Knowledge* 69).

The God of Creation

So far, we have seen how Stephen's failure to find his real-world Mercedes also undermines the effectiveness of his art. However, as we read *Portrait*'s fifth chapter, we see that this failure affects more than his individual poems. While Stephen may seem to be more interested in personal freedom than political gains, the goals of his artistic calling transcend that individual realm, as his desire to "encounter for the millionth time the reality of experience" is expanded into a call to "forge into the smithy of my soul the uncreated conscience of my race" (*P* 275–6). When we examine the textual sites where Stephen's linguistic and artistic thoughts intersect his political musings, we see his desire to construct an alternative Irish aesthetics that avoids the suffocating influences of both colonialism and nationalism.

Stephen's bitterness towards the British occupation of Ireland is explicitly articulated throughout *Portrait*'s fifth chapter. He frequently attacks the Irish informers against the rebels ("no honourable and sincere man ... has given up to you his life and his youth and his affections from the days of Tone to those of Parnell but you sold him out to the enemy" [*P* 220]); he expresses hostility towards William Gladstone, one of the leading forces behind Parnell's betrayal, and calls his commemorators at a rotunda ceremony a "race of clodhoppers!" (*P* 272); and he resignedly acknowledges that "the Ireland of Tone and Parnell seemed to have receded into space" (*P* 199). However, Stephen's most explicit connection between language and colonialism occurs during his discussion with the dean of studies over the meaning of the word "tundish." While the English dean amusedly ponders this unfamiliar "Irish" word, Stephen resents the fact that "the language in which we are speaking is his before it is mine," that England's mastery of Ireland is strengthened through each utterance of the colonial tongue. His acknowledgement that "my soul frets in the shadow of his language" may seem to complicate artistic efforts to combat this colonialism (*P* 205), but when Stephen later isolates "language" as one of the "nets" by which he must "fly" (*P* 220), he positions his art as a direct challenge to this English tongue. Thus, the Irish aesthetics that he pledges to create potentially becomes a way to "speak or write these [English] words without unrest of spirit" (*P* 205), which could enable Stephen to challenge one of the primary enforcers of colonial mastery through his art.

Additionally, Stephen rejects his contemporaries' obsession with "the sorrowful legend of Ireland" (*P* 195). Even though he desires to see an emancipated Ireland, he takes issue with nationalist art that promotes "authentic" Irish speech and deems the exclusive focus on Irish subjects to be the only worthwhile goal of art. His dismissive contemplation of the "droll statue" of Thomas Moore, the "national poet of Ireland," demonstrates his skepticism towards the nationalist sentimentality of traditional Irish poetry. He perceives the "sloth of [its] body and of [its] soul cre[eping]" over its "servile head" like "unseen vermin," and he mocks the primitive nature of Moore's art by describing him as a "Firbolg in the borrowed cloak of a Milesian" (*P* 194–5). Stephen also criticizes the Revival's glorification of West Ireland through a faux newspaper notice in his April 14 diary entry. He satirizes the movement's fascination with "pure" Irish folk by evoking John Alphonsus Mulrennan's interaction with an "old man there in a mountain cabin" with "red eyes and [a] short pipe." The mundanity of Mulrennan's exchange with this man mocks the Revival's promotion of Gaelic ("Old man spoke Irish. Mulrennan spoke Irish. Then old man and Mulrennan spoke English"), and the old man's lone statement ("Ah, there must be terrible queer creatures at the latter end of the world") pokes fun at their glorification of the primitive purity of the West. Thus, when Stephen acknowledges that he "fear[s]" and must "struggle" with this old man "with redrimmed horny eyes" (*P* 274), he confirms this nationalist literature base to be another discourse that his artistic agenda evades.

This construction of an alternative national aesthetics would seem to validate Buber's "eternal origin of art." By seeking to "forge" a new racial "conscience" that does not fall prey to the didacticism of his contemporaries, Stephen potentially constructs a politically-viable Irish poetics, enabling the artist to turn towards and affirm Ireland without automatically assimilating it into predetermined discourses of national pride. However, the amatory freedom that denies him the love that he seeks also undermines his aesthetics, as his general indifference to his "race" and his continued fascination with ideal beauty limits his ability to construct this alternative. The alienation within his personal poetics thus infiltrates his broader amatory aesthetics, and Stephen's unwillingness to affirm either his fellow Dubliners or any mention of their plight mitigates the practical effectiveness of his art.

Initially, Stephen's promotion of ideal beauty over his "race" alienates him from his audience. His initial meditations on this beauty in *Portrait*'s fifth chapter illustrate both the personal focus of his artistic platform and the alienating tendencies of that focus:

> His thinking was a dusk of doubt and selfmistrust lit up at moments by the lightnings of intuition, but lightnings of so clear a splendour that in those moments the world perished about his feet as if it had been fireconsumed: and thereafter his tongue grew heavy and he met the eyes of others with unanswering eyes for he felt that the spirit of beauty had folded him round like a mantle and that in revery at least he had been acquainted with nobility. (*P* 191)

The isolating qualities of Stephen's aesthetics are immediately apparent, as his preoccupation with the beauty he encounters "fireconsumes" his perceptions of the world and compels him to return the glances of his counterparts with "unanswering eyes." This lack of recognition shows that while Stephen may desire in theory that his art constitute a union with Dublin, in practice the "spirit of beauty" he pursues actually isolates him from the people he wishes to redeem. Because his apprehension of ideal beauty "[folds] him round like a mantle," it constructs a barrier between Stephen and his surroundings and prevents him from using his art to connect with his audience, limiting its transgressive potential to a personal nature.

Also, Stephen's reliance on ideal beauty impedes direct encounters with his artistic subjects. The symbolic love promoted by his pursuits of Mercedes and the bird girl compel Stephen to adopt a similarly symbolic attitude towards beauty that endorses the static apprehension of ideal pity and terror over the kinetic experience of personal desires and loathing, which he attributes to the "improper arts" of "pornograph[y] and "didactic[ism]." Ironically, Stephen's artistic alternative to his contemporaries' paralytic works is based on an aesthetic stasis where both the artist and audience are "arrested" by the perception of an ideal beauty (*P* 222). Whereas Marian Eide classifies this stasis as more of a "dynamic ambivalence" than a "frozen response" (3), the symbolic nature of Stephen's desired beauty impedes its "dynamic" potential because it forgoes the specifics of his surroundings to achieve an aesthetic encounter "above desire and loathing" (*P* 222). His disqualification of a girl's death in a hansom cab accident as indicative of tragedy reveals this generic advocacy of ideal pity and terror over the everyday examples of those emotions that compel compassionate responses. Stephen's promotion of symbolic beauty over the personal nature of kinetic emotions thus becomes a "prescription for paralysis in the everyday world" by sacrificing the empathetic attachment to the specific tragedies of Ireland in order to achieve a transcendent but static communion (Harkness *Aesthetics* 109).

Additionally, Stephen ignores the fact that the political goals of his aesthetic agenda are kinetic. While he may dismiss the didacticism of religious and nationalist art that compels its audience towards predetermined responses, Stephen's efforts to reveal the "uncreated conscience of his race" are complicit in the same desire and loathing that he claims to transcend. His efforts to rescue his fellow Dubliners from their paralysis by constructing this new Irish conscience indicate that his political goals are predicated on instilling predetermined reactions in his audience because they would have to throw off their devotion to Catholicism and nationalism to endorse the "conscience" he has "forge[d]." Because his interpretations of desire and beauty compel a static platform of artistic apprehension, Stephen short-circuits his ability to save his fellow Dubliners since his audience would have to forgo the social goals of his art to uncover the pity and terror that is present. Stephen may desire an embrace of "moral unity" with his audience, but his inability and refusal to connect personally with that audience limit that embrace to a static apprehension of a generic beauty that is incapable of generating the emotional response needed for the political change he seeks.

Furthermore, Stephen's emphasis on interpretation dissolves the direct encounter between artist and subject needed for effective change. When he describes to Lynch the method by which the observer apprehends the static beauty of an object, Stephen argues that "the most satisfying relations of the sensible must therefore correspond to the necessary phases of artistic apprehension. Find these and you find the qualities of universal beauty. Aquinas says: *ad pulcritudinem tria requiruntur, integritas, consonantia, claritas*. I translate it so: *Three things are needed for beauty, wholeness, harmony and radiance*" (*P* 229). By embracing the search for integritas, consonantia, and claritas as the way to uncover "universal beauty," Stephen advocates the artistic dissection of objects into components in order to appreciate their worth. Not only does this dissection exacerbate the symbolic limitations of his aesthetics (since the specific significance of the object is subordinated to its ability to reflect "universal beauty"), but the search for these three "qualities" limits Stephen's artistic endeavors to the discovery of generic components present in every entity, which reduces any personal encounter with the object to a mere treasure hunt for "wholeness, harmony and radiance." This apprehension may enable a more comprehensive understanding of an object, but its reliance on the static apprehension of the "qualities of universal beauty" forces the observer to perceive their environment not as a unique, vibrant entity, but as an "aggregate of qualities." This dissection thus imposes distance between the artist/audience and the artwork and drains their encounter of its creative potential.

This aesthetic distance is not limited simply to the perception of an object's beauty, but extends to artistic renderings of integritas, consonantia, and claritas. Stephen illustrates this detachment when he describes the artist as "remain[ing] within or behind or beyond or above his handiwork" (*P* 233) since none of these potential relationships enable them to directly "[confront] a form that wants to become a work through him," which Buber argues is needed to unlock the work's "creative power." This lack of direct relation illustrates the dissolution of Stephen's art under his aesthetic stasis, as the artwork is transformed from a subject commanding an emotional response into a mere object that is picked apart and analyzed to uncover its beauty. Just as his symbolization of the bird girl imposed distance between himself and his love object, Stephen's method of depicting the "qualities of universal beauty" erects artistic barriers that reduce the artist to an impersonal "God" who is "refined out of existence, indifferent, paring his fingernails" (*P* 233). The alienation inherent in Stephen's amatory endeavors thus pervades his aesthetic platform, and this subordination of emotion to the static apprehension of beauty further mitigates the transgressive potential of his art.

The limitations of Stephen's amatory aesthetics are confirmed by his increasingly distant attitude towards Ireland at the end of *Portrait*. While he desires to create a new unity with his homeland that will rescue his fellow Dubliners, as he prepares to embark on his exile, his ambivalence towards Dublin compromises this artistic embrace. Of course, Stephen is not obligated to remain in Ireland to represent his homeland effectively in his work, and Joyce remained capable of doing so long after he departed for the last time. However, Stephen's promotion of universal beauty over Dublin and his indifference towards his fellow Dubliners essentially creates a new Irish aesthetics that excludes Ireland, which compromises the goals of his calling. *Portrait*'s concluding diary highlights two limitations of Stephen's vocation that call his ability to "forge" a new Irish "conscience" into question.

First, Stephen's aesthetic fascination with the future dissuades him from a present-day affirmation of Dublin. Whereas Buber argues that successful I-You relationships require a directness that is "lived in the present" (*Thou* 64), Stephen's thoughts in the April 6 diary entries show his ambivalence towards such immediacy. In the first entry, his consideration of whether E.C. remembers their childhood compels him to note that "the past is consumed in the present and the present is living only because it brings forth the future." This description ignores the importance of present-day affirmations and relegates direct encounters with otherness to stepping-stones for future greatness. The artistic implications of this relegation are evident in the second entry, where Stephen considers Yeats's poem "Michael Robartes Remembers Forgotten Beauty." Rejecting Robartes's infatuation with past greatness ("Not this. Not at all"), Stephen instead "desire[s] to press in my arms the loveliness which has not yet come into the world" (*P* 273), which subordinates his immediate interactions with both love objects and aesthetic subjects to the promise of future beauty. This desire to "press" future "loveliness" "in [his] arms" thus dissuades Stephen from seeking similar embraces through his everyday interactions, which not only spurs him towards his desired exile, but also ensures that his artistic representations of Dublin will lack the directness needed to render aesthetically and politically meaningful art.

Second, the violent imagery of Stephen's imagined encounter with the West Irish peasant confirms his refusal to "affirm the person [he] struggle[s] with" (Buber *Knowledge* 69). I have already mentioned his satiric portrayal of the Revival's anthropological fascination with West Ireland, but the conclusion of this April 14 entry also highlights the aggressive nature of Stephen's antagonistic attitude towards this stereotype. His description of his encounter with the "old man" as a "struggle … till he or I lie dead" portrays Stephen's encounter with West Ireland not as an empathetic turning towards an other with whom he disagrees, but as a "fear[ful]" battle against a sworn rival, which highlights the extent to which his aesthetics rejects individuals or ideas that counter his own. Unlike Bloom, who concedes the potential legitimacy of several ideas he opposes throughout *Ulysses*, Stephen's impulse on encountering this marker of difference is to "[grip] him by the sinewy throat," brutally rejecting not only the Revival's West Irish fixation, but the "old man" himself. Even though he asserts that he "mean[s] him no harm" (*P* 274), the antagonism that pervades this encounter demonstrates Stephen's continued inability to affirm the otherness of those who oppose him. Just as this hostility towards difference compromised his personal pursuits of love, it also limits his artistic engagements with Ireland to monologic struggles that exclude any ideas that counter his amatory aesthetics, implicating his new "rac[ial]" "conscience" in the didacticism that he tries to avoid.

Ultimately, the alienation that pervades Stephen's thoughts in these entries complicates his ability to fulfill the political goals of his art. He may deem his exile necessary to create his revolutionary Irish art, but his ambivalence towards Ireland as he anticipates that exile eliminates the direct relationship between himself and his homeland that is essential to complete that objective, reducing Stephen to the "indifferent" artist that "refines [himself] out of existence." This indifference is confirmed in the April 16 entry, where he resolves to heed the "spell of arms and voices" that beckon him "Away! Away!" His exile thus becomes an opportunity for him to "press in [his] arms the loveliness which has not yet come into the world," as the "promise of [the] close embraces" of his exiled "kinsmen" compels him to continue to chase phantoms rather than affirm his fellow Dubliners (*P* 275). Stephen may not have to remain in Ireland to write effective poetry about his homeland, but his refusal to forge a meaningful attachment with anything other than his personal and artistic desires denies him the empathy needed to create a politically viable amatory aesthetics.

****

In "Framing, Being Framed, and the Janus Faces of Authority," Vicki Mahaffey describes Stephen as being "almost immune to the pity and terror aroused by a sympathetic contemplation of the other" (310). While this description is offered primarily as a contrast to Cranly's empathy, it also speaks volumes about his disinterest in the personal sufferings of others and the artistic and political limitations of that apathy. While Stephen may deem the pursuit of ideal "pity and terror" necessary to his amatory aesthetics, his "immun[ity]" to the "pity and terror" he encounters in everyday Dublin reduces his artistic endeavors to the impersonal contemplations of an "indifferent" artist. This indirect aesthetics not only drains his specific poems of their creative potential, but it also prevents Stephen from fulfilling the political objectives of his art, as his continual fascination with universal beauty effectively drains his new Irish aesthetics of its Irishness. Thus, the narcissism that felled his amatory pursuits also compromises his artistic exile, and as he sets out to "forge" this "uncreated conscience of [his] race," Stephen's refusal to view his artistic encounters as "sympathetic contemplation[s] of the other" makes it inevitable that this "conscience" will not extend beyond "the smithy of his soul."

Of course, even though Stephen commits himself to exile at the end of *Portrait*, his departure from Dublin is only temporary. In the opening pages of *Ulysses*, we find the young artist back in Ireland, and his wanderings around Dublin throughout that text enable us to watch the frequent intersections of Stephen's amatory and aesthetic longings. Once again, Stephen will have to negotiate the conflict between compassionate love and amatory freedom, and predictably he will make the same choice. Nevertheless, whereas *Portrait*'s conclusion allowed him to hope for the possibility of future greatness, in *Ulysses*, his decision will ultimately derail both his personal and aesthetic ambitions. The shift from Stephen's climactic invoking of his "old father, old artificer" (*P* 276) to his brooding over his mother's death thus solidifies his episodes in *Stephen Hero*, *Portrait*, and *Ulysses* as cautionary tales against the narcissistic refusal of the empathy needed to attain freedom within a rubric of love.

Chapter 5
Abjection and *Amor Matris* in *Ulysses*

Towards the end of *Portrait*, Cranly attempts to convince Stephen to follow his mother's wishes by making his Easter duties, arguing that "whatever else is unsure in this stinking dunghill of a world a mother's love is not. Your mother brings you into the world, carries you first in her body. What do we know about what she feels? But whatever she feels, it, at least, must be real" (*P* 263). Stephen, committed to an uncompromising religious transgression, responds by citing Pascal, Aloysius Gonzaga, and Jesus as figures who subordinated their love for their mothers to their intellectual and religious pursuits, and the resulting argument culminates in Stephen's recognition of Cranly's empathy towards others and the termination of their friendship. However, this rejection is not limited to Cranly; in refusing to make his Easter duties and subsequently leaving for Paris, Stephen has again chosen his intellectual freedom over the devotion to a real-world loved one, prioritizing the "play" of "ideas [and] ambitions" over the commitment to maternal love (*P* 263). When his father's telegram brings him back to Ireland and his mother's deathbed, Stephen is again forced to choose between amatory freedom and a display of compassion for a dying May Dedalus. Here, his refusal to pray for his mother's soul carries greater consequences, as her death and his growing isolation begin *Ulysses* on a tragic note, sending Stephen away from his Martello tower in search of something to fill the void created by a vanquished maternal love.

In that sense, Stephen's chapters in *Ulysses* seem to be characterized primarily by remorse. Numerous critics point to his preoccupation with his mother's death and his agenbite of inwit throughout the text as evidence of a young artist "paralyzed by this unresolved source of fear and guilt in his memory" (Rickard 36).[1] While these readings are compelling, they also typically cast the relationship between Stephen and the late May Dedalus in an antagonistic light, treating the mother's ghostly presence as an avenging demon that he must vanquish to fulfill his artistic calling. Even those who recognize the presence of *amor matris* in

---

[1] Similarly, John Bormanis argues that Stephen's "guilty feelings about his mother's death and the loss of her emotional support are compounded by those which he feels over his repudiation of his mother('s) country and religion by crossing her last wishes" (596). Cross also contends that "Stephen feels especially guilty about having refused the request to pray at his mother's deathbed. For him it is a matter of integrity: he has too much respect for the religion he is determined not to serve to make sacrilegious use of its forms" (66). Finally, Paul Schwaber notes that "the loss gave rise to mournfulness in him that a year later remains unmitigated, because, pained and at times frightened of her avenging rage, unconsciously he is raging at her for deserting him – for having banished him again and finally, thus depriving him forever of her always-wished-for care and concern" (64).

Stephen's remorse subordinate his desire for love to this antagonism, arguing that he is "in mourning as much for his own intransigence at not having prayed at his mother's bedside as for the love he feels unable to replace" (Hayman 19).[2] However, while the descriptions of Stephen in the "Telemachiad" appear to be merely remorseful continuations of the *non serviam* of *Portrait*'s fifth chapter, reading his struggles over his mother's death with respect to his advocacy of amatory freedom throughout *Portrait* reveals the predominance of love in his brooding. These revelations transform his subsequent wanderings around Dublin into his final quest to regain the unconditional affection needed for Stephen to maintain his persona of the transgressive artist.

The Demand for Intelligent Sympathy

When asked in "Scylla and Charybdis" if he believes that Anne Hathaway was unfaithful to Shakespeare, Stephen responds, "Where there is a reconciliation … there must have been first a sundering" (*U* 9.334–5). Similarly, before we can comment on Stephen's attempts in *Ulysses* to reclaim *amor matris*, we must return to *Portrait* and *Stephen Hero* to witness the development and dissolution of that maternal bond. By undertaking this investigation, we see that Stephen's alienation from his mother does not arise entirely out of his pursuit of intellectual freedom and exile, but is present in his initial thoughts of May Dedalus and extends throughout both of Joyce's texts. In *Portrait* and *Stephen Hero*, Stephen's struggles against Catholic repression compel him to represent his affection for his devout mother in manners that subordinate her feelings and qualify her love, rendering inevitable the conflict that transforms the aspiring lover of *Portrait* into the melancholy brooder of *Ulysses*.

Stephen's maternal dilemma finds its origins on the opening pages of *Portrait*. While these early interactions between Stephen and May Dedalus do not contain the tension of the later scenes, the tension in Stephen's maternal thoughts are still evident. For example, as his parents prepare to leave him at Clongowes, Stephen recalls his mother's advice concerning how to survive on his own at school:

> His mother had told him not to speak with the rough boys in the college. Nice mother! The first day in the hall of the castle when she had said goodbye she had put up her veil double to her nose to kiss him: and her nose and eyes were red. But he had pretended not to see that she was going to cry. She was a nice mother but she was not so nice when she cried. (*P* 5)

---

2 Schwaber also posits that "His fantasy of writing is life-defeating, holding out promise of a world without end entirely of his own: either that or the abiding wish that the fantasy counters, to have his mother back and to himself alone" (76). By contrast, I argue that these fantasies are one and the same, and the inextricability of Stephen's desire for maternal love and the fulfillment of his amatory aesthetics constitutes his central tragedy.

This recollection constitutes the first instance of Stephen qualifying his mother's love in manners that ignore the magnitude of her affection. He recognizes that her desire for him to avoid Clongowes's "rough boys" speaks to a loving concern for his well-being, but his repulsion towards her crying shows his inability to grasp the true extent of her love. While the reader recognizes these tears as signs of May Dedalus's lament over leaving her child at school, Stephen holds the tears against her, noting that his mother "was not so nice when she cried." Of course Stephen cannot be expected to understand fully his mother's devotion at such a young age, but even so, his negative reaction to her tears counterbalances his appreciation for the advice that preceded them, which demonstrates his inability to take her love at face value. By "pretend[ing] not to see that she was going to cry," Stephen erases May Dedalus's affection from the scene, a gesture that will be at the foundation of his later qualifications of her love.

Also, Stephen's confusion over the legitimacy of kissing his mother foreshadows an amatory double bind that comprises both *Portrait*'s fifth chapter and *Ulysses*. Stephen's inability to answer Wells's question correctly is frequently read as evidence of his fascination with language, but it also signifies his difficulty in responding properly to his mother's affection. Rather than defending his love for May Dedalus, Stephen tries to figure out how a yes/no question can have two wrong answers and attempts to understand what a kiss truly signifies, responses that indicate his early prioritization of intellectualizing love over actually experiencing it. Also, instead of envisioning his own mother, Stephen tries to conjure up an image of Wells's mother, symbolically shutting May Dedalus out of her own question. Stephen eventually ruminates on his mother's kiss, but he primarily uses that memory to ponder why people feel the need to kiss each other, another act that subordinates a sign of her affection to his intellectual curiosities. Thus, when an ailing Stephen fantasizes about coming home for the holidays, he cannot imagine his mother's excitement about the occasion without simultaneously wondering if it was correct of her to kiss him, demonstrating the pervasiveness of Wells's mockery in his future associations with her. Indeed, all of Stephen's subsequent interactions with his mother will be tainted by his inability to "kiss" her properly, and this early intellectualization of *amor matris* foreshadows the inevitable subordination and rejection of her affection in his construction of amatory freedom.

Stephen's ambivalence and confusion towards his mother's love becomes increasingly hostile as he embarks on his university career. As he begins to follow his aesthetic calling, Stephen increasingly represents his mother not as the "nice" parent of *Portrait*'s opening pages, but as a generic Catholic devotee who symbolizes all against which he must strive. This is understandable considering that teenage Stephen feels constrained by Irish Catholicism and that some of May Dedalus's requests would necessitate further submissions to the church. However, Stephen's totalizing rejection of the church prevents him from acknowledging his mother's love while he refuses her piety; similar to his earlier repulsions towards the tears and the kiss, Stephen's rebellion compels him to doubt the sincerity of his mother's affection, representing her concern and interest in his life as demands for conformity that he must reject. This refusal thus constitutes Stephen's answer to Wells's question, as his commitment to amatory freedom precludes him from "kiss[ing]" a mother whose religious devotion threatens his intellectual pursuits.

This maternal hostility is evident in *Portrait*'s fourth chapter. As his father inquires about possible university enrollment, Stephen recalls his mother's hesitance to this option in manners that reveal his growing alienation from her:

> Yes, his mother was hostile to the idea, as he had read from her listless silence. Yet her mistrust pricked him more keenly than his father's pride and he thought coldly how he had watched the faith which was fading down in his soul aging and strengthening in her eyes. A dim antagonism gathered force within him and darkened his mind as a cloud against her disloyalty: and when it passed, cloudlike, leaving his mind serene and dutiful towards her again, he was made aware dimly and without regret of a first noiseless sundering of their lives. (*P* 178)

Stephen may be justified in reacting negatively to his mother's hesitancy, but his specific castigations of her reveal the extent to which he sacrifices her love for his goals. Similar to E.C., May Dedalus is not given an explicit voice of disapproval, but is instead confined to the "ineluctable modality of the visible," transformed into a "thing" to be "read" by a Stephen who has just rejected the priesthood and takes any sign of hesitancy by a practicing Catholic as evidence that she is his enemy (*U* 3.1–2). Thus, what could be simply maternal concern is instead represented as "hostility," "mistrust," and "disloyalty," and Stephen's acknowledgement that a "dim antagonism ... darkened his mind" against her reveals this characterization of his mother to promote his intellectual rebellion over her concern.

Additionally, this passage demonstrates Stephen's continued inability to accept difference in his love objects. His antagonism towards his mother is not brought about by any overt attempt by her to prevent his university career, but is rather based on his recognition that "the faith which was fading down in his soul [was] aging and strengthening in her eyes." Thus, even though her protest is simply a "listless silence," the fact that she practices a religion that he has rejected is sufficient to characterize her as "disloyal." Ironically, Stephen's desire to avoid the conformity of the Catholic Church has compelled him to demand that very conformity in his counterparts, and his mother's inability to abandon her faith for him is therefore interpreted by Stephen as a rejection of his love. This refusal of his intellectual pursuits compels him to treat his mother not as the life-giving guarantor of *amor matris*, but rather as a symbol of Catholic dominion no different from the other "sentries" and "guardians of his boyhood" that are rejected in the following paragraph (*P* 178). That Stephen subsequently recognizes "dimly and without regret ...a first noiseless sundering of their lives" reveals the extent to which he desires a love object that is merely a reflection of himself, and May Dedalus's Catholic devotion subordinates her role as his mother to that of a generic churchgoer who is to blame for their growing estrangement.

Stephen's antagonistic characterization of his mother's religion reaches its climax in his refusal to take his Easter duty in *Stephen Hero*. While it is certainly legitimate for Stephen to reject this pledge to a religion he feels has tyrannized his life, the way that he conveys this to his mother emphasizes his inability to empathize with her faith and his insistence on casting maternal love antagonistically. While May Daedalus's initial request for his Easter communion certainly irritates Stephen, her idea to use the family's duty as a special intention for Isabel definitively arms him against his mother: "He was much annoyed that his mother should try to wheedle him into conformity by using his sister's health as an argument. He felt that such an attempt dishonoured him and freed him from the last dissuasions of considerate piety" (*SH* 132). Here, Stephen represents his mother's request as a nefarious scheme to trick him into submitting to the church, casting both his mother's love and his sister's health as threats to his honor that compel his rejection of his family. By articulating that this request "freed him from the last dissuasions of considerate piety," Stephen rationalizes his subsequent attacks on his mother's faith by blaming her for making her request, demonstrating his determination to view any suggestion that conflicts with his goals as a rejection of his love.

In response to her desire that he make his Easter duties, Stephen "[settles] into definite hostility," initiating an assault on the religious foundations of his mother's request (*SH* 132). Admittedly, his mother's pushing Stephen to submit to the Church itself constitutes an imposition on his otherness, suppressing his desire to elude Catholicism's influence and justifying his resistance. However, while Stephen is not wrong to refuse his mother, the extent to which he rejects her pleas demonstrates his continued inability to accept the otherness of people with dissenting viewpoints. Rather than "affirming the person [he] struggle[s] with" (Buber *Knowledge* 69), Stephen adopts a form of "religion baiting," asking mocking questions about the Ascension to provoke his mother into a reaction that can be used as proof of her role as the Catholic enemy. He refers to the Easter beliefs as "drivel" and accuses his mother of knowingly forcing him into a sacrilegious communion (*SH* 133). Once he gets his mother upset enough to tearfully threaten to burn his books, he accuses her of beginning the conversation and flippantly responds that "if you were a genuine Roman Catholic, mother, you would burn me as well as the books." To be sure, May's threat to burn Stephen's books does confirm the religious repression Stephen is resisting in this conversation, but it is also an incidental emotional response provoked by Stephen's prodding and subsequent scenes where May Daedalus attempts to read Ibsen demonstrate her desire to understand her son's dissenting beliefs. By contrast, Stephen's concluding statement that "I don't see what you're crying for" parallels his puzzlement over Emma's tears upon being propositioned (*SH* 135), as his insistence on viewing all Catholics as enemies prevents him from comprehending the feelings of his loved ones and subordinates their love to his rebellion. Thus, while this scene does highlight the religious constraints on Stephen's freedom, it also confirms Stephen's inability to empathize with others in preserving his individuality, and the severity of his dismissal of his mother reveals his prioritization of self-preservation over maternal love.

By contrast, *Portrait*'s depiction of this conflict seems tame. Here, Joyce does not show us Stephen's argument with his mother over the Easter duty, but it is reasonable to conclude that a similar dispute has taken place. Indeed, *Portrait*'s Stephen tells Cranly that an "unpleasant quarrel" took place between him and his mother "about religion" (*P* 259), and when Cranly asks him if he loves his mother, he shakes his head and tells him "I don't know what your words mean" (*P* 261). When Cranly presses further and asks if Stephen's mother has lived a happy life, he responds, "How do I know?" (*P* 262), demonstrating that Stephen's preoccupation with her Catholicism has blinded him to her specific struggles. By omitting the argument between Stephen and his mother from the finished novel, Joyce does portray *Portrait*'s Stephen in a less hostile light than his *Stephen Hero* origins, which reflects the conflicted emotions young Stephen consistently expresses about her throughout *Portrait* and exhibits more of a struggle to respond to maternal love than Stephen Daedalus's blanket rejection. Nevertheless, even though *Portrait*'s Stephen's attitude towards May Dedalus is more complex, his commitment to amatory freedom in this exchange with Cranly still prevents him from understanding or empathizing with May Dedalus, making her desire for him to take his Easter duty enough for him to argue that he does not know what it means to love one's mother. Despite the suffering and love that Cranly mentions, Stephen's rebellious commitment disqualifies that love from consideration, leaving only her Catholicism to be used to justify his separation from her.

Stephen's insistence on this separation is confirmed in *Portrait*'s concluding diary. The initial March 20 entry begins this divorce from *amor matris* by presenting an abbreviated account of his conversation with Cranly. While Stephen does mention Cranly's suggestion that he obey his mother's wishes, his presentation of this argument demonstrates his inability to take this suggestion seriously. He indicates that Cranly "had his grand manner on," characterizing his friend's arguments as righteous indignation that Stephen can easily dismiss. He also represents Cranly's advocacy as "attacking [Stephen] on the score of love for one's mother," which both represents maternal love as a weapon that Cranly wields against him and erases May Dedalus from the discussion by referring to the love of "one's" mother instead of "his" mother. Finally, just as he reacted to Wells at Clongowes, Stephen imagines Cranly's mother instead of his own, signifying both his disinterest in taking his argument seriously and his unwillingness to consider his mother under an amorous obligation.

This dismissal of his mother's love continues in the March 24 entry, where Stephen writes: "Mother indulgent. Said I have a queer mind and have read too much. Not true. Have read little and understood less. Then she said I would come back to faith because I had a restless mind. This means to leave church by backdoor of sin and reenter through the skylight of repentance. Cannot repent" (*P* 271). While the bulk of the entry reiterates his belief that his mother's concern threatens his intellectual freedom, Stephen's concluding remark illustrates just how uncompromising that freedom is. By articulating that he "cannot repent" his refusal to submit to the Church, Stephen has permanently removed a method of reconnecting not only to Catholicism (which he will not lose much sleep over), but also to his mother's love (which he will lose a lot of sleep over in *Ulysses*). This resolution is necessary for Stephen to pursue his artistic calling without being shackled down by Catholicism, but the absolute nature of this statement thus dismisses the only option Stephen has towards reclaiming maternal love.

This inextricability between maternal love, religion, and Stephen's amatory aesthetics is ultimately confirmed in the penultimate diary entry. Stephen writes on April 26 that his mother "prays … that I may learn in my own life and away from home and friends what the heart is and what it feels" (*P* 275). This hope demonstrates the extent to which May Dedalus's concern for Stephen is guided by love, as her insistence that he learn "what the heart is and what it feels" signifies a desire for Stephen to experience a love that transcends the religious concerns to which *Portrait* had previously confined her statements. However, Stephen's response to this suggestion confirms the unlikelihood of him ever feeling this form of love. His flippant "Amen" dismisses the specifics of her entreaty and instead focuses on its characterization as a "pray[er]" so as to continually portray May Dedalus as a Catholic against whom he must strive. Thus, when Stephen immediately follows this "Amen" with his desire to "encounter for the millionth time the reality of experience," he positions his exile and freedom as a rejection of maternal love, tossing aside his mother's plea for him to "learn … how [the heart] feels" so that he can "forge into the smithy of his soul the uncreated conscience of his race." In a sense, his invoking of the "old father, old artificer" in *Portrait*'s final diary entry (*P* 276) constitutes an emphatic shift away from the mother of love and religion towards the father of aesthetic creation … until his father's blue telegram brings him back to the bedside of his mother.

Ghostly Light on the Tortured Face

Throughout *Portrait*, Stephen subordinates real-world love to symbolic phantoms, crafting a framework of amatory freedom that rejects Cranly, Emma, and May Dedalus so that he can pursue his ideal Mercedes. In an event that is not narrated explicitly, but is referenced extensively in *Ulysses*, Stephen is called back to Ireland to care for his dying mother and is once again asked to make a religious concession, this time to pray for her eternal soul. While this request may seem similar to his refusal of the Easter duty, the bedside prayer carries more extensive amorous implications because its specific focus on preserving May Dedalus's well-being would constitute an empathetic embrace that would confirm the son's affection in his mother's eyes. However, to Stephen this request is also another demand to submit to Catholic tyranny, and his refusal to kneel, when combined with her subsequent death, constitutes his final rejection of *amor matris* during his mother's life.

However, this does not mean that Stephen shuts the door on maternal love after May Dedalus's death. In fact, once his mother leaves the realm of the living, Stephen becomes obsessed with reclaiming the love that he refused in real-life.

Critics are certainly correct in reading remorse in his maternal meditations, but when we read these reflections with respect to the pursuits of symbolic love that dominated *Portrait* and *Stephen Hero*, we see that more than guilt is at play. His fonder memories of his mother's life can be seen as attempts to suppress the despair and rejection that concluded it through a sanitized depiction of maternal bliss, and his focus on playing "Who Goes with Fergus" on the piano to comfort his dying mother enables Stephen to prioritize a moment of compassion and care towards her throughout his brooding. When read this way, Stephen's reflections on his mother throughout *Ulysses* are shown to be another pursuit of a symbolic love object, as his efforts to solidify a more heartwarming representation of maternal affection become attempts to reclaim *amor matris* through the suppression of his refusal of her final wish.

However, these efforts do not go smoothly. While Stephen attempts to envision a happier, loving mother, his memories inevitably return to her deathbed and his refusal to pray for her soul. Unsurprisingly, Stephen's response to this memory is to blame his mother for compelling his refusal, relying on his *Portrait* claim that he "cannot repent" and castigating the dead May Dedalus for causing his unrest. The dead mother thus undergoes what Julia Kristeva calls abjection, the banishment of signs that cannot be assimilated into oneself through representations that are considered repulsive and unclean. She writes, "What is abject, on the contrary, the jettisoned object, is radically excluded and draws me toward the place where meaning collapses. A certain 'ego' that merged with its master, a superego, has flatly driven it away. It lies outside, beyond the set, and does not seem to agree to the latter's rules of the game" (2). Scholars have noted the abject nature of Stephen's mother in *Ulysses,*[3] but the role of the "jettisoned object" becomes clear when we consider his amatory reflections in the text. Since any shift from loving to dying mother turns Stephen's depictions of her into gruesome, threatening images, abjection becomes a critical component of his quest to reclaim maternal love, as memories that reveal the futile nature of that quest are represented as loathsome and excluded from his mind so that he can continue chasing his symbolic phantom.

Nevertheless, the inability of abjection to exclude the "jettisoned object" completely ultimately undermines its effectiveness. Kristeva's observation that the suppression of the abject "draws me towards the place where meaning collapses" shows that although cracks in symbolic constructions are suppressed through abjection, their return is inevitable because "from its place of banishment, the abject does not cease challenging its master" (2). Such "challeng[es]" frequently plague Stephen throughout *Ulysses*, as his attempts to transform his mother's ghost into a gruesome threat perpetuate reappearances of the ghostly memory and

---

[3] Ewa Ziarek argues that "the compulsion to eject the maternal element from the artist's consciousness, is intensified by an emotional response of revulsion and disgust. Yet the experience of aversion, according to Kristeva, is a curious synthesis of affect and judgment, which points to the defensive expulsion of what cannot be assimilated to the self" (61).

stronger challenges to his desire for maternal love. His amatory quest is ultimately foiled as his ideal love object is overshadowed by the reemergence of the abject other he casts aside along the way.

Stephen's failure to ignore his refusal of May Dedalus's love is revealed through his interactions with Buck Mulligan and his visions of his mother's corpse in "Telemachus." When Mulligan chides Stephen for refusing to kneel at his mother's deathbed, the latter experiences "pain, that was not yet the pain of love" in his heart, and his mind turns to a dream that has tormented him since her passing: "Silently, in a dream she had come to him after her death, her wasted body, within its loose brown graveclothes giving off an odour of wax and rosewood, her breath, that had bent upon him, mute, reproachful, a faint odour of wetted ashes" (*U* 1.102–5). Not only does Mulligan's rebuke that Stephen's refusal to pray for his mother reveals "something sinister in [him]" (*U* 1.94) compels the latter to conjure up a sinister image of his mother, but given his earlier assertion that "someone killed [his mother]" (*U* 1.90), Stephen's dream reveals his desire to avoid culpability for refusing to pray for her, as its horrific nature enables him to blame her for his melancholy by transforming her into a hideous corpse, whose "mute" and "reproachful" countenance pose a threat that Stephen must vanquish.

This corpse-like imagery also reveals the prominence of abjection in Stephen's brooding. Whenever Stephen desires to imagine that he possesses his mother's affection, his thoughts prioritize fonder moments of the past over the events at her deathbed. However, when his mind turns to her plea for Stephen's prayer, he immediately represents her as a monstrous corpse whose presence threatens his soul. Kristeva calls this representational strategy "the utmost of abjection," describing "the corpse" both as a "real threat" and as "death infecting life. Abject. It is something rejected from which one does not part" (4). Stephen's construction of a "'dual mother' [that is] at once loving and terrible" demonstrates the pervasiveness of his use of abjection (Kimball *Odyssey* 90), as his inability to reclaim his mother's love compels his continued treatment of her as an enemy to his amatory freedom. This strategy may temporarily assuage his remorse, but its suppression of his mother's affection keeps Stephen from the love he seeks throughout *Ulysses* by preventing him from empathizing with her condition and leaving him with only a "pain, that was not yet the pain of love."

However, Stephen's attempts to suppress his mother's memory are only temporary. After trying to convince Stephen to "give up the moody brooding" (*U* 1.235–6), Mulligan quotes "Who Goes with Fergus" as he descends the tower steps: "And no more turn aside and brood/Upon love's bitter mystery/For Fergus rules the brazen cars" (*U* 1.239–41). Stephen's reaction to the poem reveals both the impossibility of Mulligan's suggestion and the extent of his preoccupation with "love's bitter mystery":

> A cloud began to cover the sun slowly, wholly, shadowing the bay in deeper green. It lay beneath him, a bowl of bitter waters. Fergus's song: I sang it alone in the house, holding down the long dark chords. Her door was open: she wanted

> to hear my music. Silent with awe and pity I went to her bedside. She was crying in her wretched bed. For those words, Stephen: love's bitter mystery. (*U* 1.248–53)

This passage reveals the "bitter" love at the foundation of Stephen's anguish. His juxtaposition of Fergus's song with the "bowl of bitter waters" foregrounds his guilt over his refusal of maternal love, representing his rejection of his mother's dying wish in the rhetoric of the Biblical "trial of jealousy." Gifford and Seidman's explanation of this reference to the Book of Numbers reveals the punitive nature of this representation:

> Numbers 5: 11–31 outlines the "trial of jealousy," the trial of a woman suspected of an unproven adultery. The priest presents the woman with the "bitter water," cursing her so that if she is guilty, "this water that causeth the curse shall go into thy bowels, to make thy belly to swell, and thy thigh to rot." If she is not guilty, the curse will have no effect. (18)

The association of the "trial of jealousy" with an "unproven adultery" provides a compelling analogy for Stephen's brooding, as his preoccupation with the ghostly dream constitutes his attempts to vindicate himself from the charge of betraying her affection. Juxtaposing Stephen's situation with the "bowl of bitter waters" thus represents the rejection of his mother's dying wish as his own "trial of jealousy," forcing him to stand judgment for refusing to pray for her soul. By tying the "bowl of bitter waters" to "love's bitter mystery," Stephen highlights the amorous significance of this trial, as May Dedalus's desire for him to utter "those words" represents the requests from her deathbed as a desire for his returned affection.

Juxtaposing her desire for "love's bitter mystery" with her desire for Stephen's prayer transforms his mother's dying wish into evidence of the inextricability of his double bind: since Stephen must pray for his mother's soul to secure *amor matris*, Joyce represents the maternal love Stephen seeks to be a direct threat to his amatory freedom since it would require him to submit to the Church to obtain it. Also, this scene shows that this love is not unconditional. Throughout *Portrait* and *Stephen Hero*, Stephen perpetually seeks an unconditional surrender of his love object "without any overt act of his." By contrast, the requirement that Stephen has to pray to attain maternal love foregrounds the conditional nature of that love, as his mother will return Stephen's affection only if he prays for her eternal rest. The conditional nature of the love Stephen seeks thus illustrates the inevitable frustration of his quest, as the love object he desires will reject his pleas for unconditional affection.

Stephen's response to this dilemma is again to transform his mother into an abject corpse. His subsequent meditations on her death return him to the dream where the spirit of his mother plagues his refusal of her deathbed request:

> Her glazing eyes, staring out of death, to shake and bend my soul. On me alone. The ghostcandle to light her agony. Ghostly light on the tortured face. Her hoarse loud breath rattling in horror, while all prayed on their knees. Her eyes

> on me to strike me down. *Liliata rutilantium te confessorum turma circumdet: iubilantium te virginum chorus exipiat.*[4] Ghoul! Chewer of corpses! No, mother! Let me be and let me live. (*U* 1.273–9)

The horrific nature of his mother's corpse highlights Stephen's use of abjection to overcome his maternal dilemma. His focus on her "glazing eyes" and "ghostly light" highlights its monstrous nature, representing her as villainous so as to necessitate her exclusion. Ironically, this gruesome imagery recalls the rotting bodies of those who fail the "trial of jealousy," showing Stephen's corpse imagery to be an attempt to push the "bowl of bitter waters" away from him and towards his mother. Also, Stephen's fears that the corpse emerges "*to* shake and bend [his] soul" and "*to* strike [him] down" establish an intentional malice behind his mother's presence by representing her gruesome visage as a deliberate attempt to torture his mind. His observation that the corpse "stares out of death" echoes Kristeva's description of the corpse as "death infecting life," positioning the apparition as a threat to Stephen with each appearance she makes. Thus, the antagonistic nature of his dream is not only evidenced by the monstrous corpse, but by its ability to maintain a constant challenge to the aesthetic persona that carried out its abjection.

However, the most compelling evidence of abjection's role in the visions of the corpse appears towards the end of the passage. Not only does Stephen's mother appear to him as a monstrous creature, but she constantly reminds him of his rejection of maternal love. The corpse's utterance of the "Ordo Commendationis Animae," the prayer for the dying, foregrounds his dilemma: for Stephen to reclaim maternal love, he would have to submit to a religious performance that calls his amatory freedom into question. Thus it is significant that the corpse's desire for the last rites is immediately followed by Stephen labeling the vision as a "ghoul," as evidence of his refusal of maternal love is represented in antagonistic terms that enable its exclusion. Stephen's desires for the corpse to "let [him] be and let [him] live" become the most definitive evidence of his mother's suppression in "Telemachus," as his attempts to shield himself from her ghost enable him to exclude challenges to his quest to reclaim maternal love.

Stephen's efforts to negotiate his double bind continue throughout "Nestor." While it is a critical commonplace to point to Stephen's reflections on Cyril Sargent as evidence of his preoccupation with *amor matris*, his obsession with this affection in this chapter is evident as early as his consideration of John Milton's "Lycidas." Even though Talbot's recitation of the poem in Stephen's classroom is primarily used to support Stephen's critique of the "nightmare of history" (*U* 2.377), it is telling that Joyce follows his mourning for his dead mother in "Telemachus" with one of English literature's most famous elegies in the following chapter. In that sense, it is necessary to read "Nestor" as an elegy, or rather as a failed elegy, for Stephen's indifference to Talbot's recitation demonstrates his inability to "weep" for his mother's rest.

4 Translated: "May the glittering throng of confessors, bright as lilies, gather about you. May the glorious choir of virgins receive you" (Gifford and Seidman 19).

Joyce's inclusion of "Lycidas" in "Nestor" is important not simply because of its overall relevance as an elegy, but also because of the parallel between the specific stanza that Talbot recites and Stephen's desire to overcome his grief. Indeed, these verses establish a way to come to grips with death that potentially provides an opportunity for Stephen to come to terms with his refusal to pray for his mother's rest. Initially, the stanza's opening decry of "weep no more, woful shepherds, weep no more" (*U* 2.64) echoes Mulligan's call for Stephen to "give up the moody brooding" (*U* 1.235–6), establishing the relinquishing of grief and the acceptance of the spirit's enduring life as prerequisites for overcoming an emotionally paralyzing death. Additionally, the observation that "Lycidas … is not dead/Sunk though he be beneath the watery floor" (*U* 2.65–6), while developing the shepherd's position that the departed spirit is eternal, finds its Joycean counterpart in May Dedalus, whose death does not prevent her ghost from making continued appearances in Stephen's mind. The speaker's isolation of the soul's undying existence thus means that emotional connections do not end with death, but potentially endure depending on how one chooses to remember the deceased. When read within the context of Stephen's brooding, these fragments of "Lycidas" establish a proper elegy to May Dedalus as necessary for him to restore the maternal affection he seeks throughout the text.

The efficacy of this elegy is developed throughout the rest of the stanza. While these lines are not explicitly cited in *Ulysses*, they are definitely uttered in Stephen's classroom, as Talbot's recitation of the poem's conclusion gives them an absent presence in "Nestor."[5] Specifically, we know that he recites the shepherd's contention in the middle of the stanza that Lycidas's tragic demise has been replaced by a heavenly happiness since Talbot repeats the line "*Through the dear might of Him that walked the waves*" (*U* 2.78), making it plausible that Stephen's allowing him to "turn over" the page in his recitation book enables him to finish the poem (*U* 2.80). This observation is significant because the conclusion of "Lycidas" articulates ways for the "woful shepherds" to overcome their anguish that could also quell Stephen's brooding.

Initially, the description of a tranquil afterlife in the lines that follow Talbot's error provides an alternative to Stephen's antagonistic representations of his mother's corpse in "Telemachus." Instead of focusing on his drowned corpse, the narrator contends that Lycidas "lathes" his hair "with *Nectar*" and "hears the unexpressive nuptiall Song,/In the blest Kingdoms meek of joy and love" (175–7). He subsequently insists that Lycidas is "entertain[ed]" by "all the Saints above" (178), who "wipe the tears for ever from his eyes" (181). Such peaceful descriptions of the heavenly Lycidas enable the speaker to convince his fellow

5 Patrick Hogan similarly contends that Talbot recited the entirety of that stanza, arguing that "sentences end on lines 177 and 181, but the entire concluding section of the poem runs only to line 185 … It seems most plausible to assume that the students were assigned the entire twenty-line concluding section, rather than a twelve- or sixteen-line portion of that section" (122).

shepherds to cease their mourning, to envision the tranquil image of their comrade instead of his drowned corpse, and to accept the happiness of his afterlife despite his tragic death.

When read alongside Stephen's brooding in "Telemachus," the relevance of this advice becomes apparent. Similar to the "woful shepherds," Stephen's inability to "give up the moody brooding" compels him to dwell upon his mother as a ghastly corpse instead of as the "beautiful May Goulding" (*U* 15.4173–4). For that reason, the recitation of "Lycidas" becomes a plea to Stephen to "weep no more" over her death by forgoing the preoccupation with her gruesome cadaver and instead envisioning his mother at peace. For Stephen to obey the "uncouth Swain" would be for him to accept that although his mother's faith contradicts his career path, it at least eased her pain before and after death, enabling a present tranquility that obviates the need for his grief. This acceptance of her happy afterlife would allow Stephen to perceive her spirit in a more positive light despite their differing religious attitudes, allowing him to move past his remorse.

Furthermore, this acceptance of a tranquil maternal spirit would enable Stephen to resolve his amatory double bind. Because Stephen insists on characterizing May Dedalus as a menacing corpse that threatens his freedom, the demands imposed by this spirit inevitably jeopardize his aesthetic pursuits (in this case, by forcing him to submit to a religious performance he unconditionally rejects to regain maternal love). Were Stephen to acknowledge that his mother's faith might have granted her a peaceful afterlife, then that tranquil image would supplant the gruesome corpse that demands his repentance. By shifting his maternal representations away from the deathbed, Stephen could affirm his mother's religious otherness without compromising his *non serviam*, not only because he would not need to pray for her soul if it were already in heaven, but also because he would not have to compromise himself to acknowledge that his mother's faith was sufficient for her. Rather than excluding his mother because of her dissenting beliefs, Stephen could "confirm … as creature and as creation, [she] who is opposed to [him]" and develop a loving bond with her enduring presence that would affirm her as "the personal bearer of a conviction" without compromising his intellectual pursuits (Buber *Knowledge* 69).

However, Stephen ignores this call to "weep no more." While "Lycidas" may provide a way to overcome his grief through a loving acceptance of his mother's otherness, Stephen does not listen to the entire recitation. In fact, he tunes out Talbot after the first three lines and instead contemplates his life in Paris, overlooking the speaker's description of Lycidas's enduring presence after death.[6] Then, after he sets Talbot's recitation back on track, he does not pay attention to the rest of the stanza that establishes Lycidas's tranquil heavenly existence, choosing instead to contemplate the poem's reference to "him that walked the waves" (*U*

6 "So sinks the day-star in the Ocean bed,/And yet anon repairs his drooping head,/ And tricks his beams, and with new-spangled Ore,/Flames in the forehead of the morning sky:/So *Lycidas* sunk low, but mounted high" (168–72).

2.83). His mental digressions throughout the recitation demonstrate that Stephen does not heed the specifics of the recitation, but instead uses random lines as springboards for a religious contemplation that has nothing to do with "Lycidas." These digressions prevent Stephen from acknowledging Milton's alternative to his brooding, inhibiting his ability to affirm May Dedalus in the manner needed for him to come to grips with her death and to build a loving relationship with her enduring spirit. Thus, when Stephen asks "have I heard all" (*U* 2.91), he reveals that he has heard nothing, as his inability to overcome his remorseful conscience prevents him from reaffirming his love for May Dedalus.

This missed opportunity is confirmed towards the middle of "Proteus." As Stephen considers Mulligan's once saving a man from drowning, he wonders if he could ever be so heroic. What begins as a hypothetical scenario involving an imaginary victim quickly takes on personal significance, as his insistence that "I could not save her" transforms the victim into May Dedalus, and the subsequent reference to "waters: bitter death: lost" demonstrates his continued obsession with the "trial of jealousy" that consumed his thoughts in "Telemachus" (*U* 3.329-30). Not only does this "bitter death" imagery signify Stephen's continued representation of his mother as a corpse instead of a tranquil spirit, but the defensive nature of this imagery also demonstrates his continued guilt over his death bed refusal. His insistence that there was nothing he could do to save her reveals his continued belief that he cannot help his mother without compromising his freedom, an assertion that recalls his similar equivocations in *Portrait* and *Stephen Hero*.[7] Thus, Stephen's determination to view maternal aid as a threat forces him into an amatory paralysis that prevents him from developing a more loving bond with her spirit.

This is not to say that Stephen completely ignores maternal affection in "Nestor"; however, the mechanism that he chooses to gain that affection falls short of the success potentially offered by "Lycidas." Rather than elegizing his mother, he continues to perceive his maternal obligations according to the amatory freedom that guided him throughout *Portrait* and *Stephen Hero*. Initially, Stephen tells his class a riddle and changes the answer to have "the fox [bury] his grandmother," instead of his mother, "under a hollybush" (*U* 2.115), which continues his suppression of his mother's death from "Telemachus." His alteration of the joke's conclusion confirms his failure to accept either his mother's otherness or her death productively since her "poor soul" cannot "go to heaven" if Stephen refuses to bury her (*U* 2.106–7). This tactic may enable him to continue his amatory quest by suppressing his role in his mother's death, but by improperly elegizing May Dedalus through the riddle, Stephen's denial of her difference prevents him from demonstrating the love he wishes to reclaim.

---

7 In *Portrait*, Stephen responds to Cranly's question of if he would "try to save her from suffering" by stating "If I could … that would cost me very little" (*P* 262). In *Stephen Hero*, Stephen responds to a similar question from Cranly by contending that "I would in many cases" (*SH* 138).

Also, Stephen's exclusion of his mother in his subsequent contemplations of Sargent limits his isolation of *amor matris* to a symbolic desire. He may famously describe maternal love as "the only true thing in life" (*U* 2.143), but the loving potential of *amor matris* is undermined by May Dedalus's absence in these meditations. Initially, Stephen imagines Sargent's mother, who "[bore] him in her arms and in her heart" (*U* 2.140). Then, he contemplates the "fiery Columbanus," whose religious devotion compelled him to "[leave] his mother 'grievously against her will'" (Gifford and Seidman 33). While this scenario is analogous to Stephen's departure from his mother at *Portrait*'s conclusion, he never mentions himself specifically, and any hint of May Dedalus is confined to her being likened to Columbanus's mother and to the mention of "rosewood and wetted ashes" (*U* 2.145–6). When Stephen finally refers to himself as needing maternal love, recognizing that "like [Sargent] was I" (*U* 2.168), he still does not mention his mother and abruptly ends his reflection with the "secrets" in his heart "weary of their tyranny" (*U* 2.171). As in *Portrait*, Stephen avoids dealing with his maternal relationship by imagining other people's mothers instead of his own, failing to see how a renewed affirmation of May Dedalus would enable him to experience the love he envies in Sargent and limiting his subsequent pursuits to generic love objects that will never quench his brooding.

The limitations of this suppression become evident in "Proteus," where Stephen's hesitancy to represent his mother forces him to acknowledge the pitfalls of his amatory aesthetics. Lacking the triumph and assurance of *Portrait*'s artistic episodes, Stephen's efforts to "[think] himself into confidence" are immediately nullified by his realization that nobody will acknowledge his accomplishments (*P* 74). Whereas his thoughts of E.C. enabled an ecstatic construction of the villanelle, his brooding on his mother's death compels the writing of a vampire poem that is crumpled into his pants pocket as he wonders, "Who ever anywhere will read these written words?" (*U* 3.414–5). His subsequent isolation of "a woman to her lover clinging" echoes the passionate epiphany that concluded the villanelle section, but his attempts to develop *Ulysses*'s fantasy lead him to a dead end that forces him to ask "She, she, she. What she?" (*U* 3.426). Because he cannot evoke his mother's image without simultaneously brooding on her death, he has to invoke a generic love object that is unable to spur his genius to any satisfactory degree. These failed attempts force Stephen to realize that his commitment to symbolic love and beauty has alienated him from his loved ones to the point where no love objects remain to reflect his greatness. He can continue to chase his ideal Mercedes, but Stephen now recognizes that embracing "the beauty that has not yet come into the world" without a real-world lover amounts to little more than "bow[ing] to [him]self in the mirror" (*U* 3.137).

Stephen's brooding in "Proteus" climaxes with his desire to attain the "word known to all men." His failure to envision a symbolic love object causes Stephen to lament his solitary existence and to yearn for a love that he has yet to experience: "Touch me. Soft eyes. Soft soft soft hand. I am lonely here. O', touch me soon, now. What is that word known to all men? I am quiet here alone. Sad too. Touch,

touch me" (*U* 3.434–6). Not only does the remorseful rhetoric signify Stephen's lonely existence, but it also demonstrates his continued longing for a love object that would give herself to him without compromising his amatory freedom. His pleas for this lover to "touch [him]" to ease his loneliness reveal his disinterest in initiating the act of love for which he longs, continuing to hope that his desires will be fulfilled "without any overt act of his" (*P* 67). Thus, the "word known to all men" that Stephen longs to hear is simply another form of the amatory surrender that he sought throughout *Portrait*, and by juxtaposing this "word" with the Yeats fragment "*And no more turn aside and brood*" nine lines later (*U* 3.445), he shows that his insistence on being handed the cure to his loneliness rather than actively "giv[ing] up the moody brooding" denies him the maternal "touch" he seeks.

This juxtaposition also confirms the alienating nature of Stephen's longings. Indeed, his subsequent transition from "Fergus's Song" to Mulligan's potential desertion demonstrates his inability to consider his mother's death empathetically, as the parallel he draws between Cranly and Mulligan solidifies the exclusionary nature of his maternal brooding: "Staunch friend, a brother soul: Wilde's love that dare not speak its name. His arm: Cranly's arm. He now will leave me. And the blame? As I am. As I am. All or not at all" (*U* 3.450–2). Similar to the end of *Portrait*, Stephen initiates his thoughts about Mulligan in an amatory light that abruptly give way to feelings of betrayal. By comparing him to Cranly through the touch of their arms, Stephen rhetorically unites Mulligan's rebuke of Stephen's refusal to pray for his mother ("You could have knelt down, damn it, Kinch, when your dying mother asked you" [*U* 1.91–2]) with Cranly's criticism of his refusal to take his Easter duty. For that reason, when Stephen guesses that Mulligan "now will leave me," he performs an amatory exclusion reminiscent of his termination of Cranly's friendship, representing both criticisms of his refusal to pray as rejections of his love. Rather than move towards an acceptance of his mother's death, Stephen shuts out any attempt to paint his ambivalence as problematic, transforming his concluding "All or not at all" into a renewed dedication to an uncompromising amatory freedom. Thus, in the transition from the "word known to all men" to his resolve to be "as I am," Stephen solidifies his double bind, striving to attain a maternal love but unable to initiate the action required to gain it. His continued deflection of blame and his demand that his love objects accept him "all or not at all" foreshadow the failure of his encounter with May Dedalus in "Circe" and guarantee that his subsequent attempts to gain the love he seeks will do nothing to alleviate his loneliness.

When we read Stephen's reaction to "Lycidas" with respect to *amor matris*, we see how his reliance on amatory freedom undermines his ability to gain the love he desires. While Milton's elegy could provide a way for him to regain a loving relationship with his mother, his insistence on performing the uncompromising artist denies him this alternative, compelling him to continue representing her in antagonistic terms that fail to ease his loneliness. This antagonism not only accounts for his failures in "Proteus," but recurs throughout the rest of *Ulysses*, as Stephen's obsession with the maternal threat he has created undermines his attempts to set his aesthetic pursuits back on track. What emerges in "Scylla and Charybdis," "Wandering Rocks," and "Oxen of the Sun" is a continued performance of Stephen's amatory *non serviam*, which guarantees his failure to gain either maternal love or artistic success.

"Scylla and Charybdis" begins Stephen's efforts to rebuild his amatory aesthetics. Here, he puts forth an alternative reading of *Hamlet* that both establishes a parallel between himself and Shakespeare and continues to project the blame for lost maternal love onto May Dedalus. By depicting Anne Hathaway as a malicious siren who "saw [Shakespeare] into and out of the world," Stephen constructs a strategically destructive interpretation of love that concedes her "[taking] his first embraces" and "bearing his children" while still enabling him to foreground her adulterous betrayal (*U* 9.217–9). In so doing, he reveals his continued refusal to represent his mother empathetically, instead representing her maternal care as masking an inevitable betrayal. Thus, when Stephen charges that "By cock, she was to blame," he simultaneously articulates a critical component to his literary analysis and continues to shift responsibility for his mother's death onto the deceased, a rhetorical strategy that seemingly fulfills his artistic calling in a manner consistent with his amatory freedom (*U* 9.257).

However, similar to his struggles in "Proteus," Stephen's lecture falls short of the glory that he seeks, as his *Hamlet* analysis succumbs to two limitations. First, his continued reflections on his mother's death prevent him from moving past his brooding isolation. His initial description of maternal love may equate Anne with May Dedalus, but that definition is immediately troubled by his mental return to "mother's deathbed. Candle. The sheeted mirror. Who brought me into this world lies there, bronzelidded, under few cheap flowers. *Liliata rutilantium*. I wept alone" (*U* 9.221–4). This reflection may simply rearticulate the maternal dilemma that Stephen's Shakespeare theory attempts to negotiate, but his concluding acknowledgement that he "wept alone" foreshadows his perpetual loneliness even if he does suppress his remorse. This isolation infiltrates Stephen's subsequent thoughts, as his accusations of Anne's infidelity compel him to plead for his own seduction. (And my turn? When? Come!" [*U* 9.261–2].) Stephen's awareness of being "condemned" to contemplate *amor matris* this way confirms the failure of his theory (*U* 8.499), not only because he may not know "what the hell … [he is] driving at (*U* 8.496), but also because even if he can construct an interpretation of maternal love that validates his actions, it will not assuage his mental pain.

Second, Stephen alienates his audience. Eglinton, Best, and Russell may provide his theory with the critical attention that his vampire poem lacked, but Stephen's preoccupation with resolving his maternal conflict results in an aggressively personal interpretation of *Hamlet* that undermines its receptivity. A.E. dismisses Stephen's theory as "prying into the family life of a great man" (*U* 9.181), and his focus on Anne's betrayal underwhelms Eglinton, who had anticipated "paradoxes" (*U* 9.369). As a result, even if Stephen's construction of *amor matris* helps him resolve his double bind, his resolution is so limited in its appeal that it will not advance his artistic ambitions. His omission from Russell's "sheaf of our younger poets' verses" (*U* 9.291) and his exclusion from George Moore's party show that his amatory aesthetics excludes him from the Dublin literary establishment, denying him his audience even in a crowded library. Thus, his characterization of *amor matris* in "Scylla" unravels in its very construction, and Stephen's failed attempt to suppress his mother's death becomes simply another opportunity for him to "bow to [him]self in the mirror."

The extent of this failure is evident in "Wandering Rocks," where Stephen's thoughts reveal his continued preoccupation with maternal love. As he walks past the powerhouse, he notes the "beingless beings" on Bedford Row who "throb always without you and the throb always within" (*U* 10.822–3). This observation not only demonstrates his alienation from his fellow Dubliners, but also refers to James Lane Allen's *The Mettle of the Pasture,*[8] a text whose focus on the refusal of maternal desires signifies the role his brooding plays in this alienation (*U* 10.822–3). Thus, when he desires to "shatter" the "two roaring worlds" of the "bawd and butcher"[9] between which he finds himself, Stephen reiterates his determination to overcome his double bind without compromising his religious rebellion. He acknowledges that this resolution will "stun [him]self too in the blow," but he immediately suppresses this failure, challenging his enemies to "shatter me you who can" (*U* 10.825–6). Again, Stephen has forced himself to acknowledge the unraveling of his efforts to win maternal love through amatory freedom, only to suppress that knowledge through a reclamation of his isolated artistic persona, limiting himself again to the pursuit of symbolic phantoms to gain the love he desires.

Stephen's next opportunity to win this symbolic love occurs at the bookcart on Bedford Row. As he flips through "eighth and ninth book of Moses," he comes across an incantation from Peter Salanka that he deems potentially useful: "How to win a woman's love. For me this. Say the following talisman three times with hands folded: *Se el yilo nebrakada femininum! Amor me solo! Sanktus! Amen*" (*U* 10.847–9).[10] Stephen's reaction to the incantation reveals the narcissistic nature of his pursuit, as his desire to "win a woman's love" represents her as a prize to be attained by an incantation. This characterization echoes Aquinas's depiction of narcissistic desire in "Scylla," as the "love" of a "woman" is valued because its attainment would strengthen his self-love. The command that his love object only love him reiterates the unconditional nature of Stephen's desire, representing the

---

8 Gifford and Seidman point out that the novel's protagonist "has a climactic scene with his mother, in which he refuses her wish (that he and [his] fiancée be married)" (276).

9 Stephen refers to the *dio boia* in "Scylla" as "ostler and butcher, and would be bawd and cuckold too but that in the economy of heaven, foretold by Hamlet, there are no more marriages, glorified man, an androgynous angel, being a wife unto himself" (*U* 9.1050–2). Thus, the isolation of the hangman god in his description of the "two roaring worlds" speaks to the religious submission that comprises an essential component of his double bind.

10 Translated, "My little heaven of blessed femininity! Love only me! Holy! Amen" (Gifford and Seidman 277).

love to be won by the spell as a complete submission to him. Finally, similar to the generic love objects he sought in "Proteus," Stephen chooses to "win" the love of simply "a woman" instead of directly affirming his mother or any other specific love object, limiting himself once again to the pursuit of symbolic phantoms. Thus, his application of the love charm undermines its ability to restore the love he desires, pushing him towards the nebulous submission of a fictitious love object that will inevitably elude his grasp.

The disconnect between the incantation and Stephen's desired love is inherent in his subsequent encounter with Dilly Dedalus. While their conversation has been read as evidence of Stephen's ability to "sympathize with his sister's poverty and suffering" and to "share her misery" (Dickson 24), his thoughts throughout this exchange demonstrate his disinterest in empathizing with her. As soon as he sees Dilly, Stephen's impulse is to "shut the book quick. Don't let see," an instinct that clearly signifies embarrassment but also constitutes a literal refusal to share his love with her (*U* 10.856). Also, his preoccupation with his Paris life and Salanka's love charm throughout this exchange reveal that his obsession with his mother's love renders him ambivalent towards the family plight that Dilly describes. This ambivalence is confirmed by his refusal to assist Dilly for fear that "she will drown me with her, eyes and hair," which shows that he has yet to discover "what the heart feels" and thus cannot express the empathy needed to restore the love he seeks (*U* 10.875–6). In refusing to help his poverty-stricken sister, Stephen again has limited his amatory pursuits to empty demands for symbolic love objects that only bring him "misery! Misery!" (*U* 10.880).

The emptiness of these demands is confirmed in "Oxen of the Sun," where an intoxicated Stephen performs his amatory freedom to the amusement of his drunken comrades. Here, Stephen articulates an uncompromising advocacy of artistic creation that also attempts to promote his amatory aesthetics over maternal love: "In woman's womb word is made flesh but in the spirit of the maker all flesh that passes becomes the word that shall not pass away. This is the postcreation. *Omnis caro ad te veniet*" (*U* 14.292–4).[11] Contradicting his earlier isolation of *amor matris* as the "only true thing in life," Stephen notes the temporality of maternal creation, arguing that the life-giving powers of the artist supersede those of the mother because poets confer eternal life on those about whom they write, and the fragment of the Requiem Mass that concludes this passage reveals the influence of his mother's death in this characterization. Thus, rather than embrace the memory of his mother, Stephen's advocacy of eternal artistic power subordinates the love lost at her deathbed to the aesthetic persona that justifies his refusal.

This subordination continues throughout "Oxen," where Stephen reduces his mother to a symbol of church and Ireland. His initial ridicule of "our mighty mother and mother most venerable" not only unites Erin and Mary as targets of scorn, but its maternal focus forces May Dedalus to be included as well (*U* 14.296). Thus, when Stephen mocks Mary's participation in the Immaculate Conception, he not only

[11] Translated, "All flesh will come to thee" (Gifford and Seidman 62).

condemns Catholic love, but also dismisses his mother's care as another religious threat that his artistic prowess overcomes. Similarly, he describes Ireland as a duplicitous mother by representing its crimes as a perverted form of maternal love, which passes judgment on Stephen's mother as well as his nation. By representing this love as being "suckled" with "bitter milk" (*U* 14.377–8), he transforms the life giving power of *amor matris* into sins against him that justify his rejection. His subsequent charge that his mother "[has] left [him] alone for ever" allows Stephen to characterize her death as a desertion (*U* 14.379), and his reference to their departing "kiss of ashes" denies her an identity beyond the abject cadaver from "Telemachus" (*U* 14.380). Not only does this tactic enable May Dedalus to be excluded, but by linking his maternal rejection to his critique of church and nation, Stephen reveals the relationship between his individual frustration and his social alienation, as his refusal to "affirm the *person* [he] struggle [s] with" strengthens his broader refusal to "affirm the [*people*] [he] struggle[s] with." He may suppress his maternal loss through his performance of the uncompromising artist, but that performance only confirms his inability to affirm the "many-faced otherness" of either his mother or his body politic (Buber *Man* 61), foreshadowing the unraveling of both his personal and aesthetic endeavors.

This unraveling occurs towards the end of "Oxen," where Stephen reclaims the title of "Bous Stephanoumenos" that coincided with his initial acceptance of the artificer in *Portrait* and pronounces himself "lord and giver of their life" (*U* 14.1115–6). In a reversal of the apathy in "Scylla," Lynch proclaims universal support for Stephen's aesthetics: "All who wish you well hope this for you. All desire to see you bring forth the work you meditate, to acclaim you Stephaneforos. I heartily wish you may not fail them" (*U* 14.1119–22). However, this solidarity is interrupted by Lenehan, who insensitively retorts, "Have no fear. He could not leave his mother an orphan" (*U* 14.1123). While Stephen has focused on his mother throughout "Oxen," Lenehan's reply is the first instance where she exists as something other than a religious or national symbol. This is apparent in Stephen's reaction, as rather than demonstrating the pride of his symbolic rebukes of *amor matris*, the humiliated artist's "face [grows] dark" and he is resigned to a brooding silence (*U* 14.1124). The fact that "all could see how hard it was for him to be reminded of his promise and of his recent loss" highlights the extent to which Stephen's symbolic representations of maternal love had shielded him from such "reminde[rs]" throughout the episode (*U* 14.1124–5), and the silence of the once triumphant artist reveals his success in "Oxen" to be as temporary as he initially characterized the "woman's womb." Stephen's symbolic dismissal of *amor matris* thus collapses, forcing him to recognize his inability to maintain his amatory freedom without reclaiming his mother's love.

As Stephen discovers throughout *Ulysses*, the dead will not go quietly. Kristeva's argument that the abject inevitably returns to "challenge its master" is evidenced by May Dedalus's recurring presence in the artist's broodings. Stephen's efforts either to suppress his remorse or to exclude his mother through the ghostly dream unravel, as each attempt is followed by the reemergence of the corpse whose existence undermines the legitimacy of his amatory freedom, requiring him to confront the ghost to resolve his dilemma. "Circe" thus provides Stephen a final chance to confront his mother's apparition and to seek the love he deems necessary to counteract his artistic paralysis.

May Dedalus's entrance in "Circe" foregrounds her continued abject identity:

> *Stephen's mother, emaciated, rises stark through the floor, in leper grey with a wreath of faded orangeblossoms and a torn bridal veil, her face worn and noseless, green with gravemould. Her hair is scant and lank. She fixes her bluecircled hollow eyesockets on Stephen and opens her toothless mouth uttering a silent word.* (*U* 15.4157–61)

This gruesome appearance is immediately followed by the "Ordo Commendationis Animae," a juxtaposition that shows Stephen's continued desire to suppress his remorse over his deathbed refusal by projecting May Dedalus as a threat. Stephen's reaction confirms this tactic, as his "horrorstruck" exclamation "Lemur, who are you? No. What bogeyman's trick is this?" (*U* 15.4176) denies the ghost's self-identification as the "beautiful May Goulding" and thus continues his attempts to symbolize her as something other than the loving mother whom he refused. However, while many critics paint this confrontation in an exclusively antagonistic light,[12] reading Stephen's subsequent responses with respect to his longings reveals that his interaction with the ghost is not merely antagonistic; rather, Stephen attempts to explain his actions to his mother's ghost in order to reclaim the maternal love he has lost.

Initially, Stephen tries to convince her that he was not to blame for her death. He exclaims, "(*choking with fright, remorse and horror)* They say I killed you, mother. He offended your memory. Cancer did it, not I. Destiny" (*U* 15.4186–7). The stage directions reveal Stephen's altered mental state, as his feelings of "remorse" enable him to counterbalance his "fright" and "horror" and interact with his mother's presence without automatically rejecting her as a dangerous corpse. His projections of blame onto Mulligan, cancer, and destiny are thus attempts to negotiate his way out of his amatory double bind, reclaiming his mother's affection while shifting attention away from his refusal to pray for her soul.

---

[12] Hayman views the apparition as an "emblem of the force that has brought him back from Paris and now refuses to release him from Ireland, absolve him of his guilt, and remove his fear of death" (25–6). Kimball also writes that "Of course, Stephen's ashplant is not a sword, and it does not touch crab, dragon, or mother; as it turns out, it hardly even damages the chandelier (*U* 15:4284–91). But Stephen's blow is followed in the text by the annihilation of time and space (*U* 15:4243–5) and the disappearance of the mother from *Ulysses*" (*Odyssey* 94–5). Finally, Frances Restuccia argues that "Stephen (and Joyce through Stephen) steels himself against her. He shouts out the rebellious Satanic words 'Non serviam!' (U 475), smashing the chandelier with his ashplant (possibly in an attempt to kill the ghost). Anti-Oedipal Stephen has no qualms about employing his ashplant … to fend off the real mother whom he resented in her role as agent of the punishing (religious) patriarchy" (93).

His mother's reaction seems to validate this tactic. After Stephen professes his innocence, the ghost recalls that "you sang that song to me. *Love's bitter mystery*" (*U* 15.4189–90). This memory grants new hope to Stephen, as its reference to his act of empathy confirms this confrontation as his second chance to attain the affection he has sought throughout *Ulysses*. However, his reaction to this recollection reveals his inability to capitalize on this opportunity. Rather than offering a compassionate embrace similar to his performance of "Fergus's Song," Stephen desires that his mother "tell" him "the word known to all men," sacrificing the empathy he recalled in "Telemachus" to his narcissistic longings in "Proteus." Thus, Stephen does not "confirm" his mother "as creature and as creation," but instead reduces her to a generic love object to assuage his loneliness "without any overt act of his," which denies her love even as he pleads for it and guarantees that he will fail to gain the affection he desires.

Unsurprisingly, Stephen's request is not granted, as his mother's reaction rearticulates the dilemma that characterized his rejection of her deathbed plea: "Who saved you the night you jumped into the train at Dalkey with Paddy Lee? Who had pity for you when you were sad among the strangers? Prayer is allpowerful. Prayer for the suffering souls in the Ursuline manual and forty days' indulgence. Repent, Stephen!" (*U* 15.4195–8). This reaction reveals the failure of Stephen's quest, as the ghost does not "tell" him the "word," but instead recalls the sacrifices she made for his happiness and reiterates her pleas for prayer. Stronger than the "unimaginative piety" Schwaber reads in this demand (156) or the "trivial and nagging" "words" that Rickard finds (164), the ghost's conflation of maternal love and repentance solidifies Stephen's double bind: to regain maternal love, he has to repent his refusal to pray for her soul, but to do so would destabilize his amatory freedom, not only by submitting to a prayer that his aesthetic persona rejects, but also by conceding that his earlier refusal was regrettable and thus the artistic identity he has constructed is flawed. This insistence on Stephen's repentance thus provides the ultimate rejection of his desire for unconditional maternal affection.

Stephen's rejection of his mother's plea instantaneously triggers her abjection. Stephen was willing to accept the ghost as the "beautiful May Goulding" when the conversation focused on "love's bitter mystery," but once his mother demands Stephen's repentance, he represents the vision as "the ghoul! Hyena!" (*U* 15.4200). These outbursts contrast sharply to the eagerness of his earlier desire for love and confirm the role of abjection in shielding the spurned lover from his painful rejection. Stephen's recommitment to amatory freedom culminates in his exclamation, "*Ah non, par exemple!* The intellectual imagination! With me all or not at all! *Non serviam!*" (*U* 15.4227–8). This reaffirmation of his refusal to serve thus becomes an attempt to restabilize his aesthetic persona by banishing his mother's presence, minimizing the damage caused by the rejection of maternal love under the guise of reclaiming his artistic agency.

To Kimball, this reassertion of *non serviam* is successful, as she reads Stephen's destruction of Bella Cohen's chandelier as evidence that "he has done battle with the loving and terrible mother, and he has won his deliverance" (*Odyssey* 96).[13] However, while it may seem that May Dedalus meets her end in "Circe," Ziarek correctly notes that "this ghostwoman continues to live in Joyce's text even though she has died" (63). Stephen's initial utterances upon being awakened by Bloom in "Circe" confirm that even if wielding the ashplant has banished the ghost, the "beautiful May Goulding" continues to pervade his thoughts: "Who...drive... Fergus now/And pierce...wood's woven shade.?" (*U* 15.4932–3). These fragments from "Fergus's Song" demonstrate the failure of Stephen's attempt to banish his preoccupation with maternal love, foreshadowing the recurring presence of maternal guilt in the "Nostos" episodes.

Stephen's inability to overcome this guilt is confirmed by the final image of the young artist in "Ithaca." As Stephen departs from Bloom's house, he hears the sound of the bells of St. George's Church, and his reaction highlights his continuing anguish: "What echoes of that sound were by both and each heard? By Stephen: *Liliata rutilantium. Turma circumdet. Iubilantium te virginum. Chorus excipiat*" (*U* 17.1228–31). The reemergence of the prayer for the dying demonstrates that any peace that can be attributed to the conclusion of "Circe" has worn off and the remembrance of Stephen's refusal to pray for his mother's soul has returned to torment him.[14] Thus Stephen's unswerving commitment to amatory freedom has denied him the love he has sought throughout *Ulysses* and has alienated him from his surroundings to the point where his freedom is all he has left.

****

In "Scylla and Charybdis," Stephen quotes Goethe as saying, "Beware of what you wish for in youth because you will get it in middle life" (*U* 9.451–2). While the Stephen that departs 7 Eccles Street certainly has not reached "middle life," the conclusion of his amatory struggles in *Portrait*, *Stephen Hero*, and *Ulysses* reveals him to be living proof of that adage. His desire to "meet in the real world the unsubstantial image which his soul so constantly beheld" tied his subsequent pursuits to a symbolic framework of amatory freedom, as his obsession with

---

[13] Benstock also interprets this scene as a "symbolic victory won by Stephen Dedalus," noting that "the Stephen Dedalus who emerges from the experience seems soberer and calmer" (*Ulysses* 146).

[14] Rickard reads Stephen's reaction differently, arguing that "significantly, now Stephen's mind omits the words '*te confessorum*,' which were contained in two earlier occurrences of the prayer (*U*1.277 and 15.4164). This omission of 'confessors' may again suggest that Stephen's memory of his mother is finally free from guilt" (194). However, considering that his meditations on the litany at the end of "Telemachus" also omitted "*te confessorum*" ("He walked along the upwardcurving path. *Liliata rutilantium./Turma circumdet./Iubilantium te virginum.*" [*U* 1.735–8]), his brooding on the prayer in "Ithaca" confirms that the grief that consumed his thoughts at the beginning of *Ulysses* remains at the end of the text.

encountering his ideal Mercedes enticed Stephen to treat Emma Clery, Cranly, and his mother as images of submission instead of as individuals. Since the reality of the love object cannot be encapsulated in a mere symbol, Stephen represented the inevitable disjunctions between the amorous real and the amatory ideal as refusals of his love, prioritizing his artistic calling over the obligations to his loved ones. However, whereas Stephen could rationalize his refusals of Emma and Cranly in manners consistent with his aesthetic persona, his maternal relationship proves more challenging, as his mother's death establishes a double bind from which he struggles to extricate himself throughout *Ulysses*. Ultimately, his rigid adherence to amatory freedom becomes his undoing, as his inability to repent his rejection of his mother's dying plea renders him incapable of gaining the submissive affection he desires. Thus, May Dedalus becomes Stephen's ideal Mercedes, though not in the way he desired, and the premonition of *Portrait*'s second chapter is ironically fulfilled at the conclusion of *Ulysses*, as the last glimpse that Joyce provides us of Stephen consists of him "standing in a moonlit garden with [Bloom]," uttering a "sadly proud gesture of refusal" (*P* 65).

In that sense, Stephen strengthens Joyce's cautionary tale of narcissistic desire. Whereas *Dubliners* depicted self-involved lovers falling short of their amatory escapes, in *Portrait*, *Stephen Hero*, and *Ulysses*, Joyce traces the development and performance of a comprehensive amatory framework whose primary characteristic is the ascendance of the lover through the submission of his love object. By treating his love objects as reflections of himself and refusing their empathetic embrace, Stephen's amatory freedom continues the rejection of difference that inhibits any meaningful relationships with Dublin, as his efforts to construct "the uncreated conscience of [his] race" isolate him from his intended audience and limit his art to static apprehensions of ideal terror and pity that will do nothing to change the body politic in which he finds himself entrapped. Joyce's next work would provide another opportunity to examine the self-defeating nature of an exile's narcissism; however, *Exiles* offers a different take on the relationship between love and exile. Whereas *Stephen Hero* and *Portrait* chronicled their exile's departure, *Exiles* focuses on his return, and Richard Rowan's attempts to balance his individual desires with his responsibility to "wish [Bertha] well" enable Joyce to reevaluate the continued ethical responsibilities of lovers who reject the constraints of their body politic (*E* 63). In this manner, Richard constitutes an evolution of the Joycean narcissist into a lover who tries to turn towards his beloved, even if his self-absorption prevents him from doing so effectively, which transforms *Exiles* into a key turning point in the Joycean oeuvre's amorous trajectory.

Chapter 6
Richard Rowan's Deep Wound of Doubt

In many ways, the amatory struggles of Stephen Dedalus and Richard Rowan are similar. Both characters use romance as an impetus for artistic success, struggle with the conflict between love and freedom, and pursue exiles that push them away from their lovers and their individual ambitions. Thus, it is not surprising that Richard suffers a similar fate as Stephen, as the self-centered foundations of his amatory pursuits prevent him from achieving a "uni[on] … in body and soul in utter nakedness" with Bertha, his "bride in exile" (*E* 112; 111). Critics have long noted Richard's narcissism in *Exiles*, casting him as a cruel manipulator who treats Bertha, Beatrice Justice, and Robert Hand as "moral and aesthetic pawn[s] to implement his own psychological liberation" (Henke *Desire* 92).[1] However, while Richard is certainly fascinated with dissolving the monogamous bonds that constrain him, his meditations on love throughout Joyce's play demonstrate a compassion yet to be seen in Joyce's romantic protagonists.

Considering Joyce and Nora's domestic struggles during the composition of *Exiles*, this complexity is not surprising. Indeed, Richard's guilt over his fascination with Beatrice parallels Joyce's infatuation with a Triestine English student (likely Amalia Popper) from 1911 to 1914,[2] and Robert's unsuccessful wooing of Bertha echoes Roberto Prezioso's 1913 advances towards Nora. These domestic crises thus provided the "crucial first-hand experience" for the author to be obsessed with "the themes of attraction and betrayal, marriage and infidelity and the often ambiguous nature of sexual attraction" during this time (McCourt 192–3). For that reason, it is natural that Joyce would wrestle with the duality of adulterer and cuckold as he began writing *Exiles* in 1914, and his dramatic attempt to resolve this conflict between lust and fidelity expands the scope of his amorous writings to consider not simply the failure of sentimental narcissism, but also the proper means to fulfill the loving "responsibility of an I for a You" (Buber *Thou* 66).

---

1 Bauerle also writes that "Even when Richard appears to be yielding Bertha to another, she remains his possession, and he gives her selfishly in order to keep her" ("Bertha" 116). John M. Clark similarly notes that "[Richard's] traumatic rebirth into doubt may be a necessary and from Joyce's viewpoint a desirable event, but his churlishness indicates how far he remains from genuinely matching … Joyce's compassion" (185). Finally, Eide contends that "masochism is self-involved to the extent that he boxes his corner rather than opening his subjectivity to another's partnership. Concerned only with his moral evaluation of himself, Richard's masochism inflicts pain on Bertha and, at the same time, excludes her" (43).

2 In his introduction to *Giacomo Joyce*, Ellmann notes that "its heroine, whom Giacomo relates to Beatrice Portinari and Beatrice Cenci, is related also to Beatrice Justice in *Exiles*" (*G* xxii).

This expansion is articulated most explicitly in Richard's conversation with Robert in Act II, where his rebukes of his friend's pursuit of Bertha demonstrates his understanding of both the limitations of individual passion and the ultimate objective of true love. Noting that "longing to possess a woman is not love," Richard rebuffs Robert's claim that "no man ever lived on this earth who did not long to possess … the woman whom he loves," arguing instead that the true purpose of love is "to wish her well" (*E* 63). In so doing, Richard reveals that his pursuits in *Exiles* are not purely self-motivated, as his desire to be rid of love's constraints carries with it a desire to obtain a similar freedom for Bertha, illustrating his desire for her happiness even as it misrecognizes the steps needed to obtain it. Thus, although Richard engages in manipulative actions throughout the play, he is aware on some level of his responsibility for Bertha's well-being, which makes him a crucial transition figure from Stephen's narcissism to Bloom's empathy and transforms *Exiles* into what Padraic Colum called a "sort of watershed between the work James Joyce has done and the work he is to do" (*E* 9).[3]

The False Pretender

While Richard contends that the purpose of love is to "wish [one's beloved] well," Robert endorses "the passion which burns us night and day to possess her" (*E* 63). In so doing, he demonstrates that his amatory advances towards Bertha throughout the play are inherently hollow, that beneath his insistence that he has "a deep liking" for her is the desire for possession that Joyce critiqued in *Dubliners* and *Portrait* (*E* 31). Thus, Robert becomes the embodiment of Joyce's well-documented repulsion towards amatory desire, as the author mocks Prezioso's reputation as a "*conquistatore amoroso*, a '*Don Giovanni*'" (McCourt 193) by reducing his play's lothario to "the almost comic stereotype of the seducer" (Brown 19). Through Robert's interactions with Bertha and Richard, Joyce constructs a one-dimensional, narcissistic foil to his protagonists' struggles in *Exiles*, transforming Robert into a "false [pretender]" whose seductive advances are mocked and undermined by his love objects (*E* 54).

Robert's status as a "false [pretender]" is best conveyed through his conversation with Richard in Act I. Responding to Richard's question whether he "kiss[es] everything that is beautiful to [him]," Robert notes: "This stone, for instance. It is so cool, so polished, so delicate, like a woman's temple. It is silent, it suffers our passion; and it is beautiful … And so I kiss it because it is beautiful. And what is a woman? A work of nature, too, like a stone or a flower or a bird" (*E* 41). Similar to Stephen's fascination with beauty in *Portrait*, Robert is disinterested in the specific attributes of his love objects, viewing feminine loveliness instead as indicative of a general beauty that embodies all "work[s] of nature." Indeed, his

3 Brown also recognizes that Richard anticipates Joyce's endorsement of true love in *Ulysses*, arguing that his "tentative definition" of love in Act II "perhaps prefigur[es] Bloom's definition of love in 'Cyclops'" (34).

isolation of a woman's "silen[ce]" and "suffera[nce]" of masculine advances as evidence of her worthiness mutes the specifics of her feelings and transforms her into an empty vessel whose worth is signified by his "kiss."[4] This distant desire is demonstrated further in their subsequent discussion over a kiss's value. Whereas Richard argues that a kiss is "an act of union between man and woman" (*E* 41), Robert characterizes it instead as merely "an act of homage" to a beautiful object. This distinction between "union" and "homage" highlights the fundamental difference between Richard's and Robert's attitudes towards love: while Richard values the connection forged between two people through a physical expression of love, Robert values a kiss as simply an abstract testimony to his partner's beauty, isolating him from his love object even through an act of intimacy. Also, his representation of his potential loved one as a "beautiful object" renders their relationship unequal by reducing her to a generic entity over which he wields his power. By contrast, Richard's characterization of a kiss as an "act of union" represents the intimate act as a reciprocal passionate exchange between two equal participants, which highlights the self-serving foundations upon which Robert's adoration is built.

Robert's apathy towards otherness is confirmed by their concluding remarks on feminine beauty. Scoffing at Richard's question of whether "the beautiful is what we desire," Robert argues that "what is most attractive in even the most beautiful woman" is "not those qualities which she has and other women have not but the qualities which she has in common with them" (*E* 41–2). By claiming that "those qualities which she has and other women have not" are not beautiful, Robert dismisses the otherness of his beloveds, ignoring their individual qualities and passions in favor of their ability to validate abstract feminine beauty. His accompanying list of "[common]" beautiful qualities highlights the ridiculous nature of his homage, showing his fascination with generic feminine beauty to regress to a worship of "how her body develops heat when it is pressed, the movement of her blood, [and] how quickly she changes by digestion what she eats into—what shall be nameless" (*E* 42). Thus, it is appropriate that Robert ends his argument by insisting that the excrement he celebrates "shall be nameless," since the passion he chooses to express inevitably reduces his love objects to "nameless" markers of universal beauty to which Robert can only offer a distant homage.

The most explicit examples of Robert's artificial passion occur during his numerous advances towards Bertha. While he claims to feel strongly for her, Robert rarely articulates a specific passion for her, but instead compares her to markers of natural beauty that robs his wooing of any intimacy. Echoing Prezioso's infamous claim that "'Il sole s'è levato per Lei'—the sun has risen for [Nora]" (McCourt 193), Robert notes of the previous night that "I could see the dark green

4 Clark similarly argues that "kissing a stone with the same emotion as kissing a woman can seem natural not because the stone is human … but because the woman might as well be a stone as far as her admirer's ability to identify with what she thinks and feels is concerned" (189).

masses of the trees. And you passed beyond them. You were like the moon." This observation demonstrates the symbolic foundations of Robert's desire, as he equates Bertha with "the dark green masses of the trees" and trivializes her specific beauty by comparing her to the moon. This abstract wooing continues when Robert mentions Bertha's dress, "slim body," and walk as reasons why he "saw the moon passing in the dusk till you passed and left my sight" (*E* 31). This gesture in particular betrays his ignorance of her, as his relegating her physical qualities to those of the moon literally causes him to "s[ee] the moon passing in the dusk" when she is in his line of sight. Bertha thus loses her identity through Robert's homage, and his equating her with a distant object simultaneously marks the distance in their intimate exchanges.

This distance is also demonstrated by Robert's subsequent advances. When Bertha asks if he thought of her the previous night, he responds, "I think of you always—as something beautiful and distant—the moon or some deep music" (*E* 32). Not only does Robert's description of Bertha as "something beautiful and distant" betray the lack of intimacy between them, but his equation of her "beautiful and distant" nature with "the moon or some deep music" echoes Gabriel's characterization of Gretta's reaction to *The Lass of Aughrim* as *Distant Music*, showing that Robert's wooing suffers from the same misrecognition of Bertha's desires that encapsulated Gabriel's exaltation. His subsequent declaration that "I was awake half the night. I could hear your voice. I could see your face in the dark. Your eyes" confirms the limitations of his distant metaphors (*E* 32), as he can only hear Bertha's voice and see her face in the darkness of his solitary bedroom. In that sense, her specific beauty only comes into focus when she has departed his company, and Robert's "one-dimensional fascination with [Bertha's] appearance" prevents him from understanding her otherness (Sanner 282).

Robert's symbolic advances are further undone by Bertha's awareness of his motives. When he notes that "your face is a flower too—but more beautiful. A wild flower blowing in a hedge," Bertha teasingly smiles and asks her seducer "if that is what you say—to the others" (*E* 32), recognizing that she is simply one entry in a list of admirers who also are told that they resemble the moon and wild flowers. Especially since Bertha will later refer to this behavior as endemic of "false pretenders," Robert's insistence on celebrating "the qualities which [the most beautiful woman] has in common with [others]" blinds him to the specific essence of his current conquest and dampens her receptivity to his homage. Bertha's knowledge that Robert "[has] so many admirers" thus signifies her refusal to be merely one of his "works of nature," and her concluding "thank you for saying it—and for thinking it" shows that Robert's celebrations of her natural beauty are primarily oral performances with little substance behind them (*E* 32).

Furthermore, Robert's insistence on performing the seductive lothario undermines the legitimacy of his affection for Bertha. Rather than articulating genuine feelings for Bertha, Robert limits his words and actions to those of a stereotypical lover from a sentimental romance, emptying his wooing of any authenticity. Initially he fears that he has annoyed Bertha because "you put away my poor flowers so quickly," as if her attention to his flowers is an accurate measure of her love (*E* 32). Then, when Bertha admits skepticism over his nature similes ("men speak like that to all women whom they like or admire" [*E* 33]), Robert avoids her uncertainty by "suddenly" asking her: "Bertha, may I kiss your hand? Let me. May I?" (*E* 34). His subsequent actions constitute a checklist of clichéd romantic performances, as Robert kisses Bertha's eyes, runs his hand through her hair, calls her "Little Bertha," asks her to look deep into his eyes, embraces her, and asks her to kiss him (*E* 35). The mechanical way in which Robert completes this list and the trite exclamations that accompany his actions ("Your voice!"; "At last I hold you in my arms!"; "Your lips, Bertha!" [*E* 35]) reduce Robert's wooing to the absurd performance of a lover more concerned with enacting the right demonstrations of physical passion than articulating a meaningful emotional connection with his beloved.

The empty nature of Robert's performance is emphasized by Bertha's reactions to these displays. In contrast to his desperate entreaties, Bertha ridicules Robert's generic romantic conventions, which prevents us from taking his advances seriously. For example, when Robert fears an apathetic reaction to his flowers, Bertha "*takes them from the table and holds them close to her face*," asking Robert if "this [is] what you wish me to do with them" (*E* 32). Similarly, when he runs through his checklist of physical homage, Bertha answers his requests with resigned submissions that highlight the lack of emotion in this encounter. Through responses such as "if you wish" (*E* 34), "do so," and "take it," as well as her repeated query "and then you will be satisfied?" (*E* 35), Bertha highlights the irrelevance of Robert's displays of adoration, as each of his performances is completed successfully, yet nothing significant is gained by their completion. Bertha's "[disdain of] the inflated, unnatural language [Robert] so often uses" thus robs his wooing of any emotional resonance (Bauerle "Bertha" 119), as her resigned acquiescence to his advances makes it likely that the only person he is seducing is himself.

Unsurprisingly, Robert's hollow advances render him incapable of winning Bertha. He may wish to possess her physically, but his symbolic representations of her and his clichéd romantic performances prevent any genuine emotional attachment from forming between them. The beginning of their conversation in Act I demonstrates this, as Robert's clarification of the letter that he handed Bertha the previous night falls short of the emotional declaration needed to entice her. While the letter does make Bertha aware of a vague regard, Robert immediately clarifies the "*one word which I have never dared to say to you*" to signify "a deep liking for you," which conveys merely an abstract affection instead of love (*E* 31). Ironically, Robert's inability to speak the language of love to Bertha rather than the language of seduction foreshadows her refusal of him in Act II, as his subsequent desire for her to tell him she loves him garner responses such as "I like you, Robert. I think you are good" that fall short of the romantic affirmation that he desires (*E* 88), and the fact that "*she does not answer*" his concluding plea makes it likely that he does not get the answer he seeks (*E* 88). The failure of Robert's advances are confirmed in Act III, where his persistent pursuit of her throughout the first two acts is reduced to a "dream that [Bertha] was [his]" (*E* 106) and a concession to Richard that "she is yours, as she was nine years ago" (*E* 107). Ultimately, Robert's narcissistic desire for possession and his subordination of Bertha's desires to his symbolic homage undermine his goals to the point where "only [his] dream is real" (*E* 106).

Robert's obsession with generic notions of love is demonstrated further by his relationship with Richard. As in his advances towards Bertha, Robert primarily relates to Richard through platitudes, using their conversations to note his undying devotion to his colleague. However, unlike Robert's flattery of "Little Bertha," his approach towards Richard is more antagonistic, as his obsession with Bertha compels him to view Richard as a rival suitor and to treat their interactions as a battle for ownership of her. Not only does this obsession continue to reduce Bertha to an object, it also undermines the viability of his relationship with Richard, as Robert's desire to play the cavalier hero misrecognizes his friend's desire for Bertha's freedom and alienates him further from his "master" (*E* 44).

Robert may view Richard as his rival in *Exiles*, but his initial interactions with him convey an intense congeniality that echoes his wooing of Bertha. In Act I, Robert resolves to quash the negative perception of Richard's exile out of a sense of "our friendship, our lifelong friendship" (*E* 39), and he assures him that "I fought for you all the time you were away. I fought to bring you back. I fought to keep your place for you here." Thus, when he describes his devotion to Richard as "the faith of a disciple in his master" (*E* 44), he employs strategies similar to his advances towards Bertha, using symbolic representations of his unwavering affection and loyalty to compel Richard to go along with his wishes. Robert's professed discipleship thus ostensibly serves as a catalyst for his determination to reclaim his "master['s]" place within Ireland.

However, Robert's devotion to Richard is not as genuine as it may initially seem. While he may claim to have his friend's best interests at heart, Richard is correct in characterizing his comrade's devotion as that of "the disciple who will betray him" (*E* 44). Robert might pledge to secure Richard the position of humanities chair, but his scheduling of Richard's key meeting at the same time that he has invited Bertha to his house demonstrates this commitment to be a ruse to occupy Richard so that he can seduce her. More importantly, Robert's plan demonstrates his ambivalence towards his friend's desire for freedom. Even though he claims that he "will fight for [Richard] still" (*E* 44), his characterization of Richard's decision to leave Ireland as "r[unning] away years ago …[w]ith a young girl not exactly your equal" (*E* 39) illustrates his disinterest in validating the desire for freedom that compelled Richard's escape. Instead, he represents that escape as an "episode in your past" and an "act of impulse" (*E* 38), which explains Richard's exile not as the necessary act of a smothered intellectual, but rather as a scandalous act of youthful carelessness that has been renounced by his return. For that reason, Robert's efforts to "give the lie to [Richard's] past life" prove him willing to ignore Richard's otherness and to sacrifice his happiness to secure his place within Ireland (*E* 39). Especially when we note his admission in

Act II that he originally discouraged Richard from leaving Ireland to remain close to Bertha, Robert's desire to resecure his friend's place in the country is shown to be motivated by self-interest, and his determination to view Richard as an enemy to be one-upped compels him to sacrifice his friend's freedom to facilitate his conquest of Bertha.

Robert's perception of Richard as a rival suitor is strengthened in Act II, where his panic over his ruse being discovered compels him to act as a stereotypical lover trying to steal his lady from his rival. Even though he initially dismisses his feelings for Bertha as "a lightheaded idea of mine" (*E* 62), by observing that "there was some danger" for Richard were his feelings for her to develop (*E* 61), Robert seemingly renders inevitable a confrontation where he would declare his intentions and successfully "take her from [Richard]" (*E* 62). His subsequent "brave" questioning whether Richard "think[s he] ha[s] rights over her—over her heart" constitutes a rehearsal of that confrontation, as he plays the romantic hero seeking to rescue a victimized Bertha from his rival (*E* 62). Thus, even when Robert's duplicity is exposed, his obsession with Bertha forces him to continue to treat Richard as a generic obstacle to his quest, subordinating their friendship to a generic adversarial hostility.

Robert's desire to play the romantic rival is evident even in his relinquishment of this overt hostility. When Richard denies his right to Bertha's heart, Robert's attitude shifts from confrontation to shame and he pleads for his friend to "upbraid me, curse me, hate me as I deserve" (*E* 62). However, even this change in attitude continues to cast Richard and Robert as rival suitors, this time by presenting the latter as the blackguard that unjustly tries to steal Bertha away from her true love. Not only does this approach continue to portray their friendship through an antagonistic lens, but it also demonstrates the artificiality of Robert's attitude throughout the conversation. Robert confidently declared his intentions to Richard because he perceived his obsession with individual liberty as placing unjust bonds on Bertha, but when Richard abdicates these bonds, his attempt to portray him as the villain collapses. Because his seduction of Bertha has been justified by this adversarial lens, Robert reverses the roles and casts himself as the villain that needs to be rebuked, which reveals the arbitrariness of his representational approach since he performs both the hero and villain of the same conflict. Thus, Richard's refusal to follow this romantic script reveals the hollow and self-serving foundations of his "disciple['s]" approach to their dispute.

Ultimately, Robert's perception of Richard as a rival suitor blinds him to a significant change in his friend's interpretation of freedom that could dissolve their antagonism. Robert claims in Act I to "understand your pride and your sense of liberty" (*E* 39), but this "understand[ing]" is based upon an outdated version of Richard's desire for freedom that the latter dismisses as "the language of my youth" (*E* 71). Whereas Robert views this freedom as an escape from bonds that places unjust obligations upon Bertha, Richard's fear "that I stand between her and any moments of life that should be hers" demonstrates his determination to secure the same freedom for her that he has pursued for himself, even if that results in an attachment between Bertha and Robert (*E* 69). Thus, Richard does not object to Robert's desire for Bertha, but the duplicitous way he goes about fulfilling that desire, which accounts for his refusal to play along with the attempt to frame their dispute as a generic confrontation between rival suitors. By making an open declaration of intentions in Act II, Richard forces Robert to relate to him as a friend instead of a rival and to acknowledge the changes in his beliefs that had been subordinated by his approach to their conversation. Even if Richard's freedom is ultimately narcissistic, his reinterpretation of freedom provides an opportunity for Robert and Bertha to act on their feelings without alienating him in the process, which would dissolve the antagonism through which Robert perceives their interactions and enable them to be "united … in brotherhood" (*E* 69).

However, Robert refuses this opportunity. Responding to Richard's reinterpretation of freedom, Robert claims that "my friendship for you has laid bonds on me" and views his continued seduction of Bertha as "a moment which will free us both … from the last bonds of what is called morality" (*E* 70). Richard's altered perception of freedom has thus fallen on deaf ears, as Robert's characterization of his pursuit of Bertha as "a battle of both our souls … against all that is false in them and in the world" (*E* 70) remains grounded in the "language of [Richard's] youth," and his claim that "the blinding instant of passion alone … is the only gate by which we can escape from the misery of what slaves call life" relies upon the same obsession with passion and possession that Richard rebutted earlier in the conversation (*E* 71). Thus, although Richard has altered his attitude towards freedom in a more accommodating manner, Robert's inability to look beyond the generic lens of sexual desire prevents him from embracing this accommodation, and Joyce shows him to remain "convinced of the non-existence, of the unreality of the spiritual facts which exist and are real for Richard" (*E* 116).

Robert's rejection of Richard's otherness is evident in his subsequent encounter with Bertha at the end of Act II. Although Richard allows him to pursue Bertha primarily out of a desire for her freedom, Robert continues to represent Richard as the unjust suitor whose self-serving desire for liberty imprisons his devoted lover. Initially, he asks Bertha whether "the gift of freedom which he gave you—nine years ago" has made Bertha happy (*E* 83), which subordinates Richard's reconfigured "gift" to the "language of [his] youth." Then, when Bertha still hesitates to accede to Robert's seduction, he justifies their affair by arguing that Richard "longs to be delivered … From every law, Bertha, from every bond. All his life he has sought to deliver himself. Every chain but one he has broken and that one we are to break—you and I" (*E* 87). Not only is this self-serving description of Richard's motives designed to compel Bertha to sleep with him, it ignores the change in attitude towards freedom that he described earlier in the act, as Robert reduces Richard's desire for Bertha's freedom to his youthful desire for self liberation and justifies their affair through his own advocacy of sexual passion. ("I am sure that no law made by man is sacred before the impulse of passion" [*E* 87].) In so doing, Robert subordinates Richard's hope to "wish [Bertha] well" to his own desire to possess her body, which prevents him from affirming either his "master['s]" or his lover's otherness and guarantees that his attitude towards their "lifelong friendship" will be inevitably tainted.

This inevitable alienation is confirmed by Robert's actions in Act III. Having had his advances likely rejected by Bertha, Robert adopts a two-pronged strategy that solidifies the rift in his friendship with Richard. First, he writes a newspaper article that ostensibly champions Richard as the necessary chair for the humanities department, but that simultaneously disparages his commitment to freedom through that endorsement. While Robert argues that Ireland should welcome Richard back with open arms, he also characterizes him as a "spiritual exile" who "having left her in her hour of need, ha[s] been called back to her now on the eve of her longawaited victory, to her whom in loneliness and exile [he has] at last learned to love" (*E* 99). While Robert may be correct that Richard "learned to love" during his period "in loneliness and exile," his description of him as "having left [Ireland] in her hour of need" denigrates his desire for liberation by portraying him as an ungrateful abandoner who must grovel for his country's forgiveness. This continues Robert's characterization of Richard's freedom as an "act of impulse" by representing his need for freedom as a youthful folly that requires Ireland's pardon, which proves Robert to continue to ignore the otherness that fundamentally defines his "master."

Second, Robert resolves to leave Ireland, choosing the life of exile over continued association with those whom he feels have refused his love. In so doing, he reverts back to his role as the disgraced seducer, telling Richard that "[he] failed" and that "Bertha is yours now as she was nine years ago, when you—when we—met her first" (*E* 108–9). While this resignation ends Robert's determination to steal Bertha from Richard, it also continues to cast Robert's desire for Bertha as a conflict between rivals, which solidifies Robert's position as an adversary to Richard and alienates him from his friend to the point where exile becomes his only option. Thus, the antagonism that underlies Robert's performances of clichéd romance overwhelms his ability to win the love of either Bertha or Richard, and his departure from Ireland reveals the inevitable alienation at the heart of the narcissistic desire for possession.

A Deep Wound of Doubt

Compared to Robert, Richard's attitude towards love certainly seems more generous. Whereas Robert's professions of love and friendship are primarily guided by a narcissistic desire for possession, Richard appears interested in advancing the interests of his love object as well as (and perhaps more than) his own. His contention that the purpose of love is to "wish [the loved one] well" seems to position Richard closer to Bloom than to his narcissistic predecessors on Joyce's amorous spectrum, as his desire to secure the same freedom for Bertha that he practices makes him the first protagonist to demonstrate anything resembling Buber's loving embrace. However, although Richard refuses to force monogamous bonds onto Bertha, he fails to achieve what Joyce called "the very immolation of the pleasure of possession on the altar of love" (*E* 114), for his reinterpretation of amatory freedom is still complicit in the narcissistic desire for possession even as he relinquishes his claims to Bertha.

This fascination with possession is most persuasively articulated in Richard's conversation with Archie in Act I, where their discussion of cow robbery metaphorically enables him to justify his response to Robert's treachery. Responding to his son's question of "what makes a cow give milk," Richard explains the difference between "giv[ing] a thing" and "hav[ing] a thing … taken from you" (*E* 46). By claiming that when you give something, "no robber can take it from you … It is yours then for ever when you have given it" (*E* 47), Richard "defines ultimate spiritual possession as an act of sacrificial generosity" (Henke *Desire* 90), which represents Bertha as an object that he must secure from Robert's desired robbery. Thus, even though Richard's love for Bertha separates him from Stephen's self-serving quests, his strategy for securing her freedom relies on the same "pleasure of possession" that inevitably felled his predecessors. Through his interactions with Beatrice and Bertha, we see that the intellectual desire for amatory freedom that consumed Stephen in *Portrait* and *Ulysses* remains embedded in *Exiles*, which ensures that Richard's pursuit of completely unfettered relationships will "[condemn]" him to "live side by side apart" from his love objects in "Joyce's world of exile" (Clark 190).

Richard's interactions with Beatrice initially demonstrate his aesthetic fascination with amatory desire. Similar to Stephen's pursuit of his ideal Mercedes, Richard has considered Beatrice his primary source of artistic inspiration for at least eight years, writing her letters and sending her book chapters while he and Bertha were in Rome. Upon returning to Ireland, their artistic relationship has continued, as Richard spends the majority of the play locked in his study writing new works inspired by Beatrice. However, while Richard is clearly infatuated with Beatrice to some extent (and that attraction is reciprocated), the connection between these two characters has almost no chance of being fulfilled. In Act I, he tells Beatrice that her one-time engagement to Robert "made me so reserved with you—then—even though I felt your interest in me, even though I felt that I too was something in your life … that separated me from you. I was a third person I felt" (*E* 20). This characterization of Richard as being "separated from" Beatrice is also appropriate considering that the intellectual connection that binds them was established only after he and Bertha had been settled in Rome for a year. Although Beatrice has been Richard's primary source of artistic inspiration, his exile has imposed distance between the two characters that prevents any connection between them from transcending the relationship between artist and muse. For this reason, Richard can never escape his role as a "third person" even if he replaces Robert as Beatrice's primary infatuation, and the role that "her untouchability" and "the impossibility of sexual consummation" plays in this infatuation renders any attachment between them as abstract and impersonal as Stephen's idolization of Mercedes and the bird girl (Cotter 206).

The impersonal nature of Richard's regard for Beatrice continues upon his return to Ireland. Even though this renunciation of physical exile provides them the opportunity to consummate their intellectual relationship, Richard's continued "spiritual exile" prevents him from shedding his "reserved" attitude towards her. This is apparent during their conversation in Act I, where Richard quizzes Beatrice over the extent of her attraction to him. While Joyce's protagonist articulates a vague regard for her, his primary role in this exchange is akin to an amatory anthropologist, imploring Beatrice to "tell me what your words mean" and to articulate the full extent of her attraction to him (*E* 19). In so doing, he reduces Beatrice to an "inspiring virgin" instead of a "real lover" (Rabaté "Modernity" 26), treating her infatuation as an object of inquiry rather than a genuine affection to be reciprocated. This guarantees that their connection remains encapsulated in the impersonal regard of his exile, as Richard's desire to paint a comprehensive portrait of Beatrice's adoration compels him to perform the same "cool scholasticism" in which Polhemus accuses Stephen of engaging: "a distancing form that abstracts love" (Polhemus 260).

Richard's focus on her fascination with his intellect also ignores the emotional implications of her responses. Even if his inquisition gives him a better understanding of Beatrice's feelings, his focus on her regard for his writings and ideas prevents that understanding from translating into a reciprocal affirmation of those feelings. While Beatrice reveals that Richard has always been "something in [her] life" (*E* 20) and that she comes to his home because "otherwise I could not see you" (*E* 19), Richard suppresses the emotional nature of these declarations, preferring to believe that "I expressed in those chapters and letters, and in my character and life as well, something in your soul which you could not" (*E* 20). This interest in discovering if "it is my mind that attracts you" reduces her infatuation for him to that of a fan for the writer that expresses her soul's longings (*E* 18), which prevents whatever attraction that exists between them from moving beyond the detached intellectual companionship upon which it began.

Finally, Richard's obsession with his own struggles undermines the reciprocal regard needed to affirm Beatrice's love. Richard shows some concern for Beatrice's situation, inquiring into her recovery from the illness that plagued her during his exile; however, although this temporarily establishes an emotional bond between the two characters, that connection is quickly dissolved when Richard turns his attention towards his personal problems: "O, if you knew how I am suffering at this moment! For your case, too. But suffering most of all for my own" (*E* 22). This outburst abruptly shifts the focus of the conversation away from Beatrice's struggles "to give oneself freely and wholly—and be happy" and towards the problems that initially compelled Richard's exile (*E* 22), reducing her to a sounding board for Richard to air his personal grievances. Beatrice may have momentarily moved beyond her roles of muse and enthusiast, but in so doing, she loses her role in the conversation altogether, which reveals the narcissistic foundations of Richard's regard for her and guarantees that the distance that comprised the beginnings of their relationship will remain through its completion.

The inevitable alienation between Richard and Beatrice is confirmed in Act III, where his dismissal of her regard demonstrates the extent to which his exile has tainted their relationship. Upon encountering Beatrice the morning after the events of Acts I and II, Richard describes Ireland's duplicity in a way that reveals the damage wrought by his "deep wound of doubt": "There are demons (*he points out towards the strand*) out there. I heard them jabbering since dawn ... The isle is full of voices. Yours also. *Otherwise I could not see you*, it said. And [Bertha's] voice. But, I assure you, they are all demons. I made the sign of the cross upside down and that silenced them" (*E* 98). While this statement shows Richard to still be exiled from Ireland, the inclusion of Beatrice's and Bertha's voices in this "demon[ic]" representation of "the isle" also isolates the personal implications of that exile. Significantly, Richard includes Beatrice's ardent declaration in Act I in his list of ominous "voices," revealing that the possible affair at the end of Act II has compelled him to doubt not only Bertha and Robert, but her as well. This inclusion continues the dismissal of Beatrice's affection from the beginning of the play, as the muse of Act I has now been transformed into a "demon" whose duplicitous words threaten to lure Richard into a dangerous submission. By reducing her desire to "see" him to the ominous "jabbering" of a depersonalized "voice," Richard demonstrates that whatever emotional attachment Beatrice has for him is not reciprocated, which cements the alienation at the heart of their flirtation. Thus, when he later tells Robert that he refuses the call of the "voices of those who say they love me" (*E* 109), he completes the suppression of Beatrice that began with his artistic inquisition, which confirms the emotional isolation of his embrace of exile.

Ultimately, Beatrice plays an important role in *Exiles*, though not the one she desires. Rather than serving as a love interest for Richard, Beatrice instead becomes a catalyst for his desire to grant amatory freedom to Bertha, as the liberty he takes in carrying on this flirtation makes him fear that he has denied similar opportunities to his partner. Beatrice becomes an alienated "third person" in Richard and Bertha's relationship, a person who is "something in [Richard's] life," but who cannot compel Richard to feel the same sympathetic concern and guilt towards her that he shows towards Bertha. Beatrice thus becomes a necessary sacrifice to Richard's desire to "wish [Bertha] well," and her dismissal in Act III provides another entry into the list of Joycean muses whose inability to transcend their inspirational utility denies them the affection they seek.

The narcissism of Richard's amatory desires in *Exiles* is confirmed through his multiple clashes with Bertha in the play. In Act III, Bertha lashes out at Richard's ambivalence towards her claims of fidelity, accusing him of granting her complete liberty "to make me humble before you, as you always did. To be free yourself ... With [Beatrice]! And that is your love! Every word you say is false" (*E* 103). To many, this characterization of Richard is correct, as numerous critics have accused Richard of "foist[ing] the illusion of freedom onto Bertha in order to be free himself" (Henke *Desire* 98). However, Richard does not merely desire to liberate himself from the bonds of fidelity; indeed his flirtation with Beatrice indicates that he is already free of those impositions. Instead, his actions are guided by the desire to secure liberty for Bertha, as his guilt over taking advantage of her loyalty entices him to repair that breach by bestowing a similar freedom on her. Nevertheless, while Richard may act primarily out of affection for Bertha, the abstract freedom he foists upon her ignores the reality of her love, perpetuating the alienation that has developed between them during their years in exile.

Initially, Richard's guilty conscience overtakes his ability to develop an empathetic understanding of Bertha's suffering. His attempts to secure liberty for Bertha may be more sympathetic than the actions of Duffy, Gabriel, or Stephen, but the primary beneficiary of this freedom will still be the lover instead of his beloved. This narcissism is exemplified by his conversation with Robert in Act II, where Richard reveals that his motivation for granting liberty to Bertha is the fear that "I will reproach myself then for having taken all for myself because I would not suffer her to give to another what was hers and not mine to give, because I accepted from her her loyalty and made her life poorer in love" (*E* 69). This concern, while seemingly respectful of Bertha's feelings, establishes the fear of "reproaching [him]self" for "robbing" her of her happiness as what motivates Richard rather than the robbery itself, which prioritizes his guilt over her misery. For that reason, his main goal in *Exiles* is not to alleviate Bertha's suffering, but to alleviate his personal pain over causing that suffering. Thus, even though Richard believes that he is advancing Bertha's interests, Joyce depicts him as "fighting for his own hand, for his own emotional dignity and liberation in which Bertha, no less and no more than Beatrice or any other woman is coinvolved" (*E* 120), which prevents his gift of freedom from significantly alleviating her suffering.

Additionally, Richard's refusal to compromise his own freedom undermines his ability to bestow that freedom on Bertha. While he claims responsibility for "having taken all for himself" and "ma[king] her life poorer in love," Richard ignores the most logical solution to his quandary, that the pain caused by his infidelity could be alleviated by pledging his unwavering fidelity to Bertha. Instead, he continues his intellectual flirtation with Beatrice, choosing to alleviate the inequity of freedom between he and Bertha by granting her the same liberty that he exercises. This solution may shield Richard from accusations that he is unfairly taking advantage of Bertha's faithfulness, but it ignores the fact that her pain is not caused by the inequity of infidelity, but by the infidelity itself. However, since to swear loyalty to Bertha would confine Richard to the bonds of monogamy, he refuses to consider this a viable option to his dilemma. In that sense, Richard's gift is brought about by the same commitment to amatory freedom that influences Stephen's interactions with his love objects, as he is willing to remedy the isolation between himself and Bertha as long as that remedy does not encroach on his liberty. Thus, Bertha is correct that Richard wants "to have complete liberty with—that girl," (*E* 53), though not in the manner that she perceives; while Richard may have no interest in pursuing a relationship with Beatrice, he is unwilling to sacrifice their flirtation in order to secure Bertha's happiness, which reveals the narcissistic foundations of the freedom he offers as an alternative.

Inevitably, the individual, intellectual foundations of Richard's gift blind him to Bertha's attitude towards this freedom. Richard may desire to grant Bertha the same liberty that he enjoys, but his determination to assuage his guilt through his gift of freedom prevents him from understanding that she does not want this gift. While Richard feels that to "hold [Bertha] by no bonds, even of love" is the best way to repair the breach in their relationship, he fails to consider that what Bertha ultimately desires is not the ability to participate in the same flirtations as Richard, but to engage in a committed union with him. Thus, his attempts to allow Bertha to pursue an affair with Robert are based upon abstract principles of freedom that overlook the reality of the situation in which he finds himself, revealing his obsession with personal liberty to result in the fundamental ignorance of her otherness.

Bertha's exasperated reactions to Richard's gift continually demonstrate his inability to recognize her otherness. While Richard may feel that he is right to encourage Bertha to pursue Robert, her frustration and anger demonstrate that she considers this gift to be evidence of betrayal and heartlessness. This pain is apparent in Act I, where Bertha's accusation that "you take advantage of my simplicity as you did—the first time" shows that Richard's attempts to repair the breach caused by his initial infidelity will inevitably be met by suspicions of further unfaithfulness (*E* 52). Thus, his insistence that "you have complete liberty to do as you wish—you and he" is countered by Bertha's suspicions that he is a "deceiver" who simply desires to pursue an affair with Beatrice (*E* 52; 53). This exchange demonstrates the inevitable futility of Richard's gift and illustrates that his obsession with amatory freedom has blinded him to the reality of Bertha's love for him. For this reason, "Richard has begotten the situation from which he proceeds to suffer" (*JJ* 356), as his refusal to stop Bertha from going to Robert's cottage only exacerbates her suspicion and foreshadows the irreparable breach in their relationship.

Richard's ignorance of Bertha's desire is evident not only in her frustration, but also in his irritated reactions to her suspicions. Revealing himself to be completely consumed by amatory freedom, Richard is caught off guard by Bertha's rebukes of his permission to pursue Robert and stunned that the liberty that he cherishes is not similarly desired by her. He is genuinely shocked when Bertha accuses him of further infidelities with Beatrice ("What the devil are you talking about her for?" [*E* 103]), and he responds to her inquiries over whether he wants her to go to Robert with a frustrated "why do you ask me? Decide yourself" (*E* 55). Then, when she continues to rebuke Richard in Act II, he is shocked to discover that Bertha "ha[s] come here and led [Robert] on in this way on account of me" and continues to express confusion over her hesitancy towards the freedom she has been granted (*E* 74). Such interchanges shows Richard's inability to recognize that even though he has granted Bertha the freedom to pursue Robert, she is acting primarily out of loyalty to him, demonstrating both her preference of fidelity to freedom and her continued suspicions over his refusal to "tell me what you wish me to do" (*E* 75). Even though Bertha's reactions clearly signify her ambivalence towards amatory freedom, Richard's unwavering advocacy of that freedom prevents him from coming to terms with that ambivalence, which hinders the empathy needed to repair their relationship and guarantees that his subsequent attempts to secure her happiness will further alienate them from each other.

This alienation is demonstrated throughout Act III, where Richard's refusal to acknowledge Bertha's assertions of fidelity significantly ruptures their union. While Richard feels that the "deep wound of doubt" created by the previous night is necessary to release her from her monogamous bonds, Bertha feels that it is more important for Richard to realize her continued loyalty to him, perpetuating the impasse that has characterized their interactions throughout *Exiles*. Even though Bertha's claim that "I will tell you the truth, Dick, as I always told you" is meant to ease Richard's fears over her possible infidelity (*E* 102), it is anathema to his desire to love her "in restless living wounded doubt" (*E* 112), and his insistence that "I will never know, I tell you" denies Bertha the evidence of her commitment that she feels is necessary to repair their relationship (*E* 102). For that reason, even if he wills himself into the doubt needed to be "united with [Bertha] in body and soul in utter nakedness" (*E* 112), the refusals of her fidelity that he utters to secure that union only drive her further away, causing her to feel that "you are a stranger to me. You do not understand anything in me—not one thing in my heart or soul. A stranger! I am living with a stranger!" (*E* 104). Indeed, Richard's subordination of Bertha's desire for fidelity to his desire for freedom inevitably makes him a "stranger" to her, and his inability to affirm the reality of her feelings truly makes Bertha his permanent "bride in exile" (*E* 111).

This marital exile is confirmed by the conversation that concludes *Exiles*. Initially, this final exchange seems to provide hope for Richard and Bertha to resolve their strife, as her empathetic embrace of his despair provides an alternative to the frustration that epitomized both characters' attitudes throughout the play. Even though Richard continues to profess ambivalence to her protestations of fidelity, Bertha's response is no longer one of exasperation and anger, but is rather the loving caress of one who sees her beloved every day as she did the first time they met. ("Not a day passes that I do not see ourselves, you and me, as we were when we met first. Every day of my life I see that" [*E* 111].) Here, Joyce introduces the loving potential of memory that will guide Bloom's thoughts of Molly throughout *Ulysses*, as the blissful recollections of loved ones become mechanisms for lovers to reaffirm their feelings for them despite their present problems. The ability of past bliss to compel a present affirmation is evident considering that Bertha's loving recollections are immediately followed by her renewed commitment to "follow" Richard "wherever you go" (*E* 111). Bertha thus articulates the most meaningful expression of love in Joyce's play, and her desire for Richard to "speak out all your heart to me. What you feel and what you suffer" demonstrates the empathy needed for them to reestablish the dialogic connection tempered by freedom and exile (*E* 112).

However, Richard squanders this dialogic opportunity. Even if Bertha's commitment to "try to understand everything you say" signifies an empathetic affirmation (*E* 112), Richard's vacant response reveals that her desire for recognition will not be reciprocated. Although he obeys Bertha by "speak[ing] out all [his] heart to [her]," the description in the stage directions of Richard "*speaking as if to an absent person*" reduces her to "a person who is absent and present at the same time" (Rabaté "Modernity" 34), making his confession no different than if he were talking to himself. For that reason, when he confesses his desire "to hold [Bertha] by no bonds, even of love," Richard shows the isolation inherent in that desire, as the moment when he becomes "united with [her] in body and soul in utter nakedness" simultaneously becomes the moment where he loses the ability to recognize her altogether (*E* 112). Even though Bertha pleads for Richard to "forget me and love me again as you did the first time" and to "come back to me again," it seems probable that when she "*closes her eyes*" in the play's final stage direction, they will not open again on the reciprocal affection encapsulated by when they first met. Thus, the "deep wound of doubt" that Richard creates in order to fulfill his gift of freedom deprives him of the fidelity of Bertha's love (*E* 112), condemning both lovers to "a stasis that freezes their predicament and frustrates any happy resolution" (Shaffer 210).

Throughout her interactions with Richard, Bertha remains the loving alternative to the artificiality of his desires. Similar to her ridicule of Robert's advances, Bertha's reactions to Richard's gift of freedom demonstrate the problematic nature of his beliefs, as the frustration, despair, and longing that she exudes highlight the self-serving nature of his obsession with securing her liberation. Even though Richard professes to have "allowed [her] complete liberty," Bertha's desire for Richard to "speak out all your heart to me" becomes the most liberating gesture in *Exiles*, providing both characters the opportunity to declare their desires in a manner that could move past his obsession with personal freedom. Bertha thus plays a role similar to Emily Sinico in that the "invitation of openness" that she offers at the play's conclusion reveals the closed nature of her lover's gift while establishing a dialogic alternative to their constant miscommunication that could provide them with the love they both desire, if only Richard would accept her invitation. Nevertheless, while Bertha is alive when the curtain drops on *Exiles*, her heart suffers a fate similar to Mrs Sinico's, and her plea for her "strange wild lover" to "come back to me again" is drowned out by the "tired[ness]" of Richard's "deep wound of doubt."

****

Brian W. Shaffer posits that "if Richard is a prophet of freedom he is at the same time a false messiah. Insisting that he and Bertha are now free, he nevertheless appears fundamentally bound to ideas that victimize them both" (210). This characterization provides a convincing challenge to the traditionally villainous reading of Richard, as Shaffer's representation of him as a "false messiah" who is "fundamentally bound" to faulty "ideas" enables us to recognize the self-serving nature of his actions while resisting the temptation to cast him as a purely callous and manipulative narcissist. While his foisting of amatory freedom onto Bertha damages their relationship, his actions are primarily motivated by a desire to rectify the damage he has already inflicted upon her happiness. In that sense, Richard may share Stephen's obsession with personal liberation, but he also demonstrates the sympathy of Gabriel's well-intentioned reactions to Gretta's misery. However, even the best intentions cannot overcome the ignorance of a beloved's desires, and Richard's insistence on using the gift of freedom to "wish [Bertha] well" only compounds her loneliness and furthers their isolation from each other, demonstrating the futility of non-reciprocal attachments even in benevolent instances.

Richard thus becomes a crucial transition point in Joyce's representations of love, a character who, while still lured by self-serving amatory pursuits, has moved beyond the purely personal agendas of the lovers before him to also consider the well-being of his beloved. Through his struggles with a more sympathetic love, Richard enables us to see Joyce reconciling his youthful advocacy of personal liberation with the consequences of such freedom, and the melancholic conclusion of *Exiles* allows Joyce to demonstrate the inadequacy of an unwavering exile that denies space to one's loved ones. In *Ulysses*, Joyce will provide us with another portrait of a Dubliner oppressed by a suffocating social structure, but unlike Duffy, Stephen, or Richard, Leopold Bloom will not seek the liberation of exile. Instead, Bloom will embody the compassionate love articulated throughout the Joycean oeuvre, combining Richard's desire to "wish [one's beloved] well" with Bertha's empathy in his enduring homage to Molly. It is ultimately Bloom who will enable Joyce to move past the "isle … of [demonic] voices" and towards the Hill of Howth to depict a union that, while not perfect by any means, will prove more liberating than the exiles and escapes that preceded it.

Chapter 7
The Blooms' Amatory Metempsychosis

In previous chapters, I examined the self-serving motivations behind the amatory pursuits of Joyce's characters. From this perspective, Joyce's early fiction reads like a cautionary tale against narcissistic desire, as his protagonists' promotion of their interests over those of their loved ones limits them to alienating forms of self-love that undermine their personal and political goals. With the introduction of Leopold Bloom, Joyce begins to articulate an alternative to narcissism by crafting a character whose empathy enables him to negotiate his body politic more effectively than his predecessors. For that reason, Joyce's progression from Stephen and Richard to Bloom also constitutes a textual evolution from negative portrayals of self-centered desire towards a positive love ethic that can challenge the paralysis of everyday Dublin.

However, although *Ulysses* offers an alternative to the narcissism of Joyce's earlier fiction, Marguerite Harkness is correct that the text's central love story is anything but "a psychologist's description of married bliss" (*Aesthetics* 162). Indeed, Bloom's flirtations with Martha Clifford and Gerty MacDowell show that while he may be committed to Molly, he is also complicit in adulterous tendencies. This is not surprising since to present an amorous hero who was perfect, wholesome, and loyal would inject a sentimentality into *Ulysses* that is out of character with Joyce's attitude towards love.[1] Instead, Bloom embodies the Joycean love ethic not through a performance of stereotypical romantic fidelity, but through his unwavering compassion for his wife despite whatever complications arise in their marriage. For that reason, even though he acts on his loneliness in problematic ways, he neither lets those actions cloud his devotion to Molly nor seriously contemplates rejecting her, which makes him "one of the few heroes in literature to acknowledge that the beloved 'object' is *not* an object at all but a subjective individual capable of independence, change, and self-transcendence" (Henke *Sindbook* 127). Thus, his love for Molly ultimately validates his actions

---

[1] Bloom's lack of unwavering devotion also does not conflict with Buber's dialogic love. In fact, Buber concedes that the dialogic potential of love is inevitably temporary, that "the sublime melancholy of our lot [is] that every You must become an It in our world ... Even love cannot persist in direct relation; it endures, but only in the alternation of actuality and latency" (*Thou* 68–9). However, even if the "You" in question inevitably turns into an "It," the I-You relationship can be resumed because "whatever has thus been changed into It and frozen into a thing among things is still endowed with the meaning and the destiny to change back ever again" (*Thou* 90). Thus, it is not the permanency of a specific I-You encounter that is important, but rather the continued ability to engage in such encounters, which legitimizes Bloom's advocacy of love even though his marriage is in trouble throughout *Ulysses*.

throughout *Ulysses*, transforming his odyssey into a journey that prepares him to reclaim his life's greatest love.

Cuckoo! Cuckoo!

While listening to a discussion about Parnell in "Eumaeus," Bloom ponders the "eternal question of the life connubial": "Can real love, supposing there happens to be another chap in the case, exist between married folk?" (*U* 16.1384–6). This question establishes a fundamental difference between Bloom and Joyce's earlier protagonists. Unlike Duffy, Gabriel, and Stephen, who believe they have been wronged by their loved ones, and Richard, who desires to be wronged by his loved ones, Bloom actually has been wronged, as Molly's affair with Blazes Boylan forces him to come to grips with his cuckoldry. However, the manner in which he resolves this conflict reveals a second difference from his predecessors. Whereas earlier characters obsess over their personal pain, Bloom remains "humane and sensitive to others rather than selfishly preoccupied with the wrongs done him; and basically [accepts] the lot life has to offer" (Bowen *Comic* 40). Even though marital stagnation has made him lonely, Bloom never lets personal anguish overshadow his devotion to Molly, which shapes his thoughts and actions throughout the text into a renewed affirmation of their love.

Bloom's response to his wife's infidelity is best encapsulated by the music that Molly is scheduled to perform on her concert tour. Upon learning in "Calypso" that Boylan and Molly will be rehearsing at four-thirty that afternoon, Bloom finds out that she is booked to sing "*Là ci darem* with J.C. Doyle ... and *Love's Old Sweet Song*" (*U* 4.314). We can easily grasp the ominous implications of "Là ci Darem la Mano," as the seduction duet from *Don Giovanni* not only provides an appropriate context for Molly's liaison with Boylan, but echoes Joyce's mock equation of Prezioso with the opera's titular false lover. However, what might not be immediately apparent are the ways in which that piece foreshadows not simply adultery, but reconciliation. If we are to view Mozart's opera as a lens for evaluating the Bloom-Molly-Boylan triangle, then that comparison should extend not only to the specific duet mentioned in *Ulysses*, but also to the outcome of the seduction advanced by that duet. "Là ci Darem la Mano" may enable Don Giovanni to entice Zerlina away from her fiancé Masseto temporarily, but that couple ends up together at the opera's conclusion, while the seducer's advances only push him towards inevitable damnation. Similarly, Molly's and Boylan's performance of this musical seduction may disrupt the Blooms' marriage to some extent, but whatever breach emerges from their sexual encounter stands a good chance of being resolved by the conclusion of *Ulysses*.

The possibility of reconciliation is more apparent when we consider the concert program as a whole. Even if we ignore the happy resolution of *Don Giovanni*, we can still glean hints of the Blooms' reunion through "Love's Old Sweet Song". In many ways, these two songs convey the central conflict of the Bloom episodes, as the sexual enticement of "Là ci Darem la Mano" is counteracted by the enduring love in "Love's Old Sweet Song". In fact, the optimism of the latter piece subsumes the seductive elements of its counterpart because it concedes the inevitability of obstacles to love and still concludes that the love in question will be maintained. ("Though the heart be weary, / Sad the day and long, / Still to us at twilight, /Comes love's sweet song" [Gifford and Seidman 77].) Thus, when we read the Bloom episodes with respect to both songs, we discover that despite Molly's liaison, the love at the foundation of their marriage will enable them to move past that betrayal. ("Footsteps may falter, weary grow the way, / Still we can hear it, at the close of the day" ([Gifford and Seidman 77].) "Là ci Darem la Mano" may initially spell disaster for their marriage, but the program as a whole foreshadows its likely restoration.

However, even though we can glimpse a happy resolution to *Ulysses* in "Calypso," the seduction of "Là ci Darem la Mano" still maintains an imposing presence throughout the text, as Bloom's journey towards rekindling the passion of Howth forces him to deal with the pain of cuckoldry. He may try to banish the affair from his mind by contemplating the day's minutiae, but the majority of his thoughts inevitably bring him back to Molly and her impending betrayal. In a sense, Bloom is trapped between "Là ci Darem la Mano" and "Love's Old Sweet Song" throughout *Ulysses*: he can either obsess over his wife's affair and lament their faltering marriage, or he can accept this obstacle and work towards restoring their love. And while Bloom does continually brood upon his loneliness, his unswerving commitment to Molly compels an acceptance of cuckoldry that reaffirms their relationship, subordinating the seductive allure of *Don Giovanni* to the enduring life of the "sweetest song of all" (Gifford and Seidman 77).

Initially, Bloom's inability to think negatively of his wife enables him to envision their marriage continuing after the affair. He may react harshly to Boylan and brand him the "worst man in Dublin" (*U* 6.202), but he rarely lets that hostility cloud his feelings for Molly or allows alienation to get in the way of his devotion. Although he senses her impending betrayal as early as "Calypso," he continues to run errands and do favors for his wife, such as purchasing her lotion at Sweny's and borrowing a smutty book for her. Even when his thoughts turn to her "meeting" with Boylan, he does not think bitterly of her. Instead, he reflects upon her singing abilities, wondering if she pronounces the (nonexistent) *voglio* in "Là ci Darem la Mano" correctly and admiring her "beautiful … weeping tone" when she sings the line "*Mi trema un poco il*" (*U* 6.239–40). Not only do these thoughts banish the adulterous implications of the song from his mind, but they also demonstrate his continued admiration for Molly's voice and his concern for the success of her upcoming tour. This focus enables Bloom to think fondly about Molly despite her infidelity and to use the tour to envision a future for their marriage. Thus, by continuing to demonstrate his love for Molly and to visualize a relationship after her liaison, Bloom initiates the acceptance of cuckoldry needed for them to move beyond their impasse.

Bloom's continued concern for Molly is also evidenced by his consideration of the physical harms that could result from her encounter with Boylan. In

"Lestrygonians," Bloom's contemplation of an ad for "that quack doctor for the clap" (*U* 8.96) compels him to consider whether Molly could be exposed to the disease: "If he ...? O! Eh? No .... No. No, no. I don't believe it. He wouldn't surely? No, no. Mr Bloom moved forward, raising his troubled eyes. Think no more about that" (*U* 8.102–9). Unlike Duffy and Gabriel, who fear that their lives will be disadvantaged by their loved one's problems, Bloom shows genuine concern for the health risks of Molly's encounter with Boylan, placing her safety ahead of his personal pain. Not only does this show Bloom's refusal to blanketly denigrate anyone including his rival (because even the "worst man in Dublin" would not deliberately expose his lover to the clap), but it also shows his unconditional love for Molly despite her adultery, which provides a noticeable contrast to the totalizing rejections of "unfaithful" love objects performed by his counterparts. Thus, when Bloom resolves to "think no more about that," he develops the compassionate dimension to his attempts to ignore Molly's impending affair.

Also, Bloom's refusal to act on his knowledge of the affair demonstrates his continued affirmation of Molly. Critics have characterized Bloom's inability to interrupt the encounter as a sign of weakness, arguing that his fatalistic acceptance of the affair shows that he is mired in Joycean paralysis. However, Bloom's insistence that it is "useless to go back. Had to be" (*U* 8.633) is not evidence of passivity, but is rather a conscious understanding of and concession to Molly's desires. He recognizes that Molly's rehearsal is a pretense for adultery, but that knowledge carries with it the understanding that their sexual struggles since Rudy's death have emboldened desires within Molly that he cannot presently fulfill. Thus, his refusal to break up their affair can be seen as "an identification with the desire of the other" because to walk in on Molly's encounter with Boylan would be a conscious denial of her sexual longings (McGee 127).[2] In a sense, Bloom shows himself to be concerned with Molly's amorous freedom in a manner similar to Richard's obsession with Bertha's amatory freedom; however, unlike Richard, Bloom affirms an innate desire of his loved one instead of forcing her to accept an unwanted freedom that conflicts with her desires. Kimberly Devlin is thus correct that "Bloom here is implicitly acknowledging the otherness of others" since his resignation to the inevitability of the affair becomes a conscious promotion of Molly's interests over his own, which transforms the "paradoxical choice of passivity" into a "usually unrecognized virtue" ("En-Gendered" 85–6).

Bloom's loving memories throughout the text also aid his acceptance of cuckoldry. While some scholars characterize his memories as a paralyzing form of escapism, when we read Bloom's recollections of his courtship of Molly with respect to Buber, we discover that his retreats into the past are necessary to provide

---

[2] Patrick McGee continues: "this identification is the key to Bloom and the ground of his ethical being. Though he knows that his wife has been unfaithful to him ... and though his unconscious desires and passions run rampant along every possible avenue of human sexual practice, he does not act. He subordinates his own demand for love (which is always determined within the framework of culture by ideology) to the desire of the other as the structure of his own desire" (127–8).

vitality to a relationship that has been undermined by death, isolation, and betrayal. By returning in thought to Dolphin's Barn and Howth, he allows his blissful past with Molly to recur throughout June 16, 1904, enabling the amorous energy of their courtship to "catch fire and become present, returning to the element from which it issued, to be beheld and lived … as present" (Buber *Thou* 90). Bloom's recollections in *Ulysses* become the perfect complement to his marital compassion because they provide the constant reminder of his love for Molly that enables him to move towards reconciliation.

It is fitting that Bloom's first major memory in *Ulysses* concerns the night he first kissed his wife. Indeed, his loving observation in "Calypso" that Molly has "the same young eyes. The first night after the charades. Dolphin's Barn" (*U* 4.344–5) both provides context for the text's central relationship and demonstrates that the attraction that was piqued at Luke Doyle's house is still alive on Bloomsday. Not only does Bloom's "smil[ing]" reaction to Molly's "mocking eyes" (*U* 4.344) provide the first evidence of his fondness for her despite her infidelity (since her teasing immediately follows her explanation of Boylan's visit), but his observation that Molly possesses "the *same* young eyes" indicates that the young Miss Tweedy that enticed him in Dolphin's Barn provokes the same attraction now as Mrs Bloom. That Molly's "mocking eyes" are a reaction to Bloom's explanation of metempsychosis also hints at the redemptive nature of his recollections, as the juxtaposition of the "transmigration of souls" with Bloom's remembering their first kiss enables his memories to become a renewal of past passion. His remembrance of the charades game thus provides the initial example of how his memories influence his perceptions of the present, enabling him to focus on the love still present in their marriage despite the knowledge of its inevitable breach.

However, while Bloom's recollections of that evening frequently lighten his thoughts throughout *Ulysses*, the most telling example of this memory occurs oddly through his exchanges with another woman. While his erotic correspondence with Martha Clifford does convey his temptation towards adultery, Gordon is correct that "Leopold-Henry's indiscretion with Martha … is entirely a function of his connection to Molly. She is the one running the show" (*Reality* 84). That Bloom uses these letters to indulge in masochistic fantasy and to express his loneliness is obvious, but these episodes gain memorial significance when we discover in "Sirens" that Martha also resides in Dolphin's Barn (*U* 11.897–400). By following his remembrances of Dolphin's Barn in "Calypso" with the introduction of erotic correspondence to Dolphin's Barn in "Lotus Eaters," Joyce constructs a textual link between a past flirtation with Molly and a present flirtation with a character that stands in for Molly. In much the same way that Howth will cast a shadow over Bloom's masturbation in "Nausicaa," Dolphin's Barn infiltrates his correspondence with Martha, transforming his epistolary exchange into a way to "pursu[e] a series of objects and bodily pleasures that finally lead him back to his place with Molly" (McGee 123).

The relationship between Luke Doyle's party and Martha Clifford becomes explicit in "Nausicaa," where Bloom resigns himself to the completion of Molly's infidelity. At one point in the chapter, Bloom seems to replace his remembered affection with adulterous desire, as his melancholy thoughts about Howth stir up the temptation to continue corresponding with Martha. ("Returning not the same … The new I want. Nothing new under the sun. Care of P.O. Dolphin's Barn" [*U* 13.1103–5].) However, this contemplation of an adulterous future immediately reverts to the past, and Bloom's meditations over Martha's letter give way to remembrances of the charades game. ("Are you not happy in your? Naughty darling. At Dolphin's barn charades in Luke Doyle's house. Mat Dillon and his bevy of daughters: Tiny, Atty, Floey, Maimy, Louy, Hetty. Molly too" [*U* 13.1105–8].) Not only does this transition demonstrate the intertwined nature of Marion Tweedy and Martha Clifford, but Bloom's subsequent acknowledgement of this linkage reveals the irrevocable link between past and present: "So it returns. Think you're escaping and run into yourself. Longest way round is the shortest way home" (*U* 13.1109–11). Thus, even if Bloom were using Martha to distract himself, his correspondence is so permanently tied to his history with Molly that he cannot engage present-day Dolphin's Barn without simultaneously invoking its past.[3] Bloom's statement thus confirms the power of his remembrances of Molly in reaffirming his love throughout Bloomsday, as his subsequent invoking of metempsychosis in the next paragraph ("metempsychosis. They believed you could be changed into a tree from grief" [*U* 13.1118–9]) brings us back to "Calypso" and the "mocking eyes" that provoked his initial invocation of the charades game. Through these exchanges with Martha, Bloom's memories promote the passion of Doyle's party over the loneliness of his epistolary return to Dolphin's Barn and kindle the metempsychotic reawakening of his initial passion for Molly.

Bloom's amorous memories continue with his recollections of his proposal to Molly on the Hill of Howth. These memories initially captivate him during his lunch in "Lestrygonians," as the warmth of his glass of burgundy performs a "secret touch" that "moisten[s]" his memory and brings the "wild ferns on Howth" to his mind (*U* 8.898–900):

> Pillowed on my coat she had her hair, earwigs in the heather scrub my hand under her nape, you'll toss me all. O wonder! Coolsoft with ointments her hand touched me, caressed: her eyes upon me did not turn away. Ravished over her I lay, full lips full open, kissed her mouth. Yum. Softly she gave me in my mouth the seedcake warm and chewed. Mawkish pulp her mouth had mumbled sweetsour of her spittle. Joy: I ate it: joy. Young life, her lips that gave me pouting. Soft warm sticky gumjelly lips. Flowers her eyes were, take me, willing eyes … Screened under ferns she laughed warmfolded. Wildly I lay on her, kissed her: eyes, her lips, her stretched neck beating, woman's breasts full

[3] Gordon's interpretation of the "milkwhite dolphin" (*U* 12.1772) towards the end of "Cyclops" also reads Bloom's flirtation with Martha as a reigniting of his passion for Molly, writing that "Bloom is not, mainly, heading toward the other woman in his life (see Hart and Knuth 1976, 33). He is, mainly, heading to the place where he and his first love of his life had their first kiss" (*Reality* 85).

in her blouse of nun's veiling, fat nipples upright. Hot I tongued her. She kissed me. I was kissed. (*U* 8.903–10; 912–5)

To Rickard, this recollection of Howth illustrates Bloom's "avoid[ing] the pain of this powerful memory of happier times," as his equation of this nostalgic embrace with his present-day loneliness ("Me. And me now" [*U* 8.917]") compels him to "[flee] from his memory of love on Howth to a correspondent idealization that filters out the physical" (82–3). However, even though Bloom's memory cannot be separated from his loneliness, the love contained within this recollection envelops this loneliness with the warmth needed for him to come to grips with Molly's affair.

Initially, the prominence of food in Bloom's reverie provides the spiritual sustenance necessary to quell his misery. It is not coincidental that Joyce includes a memory based on the erotic exchange of a seedcake within the food-dominated "Lestrygonians," as the burgundy and gorgonzola sandwich ingested by Bloom on June 16, 1904, hearken back to the "mawkish pulp" consumed by Molly and Bloom sixteen years earlier. In fact, Joyce unites these two events not simply through their shared act of consumption, but also through the warmth instilled in Bloom as a result of that consumption. Henke is correct in describing Bloom's memory as "sanctified by a spiritual love-communion with Molly" (*Sindbook* 128) since the reciprocal nature of their sharing the seedcake and their kissing ("Hot I tongued her. She kissed me. I was kissed.") unites their lips in a mutually erotic affirmation of their affection. In that sense, Bloom's contemplation of the connection between "me" and "me now" can be seen as more than evidence of his continued depression; especially when we consider the reverie-like rhetoric of Bloom's memory, the recollection of Howth provides the rekindling of amorous bliss that counteracts his resignation over the affair. Joyce's inclusion of this memory in "Lestrygonians" thus establishes a textual and temporal bond between the emotional communion of Howth and the physical communion of Davy Byrne's, and the warmth generated by his burgundy emboldens the renewal of the warmth of the sun over Howth that will enable him to reaffirm his love for Molly.

The positive implications of Bloom's recollection are also demonstrated by his post-lunch thoughts. As Bloom leaves Davy Byrne's, he resumes humming the music from *Don Giovanni*. However, while this action had previously signified his preoccupation with Molly's affair, here his musical thoughts take on a more positive note, as the progression from Howth to Davy Byrne's has also shifted his position in Mozart's opera from the seduction of Act II to the triumph of Act V: "He hummed, prolonging in solemn echo the closes of the bars: *—Don Giovanni, a cenar teco M'invitasti.*[4] Feel better. Burgundy. Good pick me up" (*U* 8.1039–42). Whereas Bloom's previous contemplations of *Don Giovanni* centered on Zerlina's seduction in "Là ci Darem la Mano," here he assumes the position of the spirit of Il Commendatore, Don Giovanni's vanquished enemy

4 Translated: "Don Giovanni, you invited me to sup with you" (Gifford and Seidman 185).

who resurfaces at the conclusion to initiate his rival's damnation. As he assumes this role, Bloom improves his position within his present-day *Don Giovanni* by forgoing the role of the would-be cuckold and becoming the conquered figure that returns to vanquish his enemy. This operatic renegotiation is essential for Bloom to develop a productive acceptance of his cuckoldry because when he assumes the position of Il Commendatore, he can acknowledge the wounds created by Boylan and move past them to the point where he can reassume his position with Molly. By following his recitation of the lyrics with his acknowledged nourishment from his burgundy, Joyce establishes a causal link between the memory of Howth triggered by that burgundy and his acquired desire to overcome his usurpation by Boylan. "Lestrygonians" thus functions as a critical site where Bloom's memories shape his perceptions of present-day romance, and the loving communion of Howth becomes an important "pick me up" that pushes him closer to repairing his relationship with Molly.

The efficacy of Bloom's memorial strategy is ultimately confirmed in "Sirens," where the recollections of Dolphin's Barn and Howth allow him to avoid the lamentable sirens' songs of the Ormond Hotel. Bloom's thoughts are naturally melancholy in this chapter because his witnessing of Boylan's departure for Eccles Street forces him to acknowledge that Molly's liaison is imminent. Given the heartbreaking nature of this realization, it would be simple for him to succumb to depression when the bar patrons perform "Love and War," "All Is Lost Now," and "M'appari." However, rather than yield to the pain of his present cuckoldry, Bloom uses the songs as springboards for nostalgic recollections of his marriage, which enables him to maintain his warm feelings for Marion Tweedy despite the infidelity of Molly Bloom.

Bloom's memorial coping begins during Ben Dollard's performance of "Love and War." As Bloom recognizes the opening lyrics, he recalls the humorous time when Dollard had to borrow a tight dress suit for an evening's concert. This memory diverts Bloom's attention from his loneliness by compelling him to envision both Molly's merriment over Dollard's "tight as a drum" trousers (*U* 11.555) and her witty references to his "base barreltone" (*U* 15.559). Such a diversion enables Bloom to replace his resignation over Molly's betrayal with fonder memories of his joyful wife, which brightens his spirits as the hour of his cuckoldry approaches.

The most compelling example of Bloom's memory combating his painful reactions to "Love and War" occurs later in the performance. Once he discerns that Father Cowley is accompanying Dollard on the piano, his thoughts turn to larger performances of the song by full orchestras, including the "jiggedy jiggedy" of the conductor's "bagtrousers" (*U* 11.578). No sooner does Bloom contemplate this than the evoked "jiggedy jiggedy" becomes the "jingle jaunty" of Boylan's approaches to Eccles Street (*U* 11.579). This transition demonstrates the prominence of Boylan's destination in Bloom's mind, highlighting his anguish despite his seemingly amiable thoughts of the music. Nevertheless, as Bloom continues to wrestle with "Love and War," the "jingle jaunty" of Boylan's advances gives way to "Ben Howth, the rhododendrons" (*U* 11.582), and he is able to suppress his melancholy for the moment. The memory of Howth thus buries Bloom's thoughts of Boylan, enabling him to use the "pick me up" initiated in "Lestrygonians" to avoid surrendering to his loneliness.

However, Bloom's reprieve is short lived. As soon as Dollard and Cowley finish "Love and War," Richie Goulding is reminded of a performance of Bellini's *La Sonnambula*, which compels him to whistle "All Is Lost Now." This aria, in which Elvino laments his fiancé's seeming infidelity, foregrounds Molly's adultery in Bloom's mind, as his perception of "a thrush" and "a throstle" in Goulding's whistle (*U* 11.631) recalls his perceptions of similar qualities in her performance of "Là ci Darem la Mano." ("Beautiful on that *tre* her voice is: weeping tone. A thrush. A throstle" [*U* 6.239–40].) This recollection causes Bloom to reconsider the "Jingle jaunty" of Boylan's advances (*U* 11.640), and his acknowledgment that he is powerless to stop the affair ("Too late. She longed to go. That's why. Woman. As easy stop the sea. Yes: all is lost" [*U* 11.640–1]) reveals his returning despair. "All Is Lost Now" thus restores the loneliness that was initiated by Boylan's departure, and Bloom's reaction to Goulding's "thrush" and "throstle" binds him to Elvino as a fellow cuckold powerless to improve his condition.

Fortunately for Bloom, this operatic union is short-lived. While "All Is Lost Now" may have foregrounded the seductive despair of "Là ci Darem la Mano" in his mind, the "Love's Old Sweet Song" counterpart soon arrives in the form of "M'appari," an aria from *Martha* that also laments lost love. In fact, Simon Dedalus only has to sing two lines from "M'appari" before Bloom explicitly identifies it as such ("Love that is singing: love's old sweet song" [*U* 11.681]), which transforms the song into an opportunity for him to negotiate his feelings about Molly's infidelity. Initially, his thoughts during "M'appari" echo the "falter[ing]" "footsteps" and "weary … way[s]" of "Love's Old Sweet Song", as the first verses that Simon sings constitute a mental projection of Molly's liaison with Boylan: "Jing. Stop. Knock. Last look at mirror always before she answers the door. The hall. There? How do you? I do well. There? What? Or? … Hands felt for the opulent" (*U* 11.689–92). By following this image with the line "*But alas, 'twas idle dreaming*" from "M'appari" (*U* 11.694), Joyce amplifies the seeming hopelessness of Bloom's situation, which makes his subsequent thoughts about *Martha* seem all the more productive.

This shift in the tone of Bloom's thoughts occurs as Simon continues to perform "M'appari." As Simon moves from the despair of the song's third stanza to the fourth stanza's reprisal of "when first I saw that form endearing" (*U* 11.665), Bloom shifts from lamenting his cuckoldry to remembering the night at Mat Dillon's house when he met Molly. At the moment when the tone of "M'appari" shifts from despair to hope, Bloom's thoughts undergo a similar transition, as his recollection of their conversation that night stirs up thoughts that fate brought them together. ("First I saw. She thanked me. Why did she me? Fate" [*U* 11.732]). No sooner does Bloom experience this shift than Simon performs the song's concluding cry for the singer's "lost" and "dear one" (*U* 11.740–1) to return to him, and Bloom's concurrent thoughts about Mat Dillon's echo the same desire: "Alone. One love. One hope. One comfort me. Martha, chestnote, return!" (*U* 11.742–3). In contrast to the hopelessness of "All Is Lost Now," Bloom's nostalgic remembrance replaces his despair over Molly's adultery with the hope for reconciliation embodied by the conclusion of "M'appari," transforming young Marion Tweedy into the Martha that Bloom desires to return to him. For that reason, when Simon's concluding "*Come ... To me!* (*U* 11.744; 751) compels the "consum[ing]" exclamation "Siopold!" (*U* 11.753; 752), we witness Bloom's union with the hopeful connotation of the song's concluding line, with Simon standing in for the musical invocation that he has performed. This merger created by Bloom's yearning for reconciliation thus demonstrates how his memories of happier times with Molly enable him to move past the pain of the infidelity that is simultaneously occurring, paving the way for a more productive homecoming.

John Paul Riquelme argues that "through a defining reliance on memory, Joyce's writings encourage us to remember in various ways and to recognize that remembering is part of moving forward" ("Preparatory" 12). Indeed, Bloom's meditations throughout *Ulysses* embody this characterization of memory, as the numerous recollections that come to his mind throughout Bloomsday enable him to move beyond the pain caused by Molly's adultery. This productive use of memory is confirmed by Bloom's exit from the Ormond Hotel, where his declaration that "Ben Howth. That rules the world" shows that his loving memories of Molly have enabled him to get past the despair of her betrayal (*U* 11.1183–4). As we progress through "Sirens," we witness the heartbroken cuckold that entered the Ormond become the transfigured "Lionelleopold" (*U* 11.1187) who still holds out hope that his "Martha" will "come to [him]." The "jaunty jingle" of Boylan has thus been replaced "with sweets of sin with frillies for Raoul with met him pike hoses" (*U* 11.1188), and Bloom's nostalgic negotiation through the hour of his betrayal readies him for his masochistic journey towards an amorous metempsychosis.

Throughout *Ulysses*, Bloom demonstrates himself to be one of the most capable of Joyce's protagonists in affirming his beloved. While one does not need to go as far as accepting betrayal to demonstrate true love, Bloom's thoughts about the affair show that he understands and accepts his wife's desires, and his warm recollections of their courtship and continued concern for her well-being speak to a substantial affection for Molly that is not grounded in an obsession with advancing his own interests. What ends up solidifying Bloom's productive reaction to the affair is his masochistic tendencies throughout the text, as his fascination with experiencing pleasure through pain provide him with a conduit through which he can move past the heartbreak of that affair. The perverse satisfaction aroused by Bloom's masochism enables him to accept his cuckoldry,[5] and Molly's enduring presence in these practices establishes a loving foundation for his sexual fantasies that allows him to reaffirm his commitment to her through each indulgence.

Bloom's masochistic affirmation of Molly is exemplarily demonstrated by the book that he borrows for her in "Wandering Rocks." Initially, his decision to select

[5] Bowen writes that "even if there is a painful reversal for Bloom in his recognition of Molly's infidelity, his masochism comically turns it into pleasure" (*Comic* 44).

Sweets of Sin instead of *Fair Tyrants* demonstrates his continued promotion of Molly's desires over his own, as his recognition that the former book is "more in her line" guides his decision more than the masochistic enticement of the latter (*U* 10.606). More importantly, Bloom borrows *Sweets of Sin* for Molly despite the fact that it contains an adulterous episode that echoes her affair with Boylan, which forces him to contemplate her impending betrayal in order to secure her pleasure. By reading a significant portion of the text's adulterous encounter, Bloom performatively experiences his impending usurpation, and his decision to secure that book for Molly despite its personal implications constitutes a loving embrace of masochism.

The pleasure derived from this experience is evident in Bloom's reaction to the erotic narrative. By noting that "warmth showered gently over him" and that "flesh yielded amply amid rumpled clothes" (*U* 10.619–20), Bloom demonstrates his arousal over an adulterous scene that foreshadows the adultery of the person for whom he is borrowing the book. That Bloom is turned on by the descriptions of this affair shows that he is capable of gaining satisfaction out of pain, that the fact that the scene described in *Sweets of Sin* hits close to home does not prevent him from relishing its eroticism. Especially when we consider that he is primarily aroused by the thought of "*the beautiful woman*" (*U* 10.618), Bloom's excitement shows that he is still capable of strong passion for his wife since his enchantment by the book's adulteress parallels his infatuation with Molly. The amorous benefits of this masochistic act are confirmed by the Blooms' shared fascination with *Sweets of Sin*. Bloom's fascination with the book is significant not only because it enables him to derive pleasure from a text that details the pain of adultery, but also because he recognizes that his wife would enjoy the book's eroticism. That both Bloom and Molly can gain gratification out of a book that foreshadows her infidelity towards him hints at the revitalization of their marriage, as the end result of her adultery becomes the sexual fulfillment of an adulteress and her cuckold. By choosing to borrow the text, Bloom advances Molly's desires while gaining pleasure from the pain it describes, which parallels his actions throughout *Ulysses* and foreshadows the amicable resolution of their marital impasse.

Bloom's loving masochism is also evident in "Nausicaa," where his masturbation on Sandymount Strand enables him to derive satisfaction from his own cuckoldry. Although the chapter's primary erotic exchange occurs between Bloom and Gerty MacDowell, the specter of Molly permeates "Nausicaa," which prevents us from detaching the pleasure he experiences from the pain of his wife's adultery. Oddly enough, the initial evidence of Molly's presence is provided not by Bloom, but by Gerty, as her sentimental descriptions of "her dreamhusband" contain indicators of his enduring suffering (*U* 13.431). Her observation that the sky's beauty was gradually "blotted out" by "the Bailey light on Howth" forces us to note that Bloom's fascination with Gerty occurs within full view of his and Molly's proposal site (*U* 13.408; 409), which prevents him from experiencing this masturbatory encounter without simultaneously evoking that event. Also, Gerty's description of Bloom as a "foreigner" (*U* 13.416) parallels Bloom's later recollection of Molly's reasons for choosing him. ("Why me? Because you were so foreign from the others" [*U* 13.1209–10].) This later remembrance of Molly's attraction to Bloom thus reshapes Gerty's initial fascination, establishing a bond between the two characters that forces Molly into the forefront of Gerty's erotic performance. Finally, her observation that "the story of a haunting sorrow was written on his face" (*U* 13.421–2) and her description of him as "[having] suffered, more sinned against than sinning" (*U* 13.432) make his cuckoldry a defining characteristic of his appearance, which prevents us from reading his subsequent masturbation as detached from his brooding over the affair. Gerty's descriptions thus betray the pain that Bloom is experiencing from his wife's infidelity, which transforms the orgasm he experiences later in the episode into a masochistic catharsis.

This masochistic element in "Nausicaa" is more explicit in Bloom's continued meditations on Molly's and Boylan's encounter. While his masturbation is brought about initially by Gerty's undergarments, it is important to note that "when Bloom finally comes, he does it thinking not of Gerty, but of Molly with Boylan" (Bowen "Theoretical" 265). Bloom may be aroused during the chapter's infamous fireworks display, but his subsequent "Ah!" at line 821 indicates that he did not experience a complete orgasm, and he does not fully climax until later in the episode when he contemplates the consummation of the affair: "Funny my watch stopped at half past four. Dust. Shark liver oil they use to clean. Could do it myself. Save. Was that just when he, she? O, he did. Into her. She did. Done. Ah!" (*U* 13.846–50). By withholding Bloom's orgasm until his "climactic fantasies of Molly and Blazes" (Bowen *Comic* 59), Joyce forces him literally to experience pleasure from pain, which bolsters his use of masochism to compensate for his loneliness. This decision further illustrates Bloom's sexual adoration of Molly, transforming her from *"the beautiful woman"* of *Sweets of Sin* into "*the beautiful woman*" of his personal adultery fantasy. The masochistic pleasure initiated in "Wandering Rocks" builds in "Nausicaa," enabling Bloom to promote his orgasmic fascination with Molly over his marital pain.

If "Nausicaa" constitutes the escalation of Bloom's masochistic negotiation of cuckoldry, then its climax occurs in "Circe." Indeed, Bloom's obsession with Molly's infidelity colors the majority of his hallucinations, as nearly every incident he endures in Nighttown combines his pain over her affair with the masochistic impulses that spring from that pain. In fact, one of Bloom's initial hallucinations is of Molly, whose description as a "handsome woman" with "*opulent curves*" explicitly casts her as the "*beautiful woman*" from *Sweets of Sin* (*U* 15.297–8). By juxtaposing this description with Molly's subsequent taunting of his cuckoldry, Joyce strengthens the relationship between Bloom's anguish and his masochism, as his insistence that he is "at your service" (*U* 15.296) despite Molly's mocking intimation that she is pregnant by Boylan ("So you notice some change?" [*U* 15.328]) shows his continued submission in the face of adultery. Bloom's suppression of his desires to better serve his mistress thus highlights the spousal love that undergirds his masochistic experiences throughout the rest of the chapter.

The masochistic foundations of this encounter are also indicated by Molly's departure at the beginning of "Circe." As Bloom attempts to secure her lotion from Sweny the chemist (reaffirming his commitment to running Molly's errands from "Lotus Eaters"), Molly asks him "*Ti trema un poco il cuore?*"[6] and "saunters away" (*U* 15.351–2). This allusion to "Là ci Darem la Mano" is significant not only because it reiterates the adulterous foundations of this exchange, but also because it changes the grammatical person of the song's lyric, altering Zerlina's first-person isolation of her trembling heart into a second-person seductive inquiry. By singing this altered lyric to Bloom, Molly transforms a song that signifies her husband's estrangement into an invitation for his own seduction. Even if this invitation is offered "in disdain" (*U* 15.352), it also opens up the *Don Giovanni* motif to provide space for Bloom's arousal, which turns the pleasure he gains from the pain of betrayal and the abuse inflicted throughout the rest of the chapter into the erotic fulfillment needed for him to accept his cuckolded status.

This resulting abuse begins almost immediately after Molly's departure, as Bloom is put on trial for acts of perversion committed against several women. Even though the hallucinatory nature of "Circe" prevents us from conclusively discerning what occurs in the chapter, Bloom's mental interruptions are necessary to repair his marriage for two reasons. First, to place Bloom on trial foregrounds his indiscretions instead of Molly's, which enables him to avoid the alienating blame game that felled Duffy, Gabriel, and Stephen. By focusing the adulterous allegations entirely on his alleged ogling and solicitation, Bloom shows that he does not consider Molly to be the sole marital transgressor, which enables him to resist the temptation to castigate her for her affair. This focus shows that Bloom acknowledges reciprocal culpability and avoids the blanket rejection of Molly that typified Stephen's reactions towards his "duplicitous" lovers, thus providing the means for reconciliation.

Second, the masochistic allusions throughout the trial enable Bloom to derive pleasure from his guilty and lonely conscience. Bloom's hallucinatory self-punishment is significant not simply because it subordinates his victimhood to his alleged performances of the "dirty married man" (*U* 15.385), but also because the allegations combine adulterous and masochistic allusions in manners that demonstrate his enjoyment of the flagellation. His alleged desire for Mrs Yelverton Barry to "misconduct [herself] at half past four p.m. on the following Thursday" clearly foregrounds Molly's affair in Bloom's mind, but the fact that he signs this letter James Lovebirch—the author of *Fair Tyrants*—reveals how his masochistic arousal challenges his distress over that affair. Similarly, the adulterous allegations of Mrs Bellingham ("He urged me … to defile the marriage bed, to commit adultery at the earliest possible opportunity" [*U* 15.1054–6]) point to Bloom's continued depression; however, the fact that he initiates these pleadings by calling her a "Venus in furs" hints at the pleasure that could be stimulated by contemplating this despair (*U* 15.1045). The testimony of the honorable Mrs Mervyn Talboys confirms the relationship between Molly's infidelity and Bloom's masochistic

6 Translated, "Does your heart tremble a little (beat a little faster)?" (Gifford and Seidman 457).

response, as his desired punishment for mailing Mrs Talboys a picture of "his wife, as he solemnly assured me" having "illicit intercourse with a muscular torero" (*U* 15.1067–9) is for her "to chastise him as he richly deserves, to bestride and ride him, to give him a most vicious horsewhipping" (*U* 15.1071–3). The trial thus demonstrates Bloom's masochism to be a continued response to his cuckoldry, which makes his ability to derive arousal from his marital pain a way to move past his bitterness.

The trial's resolution moves Bloom to Bella Cohen's brothel, where he experiences another hallucinatory flagellation. Similar to his previous experiences in "Circe," this encounter arises from Bloom's anxiety over Molly's affair, as Bella's fan's description of his marriage as a "petticoat government" (*U* 15.2759–60) (not to mention the "*sheepish grin*" Bloom offers as assent [*U* 15.2762]) maintains his willing submission to Molly throughout the text. What makes the resulting humiliation important from an amorous standpoint is Bello's mocking Bloom's sexual dysfunction at the end of the episode. Bello's taunting inquiry "Where's your curly teapot gone to" demonstrates the marital anxiety behind this hallucination (*U* 15.3129–30), and his subsequent references to Boylan cement Bloom's cuckolded status:

> I wouldn't hurt your feelings for the world but there's a man of brawn in possession there. The tables are turned, my gay young fellow! He is something like a fullgrown outdoor man. Well for you, you muff, if you had that weapon with knobs and lumps and warts all over it. He shot his bolt, I can tell you! Foot to foot, knee to knee, belly to belly, bubs to breast! He's no eunuch … Wait for nine months, my lad! Holy ginger, it's kicking and coughing up and down in her guts already! That makes you wild, don't it? Touches the spot? (*U* 15.3127–44)

This passage confirms Bloom's masochism to be both an assertion of guilt for Molly's infidelity and the necessary response to that infidelity. The comparison of Boylan's potency to Bloom's "eunuch"-like status demonstrates the latter's continued assumption of responsibility for the affair, as he deems his lack of complete sexual intercourse with Molly a reason for her desire to sleep with Boylan. This confirms the affirmation of otherness inherent in Bloom's masochism, not only because he acknowledges reciprocal culpability in their marital breach, but also because he comprehends the erotic desires that led Molly to betray him. Bloom's acknowledgement that his failure to "sho[ot] his bolt" effectively may have played a role in her temptation to stray thus enables him to react to the affair in a more loving manner.

The productivity of this masochistic understanding is evident in Bloom's reaction to Bello's taunts. Similar to his earlier meditations, Bloom has no problem blaming Boylan for his role in Molly's infidelity, but he avoids the temptation to chide his wife in a similar manner. He acknowledges that "I was indecently treated" and desires someone to "inform the police" (*U* 15.3146); however, this statement is not made in response to Molly's role in the affair, but rather to Bello's repeated acknowledgements of Boylan's sexual prowess. In contrast to Bloom's castigation of Boylan, he absolves Molly of her role in the affair, insisting to "Moll" that "I forgot! Forgive!" His subsequent assertion of "Moll ... We ... Still ..." (*U* 15.3151) confirms that his assignment of blame for the liaison carries with it a desire to maintain their relationship, demonstrating that Bloom's repeated attempts to derive pleasure from adulterous pain have enabled him to continue loving his wife despite her betrayal. Thus, the most explicitly masochistic episode in *Ulysses* contains within it Bloom's declaration of his commitment to Molly, and the interplay of pleasure and pain that occurs within the brothel demonstrates the affirming potential of his acceptance of cuckoldry.

The climax of Bloom's acceptance occurs when Boylan arrives to handle "a little private business with your wife" (*U* 15.3764–5). Here, the productive nature of Bloom's hallucination is evident not by the staged reenactment of Molly's and Boylan's liaison, but by Bloom's acquiescence to it. Not only does Bloom not try to stop Boylan from sleeping with her, he actively encourages it, playing the role of Molly's servant who greets her lover and watches the tryst from the keyhole. By making Bloom a more active agent in Molly's and Boylan's affair, this restaging dissolves the alienation of the initial encounter, transforming Bloom into the means by which Molly's sexual desires are fulfilled. In that sense, Bloom attains an amorous freedom similar to what Richard desired in *Exiles* by enabling his active participation in "Circe" to mitigate the secrecy and treachery that comprised the actual encounter. The masochistic nature of this restaging is confirmed by Bloom's excitement over watching Boylan and Molly have sex through the keyhole. His oral ejaculations of "Show! Hide! Show! Plough her! More! Shoot!" while "clasp[ing] himself" (*U* 15.3815–6) echo his literal ejaculation over envisioning Boylan and Molly having sex during "Nausicaa," which demonstrates that the end result of his hallucinatory humiliation in "Circe" is the masochistic orgasm needed to rectify his marriage. If Richard's "uni[on] ... in body and soul in utter nakedness" is possible, then the Blooms' reconciliation stands the best chance of constituting it, as Bloom's acceptance of cuckoldry enables them to experience an amorous freedom that will lead them back to each other.

Less Envy than Equanimity

So far, we have focused on Bloom's attempts to come to an acceptance of Molly's adultery. Throughout the second section of *Ulysses*, we have seen the struggle that Joyce's protagonist undergoes on Bloomsday, as his recollections of past happiness and his masochistic embrace of cuckoldry become complementary strategies to ensure that the affair does not cause a more sizeable rupture to their relationship. While the open-ended nature of the text's conclusion prevents a conclusive evaluation of the fate of the Blooms' marriage, we can see glimpses throughout "Eumaeus" and "Ithaca" that support an optimistic speculation, as the melancholy that dominated Bloom's mindset throughout his wanderings has given way to a reaffirmed affection for Molly. The "Nostos" episodes of *Ulysses* thus enable us to see Bloom's homecoming as a form of amorous metempsychosis, supplementing the adulterous seduction of "Là ci Darem la Mano" with the hopeful coda of "Love's Old Sweet Song".

Bloom's amorous metempsychosis is initially set up in "Eumaeus," where his interactions with Stephen promote his fondness for Molly over his previous loneliness. At first, it seems as though Bloom has not succeeded in banishing his melancholy contemplations of the affair, as the abstracted air that he puts on in response to Corley's desire for Boylan to get him a job recalls his earlier attempts to distract himself whenever he encounters the "jaunty jingle" of his rival. His vague declaration that "everybody gets their own ration of luck" and his subsequent desire to "leave that [topic] for the moment" make it seem as though the pain of Bloom's earlier wandering has not subsided, casting doubt on the success of his imminent homecoming (*U* 16.240–1). However, once they enter the cabman's shelter, that melancholy quickly subsides, and Bloom's thoughts about Molly during the rest of the episode articulate the warmth and compassion that epitomized his recollections of their courtship. Indeed, the strategies of memory and masochism interweave throughout "Eumaeus," demonstrating the success of Bloom's attempts to accept Molly's adultery and foreshadowing the triumph of his homecoming.

Bloom's reconciled attitude towards Molly is evident in his reactions to D.B. Murphy's stories. When the sailor mentions his seven years at sea and his impending return to his wife, Bloom notes that "quite a number of stories there were on that particular Alice Ben Bolt topic, Enoch Arden and Rip van Winkle" (*U* 16.424–6). While his reaction to Murphy's homecoming is replete with the cynicism of Bloom's overall opinion of the sailor, it also shapes his own return because we cannot hear Bloom mention Rip van Winkle without recalling that he pantomimed the character during the charades game in Dolphin's Barn. ("Rip van Winkle we played" [*U* 13.1112].) Thus, the passion of Bloom's courtship interrupts his present meditations, and Bloom's literary reaction to Murphy's return to Carrigaloe paints his impending arrival at Eccles Street in a more optimistic manner, providing hope that in returning home Bloom will "come to stay and make a fresh start" (*U* 16.432–3).

Bloom's subsequent thoughts also shed a positive light on his marital future. As he considers what traveling options might be available to him, Bloom thinks of the "by no means bad notion" of "trying to make arrangements about a concert tour of summer music embracing the most prominent pleasure resorts" (*U* 16.516–9). Since to undertake such a venture would necessitate the company of Madam Marion Tweedy, Bloom's idea of a future concert tour projects a future where he and Molly are still together, and his lack of hesitation or awkwardness in articulating this idea shows how natural such a future seems to him. Additionally, Bloom's idea to promote this tour under "the Tweedy-Flower grand opera company with his own legal consort as leading lady" articulates an explicit partnership between him and Molly that anticipates the maintenance of their marriage (*U* 16.525–6). His labeling this venture the "Tweedy-Flower grand opera company" also confirms his use of Martha Clifford as an epistolary return to Marion Tweedy, not only because it unites Bloom's wife with his adulterous pseudonym, but also because its reference to Molly as "Tweedy" evokes the memorial power of his letters. While it is natural that Molly's maiden name would be used for an operatic venture (since that is her stage name), by juxtaposing the Tweedy surname with the name he uses to write to Dolphin's Barn, Bloom again reaffirms his past courtship through his present and future contemplations. Marion Tweedy thus conquers Martha Clifford, and the fact that Bloom "was quite sanguine of [the] success" of this "perfectly simple matter" confirms his confidence in the future of his marriage (*U* 16.527–8), enabling the passion of Dolphin's Barn to revitalize their relationship.

The ability of Bloom's memories to replenish his present romance is supported further by his subsequent thoughts about Irish tourism. Recognizing the ability of travel to counter a humdrum existence, Bloom notes that Ireland contains several "sylvan spots for rejuvenation" that provide the "bracing tonic for the system" that all Dubliners require (*U* 16.548–50). Significantly, Bloom isolates Howth as one of these "rejuvenat[ing]" destinations and lists the "rhododendrons several hundred feet above sealevel" as one of its "historic associations and otherwise" (*U* 16.557–9), which recalls the replenishment provided by his remembered proposal in "Lestrygonians." By labeling the rhododendrons a "historic association" and by noting the attractiveness of Howth "in spring when young men's fancy" (*U* 16.560–1), Bloom unites memory and romantic passion in a characterization of Howth that reawakens the "rejuvenat[ing]" potential of the past. His contemplations of travel thus anticipate the success of his homecoming, and the emergence of his proposal within "Eumaeus" rekindles the love inherent in that memory and serves as the necessary counterpart to Molly's concluding "yes."

The optimistic foreshadowing of Bloom's homecoming is also evidenced by his continued masochistic thoughts of Molly. As Bloom listens to the Parnell discussion that occurs in the shelter, he tells Stephen of the potential Spanish origins of Katherine O'Shea and shows him a provocative photograph of Molly, a perplexing action that takes on amorous significance through frequent allusions to *Sweets of Sin*. That Bloom keeps both photo and book in the same pocket initiates the juxtaposition of the two objects, and his subsequent equation of Molly's appearance with the text's adulterous wife solidifies this connection: "He sat tight just viewing the slightly soiled photo creased by opulent curves, none the worse for wear however, and looked away thoughtfully with the intention of not further increasing the other's possible embarrassment while gauging her symmetry of heaving *embonpoint*" (*U* 16.1464–8). These allusions confirm Bloom's ability to experience pleasure from the pain of his cuckolding, as the adulterous references in the Parnell discussion compel him to think about an alternative representation of infidelity that has been proven to arouse him. By describing the photograph through the language of *Sweets of Sin*, he rekindles his earlier arousal over "*the beautiful woman*" through a visual representation of Molly's "opulent curves" and "heaving *embonpoint*." Thus, the transference of Bloom's masochistic arousal from the book to the photograph replaces the pain of cuckoldry with the *Sweets of Sin* and hints at a reconciliation with his wife.

The success of "Eumaeus" in preparing Bloom for his return to Molly is confirmed by his discussion with Stephen after departing the shelter. As they walk towards Eccles Street, Bloom strikes up a conversation with Stephen about music. In so doing, he rekindles his musical method of coping with his amorous dilemma, as the songs that he offers as praiseworthy pieces foreground his enduring affection for Molly. Initially he mentions "the music of Mercadante's *Huguenots*, Meyerbeer's *Seven Last Words on the Cross* and Mozart's *Twelfth Mass*" (*U* 16.1738–9), liturgical pieces which we know from "Calypso" that he attributes to Molly's virtuoso performance "in the Jesuit fathers' church in upper Gardiner street" (*U* 16.1747–8). Then, Bloom speaks of his "admiration of Rossini's *Stabat Mater*, a work simply abounding in immortal numbers, in which his wife, Madam Marion Tweedy, made a hit, a veritable sensation, he might safely say, greatly adding to her other laurels and putting the others totally in the shade" (*U* 16.1744–7). These references demonstrate Bloom's enduring admiration of Molly, continuing the promotion of love over loneliness that has occurred throughout the chapter. Especially when we remember his idea for a future concert tour, Bloom's regard for "Madam Marion Tweedy" provides a past, present, and future context to his love for her, enabling an enduring affirmation in "Eumaeus" that anticipates a happy resolution to his homecoming.

While Bloom's liturgical reflections demonstrate his continued affection for Molly, the possibility for reconciliation is validated when the conversation turns to opera. As he discusses his preference for "light opera" and notes his "*penchant* ... for the severe classical school such as Mendelssohn" (*U* 16.1752–5), he mentions *Don Giovanni* and *Martha* as examples of praiseworthy operas, works whose themes of seduction and lost love have colored his thoughts about Molly's adultery throughout the text. However, as he continues to proclaim the virtues of opera, Bloom "mention[s] *par excellence* Lionel's air in *Martha*, *M'appari*, which, curiously enough, he had heard or overheard, to be more accurate, on yesterday" (*U* 16.1756–8). Even though he also mentions *Don Giovanni* in this discussion, it is telling that the only specific aria that is cited as an example of admirable opera is "M'appari," whose conclusion casts a hopeful light on Bloom's return home. He may intend for this discussion to gauge Stephen's feelings for his father, but Bloom's praise of "Lionel's air in *Martha*" represents his arrival home as his own performance of "M'appari," transforming Bloom into "Lionelleopold" whose return to "Ithaca" provides the opportunity for his own Martha to "come to [him]."

If "Eumaeus" demonstrates Bloom's anticipation of a successful reconciliation with Molly, then "Ithaca" validates his optimism. Upon returning to Eccles Street, Bloom's thoughts convey little of the loneliness and misery that comprised his earlier struggles in the text, replacing these sentiments with a tranquility and compassion that anticipates his acceptance of Molly at the chapter's conclusion. This emotional change is exemplified by Bloom's perception of Molly's shadow as he urinates with Stephen. As he admires her appearance, Bloom "elucidate[s] the mystery" of this "invisible attractive person" "with indirect and direct verbal allusions or affirmations" and "with subdued affection and admiration" (*U* 17.1177;

1179–80). This description confirms that Bloom's earlier depression has given way to "affirmations" of Molly's loveliness that convey his "subdued affection and admiration." Considering that this constitutes Bloom's first encounter with Molly after her affair with Boylan, his bestowal of "affirmations" upon her "attractive" appearance initiates the prominence of love in his emotions in "Ithaca."

Bloom's reaffirmation of Molly is developed further when he has to deal with the visible signs of her affair. Fortunately, this reaffirmation is demonstrated before Bloom even returns inside, as his contemplation of "the disparition of three final stars" and "the diffusion of daybreak" recalls the charades party at Doyle's, where "he had awaited with patience the apparition of the diurnal phenomenon" (*U* 17.1257; 1261–2). This amorous memory anticipates the text's concluding reconciliation by portraying his solitary homecoming as a reiteration of his past with Molly. Thus, Bloom's return home is not simply an arrival at the scene of his cuckoldry, but is rather the renewal of the passionate connection initiated seventeen years beforehand. By presenting Bloom's return inside through the language of Dolphin's Barn, Joyce presents the second half of "Ithaca" as a scene of amorous metempsychosis, which equips Bloom to look past the evidence of Molly's betrayal and move towards a renewal of their loving bond.

This amorous metempsychosis gains further credence as Bloom contemplates the objects in his house. As he notes the rearrangement of the furniture, Bloom's eye catches sight of "a dwarf tree of glacial arborescence under a transparent bellshade, [a] matrimonial gift of Luke and Caroline Doyle" (*U* 17.1336–8). By shifting from the contemplation of daybreak to the Doyles' wedding gift, Joyce represents Bloom's homecoming as a restaging of the Blooms' progression from courtship to marriage. That the Doyles' gift is a tree amplifies this amorous depiction of their reincarnation when we recall Bloom's observation about metempsychosis in "Nausicaa." ("They believed you could be changed into a tree from grief.") Indeed, Bloom's journey from "Lotus Eaters" to "Ithaca" chronicles his progression from grief to a tree, and Joyce's introduction of this wedding gift during Bloom's homecoming solidifies the metempsychotic connection between the past and present components of their relationship.

The viability of "Ithaca" serving as the conclusion for this marital rebirth gains further credence from Bloom's contemplation of the condition of their piano. Here, the cluttered state of the piano signifies the final evidence of Molly and Boylan's affair, as the "a pair of long yellow ladies' gloves" and the "partly consumed cigarette and two discoloured ends of cigarettes" complement the rearranged furniture and the discarded lottery tickets as markers of his usurpation (*U* 17.1304–6). However, the most significant aspect of the altered piano is that the "musicrest support[s] the music in the key of G natural for voice and piano of *Love's Old Sweet Song* … open at the last page" (*U* 17.1306–7; 1309). This observation confirms the redemptive quality of the musical theme throughout *Ulysses*; not only does the absence of "Là ci Darem la Mano" magnify the importance of "Love's Old Sweet Song" still being on the music rest, but the fact that the sheet music is "open at the last page" foregrounds the redemptive conclusion of that piece. ("So till the end, when life's dim shadows fall, / Love will be found the sweetest song of all" [Gifford and Seidman 77].) By having Bloom return home to the affirming finale of this song, Joyce establishes that his wanderings throughout the text will enjoy a redemptive ending, ensuring the conclusive promotion of "Love's Old Sweet Song" over the seductive allure of "Là ci Darem la Mano" and foreshadowing the inevitability of Bloom's reconciliation with Molly.

This inevitable reconciliation is all but confirmed towards the conclusion of "Ithaca," where Bloom's consideration of the implications of Molly's affair demonstrates his desire to maintain their loving bond. As Bloom lies down in bed for the night, he ponders his conflicted emotions regarding his marriage to Molly in the wake of her adultery. Even though he entertains thoughts of leaving and concedes that feelings of "envy" and "jealousy" cross his mind, he does not let this agitation cloud his affection for his wife, allowing "abnegation" and "equanimity" to hold sway (*U* 17.2195). His acknowledgement that "the matrimonial violator of the matrimonially violated had not been outraged by the adulterous violator of the adulterously violated" signifies both Bloom's belief in shared culpability for the affair and his refusal to let whatever loneliness that was created by that affair cloud his love for Molly (*U* 2197–9). The concluding satisfaction that he gains by "kiss[ing] the plump mellow yellow smellow melons of her rump" (*U* 17.2241) thus confirms Bloom's success in accepting his cuckolded status and relishing the perverse pleasure needed to dissolve his marital pain, enabling him to reaffirm his love for Molly through his "ador[ation] of [her] adulterous rump" (*U* 15.2839).

****

In "Oxen of the Sun," Bloom is described as being "stained by the mire of an indelible dishonour, but from whose steadfast and constant heart no lure or peril or threat or degradation could ever efface the image of that voluptuous loveliness which the inspired pencil of Lafayette has limned for ages yet to come" (*U* 14.1218–22). This description perfectly encapsulates Bloom's mindset throughout *Ulysses*, as he never lets his despair over Molly's affair overshadow his devotion, and he anticipates a reconciliation that will secure their marriage "for ages yet to come." He may indulge erotic curiosities about other women, but he never renounces his love for his wife and at no point does he seriously consider ending their relationship. Instead, he allows the warmth of the past to heal his present wounds and embraces the pain that comes from his refusal to encroach on his wife's desires. This insistence on affirming Molly despite his pain differentiates Bloom from his predecessors, and the fact that Joyce has the cuckold successfully return to his beloved enables the empathy that Bloom demonstrates in *Ulysses* to become an alternative to the bitter narcissism of his earlier fiction.

However, what grants legitimacy to Bloom's amorous thoughts throughout *Ulysses* is not simply their compassion, but their eventual reciprocation at the end of the text. Indeed, it is not sufficient to confine our investigation of the central love story in *Ulysses* to Bloom's struggles with cuckoldry. To do so would ignore the desires inherent in Molly's meditations at the text's conclusion, which would render us complicit in the same narcissistic apathy towards the love object's otherness that felled the protagonists of Joyce's earlier fiction. By expanding our analysis of Bloom's homecoming to encompass "Penelope" as well as "Ithaca," we not only develop our understanding of the love initiated in 1887 and reaffirmed in 1904; we also discover the necessity of reciprocal affirmation to bolster the cooperative nature of a viable politics of love. Thus, we must now revisit the Hill of Howth and heed the concluding affirmation of Bloom's "mountain flower" (*U* 18.1606) to uncover how the "heal[ing]" of "family wounds" becomes an amorous springboard for the "constructive building of community" (hooks 144).

Chapter 8
Molly's Return to Howth

In *James Joyce and the Revolt of Love*, Utell takes issue with critics who read Molly Bloom's soliloquy as "an affirmation of the Bloom's marriage" (129). Inspired by Christine Froula's argument that critics who posit an "ending beyond the ending" where Molly serves Bloom breakfast in bed "retrofit Joyce's actual plot to their own desire" (171), Utell contends that Molly's meditations on Bloom in "Penelope" do not constitute a viable affirmation because she "remains unknowable … to the man beside her" at the novel's conclusion. Given that "Penelope" is structured as an internal monologue where the reader accesses amorous thoughts that a sleeping Bloom is denied, Utell argues that "to read 'Penelope' as an affirmation is to miss the point," for Joyce is actually "creat[ing] an infinite distance between Molly and Bloom" that makes "their profound alterity" the defining characteristic of their marriage (130; 132). Thus, the "devastating reveal of 'Penelope'" is that "we see them sharing the same story, and *neither knows it is happening*" (Utell 131–2), which transforms the Blooms' mutual otherness into an "infinite distance" that is impossible for the text's concluding "yes" to traverse.

However, even though Molly and Bloom never hear their spouse's loving reflections about each other on June 17, that does not mean that those thoughts lose their affirming potential, for the novel's dialogic structure supplements this communicative gap. In fact, it is fitting that "Ithaca" ends with a conversation between the Blooms concerning the day's events since one could describe their episodes in *Ulysses* in this manner. Indeed, Joyce's description of Molly's soliloquy as "the indispensable countersign to Bloom's passport to eternity" demonstrates this conversational structure, as his decision to "le[ave]" "the last word … to Penelope" frames the novel's concluding chapters as an amorous dialogue that places Bloom's and Molly's perceptions of Bloomsday on an equal level (*LI* 160). For that reason, the fundamental alterity of "Penelope" does not disqualify the chapter's affirming potential because her rejoinder to Bloom's reflections still establishes Molly as an active participant in a reciprocal loving exchange. Thus, the transition from "Ithaca" to "Penelope" constitutes Bloom's and Molly's turn towards each other in accordance to Buber's idea of genuine dialogue, which compels us to recognize the reciprocal affirmation inherent in their reflections on their amorous past and present, highlighting an enduring love that can move past an adulterous betrayal.

Don Poldo de la Flora

Although Molly and Bloom are at opposing ends of the text's adulterous affair, they work through that affair in similar ways. Like Bloom, Molly's thoughts in "Penelope" utilize memories to interpret her present situation, relying upon her encounters with Mulvey to shape her attitude towards Bloom. While Devlin contends that "the content of Molly's recollections often renders explicit the distance and difference between former selves," reading her reflections on Gibraltar with respect to her Dublin situation dissolves this "critical distance between past and present" ("Pretending" 87), revealing the importance of her youth in shaping her perceptions of her contemporary lovers. Whereas Bloom uses memory to reaffirm his love for his wife, Molly's memories in "Penelope" are frequently used to determine whether she should choose Boylan or Bloom, and her reflections on Gibraltar frequently use Mulvey as a yardstick by which she determines the proper characteristics of her optimal suitor and thus chooses her husband over her lover. Thus, her passionate memories of Mulvey's courtship provide the historical context needed to interpret her thoughts on Bloomsday and reawaken the passion of that past, which enables her to melt their marital stagnation through the warmth of the sun over Howth.

Mulvey's introduction demonstrates his role in guiding Molly's feelings towards Bloom on Bloomsday. While her recollections of Mulvey dominate "Penelope['s]" fourth and fifth sentences, these passages are bookended by Molly's perceptions of a train that develop the musical motif for the Blooms' reconciliation. By beginning the fourth sentence with Molly noting the similarities between the "frseeeeeeeefronnnng" of the train and the "end of Loves old sweeeeetsonnnng" (*U* 18.596; 598), Joyce shapes the passage into a rebuttal of Molly's desire for Boylan's return at the end of the third sentence. Similarly, her concluding thoughts in the fifth sentence are interrupted by the "frseeeeeeeeeeeeeeeeeeeefrong" of "that train again" and end with her "pianissimo" farting to the "sweeeee … tsong" of the engine (*U* 874; 908). By using "Love's Old Sweet Song" to frame the Mulvey passages, Joyce enables the piece's redemptive potential to pervade these reflections, and thus Molly's memories of her earliest romantic experience become a method to infuse her marriage with the passion of Gibraltar.

Also, Molly's first references to Mulvey demonstrate the role his memory plays in promoting Bloom over Boylan. By noting that she once loaned Bloom *Henry Dunbar* "with Mulveys photo in it so as he see I wasnt without" (*U* 18.655–6), Molly directly ties the conquests of her past to her success with Bloom, using Mulvey's photo as a marker of her desirability to entice her contemporary suitor. By introducing Mulvey this way, Joyce shows that the primary importance of his memory is to enable Molly to advance her relationship with Bloom, and her use of the photo during their courtship compels us to read her memories in "Penelope" as a present-day version of this strategy. Similarly, Molly's thoughts of Mulvey highlight her dissatisfaction with Boylan, as her disappointment over Boylan's terse love note contrasts with her excitement over receiving her first letter from Mulvey. By characterizing Molly's attraction to Mulvey in terms of his written correspondence ("an admirer he signed it I near jumped out of my skin" [*U* 18.762]), Joyce positions Mulvey as an amorous marker that Molly utilizes to qualify her feelings for Boylan, especially considering that this description of Mulvey immediately follows her dissatisfaction with both Boylan's letter ("I hope hell write me a longer letter the next time if its a thing he really likes me … his wasnt much" [*U* 18.730–1; 735]). When we recall her fondness for Bloom's letters, we see that Molly's love of romantic correspondence compels her to prefer Bloom's passion to Boylan's brutishness, which enables Mulvey's letter to guide her away from Boylan and towards Bloom.

Molly's subsequent descriptions of Mulvey also promote Bloom as her optimal suitor. As she recalls their walks around Gibraltar, Molly notes that she told Mulvey that "I was engaged for fun to the son of a Spanish nobleman named Don Miguel de la Flora" (*U* 18.772–4). This fictitious engagement to Don Miguel de la Flora is significant given that Molly's future husband's last name is Bloom. Of course, Marion Tweedy had not met Bloom when she created this fiancé, but in recalling this engagement to a man "of the flower," Molly ties her experiences with Mulvey to her marriage to Bloom, especially since she later refers to her husband as "the great Suggester Don Poldo de la Flora" (*U* 18.1427–8). Just as Henry Flower's letters to Dolphin's Barn constitute Bloom's engagement with the past, Molly's linking Bloom to Don Miguel de la Flora uses Mulvey to revitalize her marriage. Thus, the Mulvey passages become a transition from a fictitious marriage to her eventual marriage (from a man "of the flower" to Henry Flower), and Molly's association of this "true word spoken in jest" with the "flower that bloometh" demonstrates the viability of her memories in reaffirming Bloom (*U* 18.775).

This memorial promotion of Bloom climaxes with Molly's last encounter with Mulvey on the Rock of Gibraltar. Her descriptions of the "firtree cove" in which they laid and her seduction of Mulvey echo her encouragement of Bloom's proposal at Howth (*U* 18.790), and Molly's remembrance of this encounter directly bleeds into her contemplations of her present situation. Specifically, her reflections on its conclusion solidify the connection between Mulvey and Bloom. As she remembers them walking through the Jewish cemetery, Molly thinks about the bishop of Lystra's articulations of "womans higher functions" and "the new woman bloomers," which compels her to consider her future married identity:

> I never thought that would be my name Bloom when I used to write it in print to see how it looked on a visiting card or practising for the butcher and oblige M Bloom youre looking blooming Josie used to say after I married him well its better than Breen or Briggs does brig or those awful names with bottom in them Mrs Ramsbottom or some other kind of a bottom Mulvey I woudnt go mad about either or suppose I divorced him Mrs Boylan. (*U* 18.838–46)

Not only does this demonstrate Molly's tendency to conflate her flirtation with Mulvey with her marriage to Bloom, but the acceptance of her married surname over a list of alternatives simultaneously promotes her marriage to Bloom over several alternatives, including Boylan. Although "Mulvey" and "Boylan" do not incur the same disdain as "those awful names with bottom in them," neither is praised to the degree that Molly promotes "Bloom," which shows that the passion stirred by Mulvey at the Rock has not pushed her away from her marriage.

Mulvey's role as a facilitator of marital love is confirmed by Molly's final recollections of him in the fifth sentence, where their courtship's passion turns into an abstract regard upon his departure. Even though Molly Tweedy's thoughts of Mulvey arouse her during Mass, Marion Bloom's thoughts pale in comparison to the excitement of her earlier memories, and her wish to have given Mulvey a memento of her collapses under the acknowledgement that she gave his "clumsy Claddagh ring" to Lieutenant Gardner (*U* 18.866). At that point, Molly's passion for Mulvey gives way to the "frseeeeeeeeeeeeeeeeeeeefrong" of "that train again," which subordinates Gibraltar to "loves sweet sooooooooooong." Molly's dismissal of Mulvey may constitute the loss of the "dear deaead days" of Gibraltar "beyondre call" (*U* 18.874–5), but the redemptive potential of "Love's Old Sweet Song" demonstrates that her love for Bloom remains at the end of this section.

This redemption is confirmed at the novel's conclusion, where her thoughts of Mulvey interrupt her consideration of Bloom's marriage proposal. One could argue that her recollections of Mulvey here distance her from Bloom and temper the reconciliatory potential of the conclusion. However, even though she responds to his proposal by thinking of Mulvey and "so many things he didnt know of" (*U* 18.1582), Molly primarily uses these recollections to justify her inevitable acceptance of Bloom, a strategy that she repeats in her marriage bed sixteen years later. This is especially the case when we consider the grammatical "structure" of the "sentence" that describes Molly's evaluation of Bloom's proposal.[1] Even though her thoughts of Gibraltar consume twenty-two lines of text (1582–1604), there is not one active verb in these lines to identify a concomitant action to her "thinking of so many things he didnt know"; rather, her list of secret thoughts constitutes a gigantic prepositional phrase that clarifies the only action ("thinking") that occurs during this passage. In fact, the next identification of a direct action by Molly occurs at the list's conclusion where she "th[inks] well as well him as another" (*U* 18.1605), which shows the causal connection between her thoughts of Gibraltar and her acceptance of Bloom. Molly's memories may impose grammatical distance between his proposal and her response, but they also solidify a passionate union between Joyce's lovers that demonstrates the Moorish Wall's importance in affirming Howth Head.

While Molly's reflections on Mulvey provide an implicit promotion of Bloom over Boylan, her reaffirmation of their marriage is even more compelling when she directly compares her competing suitors. Even in her fondest recollections of the affair, her thoughts inevitably return to Bloom and prefer his affection over Boylan's sexual prowess. In that sense, Henke's contention that "Molly's thoughts about Boylan … are all suffused with an awareness of Bloom" is correct, but this connection goes beyond a simple "awareness" (*Desire* 151). Through her remembrances of her liaison with Boylan, Molly consistently promotes emotional

---

1 By "sentence," I am referring to lines 1582–1605 of "Penelope," beginning with "I was thinking of so many things he didnt know" and ending with "well as well him as another."

affection over sexual desirability, which indicates that the affair will have no significant detrimental effect on her love for Bloom.

Molly's initial thoughts of Boylan demonstrate his inevitable subordination to Bloom in "Penelope." As she considers with whom Bloom had sex that day, she recalls that "the last time he came on my bottom when was it the night Boylan gave my hand a great squeeze going along by the Tolka" (*U* 18.77–8). While she notes the excitement of her initial flirtations with Boylan, the fact that Molly chooses to mention his advances within the context of her last sexual encounter with Bloom reduces her affair to a subset of her marriage. Indeed, although Molly goes into great detail about the affair, she frequently frames her thoughts about it through her broader perceptions of Bloom. She acknowledges that he is aware of her infidelity ("he has an idea about him and me hes not such a fool he said Im dining out and going to the Gaiety" [*U* 18.81–2]), asserts that he sent Milly to Mullingar to facilitate the affair ("only hed do a thing like that all the same on account of me and Boylan thats why he did it Im certain the way he plots and plans everything out" [*U* 18.1007–9]), and blames him for her adultery ("serve him right its all his own fault if Im an adulteress" [*U* 18.1516]). Even though Molly's explanations for her infidelity castigate Bloom, their marital focus also trivializes Boylan's role in their liaison, which prevents their new sexual relationship from becoming a viable alternative to Molly's marriage.

Molly's subsequent thoughts about Boylan develop the limitations of their relationship. Even when her recollections of their affair are not explicitly framed through her marriage, Molly's opinions about Boylan inevitably invite comparisons to Bloom that promote her husband over her lover. As she considers the aftermath of their intercourse, Molly wonders "was he satisfied with me … I wonder is he awake thinking of me or dreaming am I in it" (*U* 18.121–2; 124–5). While these thoughts convey a concern for Boylan's satisfaction, they also betray an ignorance of his desires, as Molly's speculation of whether Boylan is thinking about her reveals that she does not know much about him. By contrast, Molly frequently boasts that she understands Bloom better than anybody. She scoffs that whomever Bloom had sex with would not be a threat to her "if they only knew him as well as I do" (*U* 18.45–6), and she develops this confident assertion by noting that "nobody understands his cracked ideas but me" (*U* 18.1407). Whereas Molly does not know if Boylan would think of her after the affair, she knows Bloom so well that she could "write a book out of [his crazy ideas] the works of Master Poldy" (*U* 18.580), which shows her to be more aware of her husband's otherness. This recognition shows greater long-term potential to Molly's marriage than to her affair, making it unlikely that Boylan can transcend the role of impersonal sexual partner to become an authentic alternative to Bloom.

Molly's inability to understand Boylan's otherness is emphasized further by her thoughts about his reticence. While we frequently hear her mock Bloom's observations, we barely hear her discuss anything mentioned by Boylan. Even though she acknowledges the pleasure that she experienced during their liaison, her concurrent observation that Boylan is not a conversationalist qualifies her enjoyment of the affair. This qualification is initiated at the end of the chapter's third sentence, where Molly's arousal over her second orgasm with Boylan is tempered by her observation that "he does it and doesnt talk" (*U* 18.592). This establishes the impersonal nature of their relationship, and Molly's subsequent thoughts about their affair develop this communicative distance and reveal the underlying disgust behind her acknowledgment:

> thats what you get for not keeping them in their proper place pulling off his shoes and trousers there on the chair before me so barefaced without even asking permission and standing out that vulgar way in the half of a shirt they wear to be admired like a priest or a butcher or those old hypocrites in the time of Julius Caesar of course hes right enough in his way to pass the time as a joke sure you might as well be in bed with what a lion God Im sure hed have something better to say for himself an old Lion would. (*U* 18.1371–8)

This observation shows the relationship between Boylan's impersonal advances and Molly's growing ambivalence towards him. Her recollection of him disrobing "without even asking permission" illustrates his ignorance of Molly's desires, and his posing "to be admired like a priest or a butcher" betrays his perception of her as a mirror instead of an equal participant in their sexual relationship. Her statement that "an old Lion" would "have something better to say for himself" emphasizes their lack of communication, as the silence that Molly initially attributed to his lovemaking spills over to implicate their emotional as well as physical intercourse. This silence prevents Molly from gaining the understanding of Boylan needed to affirm his otherness, and the scorn that develops through these characterizations of their affair demonstrates that the satisfaction that Molly gains from her adultery will be insufficient for Boylan to supplant Bloom.

This emotional insufficiency is highlighted by Molly's qualified enjoyment of their liaison. She may relish "the four, five, or six climaxes she purportedly enjoyed with Boylan," but her "memory is imbued with the vacuous residue of copulation without sentiment, coupling without *jouissance*" (Henke *Desire* 135). For example, Molly expresses awe over "that tremendous big red brute of a thing he has" (*U* 18.144), but her amazement quickly turns into her recognition that intercourse is "all they want out of you," a sentiment that she repeats throughout the chapter ("all the pleasure those men get out of a woman" [*U* 18.583]). This demonstrates Molly's awareness of the lack of intimacy in their liaison, as her argument that men use sex to gain pleasure from a woman reduces her to a facilitator of masculine satisfaction. In contrast to the love letters and embraces that Molly desires throughout "Penelope," Boylan's mechanical lovemaking constitutes a monologic sexual exchange that subordinates her desires to his pleasure. Indeed, one gets the sense that the "determined vicious look in his eye" carries no recognition of Molly's satisfaction (*U* 18.153), perceiving her as an emotionless body "with a big hole in the middle" instead of an equal participant in a physical union (*U* 18.151). That she recognizes this lack of reciprocity deflates the satisfaction she gains from remembering their liaison, as even her anticipation for their next encounter is qualified by her thought that men are "done with you in a way till the next time." Especially when we recall her awareness of Bloom's concern for her, her descriptions of Boylan's apathy divorces their encounters from the emotional affection she craves and undercuts the long-term viability of their affair.

Boylan's failure to supplant Bloom is confirmed by Molly's inability to imagine a substantive future with him. Throughout "Penelope," Molly considers subsequent encounters with Boylan, but each of these considerations is immediately undercut by thoughts of Bloom that foreshadow her reaffirmation of her husband. At one point, Molly considers Boylan's potential as a father ("if he was married Im sure hed have a fine strong child"), but her concession that "Poldy has more spunk in him" than Boylan represents Bloom as a more viable candidate and articulates a more viable familial future to Molly's marriage than to her affair (*U* 18.166–8). Additionally, Molly thinks of sleeping with Boylan in the carriage to Belfast and eloping with him during the concert tour (*U* 18.372–3), but her imagined tryst conjures up memories of Bloom's and Molly's trip to Howth. Furthermore, though she wishes that Boylan were in bed with her instead of Bloom, Molly articulates this as a "[wish that] he was here or somebody to let myself go with and come again" (*U* 18.584–5), which reduces Boylan to an interchangeable sexual partner. Even though her statement that she "cant wait till Monday" hints at a sexual future with Boylan (*U* 18.595), her inability to imagine an emotional future to complement their affair makes it unlikely that Molly's infidelity will entice her to reject Bloom.

Through her qualified descriptions of her liaison, Molly shows that her lust is insufficient for Boylan to supplant Bloom in her amorous future; in fact, it may not guarantee a subsequent encounter with Boylan. While Molly may seem to anticipate a future tryst, her anticipation can also be read as an actual inability to delay her satisfaction until her next rendezvous with Boylan, especially when we note her recognition that this encounter cannot occur for three days. ("Thursday Friday one Saturday two Sunday three O Lord I cant wait till Monday" [*U* 18.594–5].) When we read her statement this way, we see that her pleasure overrides her feelings for Boylan, making it probable that she would discard him if a satisfactory amorous alternative arose. Oddly enough, that alternative could be Bloom, for her final description of a sexual future in "Penelope" occurs not on Monday with Boylan, but the next morning with Poldy. Indeed, her concluding fantasy of seducing Bloom signifies Molly's desire to rejuvenate her physical relationship with him, which makes the progression from this fantasy to her memories of Howth a simultaneous renouncing of Boylan's seed for Bloom's seedcake. Boylan may have provided her with temporary sexual satisfaction, but it is ultimately Bloom with whom Molly desires to share her future, thus constituting the cuckold's final victory over his usurper.

That Was Why I Liked Him

Thus far, I have focused my analysis on Molly's preferring Bloom over his adversaries. However, the most poignant aspects of "Penelope" occur where no such comparisons are needed, where the rivals for Molly's attention fade into the background and she focuses exclusively on Bloom. Of course, her thoughts of Bloom lack the warmth and affection that typify the rhetoric of her husband's episodes. Specifically, her acknowledgement that Bloom no longer embraces her or engages in complete sexual intercourse articulates a lack of intimacy that has tempted Molly to stray. For that reason, it is somewhat understandable that Molly attempts to resolve her guilt for betraying Bloom by blaming him for her adultery, and the cynical and scornful tone that pervades her thoughts tellingly contrasts with his compassion and highlights their marital impasse. However, while she is tempted to act in manners that push Bloom away, her thoughts reveal her enduring fondness for him, which transforms her castigations of him into the "indispensable countersign" to his episodes in *Ulysses* that is needed for the Blooms to dialogically affirm their relationship.

Initially, Molly's memories of Bloom enable a more affectionate understanding of the current status of their relationship. Like Bloom, Molly frequently relies on their past experiences to work through their present situation, and her recollections of their courtship articulate a fondness for him that tempers the bitterness of her rebukes. In fact, Molly's and Bloom's memories frequently overlap, as their attempts to use the past to negotiate the present entice them to reflect on the same events in their early relationship. However, whereas Bloom describes these encounters through predominantly affectionate sentiments, Molly's excitement is qualified by mocking allusions to his eccentricities that prevent us from viewing these experiences as purely positive. This tactic enables Molly to evaluate her feelings for Bloom more productively, uniting her positive and negative attitudes towards him in a dialogic contemplation of the past that provides for a more effective affirmation of her husband.

For example, Molly's thoughts about their first meeting at Mat Dillon's house echo Bloom's meditations on this event in "Sirens." Just as Bloom reacts passionately to "M'appari," Molly recalls her "excite[ment]" as "we stood staring at one another for about 10 minutes as if we met somewhere" (*U* 18.1181; 1183–4). However, Molly's "excite[ment]" is mitigated by her sardonic characterizations of Bloom, as she scoffs at the Doyles' descriptions of his Parliamentary future ("O wasnt I the born fool to believe all his blather about home rule and the land league" [*U* 18.1187–8]) and derides Bloom's political ideas ("explaining and rigmaroling about religion and persecution he wont let you enjoy anything naturally" [*U* 18.1190–1]). However, even though her memories of this encounter are more negative than his, her derision of Bloom is bookended by recollections of her amusement over his eccentricities. Not only does her rebuke of the Doyles emerge from her statement that Bloom "used to amuse me the things he said with the half sloothering smile on him" (*U* 18.1185–6), but her subsequent castigation of Bloom's sociopolitical babbling gives way to remembrances of his sexual desires that revive Molly's amusement. ("O I laughed myself sick at him that day" [*U* 18.1195].) She may be laughing at Bloom, but the fact that this humor replaces her caustic remarks demonstrates the tendency of her affection to supersede her irritation, resulting in a net positive evaluation of their first meeting. Through this recollection, Molly engages in a dialogic assessment of the past that enables her to use her overall affection for Bloom to overcome her frustration with him.

Molly's subsequent thoughts about their courtship continue this dialogic evaluation of her past. As she scoffs at Bloom's obsession with women's undergarments, she recalls the night on Harold's Cross road when they fooled around in the rain. While Molly derides Bloom's underwear fixation and labels him a "Deceiver" for begging her to hide this experience from her father (*U* 18.318), her caustic thoughts dissolve into fonder recollections of their courtship that cast her memories in a more positive light. Not only does she subsequently acknowledge Bloom's intellect through a comparison with "that other fool Henry Doyle" (*U* 18.322–3), but Molly's memories shift from Harold's Cross road to the "night he kissed my heart at Dolphins barn," which replaces her disgust over Bloom's sexual quirks with a passion that "makes you feel like nothing on earth" (*U* 18.328–32). By transitioning from her exasperation of Bloom's physical lovemaking to her excitement of his emotional lovemaking, Molly acknowledges her affection for her husband despite her frustration over their sexual relationship. Thus, Molly's use of the past to interpret the present not only promotes Bloom over her previous lovers, it also constructs the loving framework needed to reaffirm her love for Bloom despite their sexual stagnation.

The viability of Molly's dialogic memories is shown in her comprehensive evaluation of Bloom's contemporary quirks. Similar to her recollections of their courtship, Molly's present-day evaluation of Bloom combines positive and negative assessments of his character that inevitably promote her affection over her frustration. For example, Molly does express frustration over Bloom's late return home ("well thats a nice hour of the night for him to be coming home at ... Ill knock him off that little habit tomorrow" [*U* 18.1232–4]) and scoffs at his supposed demand for breakfast in bed ("I suppose well have him sitting up like the king of the country" [*U* 18.930–1]), but what resonates the most from these thoughts is not her frustration over Bloom's tardiness, but her concern for his well-being. She may be put off by his hanging out with medicos, but her initial anxiety is a fear of Bloom's being "[led] ... astray" by "get[ting] in with those medicals" (*U* 18.926). Similarly, Molly's disbelief over his "demand" for breakfast in bed is immediately subordinated to her "love to hear him falling up the stairs of a morning with the cups rattling on the tray" (*U* 18.933–4), which illustrates her acknowledgment of his affection for her despite her frustration with his quirks. Even though she derides the substance of their conversation, that derision carries with it both a recognition of his compassion and a concern for his safety, demonstrating that her narrative snarkiness will not seriously impede her love for him.

Molly's concern for Bloom is also evident in her perceptions of his adult acquaintances. While her revived exasperation over his breakfast "request" initially compels her to minimize his affection ("I suppose Im nothing anymore" [*U* 18.1244–5]) and suspect him of infidelity, those thoughts shift to a renewed fear for Bloom's well-being, as her recollection of Dignam's obituary compels her to rebuke the other funeral attendees and to protect her husband from their influence: "theyre a nice lot all of them well theyre not going to get my husband again into their clutches if I can help it making fun of him then behind his back I know well when he goes on with his idiotics because he has sense enough not to squander every penny piece he earns down their gullets and looks after his wife and family goodfornothings" (*U* 18.1275–9). Similar to her concern with the medical students, Molly's thoughts about Bloom's peers reflect her fear of their opportunistic influence and her acknowledgment of his marital responsibility. Her castigation of Jack Power and Simon Dedalus "making fun of him then behind his back" shows that her affection for Bloom overrides her frustration with his "idiotics," as her marital insults do not mitigate her impulse to defend him against similar mockery from others. Her insistence that Bloom "has sense enough not to squander every penny piece he earns down their gullets" strengthens her assessment of her husband's sensibility, and her acknowledgement that he "looks after his wife and family" solidifies her recognition of his devotion to her and Milly. Thus, Molly's love for Bloom inevitably tempers her sarcastic descriptions of him, demonstrating that the events of Bloomsday should not damage her marital affection to any substantive degree.

Perhaps the most conclusive evidence of Molly's commitment to Bloom concerns her eventual acquiescence to his sexual eccentricities. While Bloom's desires are a central target of Molly's mockery, when she nears the conclusion of her soliloquy, her attitude towards his fetishes changes from derision to acceptance, as her projected strategy to win him back consists of an erotic encounter that caters to his sexual delights. Initially, Molly resolves to sing "Là ci Darem la Mano" while flashing her best drawers at him to "make his mickey stand for him" (*U* 18.1509–10), which combines Bloom's achieving masochistic pleasure through his cuckoldry with his obsession with women's undergarments. Then, she decides to embrace his kissing of "the plump mellow yellow smellow melons of her rump" by shoving her bare bottom in his face, enabling him to relish his role as the "adorer of the adulterous rump." Finally, she opts to "tell him I want £1 or perhaps 30/- … to buy underclothes" (*U* 18.1523), which develops her embrace of Bloom's underpants fetish while implicitly catering to his excitement over *Sweets of Sin*. This last point is particularly significant because to spend Bloom's money on exotic underwear parallels the fictional adulteress's purchase of "frillies for Raoul," which not only transforms Molly into the "*beautiful woman*" that provokes his arousal, but also reshapes Bloom into Raoul because she is purchasing these "frillies" for him.[2] Molly may have no knowledge of *Sweets of Sin*, but her fantasized reclamation of her sex life with Bloom provides an opportunity for the cuckold to reclaim his physical relationship with his adulteress. Especially when we consider her earlier criticism of Bloom's sadomasochistic literary preferences

---

[2] This transformation of Bloom into Raoul is supported further by Molly's earlier recognition that Boylan prefers nakedness over lingerie (*U* 18.438–40). Considering that it is Bloom and not Boylan who is enticed by women's underwear, Molly's concluding decision to buy lingerie constitutes an explicit promotion of Bloom over Boylan.

("theres nothing for a woman in that" [*U* 18.495]), Molly's anticipated encounter with him becomes another example of her acceptance of him despite her earlier scorn, which confirms the efficacy of her amorous dialogism in enabling her to move towards a reaffirmation of her love for Bloom.

This reclamation of the Blooms' marriage is confirmed at Howth, where Molly's recollection of their engagement transforms her fond thoughts of Bloom in "Penelope" into a climactic affirmation. Initially, her recollections of his kindness establish a compassionate bond between her justifications for accepting his proposal and the affection she attributes to him throughout the chapter. Through her recollections of Bloom's statements that "I was a flower of the mountain" (*U* 18.1576) and "the sun shines for you today" (*U* 18.1578), Molly establishes his affection as the foundation for her love for him, especially when we note that his empathy was the main reason why Molly accepted his proposal. ("that was why I liked him because I saw he understood or felt what a woman is" [*U* 18.1578–9].) When we place this historical compassion in dialogue with her concessions of Bloom's marital kindness, we discover that her recalling their engagement unifies "Howth Bloom" and "Eccles Street Bloom" through their compassion towards her and their ability to understand and affirm her desires. In that sense, Molly's recalled acceptance of Bloom's proposal constitutes an affirmation of both her past lover and her present-day husband, which transforms her meditations on their engagement into her final use of past bliss to compel her acceptance of contemporary love.

The reciprocal nature of Molly's description of their engagement also confirms the viability of their relationship. In contrast to the other amatory quests in Joyce's works, Molly's acceptance of Bloom at Howth is noteworthy in that there is no primary actor, that both Marion Tweedy and Leopold Bloom actively engage each other in a mutual desire to share the rest of their lives together.[3] He may initiate the question as they lie among the rhododendrons, but her characterization of this memory as "the day I got him to propose to me" represents her as a principal agent in facilitating this union (*U* 18.1573–4). Indeed, Molly's description of the step-by-step process she employed to aid his proposal reveals her explicit involvement in enabling Bloom to ask her to marry him, which represents both Blooms as active agents in this loving bond and contrasts to the unequal entanglements of their narcissistic predecessors.

Molly's description of her acceptance of the proposal confirms the reciprocal nature of their engagement. While she ultimately responds to Bloom's proposal with the text's concluding "yes," it is significant that upon resolving to marry him, she does not immediately respond with this affirmation. Instead, Molly "ask[s] him with my eyes to ask again" (*U* 18.1605), which constitutes an initiated proposal of

---

[3] Devlin notes that "there is no domination in this scene, nor acquiescent passivity, for both parties – like Shakespeare through his art – act and are acted on. In Joyce's lyric rendering of secular communion, the mutuality is all" ("En-Gendered" 87).

her own instead of a response to his original question.[4] That Bloom responds to her ocular proposal by reiterating his verbal proposal ("then I asked him with my eyes to ask again yes and then he asked me would I yes" [*U* 18.1605–6]) confirms the reciprocal bond forged between the two lovers. From this perspective, both Bloom and Molly say "yes" at the conclusion of *Ulysses*, and this mutual acceptance between two lovers constitutes the first reciprocal affirmation of otherness within the Joycean oeuvre.

It is thus significant that Molly's recollection of their engagement constructs a temporal bond between Howth Head and Eccles Street, for it instills her concluding memory in "Penelope" with performative contemporary implications. Utell may argue that "the final act of the novel" is "to create an infinite distance between Molly and Bloom as we are given access to her inner life – and Bloom is not" (130), but by tying her recollections of Howth to her current perceptions of their relationship, Molly actually restages her acceptance of Bloom's proposal within the confines of their marriage bed. Bloom may be asleep and no seedcake may be exchanged, but in comparing him to her past lovers and conceding his enduring compassion, Molly reenacts the thoughts that led her to accept his proposal sixteen years beforehand. In addition, even if Bloom has no direct access to Molly's thoughts in "Penelope," her recalled desire to "g[ive] him all the pleasure I could" at Howth reshapes our understanding of the next morning's fantasized encounter with Bloom that preceded this memory, as the bond created between 1888 and 1904 transforms her contemporary attempts to "make him want me" (*U* 18.1539) into a reenactment of her attempts to "[lead] him on till he asked me to say yes" (*U* 18.1580–1). For that reason, her concluding "yes I said yes I will yes" is not simply a recollection of her initial acceptance of Bloom; instead, Molly's "yes" constitutes a renewed acceptance of Bloom's proposal, enabling the passion of Howth to replenish their marital love and replacing the frustration that compelled her infidelity with a revitalized affirmation of Bloom.

Molly's soliloquy thus demonstrates the dialogic potential of the Blooms' love for each other. By narrating "Penelope" from the perspective of Bloom's loved one, Joyce enables Molly to transcend the objectifying silence that defined his previous love objects, and her concluding "yes" confirms the maintenance of a reciprocal love that counterbalances the rejection and alienation of his earlier fiction. Molly may characterize their courtship differently from Bloom and her representations of him may lack the uncompromising warmth of his narration, but her restaged acceptance of Bloom's proposal in the face of marital frustration articulates the reciprocal affirmation of otherness needed for their relationship to survive beyond June 17, 1904. By reading the "Nostos" episodes with respect to

4 It is also important that Molly asks this question "with my eyes," because this gesture reconfigures the narcissistic gaze over which Joyce's earlier lovers obsessed. Instead of constituting a vacant and impersonal reflection of Bloom's grandeur, Molly reshapes the female gaze to function as a communicative medium, and the fact that her optic question gets its desired response demonstrates the efficacy of this gesture.

Buber, we see the ability of loving dialogue to overcome a marital breach that would have crippled Joyce's previous lovers, which confirms the viability of reciprocal love as an alternative to narcissistic desire.

****

In a 1921 letter to Harriet Shaw Weaver, Joyce described "Ithaca" as "the end [of *Ulysses*] as ["Penelope"] has no beginning, middle or end" (*LI* 172). This refusal of closure to "Penelope" is significant, for to read its conclusion as Molly's reaffirmation of Bloom does not guarantee that they will live happily ever after. In fact, Buber concedes the difficulty of such amorous permanence because the potential always exists for a "You" to become an "It" again, and Molly's possible Monday rendezvous with Boylan makes this regression a real possibility. However, one does not need permanent romance to affirm a loved one; one need only possess the inherent respect for otherness at the foundation of such affirmations since that ability to view an other as a person instead of an object ensures the possibility of even lost love "catch[ing] fire and becom[ing] present" again (Buber *Thou* 90). For that reason, it may be true that Molly's and Bloom's thoughts in *Ulysses* literally fall on deaf ears and that positing an "ending beyond the ending" is to "miss the point" of the narrative. Nevertheless, Buber's amorous framework still enables us to see the Blooms' reciprocal affirmation since Molly's restaged acceptance of Bloom's proposal demonstrates her continued ability to rekindle the flames of a dwindling marriage. Molly and Bloom may not completely know each other at the end of *Ulysses*, but this "unknowab[ility]" does not doom their love to opposing sides of an "infinite distance," for Molly's renewed "yes" at "Penelope['s]" conclusion connotes the reciprocal "countersign" to Bloom's enduring affection that concludes *Ulysses* on the most lovingly productive note possible.

Thus, through the Blooms, Joyce provides his first positive endorsement of reciprocal love, and though he may have strenuously objected to the sacrament of marriage, his portrayal of Molly and Leopold Bloom shows that he endorses Buber's "basic principle of marriage." This observation is not only important to this specific love story, but it takes on social and political significance when we recall Buber's assertion that this "basic principle" translates into the "vital acknowledgement of many-faced otherness" that promotes more productive interaction and compromise within a body politic (*Man* 61). Significantly, Joyce's first portrayal of reciprocal love is accompanied by his first major contemplation of an amorous community particularly through his depictions of Bloom, which is noteworthy considering that Bloom is perhaps the least ambitious of Joyce's lovers. He may consider bizarre ideas for social reform, but Bloom never desires anything approaching Duffy's revolutionary aspirations, Stephen's aesthetic pursuits, or Richard's amatory freedom. Instead, he is content to make his odyssey through Dublin, entertaining a reformist thought here and there, but never letting the desire for greatness overshadow his obligations to Molly. It is thus ironic that Bloom's empathetic attitude towards his fellow Dubliners provides the most effective sociopolitical interaction in the Joycean oeuvre, while the broader attempts by the other protagonists towards revolution suffer the same failures as their amatory pursuits. Bloom's "steadfast and constant heart" thus enables him to affirm not only his wife, but the other people he encounters throughout *Ulysses*, transforming his empathetic embrace of otherness into a powerful loving alternative to the sociopolitical paralysis of Joyce's Dublin.

Chapter 9
The Politics of the New Bloomusalem

We have seen how Bloom's love for Molly enables him to move past the pain of his cuckoldry and towards an amorous metempsychosis. However, while this acceptance can be seen primarily as Bloom's "wish" for his wife's "otherness" and "entire being to exist," his empathy and compassion throughout *Ulysses* transcend the boundaries of their marriage, as his reflections on his fellow Dubliners demonstrate a similar acceptance of their perspectives and concern for their well-being. While it may be difficult to prove a causal link between Bloom's affection for Molly and his compassion for others, it is significant that the only protagonist in Joyce's works who affirms Buber's "basic principle of marriage" is also the only character capable of productive, dialogic interaction within Dublin (*Man* 61). For this reason, Bloom's ability to "see another's face and listen to another's words" (*U* 17.637) in both his personal and social interactions makes him the most capable of Joyce's characters of affirming the "many-faced otherness" of his loved ones (*Man* 61), which could facilitate the "overcoming of *otherness* in living unity" needed to realize Buber's dialogic community (Buber *Pointing* 102). Bloom thus becomes Joyce's most productive political agent not through his social and political ideas, but rather through his "assumption of a bond between himself and other created beings" (*JJ* 362),[1] revealing the practical viability of the Joycean love ethic.

I Am Doing Good To Others

In "Wandering Rocks," John Wyse Nolan expresses shock that Bloom has donated five shillings to the late Patrick Dignam's family, conceding that "there is much kindness in the jew" (*U* 10.980). While the racial implications of this allusion necessitate our viewing his response with a skeptical eye, Nolan's observation is accurate since a defining characteristic of Bloom is his unswerving compassion and generosity. From feeding a flock of gulls to helping a blind stripling cross the street, Bloom frequently goes out of his way to aid others, as his inherent empathy for their situations compels him to assist them to the best of his abilities. Bloom's warmth for Molly thus can also be seen in his affection for the citizens within his nation, and his actions throughout *Ulysses* demonstrate the ability of the Joycean lover to affirm the "responsibility of an I for a You" (Buber *Thou* 66).

---

[1] Bowen similarly contends that Bloom is "a rational, sensitive, compassionate, humane man. There is so much good about Bloom that an identification with him assures us that we ourselves are better" (*Comic* 7).

Bloom's social compassion is articulated initially in his thoughts about Paddy Dignam, whose death is introduced in "Calypso" and who maintains an enduring presence throughout the text. Like Stephen, Bloom spends the text in mourning. However, unlike Stephen, who views his mother's death as a psychic imposition on his amatory freedom, Bloom rarely considers the impact of Dignam's death on himself, choosing instead to contemplate how it affects the deceased, his family, and the human race as a whole. This concern is evident as he explains metempsychosis to Molly and considers whether Dignam has experienced this process: "That we live after death. Our soul. That a man's soul after he dies, Dignam's soul …." (*U* 4.352–3). Bloom had previously thought about Dignam's death in the text when he considered "stop[ping] and say[ing] a word: about the funeral perhaps" to Mr O'Rourke (*U* 4.118), but with Molly, his thoughts go deeper. By pondering whether Dignam has undergone metempsychosis, Bloom shows a concern for Dignam's death beyond what is socially obligated, which makes him a unique figure in Joyce's Dublin since, besides Martin Cunningham, nobody seems to react to this death beyond the socially required funeral and pub attendance. Thus, by shifting from his affection over Molly's question about metempsychosis to his consideration of Dignam's reincarnation, Joyce demonstrates the relationship between Bloom's marital affection and his broader social empathy.

Bloom's contemplation of Dignam's metempsychosis also highlights the difference between his and Stephen's approaches to loss. Indeed, the wording of Bloom's connection between Dignam's death and metempsychosis echoes Stephen in "Telemachus," as one cannot read Bloom's "Our soul … Dignam's soul" without simultaneously recalling Stephen's "Cranly's arm. His arm" (*U* 1.159). These two expressions demonstrate Bloom's and Stephen's disparate reactions towards others, contrasting the interconnectivity of Bloom's consideration of metempsychosis ("our soul") with the alienation of Stephen's reaction to Cranly's desertion ("his arm"). Bloom thus demonstrates his ability to feel compassion for a fallen friend, whereas Stephen's lament over his refusal of Cranly confirms him to be preoccupied with his own loss. This contrast is also apparent at the conclusions of "Calypso" and "Telemachus," as the characters' reactions to the bells of St. George's Church elevate Bloom's empathy over Stephen's narcissism. Even though they hear the same bells that chime the same time, Bloom's thoughts about the funeral compel him to express grief for "poor Dignam!" (*U* 4.551), while Stephen's hearing the "Ordo Commendationis Animae" in the chimes keeps him grounded in his self-absorbed alienation, leading him to rebuke Mulligan's role as his "usurper" (*U* 1.744). Considering that these are the last expressions uttered before both characters begin to wander around Dublin, Bloom's and Stephen's reactions to the bells prefigure their methods of interacting within their social spheres, as the empathy of Bloom's reflections throughout Bloomsday contrasts with Stephen's narcissistic brooding. Thus, Bloom's consideration of Dignam provides the first evidence of his compassion for others, transforming his love for Molly into the broader embrace of his fellow Dubliners.

The magnitude of Bloom's compassion is confirmed by his attempts to provide financial assistance to Dignam's widow and children. In "Hades," Bloom empathized with Mrs Dignam's loss after a conversation with Ned Lambert about the family's insurance, recognizing that her sorrow is much greater than his own ("Lost her husband. More dead for her than for me" [*U* 6.545]), and lamenting young Patrick Dignam being left fatherless. ("Poor boy! Was he there when the father? Both unconscious. Lighten up at the last moment and recognise for the last time. All he might have done" [*U* 6.576–8].) This compassion not only compels Bloom to contribute five shillings to Cunningham's pool of donations, but he also agrees to help the Dignams collect on Paddy's insurance policy by soliciting funds from the Scottish Widows' Fund Life Assurance Agency. ("Anyhow she wants the money. Must call to those Scottish Widows as I promised" [*U* 13.1226–7].) Here, Joyce contrasts Bloom's empathy with the artificiality of his counterparts, as the tenets of social respectability that compelled them to attend the funeral become the instruments used to persecute Bloom in "Cyclops" for being too busy securing the Dignams' insurance to stand them a drink. That they rely on Jewish stereotypes to deny Bloom's charity ("The courthouse is a blind. He had a few bob on *Throwaway* and he's gone to gather in the shekels" [*U* 12.1550–1]) shows the racial implications of this artificiality, revealing the hatred that undergirds the characters' defense of social performance. By making Bloom's financial assistance to the Dignams the source of his persecution, Joyce thus shows that the empathy his protagonist displays throughout *Ulysses* is largely absent in Dublin, positioning Bloom's compassion as an alternative to the social alienation of his body politic.

Bloom's empathy is also evident in his reflections on the pregnant Mina Purefoy. In much the same way that he thinks about Dignam's death, Bloom sympathizes with the pains that Mrs Purefoy has had to endure during her three days in labor. In fact, Bloom's thoughts frequently unite Dignam and Mrs Purefoy ("Dignam carted off. Mina Purefoy swollen belly on a bed groaning to have a child tugged out of her" [*U* 8.479–80]), and these meditations on death and life compel him to empathize not only with the individuals in question, but with humanity as a whole. ("One born every second somewhere. Other dying every second" [*U* 8.480–1].) Bloom's commiseration with Mrs Purefoy thus demonstrates how the compassion he feels for an individual transcends that local sphere to encompass a more global empathy, which bolsters his ability to affirm the "many-faced otherness" of Dublin.

Bloom's empathy towards Mrs Purefoy is apparent when he hears about her labor in "Lestrygonians." As Mrs Breen explains Mina Purefoy's hardship, Bloom offers the typical words of condolence similar to the general reaction to Dignam in the previous chapters. ("I'm sorry to hear that" [*U* 8.283]; "Poor thing! Three days! That's terrible for her" [*U* 8.289–90].) However, what separates this reaction from the social performance of sorrow are his subsequent considerations on Mina Purefoy. As he continues his walk to lunch, he imagines the pain experienced by "Poor Mrs Purefoy" (*U* 8.358) and shivers at the thought of having to undergo the same torment: "Three days imagine groaning on a bed with a vinegared handkerchief round her forehead, her belly swollen out. Phew! Dreadful simply! Child's head too big: forceps. Doubled up inside her trying to butt its way out blindly, groping for the way out. Kill me that would" (*U* 8.373–7). This observation reveals the sincerity of Bloom's compassionate words to Mrs Breen, as his consideration of what labor must feel like compels him to consider that suffering from the sufferer's perspective. His subsequent relief that "Molly got over hers lightly" (*U* 8.377) not only demonstrates his continued concern for his wife's well-being, it also shows how that love influences his compassion for others by using his thoughts of Molly to bolster his concern for Mina Purefoy rather than to brood on his cuckoldry. Thus, by recognizing that the Blooms experienced a more fortunate pregnancy than Mrs Purefoy's torment, Bloom's projected experience of childbirth illustrates his willingness to understand and empathize with others' sufferings.

Bloom's compassion towards Mrs Purefoy is confirmed by his considerations of how to alleviate labor pangs. As he contemplates the misery of enduring three days "groaning in a bed," he decries the lack of initiative in developing ways to mitigate the suffering of pregnant women:

> They ought to invent something to stop that. Life with hard labour. Twilight sleep idea: queen Victoria was given that. Nine she had. A good layer. Old woman that lived in a shoe she had so many children. Suppose he was consumptive. Time someone thought about it instead of gassing about the what was it the pensive bosom of the silver effulgence. Flapdoodle to feed fools on. They could easily have big establishments whole thing quite painless. (*U* 8.377–83)

Similar to his desire to help the Dignams, Bloom's thoughts about Mrs Purefoy progress from a contemplation of her "life with hard labour" to a desire to ease her suffering. Bloom may be incapable of "invent[ing] something to stop that," but his compassionate understanding of her pain establishes a sympathetic model of social interaction that enhances the desire to alleviate the sufferings of others. The productivity of this desire is magnified by his contemplations of Queen Victoria, as his comparison of Mrs Purefoy's labor to Victoria's considers the latter as a fellow sufferer rather than as an imperial enemy. This is especially evident when he contrasts this concern with the "flapdoodle" of Dan Dawson's speech from "Hades," as his contention that it is more important to consider the agonies of others (even the former British monarch) than to wax poetically about the "the silver effulgence" of Ireland's majestic landscape demonstrates his prioritization of human suffering over political cliché. Bloom's empathy thus demonstrates how his love for an individual can translate into an amorous social conscience that challenges the banality of his surroundings.

This elevation of Bloom's concern over patriotic cliché is best articulated in "Sirens," as his sympathy for Mrs Purefoy contrasts with the empty pity of the other bar patrons for "The Croppy Boy." Joyce earlier equated this song with hollow sympathy in "Hades" by portraying Bloom's fellow mourners as being more interested in Ben Dollard's singing of it than in the departed Paddy Dignam. It is thus fitting that this individual narcissism influences their social interactions, as a post-funeral pub gathering in "Sirens" culminates in Simon Dedalus asking Dollard for an encore. As "Lid, De, Cow, Ker, Doll" (*U* 11.1271) embrace the mournful aspects of "The Croppy Boy," Bloom considers the pleasure gained by this performance and contrasts it with his compassion for Mrs Purefoy: "Thrill now. Pity they feel. To wipe away a tear for martyrs that want to, dying to, die. For all things dying, for all things born. Poor Mrs Purefoy. Hope she's over. Because their wombs" (*U* 11.1101–3). By juxtaposing the "pity they feel" with a perceived "thrill," Bloom reveals the purely performative nature of their reactions to "The Croppy Boy," as their melodramatic connection to the song reveals a self-contained enjoyment in this musical restaging of the 1798 rebellion. By juxtaposing this performance of patriotic pity with Bloom's actual pity for Mrs Purefoy, Joyce shows how individual narcissism translates into a self-defeating social community, as the social exercise of sorrow is merely a banal act of navel gazing that promotes stereotypical political sentimentality over existing pain and suffering. Again, Bloom is the only character in the scene who can display genuine compassion instead of performed condolence, and the authenticity of his empathetic identification with Mrs Purefoy bolsters Joyce's loving depiction of Bloom's social identity.

If Bloom's reactions to Dignam's death and Mrs Purefoy's pregnancy illustrate his capacity for compassion and generosity, then his concern for Stephen shows how far his hospitality extends. While their encounter is frequently analyzed from the perspective of fathers and sons, reading their interactions with respect to Buber highlights Bloom's kindness as the necessary alternative to Stephen's narcissism. Even though Stephen's apathy throughout the "Nostos" episodes renders their conversations one-sided and limited, Bloom's attention to his well-being and his willingness to engage him substantively signify an empathetic embrace that is missing in Stephen's experiences in the text. Bloom thus provides the only affirmation of otherness that Stephen receives in *Ulysses*, which validates Zack Bowen's identification of Bloom as "the only one in *Ulysses* who would help Stephen and offer friendship, assistance, and hospitality, in short offer to show Stephen 'what the heart is and what it feels'" (*Song* 84).

Bloom thinks about the Dedalus family throughout the first half of the text, but his concern for Stephen truly emerges upon encountering him in "Oxen of the Sun." As he awaits word on Mrs Purefoy's delivery, he contemplates the despair of "his good lady Marion" upon the death of Rudy, noting that "she was wondrous stricken of heart for that evil hap and for his burial did him on a fair corselet of lamb's wool, the flower of the flock, lest he might perish utterly and lie akeled" (*U* 14.268–70). Tellingly, this dual-reflection on Molly's grief over Rudy compels Bloom to consider Stephen's well-being, lamenting the fact that "he lived riotously with those wastrels and murdered his goods with whores" (*U* 14.276). The generosity that emerges from this concern thus confirms Bloom's ability to demonstrate compassion for his fellow citizens, which sets the stage for one of the most conclusive social affirmations of otherness in *Ulysses*.

The generous implications of Bloom's reflections become immediately apparent. No sooner does he begin to show concern for Stephen's well-being than he spends the rest of the text attempting to restore security and tranquility to his life. He watches over Stephen during the remainder of "Oxen," soothing his nerves after a frightening thunderclap. ("Master Bloom, at the braggart's side, spoke to him calming words to slumber his great fear, advertising how it was no other thing but a hubbub noise that he heard" [*U* 14.424–6].) Then, he follows the medical students to Nighttown, where he holds onto Stephen's money, settles the bill over the broken lamp at Bella Cohen's, and rescues him from his impending arrest by the night watch. Bloom also gives Stephen advice as they walk to the cabman's shelter in "Eumaeus," cautioning him to avoid Nighttown ("Mr Bloom … spoke a word of caution *re* the dangers of nighttown, women of ill fame and swell mobsmen" [*U* 16.61–4]), the medicos in general ("He commented adversely on the desertion of Stephen by all his pubhunting *confréres* but one, a most glaring piece of ratting on the part of his brother medicos under all the circs" [*U* 16.95–7]), and Mulligan specifically ("I wouldn't personally repose much trust in that boon companion of yours … Dr Mulligan, as a guide, philosopher and friend if I were in your shoes" [*U* 16.279–81]). These actions constitute the first acts of concern for Stephen's well-being in *Ulysses* and demonstrate the extent to which Bloom's love for Molly compels his compassion for others.

This compassion continues throughout the rest of "Eumaeus," where Bloom's interaction with Stephen at the shelter builds upon the generosity that was initiated in "Oxen." Initially, he orders Stephen coffee and food, expressing alarm that he has not eaten in over a day. ("It occurs to me you ought to sample something in the shape of solid food, say, a roll of some description" [*U* 16.332–3].) Also, Bloom engages Stephen in conversation throughout the episode, soliciting his opinions on the Italian language, transubstantiation, and the imposition of force. In contrast to Mulligan, the newspapermen in "Aeolus," and the library patrons in "Scylla," Bloom does not humor, ignore, or deride Stephen's ideas; instead, he is the first character in *Ulysses* to attempt to relate to him on an equal level, conveying a respect for his ideas that is lacking in the text. Bloom may misinterpret Stephen's responses, but at least he attempts to understand what he is saying, which continues his fascination with other people's perspectives throughout *Ulysses*. Bloom's observation that "though they didn't see eye to eye in everything … both their minds were traveling, so to speak, in the same train of thought" thus speaks to more than simply a similarity in thought (*U* 16.1579–81); it also conveys a mutual confirmation of each other's otherness despite differing opinions, which demonstrates the practical viability of Buber's community and provides Stephen with a much needed empathetic companion.

Bloom's most elaborate attempt to help Stephen concerns Molly, which is fitting considering that his paternal regard for him sprang from her anguish over Rudy. Indeed, Bloom's initial description of Molly in "Eumaeus" establishes this connection, as he explains to Stephen that "I asked you if you wrote your poetry in Italian" because her appearance and "character" embody "the Spanish type" (*U* 16.879–81). This connection between Stephen and Molly is further developed during the discussion of music at the end of the chapter, where Bloom indicates that "my wife …would have the greatest of pleasure in making your acquaintance as she is passionately attached to music of any kind" (*U* 16.1800–2). Henke is correct that "Molly is so conspicuously a part of Bloom's identity that he *must* allude to her in order to establish intimacy with Stephen" (*Sindbook* 213), but I feel that more is at play here. Since Bloom's concern for Stephen is tied to his compassion for Molly, it seems plausible that, in inviting Stephen home to (possibly) meet his wife, Bloom embarks on a charitable project designed to improve both of their lives. ("All kinds of Utopian plans were flashing through his (B's) busy brain" [*U* 16.1652].) Given his subsequent suggestion that Stephen spend the night at his house, we can assume that Bloom envisions their interactions as laying the foundation for a more substantive relationship between Stephen and the Bloom family that will benefit everybody involved.

For Stephen, the benefits of this project are obvious. By extending this invitation, Bloom certainly has Stephen's impending homelessness in mind, as he notes that "to think of him house and homeless, rooked by some landlady worse than any stepmother, was really too bad at his age" (*U* 16.1565–7). For that reason, if Stephen were to agree to stay with them, he would inherit a surrogate family and would be provided with the mother figure whose absence has weighed on him throughout the text. For Molly, the benefits are more emotional. As Bloom has noted, Molly has been significantly wounded by Rudy's death, creating a maternal lack that (along with Bloom's paternal lack caused by the same event) has significantly damaged their marriage. By basing his concern for Stephen on his empathetic love for Molly, Bloom transforms his invitation to Stephen into a means to provide Molly with the son whose loss she still mourns. Thus, when Bloom suggests the possibility of introducing Stephen to Molly, he simultaneously acts to repair her most significant emotional wound, which validates his enduring love for her and confirms the redemptive nature of the text's conclusion.

Nevertheless, Stephen rejects Bloom's invitation, and it is uncertain upon his departure whether he will ever return to 7 Eccles Street. However, the refusal of the invitation does not invalidate the generosity behind it, as "in the temporary union of the two [characters] Joyce affirms his perception of community" (*JJ* 372). In his "sorrow for [Stephen's] forepassed happiness" (*U* 14.273), Bloom becomes the only character in *Ulysses* to empathize with Stephen's condition, and his concern for him from "Oxen" to "Ithaca" constitutes the compassionate embrace of otherness that Stephen has sought throughout the text, even if he refuses it. Joyce thus concludes Bloom's interactions with others in *Ulysses* in the most loving way possible and solidifies his characterization of him as an anomaly within his oeuvre, a character whose self-love is enhanced and strengthened by an unwavering commitment to his fellow Dubliners.

A Soft Answer Turns Away Wrath

So far, we have seen how Bloom's love for those he encounters in *Ulysses* transforms him into a more productive social participant than his counterparts. However, his ability to "see another's face and listen to another's words" carries significance beyond his compassion. In addition to his consideration of others, Bloom is able to empathize with and understand broader societal problems, which compels him to theorize ways to counteract those problems and improve Dublin as a whole. In that sense, Bloom serves as more than a model of individual love; his wanderings throughout the text are replete with political implications and demonstrate the viability of his civic interactions in providing alternatives to the sociopolitical paralysis of Joyce's Dublin.

Admittedly, it is hard to take many of Bloom's numerous political reforms seriously. Indeed, it is doubtful that his idea to "give every child born five quid at compound interest up to twentyone" (*U* 8.383–4) or to "use … dogvans and goatvans for the delivery of early morning milk" (*U* 17.1719–20) will move beyond Bloom's mind, and for all the suggestions that he comes up with, the Dublin that began Bloomsday does not change to a significant degree as the night falls on June 16, 1904. This lack of substantive progress compels some scholars to read Bloom's politics ironically, concluding as Terry Eagleton does that "his admirable humanitarianism involves a set of shallow, mildly crankish schemes for social reform, fit meat for his author's satiric debunkery" (306). However, even if Bloom's specific ideas do not stand up to critical scrutiny, we cannot dismiss the viability of his political beliefs, for his sociopolitical importance lies not in his specific schemes, but in his method of interacting with others. Thus, the empathy that comprises his everyday life spills over into his participation in the civic life, which provides us with a loving reconfiguration of the model Dublin citizen.

In "Lestrygonians," Bloom ponders the concept of parallax, which he discovered in a "fascinating little book … of sir Robert Ball's" (*U* 8.110). While Bloom's consideration of the term does not extend beyond its etymology ("Par it's Greek: parallel, parallax" [*U* 8.111–2]), Gifford and Seidman's explanation of the concept demonstrates its relevance to his outlook on otherness: "the apparent displacement or the difference in apparent direction of an object as seen from two different points of view" (160). This ability to see an object from multiple perspectives encapsulates Bloom's perceptions throughout the text, as his insistence that "you must look at both sides of [a given] question" (*U* 16.1094–5) and his tendency to view others as both he and they perceive them prevent him from settling on a fixed interpretation of almost anything. While some may classify this "anythingarianism" as a "perspectival ambivalence" that "undercuts the political significance of his revisioning," Bloom's "multivocality" enables him to understand sociopolitical ideas more comprehensively and effectively than the limited perspectives of his counterparts (Castle 226).[2] He may claim that he "never exactly understood" parallax (*U* 8.110–1), but his thoughts and actions throughout *Ulysses* constitute an emphatic embrace of the concept, which better equips him to engage his fellow citizens in sociopolitical dialogue.

---

[2] Cheng also argues that "Bloom is able to hold simultaneous perspectives, to imagine being other and thus to transcend the monologic narrowness of a single, cycloptic perspective" (177).

Bloom's political parallax is introduced in conjunction with his introduction in *Ulysses*. As he leaves Dlugacz's in "Calypso," he contemplates an exotic representation of an Oriental city, noting the "awned streets," "turbaned faces," "dark caves of carpet shops," and "cries of sellers in the streets" (*U* 4.88–90). Critics have read such characterizations as indicative of Ireland's exoticizing of the Orient, arguing that this depiction of the East provides "both a *topos* and a *tropos* for 'spiritual liberation'" that ultimately "pre-structures a hierarchical relationship that always already functions the Oriental as Other" (Cheng 77; 81). In fact, Bloom's subsequent thoughts about Arthur Griffith articulate this strategy because his transition from the "strange land" (*U* 4.86) to the "homerule sun rising up in the northwest" (*U* 4.101–2) unites the Irish fascination with the East with their desire for political emancipation. However, his subsequent consideration of this "strange land" implodes the univocality of this stereotype since Bloom acknowledges that his vision of the Orient is "probably not a bit like it really. Kind of stuff you read: in the track of the sun" (*U* 4.99–100). This recognition reveals the racial fetishization implicit in such constructions of the East, as his awareness that such a city would probably only be found in books like *In The Track of the Sun* highlights the artificial nature of the stereotype (as does his placement of Turko the Terrible within his imagined village). By juxtaposing the dominant conception of the Orient with the recognition of its fictitiousness, Bloom undercuts the political viability of such static visions of the East, which challenges the racial foundations of this Irish escapist fantasy.

However, Bloom's acknowledgement does not constitute an absolute rejection of such Eastern representations since his opinion that his fantasy is "*probably* not a bit like it really" concedes that his projection could be accurate. The open-ended nature of Bloom's criticism enables him to entertain the potential legitimacy of both the popular depiction of the Orient and its critical alternative. If he were to reject the totality of this representation, he would still fall prey to the racialized rejection of Oriental otherness by performing the enlightened Western intellectual who possesses the knowledge and mastery needed to define the East, regardless of what alternative vision replaces the stereotype. Because he is able to view the East from both perspectives, Bloom dissolves the univocality of the Irish characterization of the Orient by enabling multiple, distinct versions to be potentially legitimate. His performance of representational parallax thus constitutes an embrace of Oriental otherness, allowing its essence to flourish through a dialogic engagement with difference.

This dialogic embrace is also evident in Bloom's consideration of Agendath Netaim. Similar to his earlier contemplations of Orientalism, his perusal of this advertisement contains both a description and a reversal, as his meditations on the Zionist "planters' company" (*U* 4.192) are immediately countered by his recognition that this opportunity is not for him. However, again he offers a qualified refusal of the venture, noting that his lack of interest does not negate the value of the enterprise. ("Nothing doing. Still an idea behind it" [*U* 4.200].) As before, Bloom avoids imposing an absolute value judgment either way on

Agendath Netaim, conceding that even if an economic return to the homeland is not enticing to him, it may still benefit other members of the European Jewish community. Not only does this provide another example of Bloom's acceptance of otherness, but it also constitutes a multivocal understanding of Jewishness that allows Zionism to flourish without pinning down Jewish identity to either a totalizing acceptance or rejection of the movement. Just as his earlier thoughts on Orientalism avoided the temptation to impose a univocal Western interpretation of the East, Bloom's acknowledgment that there is "still an idea behind" Agendath Netaim demonstrates his hesitancy to designate authentic and inauthentic Jewish performances, enabling his parallactic understanding of Zionism to provide space for multiple articulations of Jewish identity.

Bloom's encounter with the citizen in "Cyclops" highlights a second benefit to this Jewish parallax. When Bloom argues in Barney Kiernan's that he "belong[s] to a race" that is "plundered," "insulted," and "persecuted" (*U* 12.1467; 1470), the citizen derisively asks him if he is "talking about the new Jerusalem" (*U* 12.1473). This reference demonstrates the univocal interpretation of Jewishness that flourishes within Dublin, as the Jewish Bloom's references to racial persecution can be interpreted only as an endorsement of Zionism. Bloom's parallactic attitude towards the "new Jerusalem" counteracts this racial totalization because its affirmation of multiple, legitimate Jewish identities introduces a fluid representation of Jewishness that can evade generic attacks based on static stereotypes.[3] For that reason, when Bloom responds to the citizen's slur by arguing that he is "talking about injustice" (*U* 12.1474), he demonstrates the ability to attack anti-Semitism without being subject to a critique of Zionism, which enables him to assert his Jewish identity outside the parameters of the citizen's discriminatory discourse. Bloom's advocacy of parallax thus demonstrates the sociopolitical benefits of Buber's affirmation of "many-faced otherness," and his resulting dialogic approach to ethnic identity enables him to negotiate his position as a productive citizen within the Dublin body politic.

The religious implications of Bloom's parallax are not limited to his dialogic acceptance of Judaism. Indeed, his contemplation of the "sermon by the very reverend John Conmee S.J. on saint Peter Claver S.J. and the African Mission" in "Lotus Eaters" conveys a broader skepticism towards organized religion's imposition of faith on non-believing populations (*U* 8.322–3). Recognizing that Catholicism and Protestantism promote such conversion "to the true religion" (*U* 8.325–6), Bloom considers this practice from the targeted population's

[3] Marilyn Reizbaum's reading of Bloom's consideration of Agendath Netaim strengthens this reading of Bloom's Jewish parallax. She contends that Bloom's noting that there was "an idea behind" Agendath Netaim despite it not being for him "signals both his sense that he does not belong there, and a sense of connection" (22). This dialogic reaction thus allows Bloom to construct a Jewish identity that includes both an embrace of and ambivalence towards Zionism. This enables him to craft his position on the movement in a more nuanced manner than the citizen can comprehend, which later enables him to use Jewish parallax to counter his rival's anti-Semitic barbs in "Cyclops."

perspective, wondering "how they explain" the mission to "save China's millions" to the "heathen Chinee" (*U* 8.326–7). This perspective contrasts with the importance Catholic Ireland places on missionary work, as his recognition that the candidates for conversion would regard the religion as "rank heresy" conveys an understanding of religious otherness that diverges from the general apathy towards it (*U* 8.327). Not only does this understanding enable the accommodation of multiple legitimate faiths, but it also promotes a broader critique of imperialism because the suppression of subaltern expression that Bloom attributes to missionary practices is at the heart of imperial strategies of conquest. His attempt to view conversion through the perspective of the converted thus constitutes a religious performance of parallax whose affirmation of otherness extends far beyond the Catholic and Protestant arenas.

However, Bloom's criticism of the sermon does not carry with it a dismissal of Catholicism as a whole. While he empathizes with the Chinese who are suppressed by an imperial religious agenda, his reactions to the mass he attends in "Lotus Eaters" convey an attempt to understand the Catholic ideas and practices that he witnesses. He tries to interpret the initials on the priest's garments ("Letters on his back: I.N.R.I? No: I.H.S." [*U* 5.372]), contemplates the type of bread used for the Eucharist ("Something like those mazzoth" [*U* 5.358]), and approves of the priest being the sole person to drink the wine ("otherwise they'd have one old booser worse than another coming along, cadging for a drink" [*U* 5.390–2]). Bloom also recognizes that Catholics experience a spiritual awakening through the Eucharist, noting that there is a "kind of kingdom of God is within you feel" within the communion that "makes them feel happy" (*U* 5.361; 359). Similar to his contemplation of the "heathen Chinee['s]" attitude towards conversion, Bloom tries to experience Catholicism through the viewpoint of the Catholic, which avoids promoting his religious perspective over his counterparts by acknowledging the legitimacy of others adhering to the religion even though he does not. Even if he finds "the whole atmosphere" of the mass to be "queer" (*U* 5.392–3), his repeated assertion that the "big idea behind it" is "perfectly right" echoes his earlier concessions of the legitimacy of Zionism despite his ambivalence towards the movement (*U* 5.360–1; 393). Such an attitude towards Catholicism solidifies Bloom's adherence to parallax, and his ability to "affirm the [people he] struggle[s] with" constitutes a dialogic embrace that is both socially and politically productive.

The most significant benefit to Bloom's multivocality is the peaceful coexistence promoted by his accommodation of conflicting viewpoints. While some may argue that the absurdity of his ideas makes it hard to take his politics seriously, Bloom's significance as a political agent is not contained in his specific beliefs, but rather in his commitment to a dialogic concept of citizenship that contrasts with the inflexible paralysis of his body politic. We have witnessed the discriminatory implications of the univocal discourses that pervade Joyce's Ireland, but we must also consider the practical limitations of such conflicting, uncompromising factions coexisting with each other. Given the tendency of these groups to dismiss dissenting voices, it is difficult to determine how Ireland could function as a viable nation when its inhabitants are too busy fighting each other to push for meaningful change.[4] Bloom's adherence to parallax becomes an alternative to this sociopolitical paralysis, as his ability to consider the perspectives of others and to acknowledge the legitimacy of belief structures that he does not share enable him to interact peacefully with his fellow Dubliners despite their differing perspectives. Thus, Bloom's parallactic approach to civic life verifies Buber's "basic principle of marriage," as the individual affirmations of otherness that comprise his loving reactions towards the people he encounters translates into the "vital acknowledgment of many-faced otherness" that not only makes Bloom embody the exemplary Irish citizen, but also transforms him into a viable model for the body politic as a whole.

A significant criticism of Bloom's parallactic politics comes from Gregory Castle, who contends that the "anythingarianism" that comprises his thoughts and interactions throughout *Ulysses* "makes it difficult to discover any kind of ideological consistency" in his beliefs. He feels that Bloom's willingness to accept multiple, conflicting viewpoints "means that his attitudes are as often complicit with as they are resistant to the social authorities of colonialism, anthropology, and the Revival" (226). While it is true that Bloom avoids giving an absolute endorsement of any of the ideologies described in Joyce's text, that does not mean that his ideas suffer from irresolution or contradiction. In fact, even though Bloom considers his surroundings from multiple perspectives, the foundation for this approach promotes a consistent, ethico-political belief system that shields him from the co-optive hazards of "anythingarianism."

To illustrate this "ideological consistency," I call attention to one of the most quoted passages in *Ulysses*: "it's no use, says he. Force, hatred, history, all that. That's not life for men and women, insult and hatred. And everybody knows that it's the very opposite of that that is really life … Love" (*U* 12.1481–3; 1485). David Ayres dismisses Bloom's endorsement of love here, reading it as an "equivocal" advocacy that "suggests the severe limitation of the secularized notion of love" (78), but as we read Bloom's actions with respect to Buber, we see the consistent, loving foundations of his individual and social interactions. For that reason, even if Bloom entertains multiple, distinct ideas, that does not mean that he lacks an "ideological consistency." In fact, his "anythingarianism" conveys that consistency, as his empathetic acceptance of otherness constitutes an unswerving endorsement of community and his refusal to reject any position completely shows how love can

---

[4] In fact, the aftermath of the Anglo-Irish war demonstrates the perils of civic participation that dismisses dissenting voices, as the disputes over the specific parameters of the Irish Free State immediately caused a bloody civil war and a socially repressive Free State under Eamon De Valera's leadership. These events eventually resulted in the Irish Republic in its current form, but the promotion of genuine dialogue and compromise in the initial construction of the Free State could have also created an accommodating Republic without the bloodshed and repression of the 1920s and 1930s. Joyce's criticism of the violence of post-independence Ireland in *Finnegans Wake* can then be seen as a confirmation of the perils of the sociopolitical refusals of otherness we see throughout *Ulysses*.

create a body politic that enables multiple, distinct ideologies to thrive. Not only does this approach evade Castle's fears of co-option (since "the social authorities of colonialism" cannot exist in a community that encourages otherness),[5] but it also shows how a consistent commitment to love in everyday interactions can lay the groundwork for effective civic participation. Thus, Bloom's explicit endorsement of love constitutes the empathetic political advocacy that arises from an everyday commitment to compassion, transforming Bloom into Joyce's model for the amorous Dublin citizen.

It is fitting that Bloom's endorsement of this loving community occurs in "Cyclops," as the conflict between Joyce's amorous citizen and a xenophobic patriot named the citizen allows Bloom to negotiate his civic identity within a hostile environment. While his advocacy of love does not occur until half-way through the chapter, the groundwork for this advocacy is evident throughout the episode, as the way that he approaches his interactions with the other bar patrons demonstrates the empathetic accommodation behind his politics. Initially, Bloom's "argument" with the citizen about "the brothers Sheares and Wolfe Tone beyond on Arbour Hill ..." shows his commitment to parallax (*U* 12.498–9). While the barfly's digressions prevent us from following a lot of this conversation, we learn enough to recognize the disparity between Bloom's and the citizen's approaches to this political debate. We may not learn the substance of any of Bloom's responses, but the narrator's mockery of his "*but don't you see?* and *but on the other hand*" (*U* 12.515) enable us to view his "contributions" as "continual attempt[s] to induce the monocular Dubliners to view objects and issues from multiple angles" (Sicker 75). Even though he seems to disagree with the citizen's interpretation of history, he never attempts to force his viewpoint on him. Instead, he tries to persuade the citizen to entertain his position, using phrases like "on the other hand" to compel a side-by-side comparison of conflicting versions of history. Such a strategy reveals Bloom's ability to articulate a dissenting point of view without it constituting a totalizing rejection of his adversary, which enables the spirit of accommodation to emerge from a contentious political exchange.

However, the citizen's response quashes that accommodating spirit. Rather than entertain Bloom's alternative interpretations of "Robert Emmet and die for your country" (*U* 12.499–500), the citizen raises a toast to "the memory of the dead" (*U* 12.519), which buries Bloom's responses under a generic performance of national pride similar to the maudlin reactions to "The Croppy Boy" (especially since the barfly notes that the citizen toasts while "glaring at Bloom" [*U* 12.520]). Then, when Bloom tries to compel him to acknowledge his arguments ("You don't quite grasp my point ... What I mean is ...." [*U* 12.522]), the citizen silences his adversary by exclaiming, "*Sinn Fein! ... Sinn fein amhain!* The friends we love are by our side and the foes we hate before us" (*U* 12.523–4).[6] Whereas Bloom

[5] hooks similarly notes the incompatibility of love and colonialism by arguing that "domination cannot exist in any social situation where a love ethic prevails ... When love is present the desire to dominate and exercise power cannot rule the day" (98).

[6] Translated: "Ourselves! ... Ourselves alone!" (Gifford and Seidman 333).

attempts to persuade his counterpart to consider the validity of his arguments, the citizen responds with patriotic slogans that serve little purpose beyond excluding his opponent's voice. Not only is his interjection specifically uttered to silence Bloom, but his use of the Gaelic League motto "ourselves alone" imposes a border between him and Bloom that denies the legitimacy of the latter's voice. When we recall the rumor that Bloom gave Arthur Griffith the idea for *Sinn Fein*, this conversation provides us with two competing versions of the movement and shows us how exclusionary rhetoric undermines more accommodating forms of political organization.

This comparison between political exclusion and accommodation continues in the famous conversation over the definition of a nation. Here, Bloom's exasperated explanation of a nation being "the same people living in the same place … or also living in different places" counteracts the bar patrons' attempts to disqualify him as a legitimate citizen in two ways (*U* 12.1422–3; 1428). First, it demonstrates the ambivalence towards intolerance at the heart of this nationalist discourse. While the discussion of what constitutes a nation is itself an important aspect of "Cyclops," we should remember that the question is a response to Bloom's contention that "all the history of the world is full of [persecution]. Perpetuating national hatred among nations" (*U* 12.1417–8). Bloom may have brought the idea of nationhood to the bar's attention, but by reading the resulting discussion with respect to the observation that initiated it, we see that the question of what a nation constitutes is largely a non sequitur designed to humiliate Bloom. Since Bloom's main point was to illustrate the predominance of persecution, the bar patrons' interrogation of his nationhood dismisses his argument, which also performs the "national hatred among nations" within Barney Kiernan's because the fact that Bloom does not "know what a nation means" defines him as an outsider and justifies his exclusion (*U* 12.1418–9). Similar to the citizen's cry of "*Sinn fein amhain*," this discussion combats Bloom's argument with a generic nationalist tactic that reveals the racial hatred behind its univocal politics.

Second, Bloom's definition of nationhood constitutes a political performance of parallax. Cheng interprets his characterization of a nation as "a people generally within a geographical location" (211–2), but I think Bloom's definition means more than that. By articulating a national classification that includes "the same people" simultaneously "living in the same place" and "living in different places," Bloom proposes a broad definition of nationhood that contains conflicting examples at its foundation. This parallactic definition accomplishes two objectives: it transforms nationhood into an affirmation of otherness since difference is granted the same legitimacy as sameness;[7] and it undermines the ability of xenophobia to use artificial borders to exclude outsiders since the outsider has now been defined

[7] Cheng notes that "Bloom's answer refuses either to hierarchize or to 'imagine' an essentialized community, but rather allows for personal or ethnic difference and heterogeneity without denying the status of 'citizens' or 'nationals' to anyone within the community" (212).

as the citizen. Thus, the univocality of the nation discussion collapses under the weight of national parallax, and we are left with an accommodating construction of nationhood that complements Bloom's stance against injustice, providing the necessary foundation for his subsequent advocacy of love.

As I mentioned earlier, Bloom's endorsement of love as "the opposite of hatred" has been dismissed as naïve, sentimental cant that demonstrates Joyce's satire. However, reading Bloom's advocacy with respect to Buber's community allows us to see a practical basis for love in his discourse against "force, hatred, [and] history." Indeed, Bloom here does not articulate a saccharinely righteous justification for "insult and hatred" "not [being] life for men and women"; instead, he dismisses those qualities on the basis that they are "no[t] use[ful]," that sociopolitical interaction based on hate does nothing to improve the conditions of the body politic. He may also convey moral objections to "force, hatred, [and] history," but his pragmatic criticisms dominate both his argumentation in "Cyclops" and his recounting of that exchange in "Eumaeus." ("I resent violence and intolerance in any shape or form. It never reaches anything or stops anything ... It's a patent absurdity on the face of it to hate people because they live round the corner and speak another vernacular" [*U* 16.1099–1103].) By limiting his endorsement of love to a pragmatic affirmation of equal social interaction ("It's all very fine to boast of mutual superiority but what about mutual equality" [*U* 16.1098–9]), Bloom demonstrates the futility of ideologies that spend more time fighting each other than improving their social conditions, which avoids the romanticization that would render him susceptible to charges of sentimentality. Bloom thus grounds his political ideology in a sensible affirmation of otherness and articulates a dialogic, cooperative politics of love that even his author could endorse.

Bloom's amorous dialogism is supported further by the "love loves to love love" passage that occurs later in "Cyclops" (*U* 12.1493). While one could read this interruption as skewering Bloom's endorsement of love, it is important to recognize not only that the "interpolated 'texts'" parody a "sentimentalized version of history" that is absent from "Bloom's words" (Lawrence 116), but also that Bloom left the tavern before this interruption occurs and is thus immune to any criticism as a result of it. Instead, what is being satirized is the citizen's mockery of "universal love" in his subsequent conversation with John Wyse Nolan (*U* 12.1489). When Nolan questions this derision ("Isn't that what we're told. Love your neighbour"), the citizen scoffs at "love, moya!" and dismisses Bloom as "a nice pattern of a Romeo and Juliet" (*U* 12.1490–2). The fact that the "love loves to love love" interruption occurs immediately after this insult demonstrates that this narrative commentary mocks the sentimentality behind the citizen's mockery rather than Bloom's pragmatic endorsement of love.[8] Thus, the

[8] Manganiello similarly contends that "the simplicity of [Bloom's endorsement of love], and the tautological parable ('Love loves to love love') which follows, does not, as is sometimes maintained, reduce the authority or genuineness of Bloom's testament, even if Joyce allows it to be mocked. The attempt of the two narrators in 'Cyclops' at mockery – by either sentimentalising or coarsening the meaning of love – is unconvincing" (232).

citizen has ignored the practical justifications for Bloom's position, choosing to continue to exclude "the new apostle to the gentiles" through his xenophobic lens of national pride (*U* 12.1489), and by following the one-eyed citizen's mockery of "universal love" with this parodic response, Joyce uses the limited, monocular nature of his Cyclops's nationalist sentimentality to highlight the compassionate accommodation of Bloom's loving politics.

The inclusivity of Bloom's politics is confirmed by his religious argumentation at the chapter's conclusion. As Cunningham ushers Bloom out of Barney Kiernan's, the frustrated canvasser responds to the citizen's anti-Semitic barbs by exclaiming that "your God was a jew. Christ was a jew like me" (*U* 12.1808–9). This outburst encapsulates the inclusiveness that Bloom has championed throughout the episode by using a parallactic religious argument to emphasize the interconnectedness of Catholicism and Judaism. Instead of promoting his Jewish identity over the Christian perspective of the citizen, Bloom argues that the citizen's Messiah "was a jew like [Bloom]," which connects the two combatants through a web of religious inclusivity. When we recall Nolan's earlier articulation of Jesus's commandment to "love your neighbour," this inclusive web becomes infused with amorous implications, demonstrating that the love Bloom champions transcends religious and political differences and accommodates even the most disparate belief systems. The citizen may try to silence Bloom's parallactic outburst by attempting to "brain that bloody jewman for using the holy name" (*U* 12.1811), but Bloom's successful escape reveals this final exclusion to be unsuccessful. The "ascen[sion]" of "ben Bloom Elijah" (*U* 12.1916) at the conclusion of "Cyclops" thus simultaneously connotes both the ascension of Joyce's amorous citizen over the citizen and the decisive victory of amorous parallax over the discriminatory tactics of monocular nationalism.

The full measure of the inclusiveness of this love ethic is confirmed in "Nausicaa," where Bloom's reflections on his argument with the citizen demonstrate the accommodating potential of that ethic. As he recalls this exchange, Bloom's thoughts gradually shift from confrontation to concession. Not only does he assume partial culpability for the escalation of their argument ("Mistake to hit back" [*U* 13.1217]), but he also entertains possible reasons for the citizen's attacks in order to moderate his adversary's malice ("perhaps not to hurt he meant" [*U* 13.1220]). This justification for the citizen's actions thus confirms the innate inclusiveness of Bloom's parallactic civic identity because he is willing to entertain a divergent perspective of their confrontation in order to ensure that the Dublin body politic can accommodate both citizens. Indeed, his characterization of the dispute as "gentle repartee" in "Eumaeus" (*U* 16.1637–8) proves this desire for accommodation by re-presenting his persecution in Barney Kiernan's as a friendly discussion of dissenting viewpoints. Through his reflections on his argument with the citizen, Bloom signifies his desire to view civic interaction within Dublin in the most cooperative manner possible, confirming the ability of his endorsement of love to provide space for even the most opposed sociopolitical agents.

Bloom's loving politics is thus more compellingly demonstrated through his interactions with others than through any explicit advocacy of "the opposite of hatred." He may not offer a concrete platform for a politically viable love, but by encouraging the consideration of multiple perspectives, Bloom expands the parameters of civic life to provide space for numerous, distinct performances of Irish citizenship, extending a compassionate embrace of "many-faced otherness" that counteracts "violence and intolerance." In that sense, it is not the specifics of Bloom's proposals, but rather his model of civic interaction, that reveals the efficacy of his politics. He may champion an absurd agenda during his coronation in "Circe," but not even the "three acres and a cow for all children of nature" can distract us from his desire for the "union of all, jew, moslem and gentile" (*U* 15.1686–8). Thus, the loving foundations of Bloom's advocacy of the "new Bloomusalem" supplant the racial hatred behind the citizen's equating him with the "new Jerusalem," and the fact that he locates "the new Bloomusalem in the Nova Hibernia of the future" enables Joyce to use Bloom's amorous parallax to envision a more accommodating Irish community (*U* 15.1544–5). For that reason, one does not have to erect "a colossal edifice with crystal roof, built in the shape of a huge pork kidney" to herald the "new Bloomusalem" (*U* 15.1548–9), for that community emerges from the compassion of Bloom's everyday interactions. His empathy in *Ulysses* thus provides a microcosmic examination of how the affirmation of difference behind a politics of love moves past the "old pap of racial hatred" and enables a "soft answer" to "turn away wrath" (*U* 16.1085–6).

****

According to Ellmann, Bloom's compassion towards others throughout *Ulysses* articulates the central theme of the text: "Casual kindness overcomes unconscionable power" (*JJ* 379). While this observation is true, it only scratches the surface of the empathy needed to counteract the discriminatory sociopolitical system that Joyce describes. His interactions with the Dubliners he encounters are certainly respectful and courteous, but the full extent of the affection he displays transcends the parameters of "casual kindness." Bloom thus validates Buber's contention that the "basic principle of marriage" coincides with the "vital acknowledgment of many-faced otherness" needed for meaningful civic interaction, as his ability to love Molly despite her adultery is indicative of his broader ability to dialogically engage a body politic that constantly tries to exclude him, and the fact that Joyce highlights Bloom's love as reciprocated through Molly's "yes" magnifies the dialogical potential of this amorous community. This desire to realize the "overcoming of *otherness* in living unity" transforms Bloom's advocacy of the "opposite of hatred" into the love ethic needed to promote dialogue and cooperation within a discriminatory and paralytic collective.

The Blooms thus convincingly demonstrate that true love "does not offer insurance against loneliness and suffering," but Joyce would never validate a loving bond that was not "characterized by grandeur as well as by misery … greatness as well as wretchedness" (Rubin 59; 55). Instead, both characters retain the capacity to love even as their present bond risks crumbling under adultery, which makes them the best equipped of Joyce's protagonists to maintain a dialogic relationship with both each other and their community. While the narcissistic lovers of Joyce's earlier fiction fail to fulfill their individual and political desires, the reciprocal affection of the Blooms' marriage enables both lovers to envision a reconciliation that extends beyond June 17, 1904. Thus, the progression from the paralysis of *Dubliners* to the concluding "Yes" of *Ulysses* allows Joyce to articulate a sustained love ethic that provides a practical alternative to the alienation of everyday Dublin.

Of course, the Joycean oeuvre does not end with "Penelope," and *Finnegans Wake* seems to indicate that the author has regained his nausea over the "lying drivel" about "love for ever." Not only does the Earwicker marriage seem inevitably doomed by Humphrey Chimpden Earwicker's scandal in Phoenix Park and his lustful advances towards his daughter Issy, but discovering a clear, consistent endorsement of a reciprocal *Wakean* love seems practically impossible due to the experimental nature of Joyce's dreamtext. Indeed, the *Wake* defies traditional narrative explication through polyglot *Wakese* and characters that morph and blend into each other, and the fact that the novel's events seem to be presented through the fragmented perceptions of an unidentified dreamer renders any sustained examination of its love "plots" even more tenuous. Nevertheless, Joyce's love ethic remains a vital component of his book of the night, and in fact his dreamtext provides a rigorous examination of love, as the seemingly random, contradictory vignettes evoke the dreamer's subconscious grappling with the numerous potential encounters between self and other, and the constant character slippages highlight the centrality of otherness and the interconnectedness of humanity within Joyce's narrative.[9] Thus, while the ensuing investigation of *Finnegans Wake* may tread close to the conceptual analyses that the text frequently elides, Buber's writings enable us to examine love's importance to the *Wake* in a manner consistent with the text's innovative approach, transforming the novel into the necessary coda to the Joycean love ethic.

9 Utell similarly argues that "with the writing of *Finnegans Wake*, man and woman as mythic, their story one of infinite renewal, their marriage one of cosmic union: this may be the final, radically ethical move Joyce makes, in and of love" (149). Philip Kitcher also contends that "many of the problems and predicaments that whirl through the dream center on the value of mutual love and marriage" (52).

Chapter 10
Amatory Darwinism in *Finnegans Wake*

Towards the end of the "Mime of Mick, Nick, and the Maggies," romantic rivals Glugg and Chuff fight each other after Glugg's final attempt to guess the heliotrope riddle and win the hand of Izod. As spectators, Izod and the twenty-eight Floras anxiously watch the battle, their vision obscured by the approaching night. Envisioning the angelic Chuff to be a more ideal suitor than the repulsive Glugg, the "treegrown girls" sum up the romantic stakes of this battle by claiming that "one's only owned by naturel rejection. Charley, you're my darwing. So sing they sequent the assent of man" (*FW* 252.27–9). These allusions to Charles Darwin brilliantly elucidate the amatory stakes of the "Mime," highlighting Glugg and Chuff's skirmish not simply as a suitor test for Izod's hand, but also as the "naturel rejection" of the outcast Glugg and the "assent" of the angelic beau ideal Chuff in a violent, evolutionary war. Especially considering that the darkness clouds the Floras' ability to "know twigst timidy twomeys, for gracious sake, who is artthoudux from whose heterotropic" (*FW* 252.19–21), and that Joyce ironically deflates this battle by locating it within the Earwicker children's nightly play, what emerges from the "Mime" is a critique of amatory Darwinism that illuminates the vehement rejection of otherness at the heart of idealized romance, casting the sibling rivalries of *Finnegans Wake* in the interrogations of narcissism in Joyce's previous love plots.

Joyce's portrayals of sibling rivalry are thus exemplary extensions of his career-long interrogation of narcissism. Indeed, Shem and Shaun's battles for the affection of Issy and the Maggies not only parody the sentimental romances that Joyce derides, but they also foreground the rejections of otherness that comprise the narcissistic plots of his earlier fiction. By creating Shem and Shaun as warring contraries and by positioning Issy's monologues as addresses to her mirror image, Joyce locates these characters' amatory rivalries within Buber's "kingdom of the lame-winged Eros" where Shaun and Issy either reject their beloveds or transform them into reflections of themselves, and Shem responds to his rejection through withdrawals similar to Stephen's self-exile. However, rather than simply replicating the narcissistic quests of Joyce's earlier protagonists, the *Wake*'s shifting dreamtext not only amplifies the implications of these amatory conflicts to demonstrate the violent repercussions of narcissism, but it also results in fluctuating characterizations of the siblings that enable the dreamer to continually interrogate amatory Darwinism through each cycle of the narrative.

Nircississies

Perhaps the character most explicitly tied to the *Wake*'s amatory themes is Issy. Not only is she at the heart of the romantic rivalry between Shem and Shaun, but her status as the two temptresses that precipitate HCE's fall in Phoenix Park and as a younger version of ALP places Issy in the middle of every romantic conflict in the text. At first glance, Issy's actions as the *Wake*'s primary love object appear to be the embodiment of narcissism, as her tempting of both brothers seemingly casts her as a coquette who is more interested in strengthening Shem's and Shaun's adoration of her than she is in actual love, and the fact that she spends most of her time admiring her mirror or in the company of twenty-eight Maggies who are also reflections of her seems to bolster a characterization of Issy who is only interested in others who are literally reflections of herself. However, while many critics have read Issy as indicative of such narcissism,[1] Joyce's multifaceted portrayal of her actually provides a criticism of the mirroring and self-absorption that she is traditionally read as upholding. Through the numerous iterations of her roles as "leap year girl" and mirror image, Issy's negotiation of her status as love object undercuts the sentimentality behind the relationships of which she is a part and forces a rigorous examination of the relationship between others.

Issy's narcissism is most evident in her appearances with/as the Maggies, twenty-eight replicas of the Earwicker daughter who are obsessed with sentimental romance and echo Issy's tempting advances towards the brothers. The Maggies' significance to the *Wake*'s love plot is effectively highlighted in I.6's quiz show, where the Shaunish contestant answers the Shemish emcee's eighth question "And how war yore maggies?" by replying:

> They war loving, they love laughing, they laugh weeping, they weep smelling, they smell smiling, they smile hating, they hate thinking, they think feeling, they feel tempting, they tempt daring, they dare waiting, they wait taking, they take thanking, they thank seeking, as born for lorn in lore of love to live and wive by wile and rile by rule of ruse 'reathed rose and hose hol'd home, yeth cometh elope year, coach and four, Sweet Peck-at-my-Heart picks one man more. (*FW* 142.30–143.2)

This question thus implicates the Maggies in the *Wake*'s amatory Darwinism. Shem's questioning how the Maggies "war" instead of "were" directly equates

[1] Adaline Glasheen contends that the *Wake*'s "ingenue lead, Issy is a triumph of feminine imbecility and sexual attraction – catty, inconsequent, affected, blithe, and treacherous – Gerty MacDowell (reincarnation of a Greek princess) playing at being an Irish princess and every young temptress everywhere" (138). Kitcher also notes that "at several points in the *Wake*, we hear Issy's voice, and it is hardly the voice of innocent girlhood; rather it oozes sex and narcissism, it is calculated both to arouse and to tease" (61). Finally, Norris argues that "by combining Isabel's role as a temptress with the mirror-image double, Joyce has utilized the narcissistic components of her characterization to create a further ingenious and subtle example of triangular desire in one of the major configurations of *Finnegans Wake*: the old man with two girl-loves" (*Decentered* 53–4).

these manifestations of Issy with combat, and Shaun's reply that they "war loving" highlights love as their explicit battleground. Specifically, the fact that they are "born for lorn in lore of love" not only ties their identity to the legacy of romance, but also leaves them "for lorn" instead of bringing any happiness, and the fact that they "live and wive by wile and rile by rule of ruse" casts their roles in the "lore of love" as "wi[v]e[s]" who snare potential suitors through duplicity, which is strengthened by Shaun's reference to their "feel[ing] tempting." Furthermore, the Maggies "smile hating," which not only reveals these symbols of affections to be further "ruse[s]," but also connotes an explicit rejection of their beloveds as a key component of their amatory "war." Joyce thus ties their gushing over the Shaunish characters in the text to futile sentimental longings for marriage and foregrounds the rejection of otherness at the heart of their overtures throughout the *Wake*, and the fact that Shaun's answer concludes with references to the "elope year" not only confirms the Maggies' marital sentimentality, but also evokes the "leap year girl," tying Issy to this narcissism.

The Maggies' perpetuation of amatory Darwinism is demonstrated by several episodes featuring the Earwicker twins and the twenty-nine girls. For example, in the Festy King trial in I.4, the "maidies of the bar" promote the Shaunish eye, ear, nose and throat witness over his Shemish rival (*FW* 92.11). That they "fluttered and flattered round the willingly pressed … stincking thyacinths through his curls (O feen! O deur!) and bringing busses to his cheeks" demonstrate their construction of the witness as a stereotypical romantic hero, an idealization that is enhanced by their equating "Show'm the Posed" with "their masculine Oirisher Rose" (*FW* 92.13–4, 16–8). Ironically, the girls' fawning over Shaun consumes his otherness, as their "pos[ing]" the witness as a virile champion replaces his specific identity with an idealized romantic hero reminiscent of the "Araby" narrator's adoration of Mangan's sister and Stephen's idealization of the bird girl. Also, whereas "Show'm the Posed" is fawned over by the girls, his Shemish counterpart repulses the "twofromthirty advocatesses within echo," who demand "Shun[ning] the Punman" (*FW* 93.7; 12–3). The fact that Shem is exiled not only for his flatulence, but also for his testimony against Festy King, magnifies the Maggies' disdain for his dissenting persona ("You and your gift of your gaft of your garbage abaht our Farvver!" [*FW* 93.19–20]),[2] and their branding him a "fenemine Parish Poser" directly contrasts with the "masculine Oirisher Rose" and further shows how the promotion of the ideal hero concomitantly rejects the unworthy, degenerative rival (*FW* 93.14). Thus, the "maidies[']" reactions to the witnesses transforms the Festy King trial into a site of amatory Darwinism, and the fact that the girls' adoration of Shaun carries with it the expulsion of Shem demonstrates the consequences of this amatory "assent of Man."

This amatory Darwinism is strengthened throughout the "Mime" in II.1. Here, Patrick A. McCarthy compellingly characterizes the chapter's "Angels and Devils"

---

[2] McHugh also notes that "Farvver" evokes "farver," which is Danish for "colours," so Shem is also rejected for his "garbage about our colours," which anticipates his attempts to guess the color of their underwear in the "Mime" and further ties the two sites of amatory Darwinism together (93).

game as "a suitor test" (*Riddles* 141), as Izod repeatedly tempts the Shemish Glugg to guess the colors of the Floras' underwear to win her love. However, the "suitor test" is rigged: "The youngly delightsome frilles-in-pleyrs are now showen drawen, if bud one, or, if in florileague, drawens up consociately at the hinder sight of their commoner guardia. Her boy fiend or theirs, if they are so pluriellled, cometh up as a trapadour, sinking how he must fand for himself by gazework what their colours wear as they are all showen drawens up" (*FW* 224.22–6). While Glugg stands a chance of guessing correctly, this description of the game demonstrates that its main purpose is to persecute the suitor. By describing the Floras and Izod as "in florileague" against the "boy fiend," the narrative not only shows that Glugg "must fand for himself" against the girls, but it also depicts the devilish Glugg as an enemy by deeming him a "boy fiend" instead of a "boyfriend" (and the fact that he is Izod's "boy fiend or theirs, if they are so pluriellled" pits Glugg against all twenty-nine girls and magnifies the conspiratorial theme). This dismissal is developed by the reference to Glugg as a "trapadour," which, while punning on his troubadour potential, both contains the "trapdoor" that devilish characters "[sink]" through in pantomimes (McHugh 224) and is spelled "trap a dour," which identifies Glugg as a dourly castoff being led into a trap. Thus, Glugg's inability to guess "heliotrope" results in his humiliation and exile, as the Floras' "tittertit of hilarity" while Glugg formulates his answer gives way to cries of "Off to clutch, Glugg! … Forweal!" when he guesses incorrectly. Their subsequent declaration that "all's rice with their whorl!" thus demonstrates the matrimonial sentimentality behind their dancing around Chuff and shows that Glugg's banishment means that all's right with their world, which confirms the rejection of otherness behind their suitor test (*FW* 225.29–31).

Additionally, the Floras' promotion of Chuff over Glugg strengthens the amatory Darwinism of the "Mime." Not only do Glugg's failed guesses result in his exile, but the Floras' repeated denigrations of his lowness demonstrate his expulsion to stem from "naturel rejection." This "rejection" is evident in the initial descriptions of Glugg, as the Floras' disgust over "all the freightfullness whom he inhebited after his colline born janitor" frames the degenerative characteristics Glugg inherited from HCE through references to Dion Boucicault's *The Colleen Bawn* to dismiss him as the devolved, inferior suitor (*FW* 224.10–1). Similarly, the fact that the Floras follow each repulsion of Glugg by celebrating "their princesome handsome angeline chiuff" demonstrates their continued obsession with casting the latter as the beau ideal of popular romantic fiction (*FW* 239.29). Reminiscent of I.4, the Floras praise Chuff as "the finehued, the fairhailed, the farahead," and they "[allaud] to him by all the licknames in the litany with the terms in which no little dulsy nayer ever thinks about implying except to her future's year and sending him perfume most praypuffs to setisfire more than to teasim" (*FW* 234.21–7). By "allauding to him" by names that women only use to refer to their "future's year" (implying "future sire" or husband), the Floras perpetuate the sentimental marriage fantasy behind their celebration of Chuff, and the fact that they seek to "setisfire" (or satisfy) Chuff rather than "teasim" confirms that they are simply manipulating Glugg and that Chuff is the only worthy winner of this test.[3] Their reference to *Don Quixote* bolsters this romanticizing of the "Mime," as the Floras cast themselves as the Dulcineas ("dulsy nayer") of their personal romantic tale. Again, Joyce demonstrates the Floras' consumption of Chuff's otherness through this sentimentalizing of the "Mime," as the Floras replace his specific agency with the "whitemost" and "goldenest" of "all the green heroes everwore coton breiches" (*FW* 234.8–10), but this time, Joyce deflates the Floras' fantasy, not simply through the *Don Quixote* allusions that cast Chuff as the misguided champion of fictitious causes, but also through the sexually charged rhetoric that dominates the Floras' adoration of Chuff and punctures their pretentions to marital piety. Thus, Joyce reveals that the girls' sentimentalism is founded on a narcissistic lust that misrecognizes the object of their affection and compromises the promotion of their beau ideal.

Furthermore, the Floras' adoration of Chuff betrays the violent rejection of otherness at the heart of their amatory pursuits since their "licknames" for their ideal lover directly promote his superiority over Glugg's repulsiveness. Indeed, their description of Chuff as "finehued" and "farahead" put him directly in opposition to the dark Glugg, and their rejection of Glugg's otherness at the heart of their "allauding" of Chuff is confirmed in their subsequent declaration: "unclean you art not. Outcaste that are not. Leperstower, the karman's loki, has not blanched at our pollution and your intercourse at ninety legsplits does not defile. Untouchable is not the scarecrown is on you. You are pure. You are pure. You are in your puerity" (*FW* 237.21–5). By describing Glugg as "unclean," "outcaste," and "untouchable," and celebrating Chuff's "puerity" as the necessary alternative, the Floras confirm the Darwinistic implications of the "Mime," as the primary purpose of the suitor test is to prove that "Lord Chuffy's sky sheraph and Glugg's got to swing" (*FW* 226.19–20). Thus, Joyce not only demonstrates that the game is a doomed sentimental fantasy, but he also highlights the exclusionary logic behind such sentimental romances, which confirms the "Mime" as an important site of his critique of narcissism.

However, whereas Issy joins the Maggies in the temptation of both brothers, her actions do not always coincide with those of her counterparts. She does bait Glugg into participating in each iteration of II.1's "trapadour" games, but she also experiences regret when Glugg is inevitably banished: "Poor Isa sits a glooming so gleaming in the gloaming; the tincelles a touch tarnished wind no lovelinoise awound her swan's. Hey, lass! Woefear gleam she so glooming, this pooripathete I solde? Her beauman's gone of a cool. Be good enough to symperise" (*FW* 226.4–8). Of course, Izod's "glooming" is not purely out of sympathy for her "[beauman]," but also because "she's promised he'd eye her" (*FW* 225.32–3), and she does quickly take comfort in the knowledge that "she'll meet anew fiancy,

3 McHugh quotes Filson Young's edition of *Trial of Frederick Bywaters & Edith Thompson*: "The terms in which a woman does not write to any man except her husband … It was to satisfy him more than to deceive him" (234).

tryst and trow" (*FW* 226.14), implicating her in the Floras' sentimental marriage fantasy. Nevertheless, while there are narcissistic elements to her temptations of Glugg, Issy's deviations in behavior from her Maggie counterparts are important to acknowledge. Considering that the Maggies are twenty-eight manifestations of Issy, to note that Issy reacts differently to the Shemish characters than her reflections ruptures Joyce's narcissistic narrative by having the Maggies function simultaneously as Issy and not-Issy. This destabilization forces us to see mirrored characters as "othered" from the self and by extension calls the entire act of lovers viewing others as their reflections into question. Within the space between herself and her mirror images, Issy constructs a self-interrogation of the narcissism she seemingly upholds, as her specific reflections on these mirrored manifestations of herself provoke bitter evaluations of her romantic situations and broaden Joyce's critique.

Issy's self-interrogation is initiated in her answer to the quiz show's tenth question. On the surface, Issy's reply seems to confirm her self-absorption, as she obsesses over cosmetics and material possessions and gushes over her reflection Maggie's beauty. Also, her imagined seductions of her love objects echo the snares of the "Angels and Devils" game. She notes that one suitor "is seeking an opening and means to be first with me as his belle alliance" (*FW* 144.11–2), making Issy that suitor's Waterloo, and she tells him to "Stoop alittle closer, fealse!" (*FW* 144.13), referencing the nursery rhyme "come a little closer, said the spider to the fly" and thus positioning her suitor as another "trapadour" (McHugh 144). Especially since she primarily addresses these responses to her mirror, Issy's monologue in I.6 is frequently read as evidence of her narcissism.[4] However, while her response does convey an infatuation with materialism and seduction, it also calls these narcissistic elements into question and continues Joyce's criticism of Darwinistic sentimentality.

Initially, Issy casts her reflection as other from herself. While she seems to admire her mirror image, her perspective on Maggie changes towards the middle of her speech, when she tells the older man pursuing her, "May you never see me in my birthday pelts seenso tutu and that her blanches mainges may rot leprous off her whatever winking maggis I'll bet by your cut you go fleurting after with all the glass on her and the jumps in her stomewhere!" (*FW* 144.36–145.4). While Issy's

---

[4] For example, Kitcher argues that "the breathless voice of Issy,[is] teasing, coaxing, and urging, as if she could restore the sexual interest of almost any man. Evidently obsessed with her own attractiveness, she is, equally evidently, taboo – off limits for HCE and for the dreamer" (123–4). McCarthy similarly contends that Issy "regards love in Darwinian terms … Although she says she would like to improve herself through reading (145.28–9), in this passage she is basically a coquette" (*Family* 17). Finally, Norris notes that "Like Gerty and Molly, Isabel is a temptress. But unlike the complex, mediated desires of men, the psychology of female desire is so narcissistic as to be primitive by Hegelian standards. In the monologues of Gerty, Molly, and Isabel, the men are virtually pretexts for fantasies about clothes, undergarments, perfumes, the accouterments of their own bodies, as though the women were their own erotic objects" (*Decentered* 53).

statement may seem like a curse on the "winking maggis" her suitor replaces her with, her specific derision is explicitly aimed at her reflection. Her reference to the woman as "blanches mainges" evokes Tristan's wife Isolde Blanchemains, who is frequently evoked in reference to Issy's mirror image, and thus positions Issy and Maggie as separate, rival Isoldes in the "Tristan" scenario she crafts (a scenario further supported by the references to "cut" and the "glass on her" when Issy describes her lover's pursuit of the "maggis"). Also, her wish that "her blanches mainges may rot leprous off her" destabilizes the division between Maggie's Isolde Blanchemains and Issy's Isolde la Belle since McHugh notes that it was actually the latter who was "given by Mark to lepers" (145). Thus, in confusing the two Isoldes and muddling the equation of Issy to Maggie, Issy prevents us from reading her response as a simple infatuation with her reflection. This rupture is further strengthened by her contention that she is "not a mishymissy" (*FW* 145.7–8), which puns on the Gaelic word "mise" meaning "me." Her response thus implies either that Issy is not Issy ("I am not me") or that Issy is not her mirror image ("I am not a me me" or "meme"), both options widening the divide between character and reflection. Jan Shelton thus effectively reads Issy's "mirror-friend" as "contiguous to but not congruent with her" (95), and this destabilization of Maggie exposes the tenuousness of consuming otherness into reflections of the self.

Furthermore, Issy recognizes the performative nature of the sentimental romances in which she is forced to participate. While Issy appears to entice her lover(s) (presumably Shaun and HCE) into a liaison, McHugh notes two occurrences in her answer that equate her lovers with Roberto Prezioso, whose advances towards Nora were pilloried throughout *Exiles*. At 146.30–1, Issy tells her lover to "move your mouth towards minth, more, preciousest" and then at 147.35–6, she asks, "Do you like that, *silenzioso?* Are you enjoying, this same little me, my life, my love?" These references to Joyce's Trieste rival shape Issy's answer into her mockery of the performance of seduction because if her addressee is a Prezioso-like seducer, then her statements equate him with the stereotypical lover that Joyce satirized through Robert's failed wooing of Bertha. Given Issy's references to their flirtations as performances throughout this passage ("The little passdoor, I go you before, so, and you're at my apron stage. Shy is him, dovey. Musforget there's an audience" [*FW* 146.36–147.2]), Issy reveals her suitors to engage in absurd, clichéd seductions that her coquetry directly challenges.

This revelation is especially significant given Issy's position within the *Wake*'s familial romances. Immediately after telling her "preciousest" to "move your mouth towards minth," Issy notes, "You know bigtree are all against gravstone. They hisshistenency. Garnd ond mand" (*FW* 146.34–5), which implicates Shem, Shaun, and HCE in the performative romantic advances against which Issy defends herself. A few lines later, after she notes that she "musforget there's an audience," Issy highlights her coquettish challenges to the twins' specific advances: "I have been lost, angel. Cuddle, ye divil ye! It's our toot-a-toot" (*FW* 147.2–3). These statements still reveal Issy's seduction of Shaun and Shem to be devoid of amorous sincerity, but by portraying the brothers as Preziosos, Issy forces us to view her amatory gamesmanship as her response to the twins' sentimental seductions, revealing them to be playing the game as much as she is. While the Maggies seem to be enraptured by sentimental romance and marriage, Issy sees through the charade of romantic idealism and her beguiling of her would-be suitors highlights and deflates the absurdity of sentimental love.

Furthermore, Issy critiques the rejection of her otherness at the heart of her suitors' advances. While the Maggies use their obsession with romantic ideals to reshape Shem and Shaun into stereotypical villains and heroes, Issy not only recognizes the artificiality of these roles, but also that her suitors have shaped her into their ideal love objects. This criticism is initially evident in Issy's references to "that espos of a Clancarbry, thefoodbrawler" (*FW* 144.5), whom she notes "My Eilish assent he seed makes his admiracion" (*FW* 144.10–1). This observation notes her suitor's admiration for Issy's Irish accent, but McHugh also notices within that "Eilish assent" a reference to Eily O'Connor, the heroine of Dion Boucicault's *The Colleen Bawn* (144), which reveals that her lover finds her enticing because of her similarity to an Irish literary heroine, a connection strengthened by the numerous instances where she is cast as Arrah-na-Pogue in II.4. That Issy's lovers force her into stereotypical roles is further developed by her reference to the clothes her suitors buy her as "your extensions to my personality" (*FW* 144.23), which equates these presents with Issy's lovers shaping her into their ideal love objects. For that reason, when Issy later playacts Isolde la Belle (*FW* 146.23–6) and Grania (*FW* 146.27–9), she reveals her enticements of the HCE-ish suitor to be her negotiations of stereotypical roles that have been forced upon her (especially since she refers to this suitor as "preciousest" two lines later).[5] Sheldon Brivic thus compellingly notes that "Issy speaks as one who has been trained to excel in playing the object of desire" (12),[6] and her recognition of her objectification as a result of this "train[ing]" strengthens her interrogation of the narcissistic romances in which she participates.

Ultimately, Issy's response serves as a scathing indict of amatory Darwinism, an attack she explicitly makes towards the middle of her answer. After rebuking her lovers for their inane, repressive treatment of her ("I mean to make you suffer, meddler, and I don't care this fig for contempt of courting" [*FW* 145.15–6]), Issy responds to her Shaunish lover's question "Of I be leib in the immoralities?" by replying, "O, you mean the strangle for love and the sowiveall of the prettiest?" (*FW* 145.26–7). This combination of Darwin and marital romance encapsulates

---

[5] Finn Fordham also describes Issy as "a composite of male fantasies, different forms of a man's desire projected onto a particular girl who … [is] asked to adopt such different roles. In this projection and objectification her particularity is being hidden and threatened" (184).

[6] Christy L. Burns similarly contends that "Joyce moves away from a simple (and silencing) objectification of woman in favor of a complex attempt to ventriloquize female desire, a move that paradoxically releases women from male control *within* Joyce's novels, even as it remains within the 'pornosophical' control of Joyce's male imaginary" (84).

the problems Joyce finds in the amatory "survival of the fittest," that it transforms love into the sentimental quest to "wive all" women, making marriage the primary "happily ever after" of amatory pursuits; that it stacks the deck in favor of the "prettiest," necessitating the rejection of otherness to promote its evolutionary ascent; and that the entire process of "wiving" all of the "prettiest" ultimately "strangle[s]" love in the process. Issy may be compelled to play the game, but she acknowledges that it is a game that she has to play in order to survive, and her seductions of the twins do not prevent her from recognizing the fallacious nature of these amatory pursuits. Issy's response in the quiz show thus enables her to expose the fallacious nature of consuming the other into a reflection of the self and the narcissistic underpinnings of the romances in which she is forced to participate.

Issy's interrogation of narcissism continues through her later episodes in the *Wake*, as each opportunity she is given to speak enables her to transcend the role of siren to which her lovers frequently relegate her and to reveal weaknesses in the sentimental narratives that they and the Maggies uphold. For example, in III.2, Izzy replies to Jaun's farewell sermon to the girls of St. Brides through similar coquettish advances, enticing Jaun to pine for her while intimating an impending marriage to a rival suitor that she swears she will toss over for Jaun. However, Izzy's seduction of Jaun is undercut by her references to her "linkingclass girl" Madge (*FW* 459.4), III.2's manifestation of her reflection Maggie whom she treats as a separate person. Not only does her farewell to Jaun begin with "Meesh, meesh" (*FW* 457.25), Joyce's Gaelic pun for "meme," but she tells Jaun to "kindly think galways again or again, never forget, of one absendee not sester Maggy" (*FW* 458.9–10), and she further notes that "I will say for you to the Allmichael and solve qui pu while the dovedoves pick my mouthbuds (msch! msch!) with nurse Madge" (*FW* 459.2–4). While these references could simply indicate Izzy's thinking of Jaun while looking in the mirror, her desire for Jaun to remember Maggy and her subsequent reference to her doppelganger as "nurse" cause her meme to transcend her mirrored space and assume a separate character. Furthermore, Izzy notes that Madge is "a fright, poor old dutch, in her sleeptalking when I paint the measles on her and mudstuskers to make her a man" (*FW* 459.4–6). Here, she not only paints measles and moustaches on her reflection to make it more other than herself,[7] but she also evokes a mirror image talking in her sleep, a personification that she subsequently develops by noting that "she loves your style considering she breaksin me shoes for me when I've arch trouble and she would kiss my white arms for me so gratefully" (*FW* 459.15–7). Like I.6, Izzy positions her reflection both as Isolde Blanchemains and as a romantic option for Jaun, but now instead of castigating her reflection, she champions Maggy as an option for Jaun while he is away from Izzy, imposing further distance between herself and her mirror image.

---

7 Shelton similarly notes that "Issy seems to engage less in simple admiration than in aggressive rewriting of her mirror image … Issy's interaction with the image in the mirror is complicated. Not only is the mirror image clearly a separate person to Issy, but it is one that she can remake into yet another image – in this case, as a mustached, spotty-faced man" (95–6).

Thus, Izzy's transformation of her reflection into a "linkingclass girl" that less and less resembles her provides a counterbalance to the narcissistic replication of the Maggies and strengthens her self-interrogation of narcissism.

Issy's reflexive critique of narcissism culminates during Yawn's inquest in III.3. Whereas previous episodes featured Issy working through the narcissistic implications of her seductions, here she is forced to defend herself from charges of narcissism, as the Four Old Men (Mamalujo) equate her with the temptresses of HCE's park scandal and explicitly highlight her perceived solipsistic foundation: "Sure she was near drowned in pondest coldstreams of admiration forherself, as bad as my Tarpeyan cousin, Vesta Tully, making faces at her bachspilled likeness in the brook after and cooling herself in the element, she pleasing it, she praising it, with salices and weidowwehls, all tossed, as she was, the playactrix, Lough Shieling's love!" (*FW* 526.28–33). By explicitly equating her with Narcissus and Ophelia, Mamalujo paints a reductive portrait of Issy that replaces her specific yearnings with a simplistic caricature of a woman undone by self-love, and the fact that they label her a "playactrix" further reduces her to a manipulative coquette. This characterization of Issy is confirmed by their declaration that "Nircississies are as the doaters of inversion. Secilias through their laughing classes becoming poolermates in laker life" (*FW* 526.34–6). This proclamation explicitly reduces Issy's identity to a "doater" of her "inver[ted]" mirror image, as her previous othering of her mirrored Maggie is overshadowed by Mamalujo's equating the two "Secilias" as "poolermates." However, while Mamalujo constructs a simplistic depiction of a "nircissis[tic]" Issy, her subsequent dialogue with to her "meme mearest" further destabilizes the relationship between lover and reflection and interrogates amatory narcissism more effectively than Mamalujo's castigation (*FW* 527.3).

Issy's rupturing of this Narcissus association is reminiscent of her answer in the quiz show chapter: in both speeches, Issy strategically adopts the siren persona that has been thrust upon her and reveals the artificiality of the stereotype. As in I.6, Issy's speech in III.3 appears to support the perception of her as a seductress in love with her reflection. She celebrates her meme's beauty, noting that "everybody knows you do look lovely in your invinsibles," complementing her on "a perfect apposition with the coldcream, Assoluta, from Boileau's" (*FW* 527.11–3), and wishing that she "could … but pass my hands some, my hands through, thine hair! So vickyvicky veritiny!" (*FW* 527.15–7). She also teasingly references potential suitors, playfully reprimanding her reflection for "go[ing] in the dreemplace and at that time of the draym" to entice "dare all grandpassia!" and recalling a tryst with another ("even my little pom got excited, when I turned his head on his same manly bust and kissed him more" [*FW* 527.31–2]). Finally, Issy ends her speech with a marriage fantasy, noting that "it will all take bloss as oranged at St Audiens rosan chocolate chapelry with my diamants blickfeast after at mine owned hos for all the catclub to go cryzy and Father Blesius Mindelsinn will be beminding hand" (*FW* 528.5–7). Thus, Issy's address to Maggie echoes the narcissistic themes that have comprised the previous seductive enticements of herself and the Maggies and seemingly validates Mamalujo's judgment.

However, Issy's presentation of these themes disrupts the fixed association of her as a narcissistic temptress. Initially, the indeterminacy of Issy's audience undermines Mamalujo's attempts to label her a simple admirer of her reflection. Issy does address "meme mearest" and later notes that "It's meemly us two, meme, idol" (*FW* 527.24), but at other points in her speech she seems to be addressing her male suitors. Her initial scolding of Maggie seemingly blames her for enticing HCE ("Of course I know you are a viry vikid girl to go in the dreemplace and at that time of the draym and it was a very wrong thing to do, even under the dark flush of night, dare all grandpassia!" [*FW* 5–8]), but it can also be read as upbraiding "dare all grandpassia" and not Maggie for "do[ing]" the "very wrong thing," which echoes her bitterness over being used by older men from I.6.[8] Similarly, the speaker's identity is indeterminate. Again, Issy uses references to Tristan's two Isoldes to reference herself and her reflection, but whereas she self-identified as Isolde la Belle and equated her meme with Isolde Blanchemains in I.6, here she wishes she could "pass" her "hands through, thine hair" and later notes that "my arms are whiter, dear. Blanchemain, idler. Fairhair, frail one" (*FW* 527.20–1). Considering that Isolde Blanchemains is associated with white hands and Isolde la Belle is associated with "fair hair," either Issy has flipped identities and become Isolde Blanchemains in III.3, or she is projecting the voice from the mirror commenting on her situation, or she is providing the voices of both self and other in a mirrored dialogue. In any case, Issy's references to Tristan's two Isoldes strengthen the differences between herself and her reflection and continue her destabilization of self-mirroring throughout the *Wake*. The resulting indeterminacy of both speaker and addressee thus undercuts Mamalujo's charges and develops Issy's self-interrogation of her identity as the narcissistic coquette.

Issy's derision of her suitors continues this destabilization of the temptress label. She first upbraids HCE, "dear old grandpassia," for "geesing and so pleasing at Strip Teasy up the stairs" when Issy's "soreful miseries first came on you" (*FW* 527.8–10), which reverses Mamalujo's portrayal of the temptresses undermining HCE by portraying the latter as spying on and pursuing Issy. Along those lines, Issy later chastises her Shaunish Tristan. She notes that "it was downright verry wickred of him, reely meeting me disguised" (*FW* 527.24–5), and after describing their tryst, she laments, "Only he might speak to a person, lord so picious, taking up my worths ill wrong!" (*FW* 527.33–4), which not only shows that her lover does not understand her, but also demonstrates Shaun's consumption of her otherness in reducing Issy to his Isolde. By highlighting her frustrations over being misused by her lovers, Issy injects her desires and yearnings into a romantic narrative that confines her to the reductive role of a coquette, and in so doing, she demonstrates the suppression of otherness at the heart of this logic.

Similarly, Issy's references to the Virgin Mary continue the rupture of stereotypical roles into which she has been cast. Fordham notes that "the dualism

---

8 Fordham notes later in the speech, "the identities of herself and her addressee are multiplying and mutually destabilizing, for Issy may be addressing her brother as much as her reflection" (180).

of Issy is a projection of the male view of woman as either virgin or whore" (178), and Issy's address to Maggie here undermines this "dualism" by frequently blending the two roles together. She references the three mysteries of the Holy Rosary in describing her primary sexual encounters, noting the "soreful miseries" of her menstruation when describing HCE's advances, asking her "meme sweety" to "be joyfold" for her conquest of Shaun (*FW* 527.21–2), and assuring her lover that she will "make it up with mother Concepcion and a glorious lie between us, sweetness, so as not a novena in all the convent loretos, not my littlest one of all, for mercy's sake need ever know, what passed our lips" (*FW* 527.35–528.3). Moreover, her description of her conquest of Shaun is couched in the litany of the Blessed Virgin Mary, as she tells her reflection, "Mirror do justice, taper of ivory, heart of the conavent, hoops of gold!" (*FW* 527.22–3). This renegotiation of the litany also strengthens Joyce's criticism of matrimonial sentimentality, as Issy transforms the "house of gold" into "hoops of gold," or wedding rings (McHugh 527), and considering that her "Tristan and Isolde" depiction of her tryst with Shaun immediately follows this, Issy thus reshapes the litany and the Tristan and Isolde myth into her tickets to fulfill her concluding marriage fantasy. In so doing, she acknowledges the stereotypical identities that have been forced upon her throughout the *Wake* and perverts the sentimentality at the foundation of them.

Finally, Issy's envisioned marriage ceremony confirms the "strangle for love" at the heart of the *Wake*'s amatory Darwinism. Whereas Issy criticized the dissolution of love at the heart of the determination to "wive all of the prettiest" in I.6, here she directly participates in her self-wiving and loses her ability to articulate her individual desires in the process. Her dialogue with Maggie can certainly be taken as evidence of narcissism (as Mamalujo sees it), but it is also the only site where Issy can articulate her specific yearnings apart from others who seek to transform her into objects to satisfy their lust.[9] Thus, it is significant that the further Issy gets into her marriage fantasy, the more her reflection fades from sight. Specifically, after the prayers at her imagined wedding, when Issy refers to her "meme nearest" as "languished hister" (which McHugh translates as "vanquished sister" [528]) and asks her to "be free to me," she is answered by the parenthetical exclamation "(I'm fading!)," (*FW* 528.10–1), and this disintegration is confirmed by the final words of Issy's speech: "And listen, you, you beauty, esster, I'll be clue to who knows you, pray Magda, Marthe with Luz and Joan, while I lie with warm lisp on the Tolka. (I'm fay!)" (*FW* 528.11–3).[10] The parenthetical exclamations could be Issy acknowledging that her self-identity is "fading" and doomed upon her marriage, or it could be Maggie acknowledging that she is doomed by Issy's new identity as a married woman. However, either option demonstrates the consequences of Issy's "wiv[ing]." If Issy can only be herself in the company of her meme, then

[9] Burns contends that Issy's "split speaking echoes not only verbal parapraxes but also the slide between unconscious desires and the struggle for self-conscious (perhaps societally ordered) control" (82).

[10] McHugh translates "I'm fay!" as "I'm doomed" (528).

the dissolution of that mirrored identity as a result of her marriage fantasy signals the dissolution of Issy's specific desires and her subsequent roleplaying of another imposed sentimental identity. This acknowledgment thus extends her recognition of the artificiality of the roles she has been compelled to play throughout the *Wake's* romantic episodes and thus confirms the dissolution of otherness at the heart of amatory Darwinism.

Issy's role in Joyce's critique of narcissism can thus be illustrated by an observation she makes in III.3: "How me adores eatsother simply" (*FW* 527.29). While this line is at one level a punnish reference to Issy and her Tristan "adoring each other simply," it also articulates the narcissistic dilemma behind Joyce's love stories: the adoration of the self simply eats the other. Issy's acknowledgement of this dilemma thus makes her a fascinating and important addition to the Joycean cast of self-lovers. On the one hand, Mamalujo is not wrong to view the Earwicker daughter as "Nircississies" since she lures Shem into numerous humiliations for her own amusement, encourages Shem and Shaun to fight over her, and frequently admires her beauty through her mirrored Maggie. Also, Issy does not affirm the otherness of anyone other than herself throughout the *Wake*; she may sympathize with Shem during his persecutions by the Maggies, but she seems more upset that his retreats prevent him from doting on her than she is in Shem's specific misery and at no point does she seem sincerely enamored with Shaun.

On the other hand, we cannot equate Issy's narcissism with Joyce's earlier protagonists because she not only possesses a self-awareness of her narcissistic impulses that those protagonists lack, but she frequently interrogates those impulses and reveals the artificiality behind such amatory pursuits. Rather than presenting us with another Duffy, Gabriel, or Stephen who try to shape their loved ones into their mirrored reflections, Joyce literally provides us with a character in love with her reflection, but her declarations of love simultaneously acknowledge the flaws of this amatory mirroring and the erasure of otherness at the heart of the *Wake's* Darwinistic romances. This self-interrogation of narcissism is enhanced by the dreamtext itself, where Joyce not only provides us with a character wrestling with the consequences of her coquetry, but also provides us with twenty-eight reflections of that persona adhering to the reductive narrative that Mamalujo assigns to Issy, which enables Issy to reveal the artificiality of that narrative the more she becomes othered to those reflections. Thus, through the dreamer's shifting characterizations of Issy and her relationship to Maggie (and the Maggies), Joyce allows a more complex wrestling with the implications of narcissism and mirroring that dovetail with the arguments of his earlier fiction.

A Tale Told of Shaun or Shem

Joyce's investigation of amatory Darwinism develops in the contentious relationship between Shem and Shaun. Not only does he position the twins as rival suitors for Issy and the Maggies, but through each persona, Joyce offers a separate perspective on how to react to others that echoes the narcissism of his earlier protagonists. While Shaun's rejection of others who believe differently from himself is reminiscent of the narcissistic protagonists of *Dubliners*, Shem's self-exile and artistic retaliation to his persecution echo Stephen's use of amatory aesthetics to counter the perceived rejections of his lovers. However, rather than simply providing us with direct reflections of his earlier protagonists, Joyce uses the manifestations of Shaun and Shem to revise and work through the problematic foundations of these narcissistic reactions to otherness. Similar to the renegotiation of mirroring that occurs through his multiple replicas of Issy, Joyce's restagings of the brothers enable the dreamer's shifting reflections on the twin encounter to overcome the ambivalence towards otherness that felled the characters of Joyce's early fiction.

Initially, Shem's struggles as the victim of "naturel rejection" demonstrate the evolution of Joyce's interrogation of narcissism. Similar to Issy's interrogations of mirroring refashioning the *Dubliners* protagonists' consumptions of otherness, Shem's status as the *Wake*'s Joycean artist results in him acting in ways reminiscent of Stephen Dedalus, as his reactions to Shaun's persecution echo Stephen's refusal to heed lovers who do not return his adoration or to serve social forces that constrain his freedom. These similarities have compelled critics to associate the two Joycean doppelgangers, with Glasheen going so far as to argue that "Shem is a burlesque of Stephen Dedalus" (262).[11] However, whereas Glasheen sees Shem as caricaturing Joyce's artist, I see him as renegotiating the amatory freedom that compelled Stephen's rejection of Dublin. Specifically, Shem's struggles with community and exile challenge Stephen's consistent performance of "*non serviam*" and provide an opportunity to reshape his refusals of others into a more affirming response.

Admittedly, the parallels between Shem and Stephen are compelling, as is evidenced by Glugg's perpetual humiliation by the Floras in II.1. Here, not only does Stephen's obsession with love objects that refuse his gaze similarly plague the *Wake*'s penman during his attempts to answer the heliotrope riddle, but Glugg's reactions to this exclusion also echo Stephen's refusal of love objects who do not return his adoration. Upon his initial repulsion, the narrator notes that "tornaments of complementary rages rocked the divlun from his punchpoll to his tummy's shentre as he displaid all the oathword science of his visible disgrace" (*FW* 227.21–3), and his specific responses to the understanding that "they're all odds against him, the beasties" confirm his solipsistic reaction to such situations (*FW* 227.27–8). Recalling Stephen's resolve to leave Ireland after losing Emma's and Cranly's love, Glugg first pledges to leave forever after being expelled by

[11] Other critics who have noted the similarities between Shem and Stephen include Kitcher, who argues that "Shem offers a potential answer to the complex of questions I have seen at the heart of the *Wake*, an answer that elaborates the fierce determination for self-fashioning with which we leave Stephen Dedalus at the end of *Portrait* – we might even think of it as the view from *Portrait*"(32); and Manganiello, whose reading of *Stephen Hero* leads him to conclude that "Like Shem, the artist in *Stephen Hero* is estranged from the world in which he moves" (79).

the Floras ("He would split" [*FW* 228.5]; "Byebye, Brassolis, I'm breaving" [*FW* 228.12]). He then vows revenge on his family, planning to "go in for scribenery with the satiety of Arthurs in S.P.Q.R.ish and inform to the old sniggering publicking press and its nation of sheepcopers about the whole plightry troth between them" (*FW* 229.7–9), echoing Stephen's self-identification with the vengeful Edmond Dantes in *Portrait*'s second chapter and demonstrating Glugg's determination to exterminate others who refuse his desires. This process repeats itself with Glugg's successive failures to solve the riddle and culminates in the Glugg-Chuff fight at the end of II.1 that recalls Stephen's envisioning Cranly as his romantic rival to justify his self-exile. Glugg's response to the Floras' taunting is understandable, but it also demonstrates the extent to which the refusal of otherness pervades Joyce's amatory Darwinism since the victim of "naturel rejection['s]" instinctive reaction is to either withdraw from the world or inflict similar retribution on his persecutors. Glugg's vengeance not only guarantees that his rivals will be "all odds against him," but it demonstrates the absence of love in any of the "Mime['s]" participants and the inevitable violence at the heart of Darwinistic romance.

However, the Shemish reversal of amatory Darwinism quickly occurs in II.2, where Joyce's restaging of the twins' rivalry for Issy within the Triv and the Quad unsettles II.1's promotion of Shaun over Shem. Here, the chapter's structure repositions the night lessons as the intellectual counterpoint to the "Mime," as Dolph's subversive marginalia rival Kev's conventional notes on opposing sides of the page with Issy's beguiling footnotes standing between them, and Dolph's marginal references to the "heliotrope" riddle and a "sweet hopeful culled Cis" confirm his preoccupation with Issy in the chapter (*FW* 265.17–8; 267.10–1). However, whereas Glugg was bested by Chuff due to his inability to answer the Floras' riddle, here Dolph's intellectual superiority enables him to turn the tables on his rival, as his assisting Kev with his homework is strategically designed to dupe him into shocking insights about the "whome of the eternal geomater" (*FW* 296.31–297.1). Rather than helping Kev "construct ann aquilittoral dryankle" (*FW* 286.19–20), Dolph capitalizes on his superior intellect by tricking Kev into drawing ALP's genitals and then flaunts his superiority as Kev experiences his horrifying epiphany. Echoing Stephen's disdain for people who do not share his intellectual acumen or pursuits, II.2 confirms the *Wake*'s Shemish manifestations to use their aesthetic prowess as revenge on the characters that exclude them, perpetuating the self-exile of another Joycean artist.

Nevertheless, the night lessons ultimately undercut the amatory Darwinism perpetuated by the "Mime." Initially, Dolph's triumph over Kev challenges the categorical promotion of Shaun over Shem in the siblings' evolutionary wars. Whereas Glugg's ignorance of the "heliotrope" color was further evidence of his degeneracy, Dolph actually bests his brother because of his superior intellect, transforming the undesirable suitor into the beau ideal and relegating the Maggies' champion to this suitor test's loser. While this does not reverse Chuff's victory in the "Mime," it does reveal the arbitrariness of such Darwinistic romances since the evolved suitor of one scenario becomes the discarded dupe of the next, and because the dreamtext prevents us from reading these episodes as linearly related, Joyce essentially constructs a love story where Shem and Shaun are both victors and losers and simultaneously experience "naturel rejection" and the "assent of man." For this reason, Dolph's victory unsettles the easy classification of the twins in the text's sibling romances and unravels the evolutionary trajectory of amatory Darwinism.

More importantly, II.2 replaces the antagonism of the previous twin rivalries with reconciliation. While Dolph's taunting results in Kev striking him in a manner reminiscent of the Glugg-Chuff fight, Kev's punch does not strengthen the rivalry between himself and Dolph, but rather causes Dolph to admit his culpability in provoking Kev and to offer a truce. Here, II.2's Shem manifestation differentiates himself from Stephen by proving himself capable of reconciling with an adversary despite acknowledging that there are differences between them. Whereas the mere hint of a romantic dalliance between Emma and Cranly was enough to encourage Stephen's exile, Dolph puts aside his differences with both siblings, and his reaching out to Kev results in a Nightletter pinned by the three children, creating a union that challenges their previous Darwinistic rivalries. While this reconciliation is not perfect, it does replace the children's refusals of each other with a more cooperative dynamic, and the fact that the Shemish Dolph offers this reconciliation demonstrates Joyce's use of the *Wake*'s penman to renegotiate the narcissistic non serviams of his previous artists into an acknowledgment of otherness that undercuts the evolutionary narcissism of the text.

However, Joyce's renegotiation of amatory Darwinism is most explicitly evident in the text's manifestations of Shaun. As I have argued, Shaun frequently embodies the ideal lover of the *Wake*'s sentimental romances, as he is portrayed as the "masculine Oirisher Rose" of the Festy King trial and the "whitemost" and "goldenest" of "all the green heroes everwore coton breiches" of the "Mime." This depiction reaches its apex in the "Tristan and Isolde" episode in II.4, where Shaun becomes "the hero, of Gaelic champion, the onliest one of her choice, her bleaueyedeal of a girl's friend" through Joyce's satire of the famous Irish romance (*FW* 384.23–4). As the *Wake*'s blue-eyed beau ideal, Shaun is celebrated not only because of his masculine prowess, but also because he is frequently associated with virtuousness, decency, and respectability and is thus seen as "the darling of the existing order" (Kitcher 117), an ideal lover persona reminiscent of Duffy's, Gabriel's, and Robert's pretentions to amatory greatness. I have already shown how this identification replaces his otherness with the persona of an ideal hero, but Shaun's adoption of this role necessitates his own rejections of otherness. Norris compellingly describes Shaun as "a hypocritical pharisee who projects his own lewdness on others and then threatens them with castigation" (*Decentered* 85), and indeed his seemingly pious pursuits of Issy are frequently predicated on objectifying his sister and the Maggies and reshaping them into love objects that will satisfy his lust.

Joyce's satire of Shaun's romantic idealism is explicit in the "Tristan and Isolde" chapter. Here, the postman and his sister become the legendary lovers of

Irish myth, and Mamalujo's equating Issy with Arrah-na-Pogue also transforms Shaun the Post into his Boucicaultian counterpoint. This tactic not only demonstrates the sentimentality behind the *Wake*'s Shaun-Issy romances, but Joyce's vulgar depictions of his Tristan dissolve Shaun's pretentions to romantic piety. By noting that Shaun was "light and rufthandling, vicemversem her ragbags et assaucyetiams, fore and aft, on and offsides" (*FW* 384.26–8), Joyce highlights more than the athletic prowess of Issy's "Gaelic champion." Indeed, in replacing Tristan and Isolde's illicit kiss with Shaun fondling Issy's breasts, Joyce reveals the lewdness concealed by the promotion of Shaun as the "bleaueyedeal." Especially since Shaun's becoming the *Wake*'s Tristan is the result of HCE's fall at the end of II.3, Joyce transforms II.4 into a mythological site of amatory Darwinism that reduces Issy to the sentimental love object to be won through the discarding of "Muster Mark" and trivializes Shaun's legitimacy as the hero of *Wakean* romance (*FW* 383.1).

Joyce's amatory critique of Shaun is even more evident in Jaun's lecture to the girls of St. Bride's in III.2, where his advice demonstrates the objectification behind his moral superiority. Upon announcing his departure, Jaun launches into a sermon of suggestions for how the girls should maintain their virtue in his absence. He advises them to "never park your brief stays in the men's convenience" and "never let the promising hand usemake free of your oncemaid sacral" (433.24–5; 27–8), and he specifically warns Izzy to "keep cool your fresh chastity which is far better far" (*FW* 440.31–2). However, similar to the pleasure for possession behind Gabriel's lust for Gretta and Robert's advances towards Bertha, behind Jaun's performance of the virtuous brother figure is a repressive desire to prevent rival suitors from impeding on his territory. This repression is not only evident in his commands, "First thou shalt not smile. Twice thou shalt not love. Lust, thou shalt not commix idolatry" (*FW* 433.22–3), but also in his explanation of the consequences of defying his orders. He threatens to "tackle" the girls "to feel if you have a few devils in you" and to "give it to you, hot, high and heavy before you can say sedro" (*FW* 439.4–6), and he tells Izzy that he will "be all over you myselx horizontally" and "draw my prance and give you one splitpuck in the crupper … that will bring the poppy blush of shame to your peony hindmost till you yelp papapardon and radden your rodatantarums to the beat of calorrubordolor" if he "find[s] corsehairs on your river-frock and the squirmside of your burberry lupitally covered with chiffchaff and shavings" (*FW* 444.18–9; 27–9; 445.14–8). Specifically, his desire to "radden" Issy's "rodatantarums" to "shame" her for her infidelities explicitly highlights his violent rejection of her otherness since "rodatantarums" evoke the rhododendrons of Bloom's memory of proposing to Molly that enables him to accept her adultery with Boylan. Thus, in contrast to Bloom's amorous masochism, the sexual foundations of Jaun's warnings implicate him in an amatory sadism that promotes his lust over the girls' desires both through his prohibitions on their seeking other lovers and through violent punishments that increase his pleasure through their painful "shame."

The sentimental foundations of Jaun's punishments also confirm his inclination to reduce the girls to love objects to satisfy his longings. Whereas Mamalujo represented Shaun as a sentimental hero in II.4, here III.2's manifestation invites the association and reveals its Darwinistic foundation, as his observation that he is "well voiced in love's arsenal and all its overtures from collion boys to colleen bawns" echoes the Maggies' "war[ring] loving" by using sentimental romance as weaponry to subdue his love objects and promote his desires over his rivals (*FW* 438.32–4). Furthermore, his declaration to Izzy that he will "contrive to half kill your Charley you're my darling for you" demonstrates the violence of the text's Darwinistic rivalries by revealing his desire to literally exterminate rival suitors in this amatory survival of the fittest. Jaun's lecture thus demonstrates the repression behind the *Wake*'s romantic sentimentality, as the Maggies' ideal lover and the champion of respectability maintains his amatory prowess through violent consumptions and rejections of otherness.

Shaun's assumptions of the beau ideal persona thus seemingly align him with the narcissistic protagonists of Joyce's earlier fiction. Neither Duffy, Gabriel, nor Robert may threaten their love objects with violence, but each protagonist similarly desires to possess their loved one's adoration as evidence of their self-worth, and Joyce's depictions of Jaun's punishments demonstrates the extent to which that desire for possession is compromised by a violent refusal of their loved ones. However, whereas Joyce kept his early protagonists grounded in their narcissism and focused his examinations on doomed quests for amatory escape, the dream's shifting dimensions enable Joyce to present Shaun in a more complicated light. While specific manifestations of Shaun coincide with Joyce's critique of narcissism, Shaun's character changes throughout the *Wake* continually alter his attitudes towards his rivals and thus constitute a more complex working through narcissism.

Oddly enough, compelling evidence for Shaun's negotiating his repulsion for the other occurs at the end of Jaun's lecture in III.2. To be sure, the majority of Jaun's advice props himself up as an ideal romantic suitor and threatens violent sexual abuse to any girl that would seek a rival in his absence. Unsurprisingly, the main rival Jaun is threatened by is a Shem manifestation, as he warns his sister to "divorce into me and say the curname in undress … of any lapwhelp or sleevemongrel who talks to you upon the road" (*FW* 441.29–32), and his subsequent reference to "the black fremdling, that enemy of our country" reveals the specific "lapwhelp" Jaun has in mind (*FW* 442.1–2). However, Jaun then leaves Izzy in the protection of Dave the Dancekerl, who is also a Shem manifestation. By having Jaun reject one Shem and promote another Shem as a guardian in the same chapter, Joyce challenges the simplistic rejection of degenerate rivals behind Shaun's Darwinistic amatory combats. Furthermore, in contrast to Gabriel's misrecognition of Michael Furey as a stereotypical rival for Gretta's affection and Robert's continual misrecognition of Richard's desire for Bertha's freedom even after he has conceded defeat, Jaun concedes to Izzy that Dave is "the sneaking likeness of us, faith, me altar's ego in miniature" (*FW* 463.6–7), which transforms the refusals of the other that have comprised their sibling rivalries with a recognition that the suitors and love object are connected in a more meaningful amorous bond. Thus, whereas the inability of Joyce's early protagonists to move past their amatory antagonism foiled their romantic quests, Jaun refashions this Darwinistic sibling rivalry into an affirmation of Izzy and Dave that enables him to develop a more accommodating reaction to otherness.

Furthermore, Jaun's insistence that Izzy can trust Dave is supported by positive descriptions of Dave's character that transform Shaun's rejections of his degenerative rival into a loving turn towards the other. Rather than denigrate the Shem manifestation's lowness, he calls Dave "my darling proxy" and "a dear old man pall of mine too" (*FW* 462.16; 18), and he concedes that "he has novel ideas I know and he's a jarry queer fish betimes, I grant you, and cantanberous, the poisoner of his word, but lice and all and semicoloured stainedglasses, I'm enormously full of that foreigner" (*FW* 463.12–5). This last statement is especially important because his acknowledgment that "I'm enormously full of that foreigner" can be read two ways, each contradicting his earlier rejection of the "black fremdling." First, "I'm enormously full of that foreigner" could mean "I'm enormously fond of that foreigner," an affectionate statement that correlates with his subsequent declaration that Jaun is "amorist. I love him" (*FW* 463.18–9). If this is true, then Jaun has transitioned from hating one Shem to loving another and thus replaced the Shaunish refusals of Shem's otherness with a more loving turn towards the "foreigner." Second, "I'm enormously full of that foreigner" could mean "I contain a lot of that foreigner within myself." This is not only itself an oxymoronic statement that implodes the self-other binary at the heart of the twins' Darwinistic rivalry, but it also correlates with Jaun's observation that Dave is "the sneaking likeness of us, faith, me altar's ego in miniature" a few lines beforehand. This recognition that Dave is the "sneaking likeness" of Jaun and Izzy thus challenges not only Jaun's earlier depictions of Shem as an enemy for Izzy to avoid, but also each persecution of Shem as "Mr Unmentionable" or "nos halfcousin of mine" in the twin rivalries of the text. Of course, the fact that we are dealing with multiple Shem and Shaun characters makes it possible for Jaun to hate one Shem and love another, but even this explanation undercuts the Shaun manifestations' persecutions of Shem because those are categorical rejections of Shem's lowness that lose legitimacy the moment exceptions start being entertained. Thus, by identifying a Shem manifestation that he loves, Jaun enables a twin dynamic not grounded in Shaun's persecution of Shem to emerge that challenges the amatory Darwinism at the heart of the novel's sibling rivalries.

Shaun's negotiation of narcissism culminates in the "drama parapolylogic" of III.3 (*FW* 474.5), where Yawn's reflections at Mamalujo's inquest recognize the interrelationship of the twins more than previous Shauns would admit and rupture the *Wake*'s amatory Darwinism. Initially, Yawn's responses seemingly recall the narcissism of his earlier manifestations, as he remains preoccupied with winning Issy ("Have you seen her? Typette, my tactile O!" [*FW* 478.26–7]) and refusing Shem ("What cans such wretch to say to I or how have My to doom with him?" [*FW* 483.17–8]). However, Yawn's thoughts abruptly shift from rejection to reconciliation, as Joyce uses Giordano Bruno's coincidence of contraries (where "every power in nature must evolve an opposite in order to realise itself and opposition brings reunion" [*LI* 226]) to reshape the "naturel rejection" and "assent of man" that comprise the twin rivalries over Issy into a more genuine dialogue. In response to Mamalujo's question "whither the indwellingness of that which shamefieth be entwined of one or atoned of two" (*FW* 488.2–3), Yawn invokes Bruno to emphasize the twins' inseparability:

> Dearly beloved brethren: Bruno and Nola, leymon bogholders and stationary lifepartners off orangey Saint Nessau Street, were explaining it avicendas all round each other ere yesterweek out of Ibn Sen and Ipanzussch. When himupon Nola Bruno monopolises his egobruno most unwillingly seses by the mortal powers alionola equal and opposite brunoipso, *id est*, eternally provoking alio opposite equally as provoked as Bruno at being eternally opposed by Nola. Poor omniboose, singalow singelearum: so is he! (*FW* 488.4–12)

Whereas previous Shauns deny Shem's legitimacy, Yawn describes the twins as both "dearly beloved brethren" and "stationary lifepartners," which not only replaces their previous hostility with love, but punningly evokes the Browne & Nolan bookstore on Saint Nassau Street to characterize the brothers as "partners" in a union of opposing forces. The legal analysis of Bruno strengthens this pairing, as Yawn deems any attempt to exterminate his Shemish rival impossible since "Nola Bruno" cannot "[monopolise] his egobruno" without simultaneously "ses[ing]" his "equal and opposite" since "Bruno" is "eternally opposed by Nola." This recognition that the oppositional relationship between the twins is not only "equal," but "[eternal]," thus prevents Shaun's "assent of man" to occur through Shem's "naturel rejection" since the degenerative rival is "equal and opposite" to the beau ideal and can never be permanently vanquished. Through this use of Bruno, Joyce thus validates Buber's contention that "the unity of the contraries" as the "mystery at the innermost core" of his idea of "dialogue" (*Israel* 17), which enables the turn to the other that the Book III Shauns rehearse to explicitly refuse the rejections of otherness behind amatory Darwinism.

Also, Yawn's memories of Shem are fonder than in previous episodes. While Jaun mostly treats Shemish rivals as "enem[ies] of our country," Yawn describes Shem as a "wellmet Capeler, united Irishmen," which characterizes him as belonging to the nation by equating him to the patriots of the 1798 rising. Additionally, Yawn calls him "the skipgod, expulled for looking at churches from behind" (*FW* 488.22–3), which is the first time a Shaunish character has depicted his Shemish counterpart as a scapegoat, and Yawn's acknowledgement that Shem has been unjustly treated simultaneously acknowledges the refusal of otherness at the heart of their rivalry. Yawn's subsequent memories of the departed Shem strengthen this attitude shift, as he directly admits that "I wronged you" and later declares that "I am no scholar but I loved that man who has africot lupps with the moonshane in his profile, my shemblable! My freer!" (*FW* 489.7; 26–8). Here, Shaun's acknowledgement that he wronged Shem and his declaration that he loves him as his brother constitute explicit affirmations of otherness that challenge the earlier repulsions of previous Shauns, and even though Yawn indicates that Shem has gone away, his reference to his departed brother as "my fond fosther, E. Obiit Nolan" at 489.13 right before he calls him "my freer!" uses Bruno's coincidence of contraries to maintain their equal connection. Since these fonder reflections emerge from Yawn's initial desire for "Typette," Yawn thus reconfigures the Darwinistic impulses of his earlier manifestations into a more affirming attitude towards Shem within his amorous meditations that build off of the reconciliatory potential of III.2's conclusion.

More importantly, Yawn's role as the medium for his family's polylogic response to Mamalujo represents Joyce's definitive challenge to amatory Darwinism. Not only is Yawn's role in HCE's defense itself an act of love, but the specific arguments from the voices that emanate from Yawn's comatose body enable the *Wake*'s lovers to explicitly challenge the evolutionary narcissism that has been foisted upon them. I have shown how Yawn's reflections on Shem critique his rejection as the devolved suitor, but he also enables Issy to interrogate the coquetry she is forced to undertake, and his depictions of the moment when "the illassorted first couple first met with each other" explicitly reconfigure the Darwinistic nature of *Wakean* romance by positioning the ALP-HCE marriage as a response to the text's previous narcissistic conflicts (*FW* 503.9). As he sets up HCE's courtship of ALP, Yawn notes "Erasmus Smith's burstall boys with their underhand leadpencils climbing to her crotch for the origin of spices and charlotte darlings with silk blue askmes chatterin in dissent to them" (*FW* 504.26–9), which Darwinistically evokes the twins' contentious discovery of "the whome of the eternal geomater," and he references "the killmaimthem pensioners chucking overthrown milestones up to her to fall her cranberries and her pommes annettes for their unnatural refection" (*FW* 504.31–3), which similarly references HCE's park scandal. By using Darwin references to position these antagonistic romantic episodes as the environment that preceded the "illassorted first couple," Yawn's subsequent depiction of HCE's union with ALP through the tree imagery on 505 becomes the loving alternative to the "sowiveall of the prettiest." In so doing, Joyce implicates the *Wake*'s numerous falls in amatory Darwinism, and by positioning ALP's love for HCE as the alternative to such rivalries, he reveals the affirmation of otherness to be the necessary challenge to the "strangle for love" that results from such conflicts. Thus, not only does the Yawn medium replace the "bleaueyedeal" of Darwinistic romance with a more accommodating lover, but Joyce's transformation of Shaun from a sentimental stereotype into a polylogic interrogator of amatory Darwinism constructs a powerful criticism of the refusal of the other that complements the doomed romantic quests of his early fiction.

This does not mean that Shaun undergoes an attitude shift throughout the *Wake* or that his fonder reflections in Book III replace his earlier narcissism with love. The Shauns of Book III are more open to otherness than their predecessors, but Yawn is not Chuff, and there is nothing to indicate that the sleeping Kevin of III.4 would be any more accommodating to Jerry if he were to awaken. However, although the dreamtext's episodic structure defies tracking a progression in Shaun's attitude towards otherness, the fact that the dreamer can envision versions of Shaun that are more than the "Gaelic champion" of sentimental romance demonstrates Shaun's evolution from his narcissistic predecessors in Joyce's fiction who are unable to overcome their desire to be ideal lovers. Thus, Shaun's multiple manifestations constitute the dreamer continually wrestling with the self's relationship to the other and the ethical responsibilities that arise from that relationship, which better allows for a perpetual negotiation of Joyce's love ethic.

****

As we have seen, Joyce uses the multiple manifestations of the Earwicker children to refashion the narcissistic viewpoints that felled his early protagonists into more affirming relationships between self and other. By reshaping his narcissistic love plots into a Darwinian "sowiveall of the prettiest," Joyce demonstrates his earlier characters' sentimental quests to be hostile battlegrounds where the "assent of man" desired by his narcissistic lovers is only attained through the "naturel rejection" of their love objects and anyone who challenges their romantic self-promotion. In so doing, Joyce's shifting portrayals of Issy, Shem, and Shaun demonstrate how each participant of the *Wake*'s amatory Darwinism is bound by the obligation to "affirm the person [they] struggle with," as the episodic dreamtext enables the children to work through their sibling rivalries and reach more accommodating familial relationships, and thus Joyce's dreamer is better equipped to work past the narcissistic impulses that flash through his mind the more often these Darwinistic episodes cycle through his head. For this reason, *Finnegans Wake*'s shifting narrative continuously works through narcissism and reshapes the self-absorbed refusals of otherness into the genuine dialogues at the foundation of Joyce's love ethic.

However, this renegotiation of narcissism is not only prominent in Joyce's individual portrayals of the children, but also in the parents for which they stand in. Given that Shem and Shaun represent the opposing characteristics of HCE and Issy is a younger manifestation of ALP, their interactions throughout the text also inform our evaluation of the text's primary romantic union. Whereas Issy reveals the flaws of marital sentimentality and Shem and Shaun hint at the possibilities of a loving turn towards otherness, Joyce's affirmation of otherness in *Finnegans Wake* truly takes shape in the struggles of HCE and ALP to reconcile their love for each other amidst the scandal in Phoenix Park. Here the true amorous potential of not just the characters in the *Wake*, but the *Wake* itself, is realized, as the negotiation of narcissism of the children's chapters lays the groundwork for ALP's loving embrace to replace HCE's refusals with an invitation of openness that provides the emphatic coda to the Joycean love ethic.

Chapter 11
Arrah Na Plurabelle

In *Joyce's Book of the Dark*, John Bishop highlights the centrality of the Earwicker marriage to *Finnegans Wake*. "Beginning with the phrase 'Eve and Adam's,'" Bishop notes, Joyce's novel "teems with forms of 'the zeroic couplet' HCE and ALP, which Joyce modulates in the course of the book, through 'minney combinaisies and permutandies' (284.12–3)," and he concludes that "these dyadic configurations show that the real hero of *Finnegans Wake*, '*The Bearded Mountain*' ... never exists independently of his 'streamline secret' and consort" (367). Bishop's observation demonstrates not only the frequency in which HCE's relationship to ALP is referenced throughout the *Wake*, but the thematic significance of their marriage to the text, particularly with respect to Joyce's love ethic. Not only do the references to "riverrun," "Eve and Adam's," and "Howth Castle and Environs" in the first lines of the *Wake* unite the two main characters and a church and thus make the HCE-ALP marriage the first image of Joyce's dreamtext (*FW* 3.1–3), but Joyce's identification of the River Liffey and Howth as the entities united at this church also equates their union to the creation of Dublin, and his specification of Adam and Eve's church evokes humanity's first marriage and further emphasizes the broader significance of their union.[1] The repetition of this universalizing tendency throughout the *Wake* thus makes the Earwicker marriage the heart of Joyce's final text, and thus the Joycean oeuvre ends with a complex examination of love whose implications transcend the marital realm.

Of course, even though *Finnegans Wake* is the only novel he wrote as a married person, Joyce would have never written a sentimental tale of connubial bliss. Indeed, Joyce represents the text's central relationship as anything but stable, as HCE engages in an unspecified transgression in Phoenix Park and seems more interested in repairing his social image and pursuing Issy than he is in maintaining the fidelity of his relationship with ALP. Such complications encourage Richard Beckman to argue that "marriage does not have a good name in *Finnegans Wake*," describing it as "the slave of biological forces and clumsy social conventions" and "the instrument of personal power" (83), an argument seemingly validated by the aggressive undertones of HCE's recollections of how he won his bride. Nevertheless, Joyce continues to develop his examination of true love through ALP, whose sufferings do not quell her love for HCE. Indeed, while HCE's desire to recover from his fall subordinates his marital love to his self-preservation, ALP's

---

[1] Brivic supports this emphasis on the marital significance of ALP and HCE by noting that "the construction that unites HCE and ALP constitutes the place where they reside. For as Niall Montgomery (422–44, cited by B. Benstock 85) first pointed out, HCE and ALP combine to form the anna-gram CHAPEL" (71).

defense of her husband and her acceptance of his otherness despite his misdeeds prove that the *Wake*'s central relationship affirms Buber's "basic principle of marriage" and lays the groundwork for the true amorous implications of the text.

I am Big Altoogooder

Like most things in *Finnegans Wake*, formulating a conclusive assessment of Humphrey Chimpden Earwicker is practically impossible. Not only does Joyce provide multiple, contradictory characterizations of HCE that make him simultaneously an invading Viking and King Roderick and at various times a publican, a sleeping mythological giant, and Humpty Dumpty, but he also keeps him offstage for the majority of the novel, providing us a limited opportunity to form a direct impression of him. This indirect access to the novel's protagonist, combined with the indeterminate nature of his crime in the park, makes it difficult to dismiss him as a cheating patriarchal tyrant who continuously gets his comeuppance through the falls of *Finnegans Wake*, for we must remember that these easy castigations are provided to us second- and third-hand by a persecuting public, the gossipy washerwomen, and a judgmental Mamalujo who are determined to magnify HCE's crimes and denigrate him regardless of the true nature of his sins. In fact, when we are provided with a protagonist forced to defend himself against the trumped up charges of an unforgiving public, we may be tempted to view HCE as an iteration of Leopold Bloom, and the echoes of "Cyclops" and "Circe" in his continued assertions of his commonalities to others seemingly support this idea of another Joycean protagonist concerned with an accommodating body politic.

And yet, HCE is not Bloom's mirror image. Both characters are seemingly unjustly maligned by a vitriolic public and respond by asserting that they are more alike than their persecutors care to admit, but they do so for different reasons, and it is difficult to see Bloom's accommodating refutations of anti-Semitism in HCE's protestations of innocence. While Bloom's retorts to the citizen challenge the bigotry at the heart of his monocular nationalism, HCE's assertions of universality are primarily designed to convince others that he is innocent of the charges against him. While Bloom's lack of an analogous crime against which to defend himself makes this difference understandable, it is noteworthy that Bloom's instinct is to defend his race while HCE's motivation is to defend himself, and the narcissistic implications of HCE's defenses take on amatory significance in his attempts to cover over his fall by fashioning himself as a romantic and civic hero. In the limited instances in which Joyce allows HCE to speak, he primarily avoids culpability for the scandal by stressing that he is a "big altoogooder" (*FW* 358.15–6), and he uses memories of wooing ALP as evidence of his virility to challenge the crowd's buffoonish caricatures of him. This provides another important distinction between Earwicker and Bloom, for whereas Bloom uses his memories of Molly Tweedy to strengthen his love for her, Earwicker more closely evokes Gabriel

Conroy by covering over his present-day marriage to ALP through references to his courtship, which replaces the otherness of his primary love object with a sentimental romantic past designed to promote his ideal self-image.

The narcissistic implications of HCE's self-fashioning are evident in the pub scene of II.3, where the publican is forced to defend himself against the derisive gossip of the *Wake*'s twelve citizens. Reminiscent of "Cyclops," Joyce's protagonist finds himself the butt of every derisive conversation that occurs in the pub, as the customers' comments about HCE's scandal are compounded by the stories of the Norwegian captain and Buckley and the Russian general that are explicitly designed to indicate his guilt. Given both stories' portrayals of the HCE-like protagonists as bumbling disgraces who get their deserving comeuppances, it is understandable that HCE would spend the majority of the chapter protesting his innocence against his customers' scorn, and Kitcher highlights the romantic significance of his defense by arguing that "the attempt to renew his amatory life percolates through this speech with an ever increasing frequency of suggestive vocabulary" (174). However, these defenses frequently deny the heart of "his amatory life," as HCE's insistence that he is mightier than the pub stories give him credit for rejects the reality of his marriage for another narcissistic fairy tale.

The denial of marriage at the heart of HCE's defenses is initially seen in his reaction to the story of the Norwegian captain. Indeed, the disparaging associations to Earwicker pervade this pub tale, as the Scandinavian nature of the duplicitous captain highlights the citizens' frequent associations of HCE's assumed foreign heritage to the ancient invaders of Ireland, and the numerous portrayals of the captain's cheating the story's tailor dovetail the customers' frequent allusions to HCE's crimes. This use of the story climaxes in the description of the captain's marriage to the tailor's daughter, as the storyteller's description of how the captain was ultimately felled parallel not only HCE's marriage to ALP, but his present stagnation as well. Initially, the ship's husband references the captain's marriage as the price he must pay for robbing the tailor, not only noting that "I've fined you a faulter-in-law, to become your son-to-be, gentlemens tealer" (*FW* 325.15–6), which notes that the husband has both "found" the captain a father-in-law, and "fined" the captain a father-in-law as punishment for his crimes, but also by calling him "tsay-fong tsei-foun" (*FW* 325.14), which McHugh translates as Chinese for "tailor robber" and thus explicitly ties the captain's marriage to his robberies (325). The ship's husband's subsequent assertion that they will have "no more of your maimed acts after this" or he will "rehearse your comeundermends and first mardhyr you entirely" develops this equation of marriage and retribution (*FW* 325.33; 326.2–3), equating the wedding with the captain's punishment and threatening a violent parole violation for any subsequent crimes. The equation of the captain's marriage with the Earwicker union is explicit throughout the ending of the tale, as he refers to the "nowedding captain" as "the rude hunnerable Humphrey" and names the tailor's daughter "anny living plusquebelle" (*FW* 325.27–8; 327.6), and the acrostic HCE that signifies Earwicker's presence throughout the text is repeated several times throughout this section of the tale ("hero chief explunderer" [*FW* 326.9]; "Heri the Concorant Erho" [*FW* 328.25]; "Horuse to crihumph over his enemy" [*FW* 328.34–5]). Thus, the "scat story to the husband's capture" portrays HCE's nuptials as his imprisonment (*FW* 325.19), and the customers' re-presentation of the Earwicker marriage gives them further ammunition to disparage their publican.

The references to HCE's current crimes magnify the persecutorial nature of the Norwegian captain story. For example, not only does the storyteller name ALP as the tailor's daughter to be betrothed to HCE's "nowedding captain," but he subsequently describes ALP as "the lippeyear's wonder of Totty go, Newschool" who is "readoromanscing long evmans invairn, about little Anny Roners and all the Lavinias of ester yours and pleding for them to herself in the periglus glatsch hangs over her trickle bed" (*FW* 327.7–8, 11–4). Here, the references to a leap-year girl who is associated with "Esthers" and is pleading to herself in a looking glass all signify Issy, and while her relationship to a young ALP makes these references in a story about her mother's courtship understandable, they also signify HCE's present lust for his daughter that both creates tension in his marriage and evokes the two young temptresses of the park scandal. This last result is particularly significant to the end of the Norwegian captain story, as this depiction of Issy is embellished by numerous references to the raven and the dove, which also signify the temptresses ("twentynine to her dozen and coocoo him didulceydovely to his old cawcaws huggin and munin for his strict privateer" [*FW* 327.35–6]). The later reference to the captain being "cawcaught" and "coocaged" not only solidifies the equation of HCE's marriage and his imprisonment (*FW* 329.13), but also confirms the story's allusion to the park scandal, as the "caw" and "coo" allude to the raven and dove that "ca[tch]" and "[cage]" HCE and the vocal sounds of "cawcaught" and "coocaged" replicate HCE's stammer that signifies his guilt over the scandal throughout the *Wake*. Thus, "the Norwegian Captain and the Tailor" becomes a weapon for the customers to equate HCE's marriage with his fall and to deride him further for his unspecified crimes.

Given the marital associations of the Norwegian captain story, HCE's subsequent response to the servant Kate's request for him to come upstairs is telling. Immediately following the conclusion of the story, Kate brings HCE a seductive message from ALP, written in "amnest plein language" (*FW* 333.27), telling him that "she was a wanton for De Marera to take her genial glow to bed" (*FW* 334.4–5). However, given that this immediately follows the "scat story to the husband's capture," for HCE to acknowledge this request would further highlight his role in their present-day marriage that has been derided by his customers throughout the chapter, especially considering that the letter's "amnest plein language" would apparently "pierce his ropeloop ear" (*FW* 333.28). This statement not only implies "pierc[ing]" his leap year and highlights his lust for Issy, but also connotes his moniker Persse O'Reilly (as does the subsequent reference to "Podushka" at 333.28, which McHugh translates as Czech for oreiller [333]) and thus recalls Hosty's ballad that scorns HCE for the park scandal. Thus, ALP's turning towards her husband only foments his thoughts about a younger version of her, and rather than calling further attention to his marriage, HCE ignores ALP's request and continues to keep bar throughout II.3, which signifies an explicit rejection of his wife's love in an effort to repair his wounded self-image.[2]

HCE's obsession with his self-image is strengthened later in II.3 after Butt and Taff's radio performance of "Buckley and the Russian General." Here, another derisive story of a stumbling fool who gets what is coming to him is loudly applauded by the customers, as they note that "bud did down well right" to shoot the general for his offense (*FW* 355.8), and their determination that "as to whom the major guiltfeather pertained it was Hercushiccups' care to educe" confirms the radio play as another tale told to exclude HCE for his transgressions (*FW* 355.11–2). For this reason, HCE's speech that immediately follows constitutes another chance for him to replace their castigations of his fall with a more flattering self-portrait, and the text's framing of this speech through Thomas Moore's ballad "After the Battle" further validates Kitcher's reading of it as a specific attempt to repair his amatory prowess ("Nightclothesed, arooned, the conquerods sway. After their battle thy fair bosom" [*FW* 355.19–20]).[3] However, the Moore reference also paints HCE's defense with a sentimental brush and thus anticipates its self-centered foundations, as his attempts to portray himself as a romantic hero fall short of affirming the reality of his marriage and only precipitate his rejection at the chapter's conclusion.

Initially, HCE seems like he will pursue a similar line of argumentation to Bloom in "Cyclops." Noting that the crimes the Russian general (and by extension himself) is accused of are "tootrue enough in Solidan's Island as in Moltern Giaourmany and from the Amelakins off to date back to land of engined Egypsians" (*FW* 355.21–3), he asserts that nobody is blameless for the transgressions of which he is accused, "for whole men is lepers" (*FW* 355.33). This assertion of universal interconnectedness is strengthened by HCE's rewording of Shem's "farst wriggle from the ubivence, whereom is man, that old offender, nother man, wheile he is asame" (*FW* 356.12–4), which seemingly echoes Bloom's arguing that Christians and Jews are the same in response to the citizen's anti-Semitism. However, whereas Bloom preaches universal interconnectedness to advocate tolerance, HCE preaches universalism to demonstrate his personal innocence, as his insistence that "I am big altoogooder" shows that his desire to equate the general's transgressions with those of the common man is mostly an attempt to repair his wounded image (*FW* 358.15–6). Thus, while his defense of the Russian general and his advocacy of the interconnectedness of humanity echoes Bloom's compassion in *Ulysses*, the narcissistic motivations that compel his defense undercut his speech and only magnify his fall at the end of the chapter.

Specifically, HCE's attempts to overshadow the customers' castigations of him through universalism are punctured by the numerous references to the park

---

[2] Kitcher similarly argues that "HCE does not go up. Instead he keeps the bar open, perhaps because he is so concerned with social acceptance, with the camaraderie of his customers, with fitting in" (14).

[3] Reference to Moore's ballad noticed by McHugh on 355.

scandal that he accidentally utters during his defense. While he attempts to defend the sexual transgressions the customers deride through general accounts of their normality, his generalized pleas give way to specific references to his crime that unravel his strategy. This primarily occurs during his recounted thumbing through Aubrey Beardsley's illustrated edition of Oscar Wilde's *Salome*, itself a play about a protagonist undone by a temptress, as the pictures he cites as particularly appealing betray references to the temptresses in the park. He notes the "ravening shadow" and "dovely line" of the pictures (*FW* 357.16–7), a misstep he repeats through his subsequent references to the "colombophile and corvinophobe alike" (*FW* 358.12–3), which McHugh translates as Latin raven and dove references (358), and his botched references to the song "I Lift up My Finger & I say Tweet Tweet," in which he misrecites the "tweet tweet" as both the raven's "cawcaw" and the dove's "coocoo" (*FW* 357.20; 358.1). HCE also accidentally references Phoenix Park multiple times during his speech, compromising his claims of general erotic fascination through specific references to both General Gough's statue (*FW* 357.31) and the Furry Glen in the park (*FW* 357.31–2). Thus, even though HCE intends for his speech to cover over his specific culpability with general references to the sins of humanity, his specific scandal punctures through his strategy and undercuts his attempts to repair his self-image.

Ultimately, HCE's desire to respond to the pub's castigation through general assertions of innocence precipitates his downfall at the conclusion of II.3. Only a few lines after he asserts that he is a "big altoogooder," the narration mocks his protestations of innocence by saying that "he declared that "win a gain was in again, Flying the Perseoroyal" (*FW* 358.19–20), in which the perceived resurrection of Finnegan is overshadowed by equations of HCE to both the Flying Dutchman of the Norwegian captain tale and Persse O'Reilly. This demonstrates that HCE's attempts to overshadow his culpability and reassert his amatory prowess have only fomented the citizens' scorn, as their subsequent castigation of HCE after closing time precipitates the Roderick O'Conor sequence in which HCE, as the last high king of Ireland, drinks the dregs of his customers' drinks and collapses in a drunken stupor. The fact that HCE's generalized self-endorsement precipitates the fall of Roderick O'Conor thus demonstrates the futility of his attempts to repair his amatory self-image by denying the reality of his marital situation, as both his explicit refusals of ALP and his specific transgressions lock him into a defense strategy that renders his usurpation and fall inevitable.

The hazards of HCE's amatory refusals are further illustrated in III.3, where the Earwicker voice that emanates from the sleeping Yawn fashions himself as the masterbuilder of Dublin whose grand love affair with Anna Liffey validates his innocence. Similar to II.3, here Earwicker's voice rises to address the charges of a judgmental Mamalujo determined to get to the bottom of his crime in the park. However, whereas the scenarios between the two scenes are similar, a couple of important differences between the two HCE speeches are worth noting. First, III.3's HCE explicitly denies culpability for the crime in the park. Whereas the publican of II.3 attempted to cover over his scandal through general references to universal sins, here Earwicker's voice protests his innocence, branding the cad a drunk (*FW* 534.29–30), dismissing the "meisies" who tempted him as "sulken taarts," and labeling the "hole affair" as "rotten muckswinish porcupig's draff" (*FW* 535.16; 20–1).

More importantly, the HCE of III.3 explicitly declares his love for ALP. While the II.3 publican refused his wife's invitation to come to bed, the voice of III.3 frequently references his courtship of her. At one point, HCE directly addresses his "dear lady" (*FW* 535.31), asking her to preference his good qualities over his misdeeds ("judge on my tree by our fruits" [*FW* 535.31–2]) and to "pity poor Haveth Childers Everywhere with Mudder" (*FW* 535.34–5). Then, in his subsequent accounts to Mamalujo, the Earwicker voice fondly recollects the early days of their courtship, saying that he "did umgyrdle her about, my vermincelly vinagerette, with all loving kindness as far as in man's might it lay and enfranchised her to liberties of fringes" (*FW* 548.18–9). His subsequent depictions of this "loving kindness" take on mythic proportions, as he notes that he "spread before my Livvy .. my selvage mats of lecheworked lawn, my carpet gardens of Guerdon City, with chopes pyramidous and mousselimes and beaconphires and colossets and pensilled turisses for the busspleaches of the summiramies and esplandas and statuesques and templeogues" (*FW* 553.4, 8–12). This shapes his role as masterbuilder into the ideal romantic suitor presenting the seven wonders of the world to his beloved, and his subsequent observation that he "laid down before the trotters to my eblanite my stony battered waggonways, my nordsoud circulums, my eastmoreland and westlandmore, running boullowards and syddenly parading" transforms the creation of Dublin into HCE's loving gift to Anna Liffey (*FW* 553.28–31). Thus, in the progression from II.3 to III.3, HCE's manifestations seem to have evolved from ignoring ALP to celebrating her, and his concluding observation that "she lalaughed in her diddydid domino to the switcheries of the whip" seemingly replace the stale marriage of the pub chapter with an ardent embrace (*FW* 554.8–9).

However, while HCE's descriptions for ALP are more passionate in III.3, several factors complicate our ability to assign a genuine affirmation of her to the Earwicker voice. For one thing, the HCE manifestation at Yawn's inquest still uses his amorous past to avoid guilt for the park scandal. Whereas the II.3 publican avoided acknowledging his marriage out of fear of culpability, his III.3 manifestation explicitly uses his love for ALP as evidence that he could never have transgressed in the park. The relationship between his love and his defense is evident in the opening lines of the speech, as he says that "by my halfwife, I think how our public at large appreciates it most highly from me that I am as cleanliving as could be" and he contends that "on my verawife I never was nor can afford to be guilty of crim crig con of malfeasance trespass against parson with the person of a youthful gigirl frifrif friend" (*FW* 532.15–6, 18–20). His subsequent insistence that "our private chaplain of Lambeyth and Dolekey" "can speak loud to you some quite complimentary things about my clean charactering, even when detected in the dark .... when I introduced her .... to our fourposter" continues

HCE's strategy of pointing to his marriage as proof of his clean record (*FW* 533.8, 12–6). Thus, even though HCE's depictions of his "bestpreserved wholewife" are more passionate in III.3 than in previous chapters (*FW* 533.4), his reliance on this passion as evidence of his innocence reduces his marital love to a means to an end rather than an authentic affirmation of ALP.

Along those lines, HCE's protestations of innocence continue to betray his culpability. Similar to II.3, HCE's attempts to portray himself as a "cleanliving" citizen are constantly punctured by incriminating admissions that only magnify the perception of his guilt. Not only are his early assertions of innocence compromised by his guilty stammer (e.g., the above denial of a "youthful gigirl frifrif friend"), but he later follows his depiction of erecting the National University of Ireland by asking, "was I not rosette on two stellas of little egypt? had I not rockcut readers, hieros, gregos and democriticos?: triscastellated, bimedallised" (*FW* 551.30–2), which implicates him with the two Stellas and the three soldiers in the park. His subsequent depiction of building Dublin magnifies his guilt, as his love present to ALP includes references to Furry Glen (*FW* 553.22) and the Magazine Wall (*FW* 553.24) in Phoenix Park, and his subsequent reference to "a Queen's garden of her phoenix" references The Queen's Garden at the Phoenix, the original name of Phoenix Park (*FW* 553.24–5; noticed by McHugh on 553). Again, HCE's attempts to avoid culpability for the scandal are undercut by incriminating statements that signify his guilt, and since these statements are explicitly made in reference to his passion for ALP, the Earwicker voice's slips undercut the viability of his affirming portrait of his wife with each mistake he makes.

The continued recurrence of the park scandal in HCE's memories of ALP not only demonstrates his failure to use his marriage as a means to an end, but it also demonstrates a key flaw in the Earwicker voice's portrayals of marital love: all of his depictions of marital bliss with ALP are confined to the past. Whereas the Blooms used memories of their courtship and proposal to rekindle their present-day love, HCE prioritizes his memories of newlywed ALP over his present-day wife, which simply repeats his II.3 persona's refusals of any reminders of the current state of his marriage. The pitfalls of this approach are especially problematic in HCE's strategy at the inquest because past marital bliss alone cannot refute charges of a more contemporary transgression. In fact, HCE's prioritization of the past actually incriminates him in an adulterous lust, as his love for the past ALP materializes in his incestuous desire for Issy, and this lust infects the amorous viability of his speech. Indeed, at the very beginning of his defense, when HCE describes his attraction to "the ripest littlums wifukiea round the globelettes globes" (*FW* 532.30–1), he declares, "I kickick keenly love such, particularly while savouring of their flavours at their most perfect best when served with heliotrope ayelips, as this is, where I do drench my jolly soul on the pu pure beauty of hers past" (*FW* 532.36–533.3). Not only is this protestation of love compromised by HCE's guilty stammer, but his reference to ALP's "heliotrope ayelips" also evokes the color of Issy's underwear that was the answer to the riddle in II.1 and reveals how his lust for his daughter compromises his affirmation of his wife. Thus, the

Earwicker voice's focus on the past is undercut by a marital stagnation that he cannot suppress, and his reliance on past love as proof of his "cleanliving" further incriminates him in adulterous obsessions at home and in the park.

Finally, HCE's loving depictions of ALP are undone by the violent depictions of their courtship. While his speech concludes with a seemingly endless list of gifts he presented to his beloved, the Earwicker voice's earlier accounts of their marriage are characterized by disturbingly aggressive rhetoric that compromises the authenticity of his marital affirmation. He initially notes that "I waged love on her: and spoiled her undines. And she wept: O my lors!" (*FW* 547.7–8), which equates his wooing to a warlike advance and depicts their sexual union in terms more akin to rape. His subsequent observation that he "thumbed her with iern of Erin and tradesmanmarked her lieflang mine for all and singular" also portrays their marriage as HCE's gaining ownership over ALP, a portrayal of amatory possession that is strengthened by his subsequent acknowledgment that "I pudd a name and wedlock boltoned round her the which to carry till her grave, my durdin dearly, Appia Lippia Pluviabilla" (*FW* 548.5–6).[4] Even his subsequent assertions of "loving kindness" are compromised by his desire to possess ALP. He notes that he bestowed his gifts "fortiffed by my right as man of capitol" (*FW* 548.16–7), and he "did *umgyrdle* her about" with his presents, which McHugh translates as German for "girdle" and thus reveals his gifts to be methods to bind ALP to him further (548). Also, the corrective nature of some of HCE's presents confirms the lack of affirmation in his passionate descriptions of ALP. While he does portray the creation of Dublin as his labor of love for ALP, he also identifies "spiceries for her garbage breath" (*FW* 550.9), "Biorwik's powlver and Uliy's oils" for "my saffronbreathing mongoloid" (*FW* 550.17–8), and other such presents to ensure that his "shopsoiled doveling" was "kinly civicised" (*FW* 550.23). These corrective gifts, combined with his later observation that "with fairskin book and ruling rod, vein of my vergin page, her chastener ever I did learn my little ana countrymouse in alphabeater cameltemper" (*FW* 552.36–553.3), demonstrate that HCE not only wished to possess ALP, but to reshape her into a more presentable, civilized wife, which recalls Gabriel's attempts to whitewash Gretta's "country cute[ness]" in "The Dead." Thus, despite the passionate overtones of the Earwicker voice's depictions of their courtship, his specific portrayal of their marriage constitutes an explicit refusal of ALP's otherness that reduces their relationship to a narcissistic marital possession.

Ultimately, HCE's defense at Mamalujo's inquest in III.3 falls short of portraying him as a loving husband who is innocent of the park scandal. While

---

[4] Devlin also argues that "This vision of the 'beyashmakt' woman returns in one of the accounts of ALP's marriage to HCE, a context that clarifies even more markedly the wish for female subjugation that motivates the exotic and erotic imago from popular eastern lore. The account highlights HCE's capture and appropriation of ALP, the fetterchain from Circean fantasy finding its Wakean transformation in the locked chain of a chastity belt" (*Wandering* 152–3).

the voice protests his love for ALP as evidence that he is a decent person, his focus on their romantic past suppresses the reality of their current relationship, and his specific memories of their courtship betray his preference for owning a civilized, docile wife instead of affirming the woman he actually married. The prevalence of this desire for amatory possession is confirmed in the scene in the Porter house in III.4. For example, HCE's lust for Issy is evoked by Mr Porter's "present[ing]" his "wappon, blade drawn to the full" to "the infant Isabella" while Mrs Porter comforts the crying Jerry (*FW* 566.21–3), and the fact that his arousal subsequently compels his desire to sleep with his wife confirms that his love for her is guided by his lust for an earlier version of Mrs Porter. Also, Mr Porter expresses his desire to sleep with his wife in rhetoric that confirms his desire to possess her. After Mrs Porter has calmed Jerry down, her husband demands that they continue their lovemaking by arguing that he has a right to have sexual relations with her ("Legalentitled. Accesstopartnuz. Notwildebeestch. Byrightofoaptz. Twainbeonerflsh. Haveandholdpp" [*FW* 571.28–9]). That his desires are couched in terms of what he is legally entitled to rather than in his marital love for Mrs Porter confirms Mr Porter to be another HCE manifestation determined to possess and use his wife for his own gratification rather than affirm an equal partner. Thus, the Porters do have sex towards the end of III.4, but any trace of passion is absent from Mr Porter's gratification, as their lovemaking is couched in cricket metaphors that emphasize his domination of Mrs Porter and make him seem ridiculous ("The way he was slogging his paunch about, elbiduubled, meet oft mate on, like hale King Willow, the robberer" [*FW* 583.27–8]), and his climax is simply referenced as "his reignbolt's [being] shot" (*FW* 590.10). Through this depiction of the feeble Mr Porter, Joyce confirms the lack of amorous passion at the heart of HCE's perceptions of ALP and thus provides us with an important foil to Bloom, a person similarly persecuted by a hostile crowd and infatuated with his amorous past, but whose interest in repairing his self-image and asserting his amatory prowess blinds him to the one person who still affirms him regardless of how far he has fallen (and will continue to fall).

I am Leafy Speafing

Through her many manifestations in *Finnegans Wake*, ALP reveals herself to be the amorous counterpoint to HCE's narcissism. Not only does she vindicate her husband by dictating her mamafesta and supplying gifts to his detractors, but Joyce's descriptions of ALP directly counteract the flaws in HCE's attempts to rebuild his amatory prowess in two ways. First, ALP is explicitly associated with otherness, as her personas frequently root through the detritus that HCE wishes to deny. Whether it is Biddy Doran the hen digging the redemptive letter out of a midden heap or Anna Liffey's cleansing her husband's dirty laundry through her filthy waters, ALP's defenses of HCE are frequently associated with mire and excrement, and the fact that she can use the filth that HCE denies to construct a loving embrace demonstrates the affirmation of otherness at the heart of her turn towards HCE. Second, ALP recognizes the vitality of the present. At the beginning of the *Wake*, I.1's narrator highlights ALP's ability "to steal our historic presents from the past postpropheticals so as to will make us all lordy heirs and ladymaidesses of a pretty nice kettle of fruit" (*FW* 11.30–2), and this grammatical association of ALP with the historical present reveals an important distinction between the Earwicker spouses. Whereas HCE denies his present problems by focusing on his courtship with a young ALP and lusting after her past beauty in Issy, ALP uses the disasters of the present to redeem her husband and revitalize their marriage, and her concluding soliloquy unites fond memories of the past with acknowledgements of their troubled present in an amorous redemption akin to Bloom's and Molly's use of memory in *Ulysses*. Thus, whereas Beckman sees "tremendous loyalty" rather than "affection" in her "fierce defense of him against all charges of guilt" (90), ALP's actions are explicitly designed to force HCE to acknowledge and affirm their relationship despite their marital problems, transforming the park scandal into a loving embrace.

Early evidence of ALP's amorous role can be found in the Prankquean episode of I.1, where Joyce's parody of Grace O'Malley's conflict with the Earl of Howth isolates the differing perspectives and roles that ALP and HCE adopt in their marriage. At first glance, portraying ALP as a pirate invader who steals the Earl's children may not seem the most flattering way to depict a romantic heroine, but Joyce's specific take on this legendary encounter effectively counterbalances HCE's suppression with ALP's openness. By depicting Jarl van Hoother as locked up in his castle and refusing the Prankquean's three requests for porter, Joyce associates this HCE manifestation with the refusals of his later counterparts, as his ignoring the Prankquean's requests will be later echoed in his rejections of ALP's seductive invitation in II.3 and his promotion of the young ALP over her present-day counterpart in III.3. Thus, Joyce's specific depictions of the Jarl shutting the Prankquean out so that he can "lay cold hands on himself" and "shake warm hands with himself" highlight the narcissism of his refusals (*FW* 21.11; 36), preferring a masturbatory isolation over an invitation of openness and tainting his subsequent refusals of ALP with a similar masturbatory implication.

By extension, the Prankquean's intrusions and riddles can be seen as her forcing the Jarl to affirm the wife he wishes to deny. This is especially true if we follow one of McCarthy's interpretations of her riddle ("Mark the wans, why do I am alook alike a poss of porterpease? [*FW* 21.18–9]) as "part of an attempt to force the Jarl to recognize that he and the Prankquean are closely related," essentially "asking 'why do I look like I could pass as a Porter, please?'" While McCarthy sees the answer to this version of the riddle as ALP revealing herself "either as the wife of, or more importantly, as the daughter of the Jarl" (*Riddles* 109), the more damning answer to HCE is that she is both, as his shut-in life with his "dummy" (the episode's Issy manifestation) is disrupted by the Prankquean's riddle that forces him to acknowledge that his beloved is not only the beautiful girl on his rug, but also the older outsider demanding recognition (*FW* 21.12). From this perspective, each of the Jarl's refusals of the Prankquean are punished by her stealing one child and transforming it into its opposing twin and thus replacing the self-contained existence the Jarl has fashioned for himself with a more accommodating household.

This unsettling of the Jarl's self-contained fantasy climaxes in their direct encounter where the Jarl "clop[s] his rude hand to his eacy hitch" (both "his easy hitch" and "his ECH," confirming the masturbatory nature of his action) and orders the scene's Issy manifestation to "shut up shop, dappy" (*FW* 23.3–5). However, whereas the previous refusals of the Prankquean excluded her from his household, this direct encounter triggers a Viconian thunderword that signals the beginning of a new age, and the aftermath demonstrates the openness that has been triggered by the Jarl's encounter with the Prankquean: "And they all drank free. For one man in his armour was a fat match always for any girls under shurts" (*FW* 23.5–9). While this could be read as the armored HCE conquering the seductive Prankquean, the idea of the Jarl being a "fat match" for her also implies a union, and the presence of the word "amour" in Joyce's portmanteau word for armor emphasizes the amorous significance of their match. The peaceful descriptions of the Jarl's family further demonstrate the loving nature of this aftermath, as ALP holds Issy ("the prankquean was to hold her dummyship"), the warring twins reconcile ("the jimminies was to keep the peacewave"), and HCE "was to get the wind up" (*FW* 23.12–4). Multiple interpretations of the Jarl "get[ting] the wind up" demonstrate the unsettling this result accomplishes to his self-enclosed life. For example, the traditional meaning of the phrase connotes being upset or disturbed, which the Prankquean's demand that the Jarl acknowledge her certainly accomplishes. However, one cannot read the Jarl "get[ting] the wind up" without also being reminded of the Willingdone "g[etting] the band up" (having an erection) in his encounter with the "jinnies" in the Museyroom episode thirteen pages earlier. From this perspective, the Jarl is not only disturbed by the Prankquean's demands, but he is also aroused, and by having the Jarl's masturbatory life giving way to an arousal by the Prankquean he wishes to refuse, Joyce demonstrates the amorous potential of ALP's forcing her husband to acknowledge the otherness he evades throughout the text.

The Prankquean's struggles to force the Jarl to acknowledge that she is "alike a poss of porterpease" are replayed through many of ALP's encounters with HCE, as she not only seeks to defend him from his detractors, but also to revitalize their marriage by encouraging his return to her. Multiple examples of ALP's attempts to recharge their marriage are demonstrated in I.8, where the washerwomen's tale about Anna Livia highlights her unwavering adoration of HCE despite his constant refusals of her. Admittedly, we have to take this story of the Earwicker marriage with a grain of salt since it is narrated through the washerwomen's vitriolic gossip, but even if we downplay their castigations of both HCE and ALP, their descriptions of ALP's actions demonstrate her vigilant attempts to make her husband satisfied with their marriage despite his repeated refusals of her. Quickenough describes ALP's making HCE breakfasts that are thrown back at her (*FW* 199.15–27), singing love songs that are silenced (*FW* 200.4–15), and even supplying him with girls to "go in till him, her erring cheef, and tickle the pontiff aisy-oisy" (*FW* 198.12). This last action is especially significant concerning ALP's attempts to rekindle HCE's love, as she not only satisfies his lust by providing him other women, but she actually "call[s] them in, one by one" and "leg[s] a jig or so on the sihl to show them how to shake their benders and the dainty how to bring to mind the gladdest garments out of sight" (*FW* 200.22–6). By teaching these women how to arouse HCE, ALP becomes the direct source of her husband's arousal and she facilitates his gratification through women who are duplicating her advances, resulting in HCE having sex with women who become iterations of his wife.[5] McHugh's translations of the washerwomen's labeling ALP a "proxenete" are thus instructive here (*FW* 198.17), as his notation that the word both is French slang for "bawd" and literally means "one who negotiates something, esp[ecially] a marriage" enables ALP to use bawdy means to renegotiate her marriage to HCE (198).[6] Thus, it is ALP as well as HCE who "minx[es] marrage and making loof" (*FW* 196.24), and her ability to satisfy her husband through women who perform her own advances towards HCE potentially transforms a "marr[ed]" mirage of a marriage into a mixture of matrimonial love and lovemaking.[7]

However, while HCE gains temporary gratification through ALP's procurement of alternative river women, her defense of him following the park scandal constitutes her most affirming embrace of him. In fact, the chapter's scenario of the washerwomen both airing and cleaning HCE's dirty laundry in the filthy waters of Anna Liffey is an effective depiction of ALP's role as HCE's redeemer, not only because her actions appease a scorning crowd eager to persecute him, but because she facilitates this appeasement by acknowledging the filth that her husband wishes to suppress. The washerwomen note ALP's role as redeemer by mentioning her penning the letter that both accuses and vindicates him, as Quickenough exclaims that "I'm dying down off my iodine feet until I lerryn Anna Livia's cushingloo, that was writ by one and rede by two and trouved by a poule

---

5 This connection between ALP and the women she provides for HCE is strengthened by Joyce's naming them after rivers and thus explicitly equating them to Anna Liffey at 200.19–20.

6 Brivic's equation of ALP's gesture to the negotiations of amatory possession in *Exiles* and *Ulysses* may strengthen the idea of her providing HCE with women as a gesture of her love. He argues that "she might often have to hire [servants] knowing (or denying) that her husband was likely to have ideas about them ... Since the tendency to notice alternatives would be at least as true for the husband, it leads to the implication that one either restricts one's mate or grants the freedom to connect to some extent with others. This question is emphasized in *Exiles*, where Richard allows Bertha to commit adultery, and in *Ulysses*. To give such freedom is for Joyce a central expression of love, and to withhold it is to deny love" (40).

7 Brivic similarly contends that "the washers accuse HCE of 'minxing marrage and making loof' (*FW* 196.36). The charge can be interpreted in many ways, including adultery, or marrying one person and loving another; but I think that the idea of mixing works against this level. This term suggests that the two activities could be combined in one relationship, which might not be a bad thing" (68).

in the parco!" (*FW* 200.35–201.2). This depiction of the letter as a "cushingloo" highlights its simultaneous revealing and redeeming HCE's crime, as the "loo" not only references the Irish ballad "Cusheen Loo" (McHugh 200), but also evokes loo's slang definition as a toilet, implying that the letter that will save ALP's husband will contain the filth against which it is defending him. Also the fact that Quickenough is "dying down off my iodine feet" to read it demonstrates more than her status as a gossip; it also shows that ALP intends for HCE's dirty laundry to be aired, directly positioning the revelation of his otherness as the solution to his persecution.

The gossips' subsequent reference to ALP's delivering gifts to HCE's enemies accomplishes similar objectives, as her presentation of presents to the derisive crowd moves her strategy beyond defending her husband and towards undermining his ostracism from the body politic. Two potential readings of ALP's gesture demonstrate its inherent affirmation of otherness.[8] One could see ALP as bribing the people who scorn her husband, alleviating their anger through desirable gifts that could encourage their reacceptance of HCE despite the park scandal. If we follow this reading, then the combination of letter and presents demonstrates the necessity of affirming the otherness HCE seeks to deny, as ALP airs his dirty laundry and then encourages others to move past their animosity and involve HCE in a more accommodating community. However, Devlin offers an even more enticing consideration. Noting that "ALP's seemingly generous distribution of Christmas parcels takes on unsavory overtones when we remember that on a naturalistic level Anna Livia is the anal Liffey of 'dear dirty Dublin,'" Devlin contends that "her presents may be the trash people have thrown into her which in flood she vengefully returns to them" (*Wandering* 157). Whether her return of the people's "trash" is purely vengeful is up for debate, but I like the idea of "anal Liffey" delivering back to her fellow Dubliners the detritus they have thrown into her. If ALP's letter forces HCE to come to grips with his otherness by airing the dirty secrets he suppresses, then ALP's dirty "Christmas parcels" may accomplish something similar, forcing HCE's persecutors to acknowledge the otherness about themselves that they deny. If this is the case, then ALP's gift-giving nullifies the crowd's persecutorial attitude towards HCE by airing everyone's dirty laundry and forcing the hostile Lucalizod crowd to reshape itself into a more accommodating community. Thus, ALP's role as both penwoman and postwoman in I.8 provides another opportunity to show how her forcing her love objects to recognize the otherness of not only her, but of themselves and each other signifies both a personal and social amorous invitation.

---

[8] Joyce's equation of ALP's knapsack with Pandora's Box could also compel a third reading that sees ALP's delivery of presents as a purely vengeful act of punishing the people who persecuted HCE. However, I am not inclined to see ALP's gift delivery as entirely vengeful given Joyce's contention that "all Pandora's gifts are not maladies" in a March 24, 1924 letter to Weaver (*LI* 213).

The success of ALP's actions in the washerwomen chapter is difficult to discern. While ALP does take decisive steps towards vindicating her husband, HCE's attitude throughout the chapter remains scornful and disdainful towards the wife that his personas refuse throughout the *Wake* and there is no indication that her invitation of openness is accepted at the end of the chapter. However, the efficacy of her amorous actions could be evidenced in the washerwomen's possible encounter with the ghost of Finn MacCool towards the end of I.8, as Doddpebble wonders, "Is that the great Finnleader himself in his joakimono on his statue riding the high horse there forehengist? Father of Otters, it is himself!" (*FW* 214.11–3). While Quickenough quickly shoots down Doddpebble's suspicion, telling her to "throw the cobwebs from your eyes, woman, and spread your washing proper" (*FW* 214.16–7), the resurrection imagery at the end of the chapter is telling. Considering that an episode comprised of ALP's attempts to vindicate her fallen husband ends with the possible return of the fallen giant in Phoenix Park, Joyce highlights the potential for ALP's acknowledgment of the park scandal and continued affirmation of HCE to trigger his resurrection, a theme that will be reiterated through the subsequent ALP personas' defenses of HCE. Indeed, as Joyce concludes his work with even more explicit defenses from ALP, we see the potential of a loving affirmation in her refusal to suppress HCE's crime, demonstrating the direct encounter with otherness that is needed to repair their marriage.

ALP's affirming reaction to the park scandal is further evident in her testimony to Mamalujo in III.3, where the different ALP voices that emanate from Yawn highlight both HCE's scandal and ALP's forgiveness. Here, the defense of HCE manifests itself in the form of three voices, the first two echoing the temptresses and the third constituting ALP's forgiveness. This three-fold structure of the marital defense is itself an extension of ALP's approach to affirming her husband, as it foregrounds the scandal that HCE's voice will unsuccessfully attempt to suppress later in III.3, yet it moves past that transgression through the third voice's characterization of his downfall. Similar to her airing of HCE's dirty laundry and delivery of presents in I.8, ALP's voice follows her references to HCE as a snake in the grass "camouflaged as a blancmange and maple syrop" to tempt "the Emfang de Maurya's class" by castigating everyone involved in the gossip that precipitated his fall" (*FW* 494.20–1). She chastises the cad and his wife for spreading HCE's guilty confession (*FW* 23–5); she denigrates Sully as the "wreuter of annoyimgmost letters and skirriless ballets in Parsee Franch who is Magrath's thug and smells cheaply of Power's spirits," deeming him "not fit enough to throw guts down to a bear" (*FW* 495.2–5); and she indicates that "Synamite is too good" for the people who trashed her husband's reputation (*FW* 494.33). Thus, ALP not only acknowledges her husband's misdeeds and attempts to work past them, but she lambastes the people whose refusals of HCE's otherness caused his ostracism, demonstrating the love at the foundation of her testimony.

More importantly, ALP's loving depiction of her marriage replaces HCE's transgression with an amorous affirmation. After criticizing everyone responsible for his decline, ALP highlights the affection she feels for HCE and the lovemaking between them that persists despite his breach in the park. Specifically, upon declaring that Sully should be hung for destroying HCE's reputation, ALP notes "how we will make laugh over him together, me and my Riley in the Vickar's bed!" (*FW* 495.16–8). This observation not only forecasts an affectionate future for the Earwickers, but her characterization of their lovemaking as "mak[ing] laugh over him together" shows their ability to suppress Sully through their marital affection, and that she resolves to make love to "my Riley" transforms the derisive Persse O'Reilly into an affectionate pet name, which further shows ALP's ability to affirm HCE beyond (and through) his transgression. Similarly, ALP says that HCE "cawls to me Granny-stream-Auborne when I am hiding under my hair from him and I cool him my Finnyking he's so joyant a bounder" (*FW* 495.18–20). Here, the portmanteau words "cawls" and "cool" magnify ALP's renegotiation of the park scandal by reshaping the raven and dove imagery into the loving gestures of husband and wife, which shows that ALP affirms HCE for who he is rather than reshaping him into a more attractive love object, and the fact that she "cool[s]" him "my Finnyking" uses the dove's coo to evoke Finn MacCool and echoes the resurrection potential of I.8's conclusion. Furthermore, the use of the present tense to describe their affectionate names for each other challenges HCE's later obsession with the past by indicating that their loving affirmations of each other are an ongoing occurrence, and thus her testimony combines explicit references to HCE's transgression and evidence of continued affection to demonstrate the both the persistence of their love and its redemptive potential. Thus, when she ends her testimony with the concluding signature "Your wife. Amn. Anm. Amm. Ann" (*FW* 495.33), she transforms her testimony into another manifestation of her letter and ruptures the inquest of HCE's crimes with an affirmation of marital love.

ALP's affirmation of HCE culminates in the closing sections of Book IV, where her revelation of the letter and her monologue confirm her enduring love for her husband despite the strains in their relationship. Similar to ending *Ulysses* with the "clou" of "Penelope," Joyce gives ALP the last word in two respects, as he ends his novel of social ostracism with the letter that vindicates the pariah and he concludes his novel of marital strife with a loving testimony to its persistence. The letter's role in the *Wake*'s examination of love will be addressed in the next chapter, but from a marital perspective, ALP's soliloquy effectively positions her affirmation of HCE as the "indispensible countersign" to HCE's refusals of her throughout the text. For one thing, Joyce's framing of the soliloquy provides a productive counterpoint to the Prankquean episode since ALP again finds herself demanding to be recognized by an absent husband who ignores her presence. However, here ALP directly addresses HCE, inviting him to "rise up now and aruse" and accompany her on a journey through the past scenes of their relationship (*FW* 619.28–9). Norris is thus correct that "the act of raising her fallen husband … takes the form of the simple, loving injunction" ("ALP" 200), as her invitation echoes Molly's reacceptance of her husband in "Penelope" and in expands its amorous potential by replacing Molly's mental meditations with

ALP's direct address to HCE, transforming her affection into a powerful turn to the other that is strengthened through each iteration of the *Wake*.

Initially, the loving tone of ALP's soliloquy demonstrates her continued fondness for HCE. She indicates being "sharm[ed]" by his calling her "leafy, your golden" (*FW* 619.31; 29), noting that "there's a great poet in you too" (*FW* 619.31–2), and she lays out HCE's best clothes because "I want to see you looking fine for me" (*FW* 620.1–2). The affection behind her invitation to "give me your great bearspaw" (*FW* 621.20–1) echoes both Bloom's loving thoughts of Molly throughout *Ulysses* and Molly's joyful remembrance of being called a "flower of the mountain," and ALP's subsequent assurance that HCE will be "glad that I waked you! My! How well you'll feel! For ever after" (*FW* 625.33–4) reveals this journey as another opportunity for her to promote his happiness. The warmth of ALP's "loving invocation" thus demonstrates her ability to continue to affirm the otherness of her beloved despite the difficulties of their relationship, which hints at the reconciliatory possibilities of her monologue.

Additionally, ALP's memories bolster this redemptive potential. Unlike HCE, who buries the present in his contemplations of past love, ALP utilizes memory to embellish her thoughts of their marriage, which enables her to treat past romance as a catalyst for present desire. Just as Molly uses Mulvey and Gardner to influence her perceptions of Bloom, ALP compares HCE to her past lovers, noting that "You make me think of a wonderdecker I once. Or somebalt thet sailder, the man megallant, with the bangled ears. Or an earl was he, at Lucan? Or, no, it's the Iren duke's I mean. Or somebery erse from the Dark Countries" (*FW* 620.6–10). Similar to Molly's promotion of Bloom over her Gibraltar lovers, ALP's inability to describe any of her past lovers beyond "an earl was he" and "somebery erse from the Dark Countries" undermines our ability to consider these characters as legitimate rivals for her affection. The washerwomen of I.8 may utter similarly confused accounts of young ALP's prior lovers to foment their gossipy attacks on the Earwickers, but here the vague nature of these recollections actually aids in her affirmation of her husband by contrasting her indeterminate past suitors with her comprehensive representations of her present love throughout the monologue, which magnifies the amorous potential of her descriptions of their marriage.

Specifically, ALP's memories of her courtship with HCE revitalize their present journey. She recalls the day they first met ("Here, weir, reach, island, bridge. Where you meet I. The day. Remember!" [*FW* 626.7–8]), their marriage night ("Our native night when you twicetook me for some Marienne Sherry and then your Jermyn cousin who signs hers with exes" [*FW* 624.36–635.2]), and Issy's birth ("And blowing off to me, hugly Judsys, what wouldn't you give to have a girl. Your wish was mewill" [*FW* 620.26–7]). Not only do these memories enable their passionate courtship to interrupt their marital stagnation, but ALP frequently ties this passion directly to the walk she wishes to take with HCE, as her desire to "go duct to Danegreven" is brought about by her recollections of "when I ran berrying after hucks and haws" (*FW* 622.20; 17–8) and "[gave] Shaughnessy's mare the hillymount of her life" (*FW* 623.22–3). In contrast to III.3's HCE voice ignoring his marital present by focusing on his amorous past, here ALP establishes a redemptive link between past, present, and future, especially when we consider that the trip to Howth spurred by these recollections would enable them to "watch would the letter you're wanting be coming may be" (*FW* 623.29–30).[9] Thus, when ALP argues that "It's Phoenix, dear. And the flame is, hear!" (*FW* 621.1–2), she unites the name of the park HCE attempts to suppress throughout the text with the resurrection of the Phoenix flame, which transforms their concluding walk into an opportunity to work through the park scandal and enable their marriage to "catch fire and become present" (Buber *Thou* 90).

However, ALP does not allow her rhetoric to descend into maudlin sentimentality. Brivic may read her desire to "close me eyes" and "lave" HCE's faults (*FW* 621.29; 33) as her construction of an "ideal incubus" that projects a "series of images of the phallus not as an actual penis, but as a magic wand" (93; 92),[10] but I do not see her attempting to whitewash his crimes in order to represent a pristine love object. In fact, ALP is quick to articulate her marital frustration, noting that their relationship forced her to suppress her dreams ("I wrote me hopes and buried the page when I heart Thy voice" [*FW* 624.4–5]) and that HCE's scheming has harmed their marriage ("All your graundplotting and the little it brought!" [*FW* 624.12–3]). She even acknowledges that HCE promotes Issy over her as his beloved, recognizing that "you're changing, sonhusband, and you're turning, I can feel you, for a daughterwife from the hills again" (*FW* 627.1–3). Rather than filtering HCE's philandering through a rose-tinted romantic idealism, ALP qualifies her loving thoughts with concessions of their marital problems, which recalls the combination of affection and disgust that Molly uses to describe Bloom. ALP may desire to view HCE as "the child we all love to place our hope in for ever" (*FW* 621.31–2), but she also portrays this "child" as a "bumpkin" and a "puny" (*FW* 627.23–4), which enables her to articulate a more comprehensive assessment of him grounded in a realistic marital love.[11]

---

9 Norris also recognizes the redemptive potential of ALP's memories, arguing that "in reversing her memories, she reverses, as it were, the husband's fortunes and their decline" ("Last" 25–6).

10 Devlin similarly notes that "this politely veiled female eye, which blocks out unpleasant sights and replaces them with happier ones, provides an apt figure for the final monologue's dominant discourse: the kindly, optimistic, and circumlocutory speech is the verbal equivalent of ALP's censored gaze" (*Wandering* 164).

11 Some critics argue that these hostile representations constitute ALP's definitive rejection of HCE. For example, Beckman argues that "man, the husband, she will scorn in her dying thoughts. The colossus is reduced to a 'Cooloosus' (*FW* 625.22)—a rear end. She alone has defended him, but she regrets her effort" (97). Devlin also writes that "at the end of her speech, the dream wife acknowledges even more frankly the discrepancy between her wishful estimation of her husband and the reality of his achievements … The female voice grows more and more overtly dissatisfied, ALP ending her speech with both a verbal and physical rejection of her spouse" (*Wandering* 173). But these negative characterizations of HCE also enable us to view ALP's love more realistically: even if ALP derides HCE

Where Brivic sees ALP constructing an "ideal incubus," I agree with Norris that she "not only forgives past transgressions but assumes the heroic mission of saving her husband from slander and raising him from his fallen state" ("ALP" 207). ALP may pledge to "lave" HCE's wrongdoings, but it is more likely that she desires to move past the "horner corner" and "old mutthergoosip" that plagues him throughout the *Wake* than it is that she wants to believe that he is faultless (*FW* 623.3–4). Her argument that "all men has done something" (*FW* 621.32), while echoing HCE's generalization of his transgressions in II.3, consciously acknowledges that he has transgressed, and her subsequent conditions that he must not "start your stunts of Donachie's yeards agoad again" (*FW* 624.16–7) and "must redoform again" (*FW* 624.20) for them to "cohabit respectable" show that she recognizes his betrayals and still desires to share her life with him (*FW* 624.8). By directly confronting HCE's transgressions and still envisioning a future with him, ALP turns to and affirms the otherness of her husband, which establishes a solid reconciliatory foundation for her monologue.

This hope for reconciliation is confirmed by the *Wake*'s conclusion. While some contend that ALP's departure signifies her irreparable separation from HCE, reading her return to the sea with respect to her marital affection demonstrates that this return carries with it the possibility for renewal. Even though she feels "looneley in me loneness" and considers "slip[ping] away before they're up" (*FW* 627.34–5), ALP ultimately promotes "[her] only" (*FW* 628.4) over her "cold mad feary father" (*FW* 628.2), desiring to "rush … into [HCE'S] arms" so that he can "save [her]" from the sea's "therrible prongs" (*FW* 628.4–5). As before, ALP balances resignation with affection, and the warmth that has guided her thoughts of HCE throughout her soliloquy compels her to prioritize her love for him over her "loneness."

Also, her parting words confirm the power of memory to maintain an amorous connection despite the lovers' physical separation. As she resigns herself to returning to her "cold mad feary father," she uses her remaining leaf ("I'll bear it on me. To remind me of" [*FW* 628.7]) and their concluding kiss ("Take. Bussoftlhee, mememormee!" [*FW* 628.14]) as memorial markers to preserve their love even when she is gone. More importantly, ALP concludes by observing, "Lps. The keys to. Given!" (*FW* 628.15), which confirms the efficacy of these markers not only because this description of their kiss recalls HCE's past pledge to "give me the keys of me heart" (*FW* 626.30–1), but also because the image of her "l[i]ps" providing "the keys" to HCE's liberation through her letter enables ALP to transform herself into the *Wake*'s Arrah-na-Pogue. This replaces the narcissistic imposition of the Boucicaultian identity onto Issy with her self-assumption of the romantic heroine and reshapes HCE's obsession with the past into a memorial affirmation of their marital present. Once again, the ability of past

towards the end of the *Wake*, her loving addresses to him as she returns to the sea connote her ultimate reacceptance of their love, which enables their marriage to reignite through the text's cyclical structure.

bliss to revitalize present desire enables ALP and HCE to move past their marital impasse, only this time the temporal connection is solidified by the "commodious vicus" of the text's "recirculation" (*FW* 3.2), and the *Wake*'s circular structure guarantees that the separation that concludes the novel will inevitably give way to a reconciliation upon our return to its opening pages. Joyce thus concludes his final work by presenting us with a lover who ends her journey admittedly "a lone," but unquestionably "a loved" (*FW* 628.15), and though she may leave HCE to return to the sea, each iteration of the *Wake* will inevitably carry her "riverrun" back to "Howth Castle and Environs."[12]

****

In his essay on the composition process of Book IV, Dirk Van Hulle documents Joyce's original intentions for ALP's letter in *Work in Progress*. Quoting Joyce's notes on page thirty of the red-backed notebook (BL 47471b), Van Hulle observes that ALP's letter airing and defending HCE's crimes was originally intended to be delivered successfully by Shaun to HCE, and that his discovery of the contents of the letter "at last gave HCE the raspberry. Groaning of spirit, he lifted his hands & many who did not dare it, heard him say: I will give £10 ^[1]tomorrow & gladly[1]^ to the 1st fellow who will put that W in the royal canal. (BL 47471b f.30, simplified; JJA 46:233)" (qtd. in Van Hulle 447). While both the delivery of the letter and HCE's reaction were omitted from the final version of *Finnegans Wake*, Joyce's original plans for the letter still highlight the difference between HCE's and ALP's reactions to the park scandal, as ALP's desire to acknowledge and work past it is challenged by HCE's insistence on suppressing any knowledge of his misdeed in an effort to rebuild his amatory appeal. These differing reactions to the scandal in turn speak to a fundamental difference in their reactions to the current state of their marriage: whereas ALP's defenses of HCE constitute her enduring affirmation of both her husband and their marriage, HCE's suppressions of the present are indicative of his broader tendency to rely on past romance to the detriment of his current relationship and to subordinate his love for ALP to his lust for an Issy that evokes the past beauty of his wife. HCE's inability to completely suppress his culpability highlights the flaws in this narcissistic perception of marriage, but even though his desire to galvanize his amatory prowess provokes his numerous falls throughout the *Wake*, ALP's persistent affirmation of his otherness and her invitations for him to return to her keep the possibility of his redemption and resurrection alive. Thus, although Joyce's depictions of marriage in the *Wake* are

[12] Beckman objects that "the picture of marriage" in the *Wake* "seems bleaker than the one in *Ulysses* because loyalty seems to be one-way" (90–1). Nevertheless, even if her love is presently unrequited, ALP never loses the ability to turn towards and affirm her beloved. Like Bloom, she remains capable of looking past HCE's transgressions and hoping for a reconciliation, which allows us to entertain the possibility of their marriage "catch[ing] fire and becom[ing] present" through the iterative cycles of the *Wake*.

not terribly flattering, his portrayal of ALP consistently affirms Buber's "basic principle of marriage": "I wish his otherness to exist because I wish his entire being to exist," and the cyclical nature of the *Wakean* narrative ensures that the Earwicker marriage is perpetually affirmed, building off of the affirmation of "Penelope" and ending the Joycean love ethic in one of the most ethically productive manners possible.

These differences between HCE's and ALP are further complicated when we consider the role of the dreamer in Joyce's portrayals of the Earwicker marriage. While a conclusive determination of the dreamer's identity is probably impossible, if critics who contend that the dreamer is HCE are correct, then we must reevaluate our assertions of Earwicker's narcissism and reflect on the significance of him envisioning these oppositional takes on his marriage.[13] By reading the marital strife between Earwicker and Plurabelle as the dreamer wrestling with the complications of his marriage, HCE's refusal and ALP's affirmation provide him with different possibilities of how to deal with his present relationship, transforming HCE's narcissistic rejections of ALP into an integral component of the dreamer's dialogic consideration of marriage. For this reason, Joyce's decision to give the "last" word to ALP takes on further significance, for by having HCE's rejection of ALP give way to Anna Livia's persistent affirmation, the marital episodes of the *Wake* can be seen not only as HCE coming to grips with the state of his marriage, but more importantly as his acknowledging and reciprocating his wife's loving turn towards him. Thus the Prankquean's desire to be affirmed by the Jarl becomes a microcosm for the novel's marital themes as a whole, only in the dreamer's mind, her riddle is successfully answered, and the reciprocal affirmation of otherness at the heart of the dreamer's marital renegotiation further magnifies the *Wake*'s loving potential.

ALP's enduring love for HCE is not only important on a marital level, but it also affects the political effectiveness of Joyce's most democratic text. If we recall Buber's contention that affirming the "basic principle of marriage" triggers the "vital acknowledgement of many-faced otherness" needed for effective "dealings with the body politic," then ALP's explicit acknowledgment of her husband's missteps and her persistent affirmation of HCE despite those transgressions provide an effective sociopolitical alternative to the squabbling and derision that pervade the *Wake*. Especially considering that HCE's matrimonial breach is the foundation for the text's primary social conflict, ALP's loving affirmation not only

[13] Critics who see the dreamer as potentially HCE include Shari Benstock, who writes that "since HCE's consciousness controls the dream, it is difficult to separate public suspicion and the compounding evidence from Earwicker's apprehensions" (187); Bishop, who argues that "Joyce draws on the inventive 'sigla H.C.E.' (32.14) less to 'allude to' than to identify the 'one stable somebody' who sleeps (107.30), unnamable because unconscious, at *Finnegans Wake*" (139); and Devlin, who contends that "The subjective consistency of the various speech acts in the dream has led several critics to assume, quite logically I think, that HCE is the dreamer: he is identified as such *not* because he is the main speaking subject – his speeches form only a small portion of the dreamtext—but because he is the main discursive subject of the *Wake*'s various utterances" (*Wandering* 6).

moves towards repairing that breach, but also works towards replacing the social scorn that ostracizes characters who deviate from the norm with a loving dialogue, a relationship between personal and social love that is strengthened by both the letter and ALP's gift delivery in I.8. It is thus important that our examination of the role of *Finnegans Wake* in Joyce's love ethic concludes with a consideration of its political potential to see how the vitriol behind its "mutthergoosip" is challenged by the Liffey, the mamafesta and, ultimately, by the *Wake* itself.

Chapter 12
Joyce's Amorous Collideorscape

Towards the beginning of the lessons chapter, the narrator describes the twins studying the "memoiries of Hireling's puny wars" (*FW* 270.30–1), in which the *Wake*'s romantic narratives are equated to the ascent of the Roman Empire. Not only do the textbook's descriptions of "Sire Jeallyous Seizer … with his duo of druidesses in ready money rompers and the tryonforit of Oxthievious, Lapidous and Malthouse Anthemy" shine an imperial light on HCE's park scandal (*FW* 271.3–6), but similar references to Issy's relationship with her reflection ("so bright as Mutua of your mirror holds her candle to your caudle, lone lefthand likeless, sombring Autum of your Spring" [*FW* 271.9–12]), the twins' battles for Issy's love ("the gossans eye the jennings aye" [*FW* 271. 18–9]), and HCE's conquest of ALP ("Leda, Lada, aflutter-afraida, so does your girdle grow!" [*FW* 272.2–3]) similarly place the family's amatory struggles in a broader light. The textbook also notes the disastrous consequences of these pursuits, highlighting the brothers' self-destruction by arguing that "if you're not ruined by that one she won't do you any whim" (*FW* 271.15–7) and elucidating the relationship between desire and violence by contending that "it's tails for toughs and titties for totties and come buckets come bats till deeleet" (*FW* 272.6–8). Thus, when the text concludes that "as they warred in their big innings ease now we never shall know" (*FW* 271.22–4), it places the Earwicker family's romantic squabbles at the heart of the world's historical conflicts, elucidating a destructive dimension to the text's universalization of its main characters.

However, this does not simply portray the Earwicker family as the universal archetypes of humanity, but it also elucidates the sociopolitical ramifications of the novel's amatory episodes. As he does in his earlier fiction, here Joyce ties the personal failures of his lovers to the broader social conflicts that they inhabit, which demonstrates Buber's connection between the individual affirmation of otherness and the "vital acknowledgment of many-faced otherness" that facilitates genuine dialogue within a body politic. Specifically, it is important to note Joyce's focus on the *Wake*'s narcissistic romances in this section, as the rejection and consumption of otherness that comprise these exchanges are directly linked to historical episodes of imperial conquest and warfare. This link between amatory narcissism and sociopolitical violence is strengthened by the subtle references to Bruno's coincidence of contraries towards the middle of this passage, as the text notes, "From the butts of Heber and Heremon, *nolens* volens, brood our pansies, *brune* in brume" (*FW* 271.19–21; italics mine), and the reference to Bruno's *Eroici Furori* in Shem's accompanying marginalia strengthens the section's Brunonian implications (*FW* 271.20–3). Thus, by having Bruno references dissolve into inevitable narcissistic bloodshed, Joyce demonstrates the disastrous consequences of rejecting the union of opposites and confirms the sociopolitical importance of the individual's loving turn to the other, and these themes become both the heart of the *Wake*'s political episodes and the conclusion of Joyce's politics of love.

Clashes of Wills gen Wonts

One of the primary ways that Joyce unites the personal and social rejections of otherness occurs through the persecution of HCE. Similar to *Ulysses*, Joyce makes HCE's transgression the subject of malicious gossip by a body politic who already rejects him as an outsider. However, whereas Joyce mostly presented Bloom's degradation by a Dublin populace snickering about his wife's alleged promiscuity, in *Finnegans Wake*, Joyce explicitly unites romantic and social rejections of otherness by tying HCE's social downfall to an encounter with a cad that both mirrors his transgression in Phoenix Park and is replicated in the other social encounters in the *Wake*. This approach not only explicitly unites HCE's marital breach with his social downfall, but by portraying this encounter with the cad as a mutual misrecognition of otherness, Joyce highlights the lack of a reciprocal affirmation between self and other as the catalyst for HCE's social persecution and demonstrates the importance of mutual celebrations of otherness in fostering genuine social dialogue.

To demonstrate the progression in Joyce's portrayal of this connection between amatory and social narcissism, we must compare HCE's persecution by Lucalizod to Bloom's persecution by Dublin since Joyce uses the seemingly parallel episodes of his last two novels to make similar comments on the social ramifications of love. This is not to say that Bloom and HCE are directly parallel to each other since such direct comparisons are stymied by the *Wake*'s polylogism, but there are important similarities between Joyce's portrayals of these protagonists. As I said above, both characters are derided by hostile crowds for perceived sexual perversities that are primarily a smokescreen for an inherent social hostility towards their foreignness. However, Joyce's depiction of the characters' responses to this hostility is significantly different. Whereas Bloom consistently preaches tolerance to his unforgiving body politic and empathizes with the citizens that deride him, HCE's self-absorbed focus on his own troubles causes him to misrecognize the people he encounters and to contribute to his own persecution.

This narcissistic misrecognition is initially evidenced in his encounter with the cad, where Joyce describes HCE as "carryin his overgoat under his schulder, sheepside out, so as to look more like a coumfry gentleman and signing the pledge as gaily as you please" (*FW* 35.13–5). This description demonstrates HCE's preoccupation with covering over his disgrace with the appearance of propriety (especially considering McHugh's translation of the "schuld" in "schulder" as German for guilt [35]), which begins HCE's tendency to suppress his otherness by promoting an ideal self-image of himself. This obsession with suppressing his scandal thus taints his encounter with the cad, as he misrecognizes the other's request for the time as the "softnosed bullet[s]" of an accusing "sap" and responds with stuttering professions of innocence that magnify his perceived culpability (*FW* 35.25–6). HCE's reaction thus constitutes a multi-faceted rejection of otherness since he both prevents the cad from turning towards him by replacing his identity with a fictitious persona of respectability, and he dismisses the cad's identity with an antagonistic perception of a hostile other that's directly derived from his guilty self-absorption. Whereas Bloom's inability to attain a reciprocal affirmation of otherness is brought about by a hostile body politic who refuses him, HCE directly undercuts his ability to engage in reciprocal dialogue with the cad, and this mutual misrecognition of otherness becomes the catalyst for HCE's social fall.

The role HCE's encounter with the cad has in his social downfall quickly becomes apparent, as his stuttering professions of innocence are transformed into harsher proof of his guilt the more the gossip about the encounter spreads. This social derision initially takes the form of "The Ballad of Persse O'Reilly," a savage song that not only excoriates HCE for the park scandal, but also uses his transgression as an excuse to mock his general annoyance to the body politic: "He was fafafather of all schemes for to bother us/Slow coaches and immaculate contraceptives for the populace,/Mare's milk for the sick, seven dry Sundays a week,/Openair love and religion's reform" (*FW* 45.15–8). This specific stanza parallels Blooms' persecution by making HCE both the inventor of hair-brained social reforms and the advocate of "openair love and religion's reform," evoking Bloom's mocked advocacy of love as "the opposite of hatred" in "Cyclops." However, whereas Bloom's championing love and tolerance gives him a victory over the citizen, HCE is set up for another fall, as his advocacy of love and perceived perversity become weapons that Hosty wields to advocate "bury[ing]" the "brave son of Scandiknavery" (a portmanteau that explicitly equates HCE's foreignness with his perceived delinquency) at the end of the ballad (*FW* 47.24–5). Indeed, the aftermath of the ballad's construction demonstrates the extent to which HCE is "bur[ied]" by an unforgiving Lucalizod, as he is assaulted by a man with a revolver in another iteration of the encounter with the cad, imprisoned in his pub and insulted by an angry "northroomer" outside his gates (*FW* 69.32), and ceremonially buried at the bottom of Lough Neagh. Thus, in contrast to Bloom's successful advocacy of love, Joyce uses HCE's continual persecution both to demonstrate the inevitable consequences of the social rejection of otherness and to highlight the limitations of a narcissistic response to such persecution.

The destructive consequences of HCE's narcissistic response to his social persecution culminate in II.3, where HCE defends himself from the derisive comments of a hostile body politic. Again, II.3 explicitly parallels "Cyclops," as Joyce places both HCE and Bloom in bars and forces them to challenge the barbs of drunk, scornful customers. However, Joyce again has HCE fail where Bloom succeeds, as his identifications with the fools of the pub stories and his continued assertions of innocence only increase the citizens' castigation of him. I previously read HCE's contention that "whole men is lepers" as a narcissistic attempt to use a generalized depiction of sinful humanity to maintain his personal innocence (*FW* 355.33). However, whereas Bloom escapes the citizen's biscuit tin after highlighting the interconnectedness of Christianity and Judaism at the end of "Cyclops," HCE's obsession with maintaining his ideal persona of respectability provoke accidental admissions of guilt that repeat his encounter with the cad on a larger social scale. Specifically, his use of universal sin to prove that he is "big altoogooder" and his subsequent justifications for his transgression later in II.3 not only betray references to the raven and dove, which I noted in Chapter 11, but also accidentally evoke Persse O'Reilly (*FW* 357.18) and the encounter with the cad (*FW* 358.9–10). Once again, these self-defeating protestations of innocence result in the customers "disassembling and taking him apart, the slammocks, with discrimination for his maypole and a rub in passing over his hump" (*FW* 358.33–5), and when Sackerson ushers them out of the pub at closing time, they converge in a seven-page excoriation of HCE reminiscent of "the Ballad of Persse O'Reilly." In that sense, HCE finds his fate more aligned with Stephen's stumbling exit from *Ulysses*, for in contrast to Bloom ascending like "Ben Bloom Elijah" at the end of "Cyclops," the end of II.3 finds HCE transformed into "poor old Roderick O'Conor Rex" making a monumental fall from which the HCE manifestations of the rest of the text will struggle to recover (*FW* 380.33). Thus, through the many iterations of HCE's and the cad's misrecognitions of each other and the persecution that emerges from this failed encounter, Joyce confirms the relationship between individual and social "acknowledgments of many-faced otherness" and the destructive repercussions of the reciprocal rejection of Buber's "basic principle of marriage."

The sociopolitical failure of *Wakean* narcissism further manifests itself in the text's political episodes. Again, Joyce draws upon arguments he made in earlier works, demonstrating the "old pap of racial hatred" that he attributes to imperialism and nationalism to stem from the individual rejection of the other. Whereas the social implications of this refusal are manifest in the multiple iterations of HCE's encounter with the cad, Joyce highlights the political ramifications of the *Wakean* love ethic through his universalization of the park scandal itself, as the multiple manifestations of HCE, the two temptresses, and the three soldiers directly unite amatory desire and political violence. Joyce's portrayal of HCE again becomes instructive here, as he does not simply portray Earwicker as a Bloomean victim of social persecution, but he combines his foreign origins and self-absorption to depict him also as the *Wake*'s principal imperialist. This is initially demonstrated in I.1's Museyroom episode. Here, the park scandal takes on explicitly imperial undertones, as HCE becomes the Willingdone, an amalgam of William III and the Duke of Wellington, battling the three lipoleums for the attentions of the two jinnies. Moreover, because HCE's park scandal is itself derived from his lust for his daughter, the Museyroom sequence also implicates HCE battling Shem, Shaun, and Shimar Shin (a Shem-Shaun hybrid) for Issy in the episode's imperial overtones. For this reason, HCE's rejection of ALP for her youthful counterpart(s) becomes the imperial rejection of subaltern otherness not just through the Willingdone being "a composite figure of patriarchal English domination" (Cheng *Empire* 265), but through his rivals individually evoking the Irish, Scottish, and Indian victims of

British imperialism and collectively becoming "the lipoleum boyne" (*FW* 8.22), a label that both marks their status as the boys (or HCE's sons) and evokes William III's bloody victory at the Battle of the Boyne that strengthened England's control over Ireland. Thus, by representing the lustful HCE as an imperial invader, Joyce highlights the relationship between the amatory consumption of otherness and the desire for colonial mastery, and his continual portrayal of HCE as both persecuted and persecutor unravels the stability of such repressive discourses.

This imperial portrayal of the narcissistic HCE is also evident in his universalized relationship with ALP. I have already argued that HCE's perceptions of ALP subordinate their current marriage to an obsession with her past beauty, and Joyce highlights the exploitative potential behind this suppression throughout the *Wake*. Not only is HCE frequently portrayed as the Viking invader colonizing Ireland during scenes of their courtship, but HCE himself articulates the political suppression of otherness that extends from his refusal of ALP in III.3. HCE's voice may contend that he created Dublin as a gift for his beloved Anna Liffey, but the specific descriptions of the city's construction reveals the lower class exploitation that made this love token possible. While he insists that "in the humanity of my heart I sent out heyweywomen to refresh the ballwearied," the ensuing list of home advertisements that describe HCE's created city reveals the extent to which this "refresh[ment]" "devaleurise[s] the base fellows for the curtailment of their lower man" (*FW* 542.36–543.3).[1] Just as HCE covers over the harsh realities of his present in favor of a more respectable past, here the multiple juxtapositions between the alleged "respectab[ility]" of these advertised establishments and their deplorable living conditions reveals HCE's construction and suppression of urban poverty in order to create the appearance of a "respectable" Dublin (*FW* 543.22–545.23).[2] Thus, through the political manifestations of HCE, Joyce reveals

[1] HCE's boasting that he "devaleurised the base fellows" also equates him with Eamon De Valera, whose social crackdowns during his reign as leader of the Irish Free State also suppressed "the base fellows for the curtailment of their lower man" (Manganiello 177). Not only does this then make HCE both imperial sovereign and Free State leader, but since Shaun is also attributed to De Valera, this description equates both HCE and his rival son with De Valera, which further troubles the simplistic self/other distinctions behind imperial and nationalist suppressions of otherness and magnifies Joyce's critique of both institutions.

[2] McGee similarly notes the imperial and exploitive nature of HCE's boasts, arguing that "he has devalued, through the expropriation of surplus value, the social base in order to control and curtail the desires of the body, including the desire for freedom in the form of free time. He concludes this long passage with a reenactment of the charter of 1173, by which Henry II granted the city of Dublin to the city of Bristol, an event that is the very image of paternal social command" (268). Rabaté also contends that "Joyce suggests that the history of Dublin, like that of any capital city, confirms that its formation must indeed have been 'dirty.' Facing such a mixture of concrete accomplishments … and the underside showing the exploitation of the majority, progress appears indissociable from abjection and subjection" (*Egoism* 191).

Ireland's colonial and socioeconomic struggles to stem from the narcissistic desire to consume the other that is at the heart of his amatory critique.

Joyce also locates the destructive consequences of narcissism on the other side of the imperial conflict, as the refusal of otherness is prevalent in his criticisms of Irish nationalism in the *Wake*. This manifests itself both in general associations of nationalist exclusion to the crowd's persecutions of HCE, such as the interjections of the Sinn Fein motto into the construction of the "Ballad of Persse O'Reilly" (*FW* 42.11–2) and the narration of the Norwegian captain tale (*FW* 324.15–6), and through his specific portrayals of Shaun, whose "paint[ing] our town a wearing greenridinghued" dovetail with violent scorn towards his "black fremdling" brother in Book III (*FW* 411.24).[3] Specifically, Joyce's reflections on post-independence Ireland add a new dimension to his career-long critique of nationalism, as his negative depictions of Shaun are frequently read as specific attacks on Eamon De Valera.[4] Indeed, De Valera's opposition to the Anglo-Irish treaty that fomented the Irish Civil War finds parallels in the increasingly hostile twin rivalries of III.1 and III.2, and Platt compellingly equates the "articulation of morality, family values and community" in Jaun's lecture to the girls of St. Bride's with "the victory of a repressive culture of tradition and conformity" as a result of "De Valera's Ireland" (66). While Joyce always understood the repressive element behind the nationalist movement, the Joyce of *Finnegans Wake* watched the inevitable consequences of monocular nationalism, as the inability to engage in productive dialogue over the parameters of the Free State plunged the newly-independent country into bloodshed and replaced imperial oppression with harsh censorship and social regulation. Thus, when the narrator argues that "Molochy wars bring the devil era" at the end of III.2 (*FW* 473.7–8), he not only "mark[s] out" De Valera "as the anti-Christ," as Manganiello argues (175), but his equation of De Valera's "devil era" with "Molochy wars" highlight the needless sacrifices brought about by Ireland's primary political monologist, using the Shauns of Book III to demonstrate the destructive consequences of the nationalist refusal to engage in compromise and dialogue.

Ultimately, Joyce's critique of this refusal of compromise is not limited to the Irish Free State, and here is where the most significant political impact of his

---

[3] Critics have frequently equated Shaun with the repressive side of Irish nationalism. For example, M. Keith Booker argues that "standing as a figure of both religious and political oppression, the patriarchal authoritarian Shaun the Post exemplifies the links in the *Wake* among politics, patriarchy, and religion" (199). Andrew J. Mitchell contends that "a nationalism of Shaun's sort, therefore, would be better termed isolationism, for it is more an anti-inter-nationalism than a nationalism in any positive sense. His position entails an elimination of the other or, at the very least, a denial of alterity" (65). Finally, Len Platt notes that "in the Shaun identity the complex concatenation of Aryanism and fascism with Celticism and Irish republicanism becomes particularly focused" (61).

[4] According to Manganiello, "that the Shaun of *Finnegans Wake* represents in part de Valera, a theory first introduced by John Garvin, has now become a generally accepted view in *Wake* criticism" (175).

interrogation of narcissism takes shape. Throughout the *Wake*, Joyce demonstrates the inevitable chaos and bloodshed that has historically been fomented by the martial rejection of otherness, as each political episode features warring characters whose inability to reconcile their differences and turn towards each other lead to their mutual destruction.[5] This critique of violence is initiated on the novel's second page, where the narrator notes the "clashes here of wills gen wonts, oystrygods gaggins fishygods" and then references the eighteenth century insurrections of the Whiteboys and the Battle of Verdun (*FW* 4.1–6), characterizing the past as a repetitive cycle of violence. This tactic is expanded in the Museyroom episode, where HCE's Willingdone conquers the three lipoleums only to be blown up by Shimar Shin. However, while Joyce frames this iteration of the park and family scandals as both sides' personal Waterloos, he also references over thirty additional battles ranging from the battle of Marathon to World War I (McHugh 8–10), demonstrating that "in the dream, history merely repeats itself without our having learned any lessons, and all battles are version of one another" (McCarthy *Family* 11). Given the frequent parallels between the Earwicker conflicts and historical violence in other episodes (the mutual destruction of the Shaunish Mookse and Shemish Gripes that evokes the conquest of Ireland; the twins' usurpation of HCE in the "Buckley and the Russian General" skit that evokes the Crimean War), Joyce confirms that the reciprocal rejection of otherness at the heart of the novel's amatory episodes is indicative of the sociopolitical refusal of the other that historically has been the foundation of imperialism, exploitation, and warfare.

However, Joyce provides an alternative to this sociopolitical monologism through ALP, whose constant affirmations of otherness not only accept and defend HCE, but also promote accommodation to the novel's other warring parties. Just as the narrative's polylogism enables the multiple manifestations of Joyce's narcissistic characters to demonstrate the broader hazards of refusing the other, ALP's differing manifestations expand the scope of her love to replace the text's conflicts with the affirmation of opposing forces. This role is initially demonstrated after the Museyroom, where the janitrix's tale of familial destruction is countered by the appearance of the "gnarlybird" (*FW* 10.32), ALP's hen manifestation that digs out the affirming letter from the midden heap, and the narrator's subsequent depiction of the "gnarlybird" as a "peacefugle, a parody's bird, a peri potmother" demonstrates the potential of her love letter to replace the destructive tendencies of the Museyroom sequence with a peaceful acceptance of difference (*FW* 11.9). The efficacy of this loving alternative is strengthened by the narrator's subsequent reference to ALP "steal[ing] our historic presents from the past postpropheticals so as to will make us all lordy heirs and ladymaidesses of a pretty nice kettle

[5] Norris develops this relationship between personal and political violence by noting that "the same competitive dynamics that prompt rivalry in love also prompt rivalry in war. Joyce features those military conflicts in *Finnegans Wake* – Clontarf, Balaklava, Waterloo – that are marked not only by imperialistic consequences, but also by strong interpersonal rivalries that simulate paternal and fraternal conflicts" (*Decentered* 49).

of fruit" (*FW* 11.30–2), which not only replaces HCE's obsession with the past with an affirmation of the present, but also replaces the historical violence of the Museyroom's past with a more accommodating present. Thus, by positioning ALP as the response to the Museyroom's familial violence, Joyce demonstrates the loving potential of her acceptance of otherness to replace the destructive refusal of difference with a more accommodating alternative.

ALP's loving alternative is further demonstrated by her role as the River Liffey, as Joyce uses her fluvial manifestation as a bridge that reconciles warring contraries. The amorous potential of ALP's "riverrun" is primarily evident with respect to the warring twins (*FW* 3.1), as Joyce frequently separates Shem and Shaun on opposing banks of the Liffey and positions ALP as the bridge uniting the two brothers.[6] In Book I, the distance between the twins frequently leads to their destruction, as their inability to bridge the gap between them causes the Mookse and Gripes to destroy each other and Quickenough and Doddpebble to devolve into a tree and a stone. However, Anna's river not only divides the warring brothers, but provides the possibility for their mutual affirmation. We have already seen how the dirty "anal Liffey" promotes the reconciliation of HCE and Lucalizod in I.8, but the Shemish Mercius hints at a similar reconciliation between himself and the Shaunish Justius at the end of I.7 by noting that "the days of youyouth are ever mixed mimine" and warning him that "our turfbrown mummy is acoming" (*FW* 194.4, 22). Chronologically, Mercius's statement seemingly anticipates the ALP of I.8, but from an amorous perspective, he could be evoking the ALP of Book III, as Shaun's barrel ride down the Liffey becomes the site where he reconciles his attitude towards Shem's difference in a more accommodating manner. Especially if we read Book III's Shaun in part as a De Valera-esque proponent of a repressive Free State, ALP's role as the Liffey enables her accommodation of difference to wash through Joyce's portrayal of the violent history of Ireland, from the Laudibiliter through the Civil War. Thus, just as the narcissism of the *Wake*'s romantic conflicts manifests itself in the political violence of the historical episodes, ALP's amorous embrace of HCE is indicative of a broader affirmation of otherness that can replace conquest and destruction with genuine dialogue.

A Polyhedron of Scripture

In *The Decentered Universe of* Finnegans Wake, Norris argues that "through the incarceration theme in *Finnegans Wake*, Joyce shows the relationship of society and the artist to be one of mutual aggression" (113). Certainly Shem would

[6] Eide also argues that "ALP's river language performs Joyce's ethics as it undoes the political and moral certainties upon which her sons base their identities. Her language is tidal, as is the river Liffey, ebbing and flowing, suggesting and contradicting, posing a possibility and entertaining equally its opposite. Behind this unsettling fluid prose is the suggestion of another intention in her language: to remind her sons of their ethical responsibility to one another, a responsibility that stems from their differences" (85).

seem to validate this antagonistic conception of the *Wakean* artist, as he is not only ostracized by the Lucalizod crowd, but he frequently vows to use his art to avenge his persecution by airing everyone's dirty secrets. However, while there is certainly "mutual aggression" in this "relationship of society and the artist," the ultimate role of art in *Finnegans Wake* is more loving than it may seem. Similar to his earlier fiction, Joyce positions art as a driving factor of the relationship between individual and social affirmations of otherness in the *Wake*, identifying literature as a potential method for reconfiguring the body politic. However, whereas *Portrait* and *Ulysses* demonstrated the limitations of amatory aesthetics through Stephen's failed pursuits of the "uncreated conscience of [his] race," the *Wake* posits an amorous alternative through its negotiation of the necessary relationship between artist and subject. While the text has its fair share of narcissistic artists, Joyce demonstrates the ability of art to transform the body politic in a more accommodating manner through both ALP's letter and the *Wake* itself. The amorous aesthetics that emerge through the iterations of the *Wake* thus make Joyce's final novel a fitting coda for his love ethic by transforming the artist into a loving redeemer of the wor(l)d.

To uncover this redemptive potential of the *Wakean* artist, we must recall Buber's characterization of "the eternal origin of art." In Chapter 5, I noted Buber's contention that the direct encounter between individuals also occurs in the confrontation between an artist and a "form that wants to become a work through him." For this reason, the artist must not treat their subject as a means to an end or reduce it to an "aggregate of qualities" since only by "speak[ing] with his being the basic word [I-You] to the form that appears" can "the creative power [be] released and the work [come] into being" (*Thou* 60–1). As we saw in the fifth and sixth chapters, Stephen's obsession with using his subjects to validate his aesthetic calling undermined the efficacy of his art because he ignored the direct encounter between artist and subject and refused to affirm the "form[s]" he encountered "with his being," and the limitations of this refusal of aesthetic otherness are also present in *Finnegans Wake*. The most explicit example of narcissistic art is the derogatory "Ballad of Persse O'Reilly," but Shem also struggles with the amatory foundations of his art throughout the *Wake*'s first two books. Here the parallels between the amatory aesthetics of *Portrait* and *Finnegans Wake* are most evident, for whereas Stephen desires to use art to "forge in the smithy of *my* soul the uncreated conscience of my race," Shem responds to his societal alienation through an excretory aesthetics whose composition is explicitly narcissistic. By locking himself in his "inkbattle house" to "ma[k]e synthetic ink and sensitive paper for his own end out of his wit's waste" in order to "wr[i]te over every square inch of ... his own body" (*FW* 185.6–8, 35–6), Shem uses artistic materials created by himself from himself in order to write on himself. This solipsistic approach may be borne out of necessity since he has been denied other materials, and Eide notes the potential self-reflective benefits of Shem's art by characterizing it as "a reminder that the abject is as much a part of the subject as the skin on which he writes," which "celebrates otherness within" (23).[7] However, it also ensures that he is the only person who can participate in his aesthetic project, which prevents him from using his art to engage his hostile body politic in any productive manner. This inability to engage Lucalizod effectively is compounded by the vengeful intent of his art, as his pledges to expose the scandalous secrets of his rivals in both I.7 and II.1 replace the direct encounters Buber advocates with an aesthetic retaliation that magnifies the distance between self and other. Thus, just as Stephen's amatory aesthetics perpetuates his exile from Dublin without fulfilling his calling, Shem's replaces a potential artistic turn to the other with a self-exiled excretory vengeance that fails to facilitate his desired reconciliation with his community.

However, while Shem's primary artistic pursuits echo Stephen's failed amatory aesthetics, his role as the penman of ALP's letter provides a bridge towards a more accommodating artistic approach. Indeed, McGee persuasively contends that "if Shem composes the book from his own feces and urine as an act of defiance against the domination of capital and its work ethic … he nonetheless writes down the desire of his mother" (259), and this is the distinction between Shem's and Stephen's artistic pursuits. Whereas Stephen can only focus on his own desires through his art, Shem's participation in the letter's construction demonstrates his ability to artistically promote people other than himself, as he not only becomes "the instrument of [ALP's] desire," but his penning HCE's defense also constitutes an artistic turn towards his father. Especially since he vengefully desired to excoriate HCE through his art in II.1, Shem's participation in his father's defense constitutes a renegotiation of his amatory aesthetics into a more affirming project and transforms the letter into Joyce's advocacy of amorous art, an endorsement that becomes more explicit in the *Wake*'s specific focus on the letter.

The loving potential of ALP's letter is ironically confirmed by Mamalujo, who spend III.3 interrogating the voices that emerge from the comatose Yawn in an effort to condemn HCE. As the Four Old Men transition from their questions about Shem to the letter, they refer to ALP's creation as "that letter selfpenned to one's other, that neverperfect everplanned" (*FW* 489.33–4). While they subsequently dismiss the letter's importance by noting that "any owl rooster can peck up bostoons" (*FW* 489.36–490.1), their initial description explicitly brings the letter in line with Buber's amorous aesthetics, as the idea of a composition being "penned" by the self" and written "to one's other" transforms ALP and Shem's creation into a direct literary encounter with HCE that "affirm[s] him as creature and creation" despite his transgressions. Unlike Shem's excretory artistic retaliations, the construction of the letter contains no self-serving motives, but is designed to acknowledge ALP's love for HCE despite his marital missteps and to defend him against an exclusionary public.

---

[7] Kitcher also notes that "Shem is engaged in the ordering of his life, the explicit rendering of it as a work of art, not in a spirit of narcissism, but as a self-conscious counterpoint to the reflective engagement with all sides of his existence – seeing life 'foully.'" (117).

The letter's amorous implications are confirmed by its emergence in Book IV, where ALP acknowledges her husband's waning interest in her ("I wisht I wast be that dumb tyke and he'd wish it was me yonther heel … Our shape as a juvenile being much admired from the first with native copper locks" [*FW* 617.31–4]) and recognizes his possessive attitude towards her through references to the "Married Woman's Improperty Act" (*FW* 617.34–5), yet still defends him from his persecutors. Similar to III.3, ALP blasts the "three Sulvans of Dulkey" and notes "what a sellpriceget the two Peris of Monacheena" (*FW* 616.10–2), which both acknowledges HCE's fall in the park and labels the temptresses and soldiers as betrayers persecuting her Parnell-esque Earwicker. Also, she prays that "the low forget him their trespasses against Molloyd O'Reilly" (*FW* 615.36–616.1), which combines her acknowledgement of the park scandal and her love for HCE in the affectionate appellation "Molloyd O'Reilly," transforming the nickname at the foundation of HCE's social rejection into a term of endearment. Thus, when she notes that "Mucksrats which bring up about uhrweckers they will come to know good" (*FW* 615.16–7), she illustrates her letter's redemptive potential since she not only says that the gossipers "will come to no good," or will fail in their exclusionary efforts, but also that they "will come to know good," or that they will come to recognize the good in HCE instead of denigrating him for his missteps. Thus, whereas McCarthy contends that ALP's letter "is apparently meant to defend him but that inadvertently resurrects all of the charges against him" (*Family* 8), I see her creation as a continuation of her attempts to "defend him" *by* "resurrect[ing]" the charges, for her affirmation of both his positive and negative qualities constitutes the artistic direct encounter with otherness needed for the letter's "creative potential" to be unlocked.

This aesthetic potential is strengthened through Joyce's investigation of the relationship between the letter and its audience. Just as the artist's reduction of their subject to an "aggregate of qualities" confines their work to the I-It world of experience, so too is the audience's response to a work affected by their analytical approach, and Joyce demonstrates the limitations of a purely interpretive dissection of art through the academic examination of ALP's mamafesta in I.5. Though the narrator acknowledges the dialogic potential of both the letter as a "polyhedron of scripture" and its creator as a "Bringer of Plurabilities" (*FW* 107.8; 104.2), he never discusses the contents of the letter itself, but is instead content to subject the document to several interpretive lenses that all fall short of acknowledging its amorous potential. In what Kitcher describes as Joyce's "lampooning all efforts of academic interpretation" (73), the narrator argues that the importance of "the enveloping facts" of the letter require "look[ing] sufficiently longly at a quite everydaylooking stamped addressed envelope," which subordinates ALP's defense of HCE to a rigid analysis of the letter's "outer husk" (*FW* 109.7–8, 14). Then, the narrator focuses on the hen's discovery of the letter and subjects the document to psychoanalytic and historical interpretations that similarly fall short of uncovering its redemptive importance. The narrator does acknowledge that "all schwants (schwrites) ischt tell the cock's trootabout him" and that "he had to see life foully the plak and the smut, (schwrites)" (*FW* 113.11–4), but this dry transcription of ALP's intentions further reduces the document to a "thing among things" to be picked apart by his interpretive abilities, and his constant parenthetical reminders that these are ALP's intentions and opinions impose further distance between the letter and its audience. Thus, by replacing a direct encounter with the artistic creation with a dry academic dissection of its qualities, Joyce's narrator ignores the affirmation of otherness at the heart of ALP's defense of HCE and overshadows its amorous artistic power.

By contrast, Joyce's inclusion of the letter in Book IV facilitates the direct encounter between art and audience, as ALP's celebration of HCE's otherness enables her reader to witness the redemptive power of her missive. This difference in these two episodes is especially evident in ALP's transitional phrase "about that coerogenal hun" at 616.20, which echoes the I.5 narrator's transition "about that original hen" at 110.22 that initiates his explanation of Biddy Doran unearthing the document. This parallelism demonstrates a significant difference in the portrayals of the letter in the two chapters: whereas the academic's interest in the "original hen" highlights his focus on explaining the "enveloping facts" behind the letter's composition to the detriment of its defense of HCE, ALP's interest in "that coerogenal hun" signals her intent to celebrate HCE's life, both his positive attributes and his mistakes, in order to promote his otherness over his ostracism. Especially if we consider the primary audience of ALP's letter to be HCE, Joyce's comparison of the letter in Book IV to its academic dissection in I.5 highlights the redemptive possibilities of his amorous aesthetics, as the "letter selfpenned to one's other" creates the direct encounter between artist and subject/audience that enables its affirmation of otherness to replace the *Wake*'s sociopolitical scorn with a more amorous and accommodating dialogue that could revitalize the Lucalizod community.

Ultimately, the letter's demonstration of Buber's "origin or art" is most powerfully articulated in its status as a microcosm for *Finnegans Wake*. If we accept the critical commonplace that ALP's letter is a version of the *Wake* itself,[8] then the loving turn towards the other created by ALP's defense of HCE becomes magnified when we consider the amorous implications of Joyce's final novel. Since Buber identifies art as an important site where the direct encounter between self and other can foster genuine dialogue, the *Wake* is an integral example of the dialogic potential of Joyce's amorous aesthetics. Not only does its shifting narrative defy attempts to arrest it as a static text, but Joyce's *Wakean* language

[8] Critics who equate ALP's letter and the *Wake* include Devlin, who sees the letter "marked as an evidentiary advertisement of polymorphous wishes and fears – a representation in miniature of the dreamtext itself" (*Wandering* 38); Henke, who argues that "each of the multiple versions of the letter serves as a textual paradigm for the *Wake* itself, acting as a semiotic microcosm of the linguistic macrocosm in which it has, like a puzzle or rebus, been playfully embedded" (*Desire* 185); and Manganiello, who writes that "the letter represents all writings and all documents, particularly *Finnegans Wake* itself" (182).

of multilingual puns and portmanteaus renders the narration itself dialogic, enabling a babel of voices to coexist side-by-side and participate in a polyglot storytelling medium (a technique exemplarily evidenced by the thunderwords that unite multiple linguistic markers of the same word in a dialogic Viconian progression). Especially considering Joyce's career-long criticism of the "nets" of "language" (*P* 220), his *Wakese* constitutes an emphatic celebration of difference and dialogue over the monologic narratives that he interrogated throughout his literary career. Thus, by continuously re-presenting Ireland through this polyglot discourse, Joyce's dreamtext concludes his oeuvre by reshaping the paralyzed Dublin whose repressive instruments compelled his exile and continued to plague post-independence Ireland into a polyvalent Irish community that is perpetually maintained by otherness.

The multiple manifestations of Joyce's characters further demonstrate the ethical and political potential of the *Wake*'s amorous aesthetics. As I mentioned earlier, Joyce's numerous iterations of his main characters do not simply universalize his familial themes, but they also strengthen his criticism of the sociopolitical rejection of otherness. Specifically, by transforming each character into several versions of themselves that transcend spatiotemporal boundaries, Joyce challenges the facile constructions of self and other used to justify exclusion and conquest since every self is othered to an exponential degree, and he reconfigures the Lucalizod of the *Wake* into a dialogic community by constructing a body politic whose citizens are defined by difference. This promotion of difference carries further political force when we consider Joyce's contradictory manifestations of the same characters. Joyce may narratively demonstrate Bruno's coincidence of contraries through the Shem-Shaun conflicts, but by creating a dream space where HCE can be both Viking invader and Roderick O'Conor, both William III and Charles Stuart Parnell, he explicitly undermines the exclusionary separations of self and other at the heart of political strategies of imperialism and warfare, replacing the impetus to reject and reshape otherness into reflections of the self with a more accommodating desire for individuals to "affirm the [people] they struggle with" because they *are* "the [people] they struggle with."[9] The "plurabilities" of *Finnegans Wake* thus confirm the political force of the Joycean love ethic, as his polyglot celebration of a dialogic Dublin transforms his final novel into the exile's amorous turn towards his homeland, celebrating its past despite its flaws and envisioning the road to its resurrection.

---

[9] Cheng similarly argues that "all attempts to assert the Self by denying the Other are problematized as unstable in the multipleness of *Finnegans Wake*" (269). Williams also characterizes "the babel of voices in *Finnegans Wake*" as Joyce's attempt "to avoid the imperialism of the Cyclopean or one-eyed view, to encourage parallax or the second look, or, as Bloom out of the blue says in Hades, to imagine ourselves as someone else" (*Politically* 85).

Afterword

In his conclusion to *Joyce, Race, and Empire*, Vincent J. Cheng notes that "as narratives of resistance to repressive ideologies, Joyce's texts – especially *Finnegans Wake* – do seem both utopian and hopelessly esoteric as agents for a pluralistic vision of a polylogic, universal discourse which can displace the monologic discourses of both nationalism and imperialism." While his argument that "their effectiveness in political terms, while real, is largely indirect" and felt mostly "as fictional correspondences to cultural or social theories" or "as practical applications of theoretical arguments for certain ideological positions and theories" is almost certainly true (294), we must further consider the idea of the *Wake*'s "resistance" to "repressive ideologies" as "utopian," for a utopian *Wake* would clash not only with Buber's meliorism, but with Joyce's jabs at political utopianism throughout his career. Certainly Joyce's polylogic dreamtext creates a fantastic narrative where shape-shifting characters unite with historical predecessors in a universalized tableau of humanity, but just because the *Wake*'s *narrative* is utopian does not necessarily mean that its *politics* is utopian as well. For one thing, HCE's redemption is not assured at the end of the *Wake*, as it is not certain that ALP's affirming love letter will be endorsed by Lucalizod. (In fact, the public derision of the Porters' lovemaking in III.4 seemingly indicates that HCE is still a pariah at the novel's conclusion.) The cyclical nature of the *Wake* may further complicate matters, for even if ALP and HCE are reunited through each iteration of the narrative, that reconciliation is still followed by an infinite repetition of falls by "Bygmester Finnegan" and a reemergence of the social scorn that compelled ALP's letter in the first place (*FW* 4.18). Joyce does envision a polylogic Irish community through both the narrative and form of *Finnegans Wake*, but he holds no illusions over the ease in which discrimination can be replaced by accommodation, and the numerous repetitions of HCE's fall and resurrection constitute a politics of love that is far from idealistically envisioned.

In fact, the dreamtext ironically creates the conditions for a realistic amorous politics that naturally develops from both Buber's and Joyce's love ethics. Given that the narcissistic episodes of the text suggest the dreamer's constant wrestling with the lover's responsibilities to their beloveds and that the cyclical narrative prevents any permanent resurrection or stable state of amorous bliss, *Finnegans Wake* becomes the exemplary medium where Buber's assessment of love can be realized. Indeed, HCE embodies Buber's concession that "love cannot persist in direct relation," as his repetitious stumbles in Phoenix Park and subordinations of ALP for Issy demonstrate the reality that "every You in the world is doomed by its nature to become a thing or at least to enter into thinghood again and again" (*Thou* 68–9). However, just as the Blooms' love provides the potential for Molly's next rendezvous with Boylan to be overcome, so too does ALP's perpetual defense of HCE highlight the capability for their marriage to be affirmed no matter how many times HCE falls, allowing the love at the foundation of the *Wake* to "catch fire and become present" like the Phoenix imagery of Book IV's resurrection. From this perspective, the *Wake*'s cyclical, polylogic narrative thus enables Joyce to not simply envision a Dublin of "plurabilities," but to create an Irish community where both individuals and citizens constantly wrestle with their responsibilities to each other, where discrimination is replaced with accommodation only to slide back into discriminatory impulses and to replace those with more loving affirmations (and then to fall again). It is thus the capability to love that remains a constant force of the dreamer's ethical and political negotiations of the *Wake* and thus validates Bishop's argument that "far from being the work of the cold and cerebral writer, the *Wake* is a work of exorbitant and almost overwhelming passion and compassion" (371), an amorous text whose inability to be confined by borders or reduced to a monologic narrative renders it an effective vehicle for a pragmatic politics of love.

This multivocal engagement with otherness also makes *Finnegans Wake* the necessary coda for Joyce's love ethic, a text that successfully unites Stephen's desire to "forge in the smithy of my soul the uncreated conscience of my race" with his mother's "pray[er]" to "learn … what the heart is and what it feels." It seems as though the Joycean oeuvre has always been leading to this moment, from *Dubliners*'s stories of amatory escape, to Stephen's pondering the necessary relationship between compassion, freedom, and art, to Richard's struggles with "wish[ing Bertha] well" and the "pleasure of possession" in *Exiles*. *Ulysses* highlights the potential for an effective amorous dialogue through both the Blooms' affirmations of each other and the narrative's parallactic structure, and *Finnegans Wake* celebrates an amorous ethics and politics that is pure parallax, transforming the confusion of Babel into a dialogic storytelling medium and uniting disparate, contradictory characters in a polylogic community whose loving potential is perpetually affirmed by ALP's letter and soliloquy. In that sense, the Joycean oeuvre can be seen as the author's own perpetual negotiations of his attitudes towards love, moving beyond the nausea over "pure men and pure women and spiritual love and love for ever" and the rejections of the "politics of a universal lover" towards a more positive endorsement of an amorous aesthetics that strengthens his career-long criticism of the discriminatory forces of imperialism and nationalism. Recognizing this may make Joyce a bit queasy, but this should not dissuade us from acknowledging his ability to look past the banal sentimentality of ideal romance and assert a pragmatically-viable love ethic, thus making him the author of some of the twentieth century's most meaningful love stories.

Bibliography

Ayres, David. *Modernism: A Short Introduction.* Malden, MA: Blackwell Publishing, 2004. Print.

Baccolini, Raffaella. "'She Had Become a Memory': Women as Memory in James Joyce's *Dubliners.*" *ReJoycing: New Readings of* Dubliners. Eds. Rosa M. Bolletieri Bosinelli and Harold F. Mosher Jr. Lexington: University Press of Kentucky, 1998. 145–64. Print.

Balsamo, Gian. "The Necropolitan Journey: Dante's Negative Poetics in James Joyce's 'The Dead.'" *James Joyce Quarterly.* 40.4 (Summer 2003) 763–82. Print.

Bašić, Sonja. "A Book of Many Uncertainties: Joyce's *Dubliners.*" *ReJoycing: New Readings of* Dubliners. Eds. Rosa M. Bolletieri Bosinelli and Harold F. Mosher Jr. Lexington: University Press of Kentucky, 1998. 13–40. Print.

Bauerle, Ruth H. "Bertha's Role in *Exiles.*" *Women in Joyce.* Eds. Suzette Henke and Elaine Unkeless. Urbana: University of Illinois Press, 1982. 108–31. Print.

———. "Love—that word debated by All." *James Joyce Quarterly.* 36.4 (Summer 1999): 813–23. Print.

Beals, Corey. *Levinas and the Wisdom of Love: The Question of Invisibility.* Waco, Baylor University Press, 2007. Print.

Beckman, Richard. "Perils of Marriage in *Finnegans Wake.*" *James Joyce Quarterly.* 33.1 (Fall 1996): 83–99. Print.

Benstock, Bernard. *Narrative Con/Texts in* Dubliners. Urbana: University of Illinois Press, 1994. Print.

———. *Narrative Con/Texts in* Ulysses. Urbana: University of Illinois Press, 1991.

Benstock, Shari. "The Genuine Christine: Psychodynamics of Issy." *Women in Joyce.* Eds. Suzette Henke and Elaine Unkeless. Urbana: University of Illinois Press, 1982. 169–96. Print.

Bishop, John. *Joyce's Book of the Dark:* Finnegans Wake. Madison: The University of Wisconsin Press, 1986. Print.

Bixby, Patrick. "Perversion and the Press: Victorian Self-Fashioning in 'A Painful Case.'" *A New and Complex Sensation: Essays on Joyce's* Dubliners. Ed. Oona Frawley. Dublin: The Lilliput Press, 2004. 112–21. Print.

Boldrini, Lucia. "The Artist Paring His Quotations: Aesthetic and Ethical Implications of the Dantean Intertext in *Dubliners.*" *ReJoycing: New Readings of* Dubliners. Eds. Rosa M. Bolletieri Bosinelli and Harold F. Mosher Jr. Lexington: University Press of Kentucky, 1998. 228–46. Print.

Booker, M. Keith. "*Finnegans Wake* and *The Satanic Verses*: Two Modern Myths of the Fall." *Critique.* 32.3 (Spring 1991): 190–207. Print.

Bormanis, John. "In the First Bloom of Her New Motherhood: the Appropriation of the Maternal and the Representation of Mothering in *Ulysses.*" *James Joyce Quarterly.* 29.3 (Spring 1992): 593–606. Print.

Bowen, Zack. *Bloom's Old Sweet Song: Essays on Joyce and Music*. Gainesville: University Press of Florida, 1995. Print.

———. Ulysses *as a Comic Novel*. Syracuse: Syracuse University Press, 1989. Print.

———. "Theoretical Bloom." *Twenty-First Joyce*. Eds. Ellen Carol Jones and Morris Beja. Gainesville: University Press of Florida, 2004. 259–70. Print.

Brandabur, Edward. *A Scrupulous Meanness: A Study of Joyce's Early Work*. Urbana: University of Illinois Press, 1971. Print.

Brivic, Sheldon. *Joyce's Waking Women: An Introduction to* Finnegans Wake. Madison: University of Wisconsin Press, 1995. Print.

Brown, Richard. *James Joyce and Sexuality*. Cambridge: Cambridge University Press, 1985. Print.

Buber, Martin. *Between Man and Man*. Trans. Roland Gregor Smith. London: K. Paul, 1947. Print.

———. *I and Thou*. Trans. Walter Kaufmann. New York: Scribners, 1970. Print.

———. *Israel and the World: Essays in a Time of Crisis*. Syracuse: Syracuse University Press, 1997. Print.

———. *The Knowledge of Man: Selected Essays*. Ed. Maurice S. Friedman. Trans. Maurice Friedman and Roland Gregor Smith. Atlantic Highlands, NJ: Humanities Press International, 1988. Print.

———. *Pointing the Way*. Ed. and Trans. Maurice S. Friedman. New York: Schocken Books, 1974. Print.

Burns, Christy L. *Gestural Politics: Stereotype and Parody in Joyce*. Albany: State University of New York Press, 2000. Print.

Byrne, J.F. *Silent Years: An Autobiography with Memoirs of James Joyce and Our Ireland*. New York: Farrar, Straus and Young, 1953. Print.

Castle, Gregory. *Modernism and the Celtic Revival*. Cambridge: Cambridge University Press, 2001. Print.

Cheng, Vincent J. *Joyce, Race, and Empire*. Cambridge: Cambridge University Press, 1995. Print.

Clark, John M. "Writing 'Jerusalem' Backwards: William Blake in 'Exiles.'" *James Joyce Quarterly*. 26.2 (Winter 1989): 183–98. Print.

Colum, Mary. *Life and the Dream*. Garden City, NY: Doubleday and Company, Inc., 1947. Print.

Colum, Padraic. "Introduction." *Exiles*. New York: Viking Press, 1961. Print.

Cotter, David. *James Joyce and the Perverse Ideal*. New York: Routledge, 2003. Print.

Cross, Richard K. "*Ulysses* and *Under the Volcano*: The Difficulty of Loving." *Joyce/Lowry: Critical Perspectives*. Eds. Patrick A. McCarthy and Paul Tiessen. Lexington: University Press of Kentucky, 1997. 63–83. Print.

Day, Robert Adams, Hans Walter Gabler, Philip Gaskell, Arnold Goldman, Clive Hart, David Hayman, and John Kidd. "The Love Word – Panel Discussion." *James Joyce Literary Supplement*. 3 (Fall 1989): 17–8. Print.

Deane, Seamus. "Dead ends: Joyce's finest moments." *Semicolonial Joyce*. Eds. Derek Attridge and Marjorie Howes. Cambridge: Cambridge University Press, 2000. 21–36. Print.

Devlin, Kimberly J. "En-Gendered Choice and Agency in *Ulysses*." Ulysses *in Critical Perspective*. Eds. Michael Patrick Gillespie and A. Nicholas Fargnoli. Gainesville: University Press of Florida, 2006. 70–87. Print.

———. "Pretending in 'Penelope': Masquerade, Mimicry, and Molly Bloom." *Molly Blooms: A Polylogue on "Penelope" and Cultural Studies*. Ed. Richard Pearce. Madison: The University of Wisconsin Press, 1994. 80–102. Print.

———. *Wandering and Return in* Finnegans Wake. Princeton: Princeton University Press, 1991. Print.

Dickson, Jay. "Defining the Sentimentalist in *Ulysses*." *James Joyce Quarterly*. 44.1 (2006): 19–37. Print.

Dillon, Eilís. "The Innocent Muse: An Interview with Maria Jolas." *James Joyce Quarterly*. 20.1 (Fall 1982): 33–66. Print.

Doherty, Gerald. Dubliners*' Dozen: The Games Narrators Play*. Madison: Fairleigh Dickinson University Press, 2004. Print.

Eagleton, Terry. *The English Novel: An Introduction*. Malden, MA: Blackwell Publishing Limited, 2005. Print.

Eide, Marian. *Ethical Joyce*. Cambridge: Cambridge University Press, 2002. Print.

Ellmann, Richard. "A Crux in the New Edition." *Assessing the 1984* Ulysses. Eds. C. George Sandulescu and Clive Hart. Totowa, NJ: Barnes & Noble Books, 1986. 28–34. Print.

———. "The Big Word in 'Ulysses.'" *The New York Review of Books*. 31.16 (25 Oct. 1984). Web. 7 Oct. 2006.

———. *James Joyce: New and Revised Edition*. Oxford: Oxford University Press, 1982. Print.

———. "Preface." *Ulysses*. Ed. Hans Walter Gabler. New York: Vintage Books, 1986. ix–xiv. Print.

Finneran, Richard J. "That Word known to All Men in *Ulysses*." *James Joyce Quarterly*. 33.4 (Summer 1996): 569–82. Print.

Fordham, Finn. *Lots of Fun at* Finnegans Wake*: Unraveling Universals*. Oxford: Oxford University Press, 2007. Print.

Fox, Cheryl. "Absolutely: Redefining the Word Known to All Men." *James Joyce Quarterly*. 29.4 (Summer 1992): 799–804. Print.

Friedman, Alan W. *Party Pieces: Oral Storytelling and Social Performance in Joyce and Beckett*. Syracuse: Syracuse University Press, 2007. Print.

Friedman, Maurice. *Martin Buber and the Eternal*. New York: Human Sciences Press Inc., 1986. Print.

———. *Martin Buber's Life and Work: The Middle Years 1923–1945*. New York: E.P. Dutton, Inc., 1983. Print.

Froula, Christine. *Modernism's Body: Sex, Culture, and Joyce*. New York: Columbia University Press, 1996. Print.

Gifford, Don. *Joyce Annotated: Notes for* Dubliners *and* A Portrait of the Artist as a Young Man. Berkeley: University of California Press, 1982. Print.

Gifford, Don and Robert J. Seidman. Ulysses *Annotated: Notes for James Joyce's* Ulysses. London: University of California Press, 1988. Print.

Glasheen, Adaline. *Third Census of* Finnegans Wake*: An Index of the Characters and Their Roles*. Berkeley: University of California Press, 1977. Print.

Gordon, John. *Joyce and Reality: The Empirical Strikes Back*. Syracuse: Syracuse University Press, 2004. Print.

———. "Love in Bloom, by Stephen Dedalus." *James Joyce Quarterly*. 27.2 (Winter 1990): 241–55. Print.

Harkness, Marguerite. *The Aesthetics of Dedalus and Bloom*. Lewisburg, PA: Bucknell University Press, 1984. Print.

———. A Portrait of the Artist as a Young Man*: Voices of the Text*. Boston: Twayne Publishers, 1990. Print.

Hayman, David. Ulysses*: The Mechanics of Meaning*. Englewood Cliffs: Prentice-Hall, 1970. Print.

Henke, Suzette. *James Joyce and the Politics of Desire*. New York: Routledge, 1990. Print.

———. *Joyce's Moraculous Sindbook: A Study of* Ulysses. Columbus: Ohio State University Press, 1978. Print.

———. "Reconstructing *Ulysses* in a Deconstructive Mode." *Assessing the 1984* Ulysses. Eds. C. George Sandulescu and Clive Hart. Totowa, NJ: Barnes & Noble Books, 1986. 86–91. Print.

Henke, Suzette, and Unkeless, Elaine, eds. *Women in Joyce*. Urbana: University of Illinois Press, 1982. Print.

Hogan, Patrick Colm. *Joyce, Milton, and the Theory of Influence*. Gainesville: University Press of Florida, 1995. Print.

hooks, bell. *All About Love: New Visions*. New York: Harper Perennial, 2001. Print.

Hyman, Suzanne Katz. "'A Painful Case': The Movement of a Story through a Shift in Voice." *James Joyce Quarterly*. 19.2 (Winter 1982): 111–8. Print.

Ingersoll, Earl G. *Engendered Trope in Joyce's* Dubliners. Carbondale: Southern Illinois University Press, 1996. Print.

Jackson, Roberta. "The Open Closet in *Dubliners*: James Duffy's Painful Case." *James Joyce Quarterly*. 37.1/2 (Fall 1999/Winter 2000): 83–98. Print.

Joyce, James. *Dubliners*. New York: Penguin Books, 1992. Print.

———. *Exiles*. New York: Viking Press, 1961. Print.

———. *Finnegans Wake*. New York: Penguin Books, 1999. Print.

———. *Giacomo Joyce*. London: Faber and Faber, 1968. Print.

———. *Letters of James Joyce*. Volume 1. Ed. Stuart Gilbert. New York: Viking Press, 1957. Print.

———. *Letters of James Joyce*. Volume 2. Ed. Richard Ellmann. New York: Viking Press, 1966. Print.

———. *A Portrait of the Artist as a Young Man*. New York: Penguin Books, 1992. Print.

———. *Stephen Hero*. Ed. Theodore Spencer. New York: New Directions Books, 1944. Print.

———. *Ulysses*. Ed. Hans Walter Gabler. New York: Vintage Books, 1986. Print.

Joyce, Stanislaus. *My Brother's Keeper: James Joyce's Early Years*. Ed. Richard Ellmann. Cambridge: Da Capo Press, 2003. Print.

Kimball, Jean. "Love and Death in *Ulysses*: 'Word known to all men.'" *James Joyce Quarterly* 24.2 (Winter 1987): 143–60. Print.

———. *Odyssey of the Psyche: Jungian Patterns in Joyce's* Ulysses. Carbondale: Southern Illinois University Press, 1997. Print.

Kitcher, Philip. *Joyce's Kaleidoscope: An Invitation to* Finnegans Wake. Oxford: Oxford University Press, 2007. Print.

Kristeva, Julia. *Powers of Horror: An Essay on Abjection*. New York: Columbia University Press, 1982. Print.

Lamos, Colleen. "Duffy's Subjectivation: The Psychic Life of 'A Painful Case.'" *European Joyce Studies 10: Masculinities in Joyce: Postcolonial Constructions*. Amsterdam: Rodopi, 2001. 59–71. Print.

Lawrence, Karen. *The Odyssey of Style in* Ulysses. Princeton: Princeton University Press, 1981. Print.

Leighton, Jean. *Simone de Beauvoir on Woman.* Cranbury, NJ: Associated University Presses, 1975. Print.

Leonard, Garry M. *Reading* Dubliners *Again: A Lacanian Perspective*. Syracuse: Syracuse University Press, 1993. Print.

Lewis, Pericles. *Modernism, Nationalism, and the Novel*. Cambridge: Cambridge University Press, 2000. Print.

Mahaffey, Vicki. "Framing, Being Framed, and the Janus Faces of Authority." *Critical Essays on James Joyce's* A Portrait of the Artist as a Young Man. Eds. Philip Brady and James F. Carens. New York: G.K. Hall and Company, 1998. 290–315. Print.

Manganiello, Dominic. *Joyce's Politics*. London: Routledge and Kegan Paul, 1980. Print.

McCarthy, Patrick A. *Joyce, Family,* Finnegans Wake. Eds. Luca Crispi and Catherine Fahy. Dublin: The National Library of Ireland, 2005. Print.

———. *The Riddles of* Finnegans Wake. Rutherford, NJ: Fairleigh Dickinson University Press, 1980. Print.

McCourt, Frank. *The Years of Bloom: James Joyce in Trieste 1904–1920*. Dublin: The Lilliput Press, 2000. Print.

McGee, Patrick. *Joyce Beyond Marx: History and Desire in* Ulysses *and* Finnegans Wake. Gainesville: University Press of Florida, 2001. Print.

McHugh, Roland. *Annotations to* Finnegans Wake, *Third Edition.* Baltimore: The Johns Hopkins University Press, 2006. Print.

Milton, John. "Lycidas." *Complete Shorter Poems*. Ed. John Carey. London: Longman Group UK Limited, 1968. Print.

Mitchell, Andrew J. "Meaning Postponed: *Finnegans Wake* and *The Post Card*." *James Joyce Quarterly*. 44.1 (Fall 2006): 59–76. Print.

Moore, Donald J. *Martin Buber: Prophet of Religious Secularism*. New York: Fordham University Press, 1996. Print.

Mosher Jr., Harold F. "Clichés and Repetition in *Dubliners*: the Example of 'A Little Cloud.'" *ReJoycing: New Readings of* Dubliners. Eds. Rosa M. Bolletieri Bosinelli and Harold F. Mosher Jr. Lexington: University Press of Kentucky, 1998. 53–67. Print.

Norris, Margot. "Anna Livia Plurabelle: The Dream Woman." *Women in Joyce*. Eds. Suzette Henke and Elaine Unkeless. Urbana: University of Illinois Press, 1982. 197–213. Print.

———. *The Decentered Universe of* Finnegans Wake*: A Structuralist Analysis*. Baltimore: The Johns Hopkins University Press, 1974. Print.

———. "The Last Chapter of *Finnegans Wake*: Stephen Finds His Mother." *James Joyce Quarterly*. 11.4 (Fall 1987): 11–30. Print.

———. *Suspicious Readings of Joyce's* Dubliners. Philadelphia: University of Pennsylvania Press, 2003. Print.

O'Brien, Eugene. "'You can never know women': Framing Female Identity in *Dubliners*." *A New and Complex Sensation: Essays on Joyce's* Dubliners. Ed. Oona Frawley. Dublin: The Lilliput Press, 2004. 212–22. Print.

Platt, Len. *Joyce, Race and* Finnegans Wake. Cambridge: Cambridge University Press, 2007. Print.

Polhemus, Robert. *Erotic Faith: Being in Love from Jane Austen to D.H. Lawrence*. Chicago: University of Chicago Press, 1990.

Rabaté, Jean-Michel. *James Joyce and the Politics of Egoism*. Cambridge: Cambridge University Press, 2001. Print.

———. "The Modernity of *Exiles*." *European Joyce Studies 1: Modernity and its Mediation*. Ed. Christine Van Boheemen. Amsterdam: Rodopi, 1989. 23–36. Print.

Reizbaum, Marilyn. *James Joyce's Judaic Other*. Stanford, Stanford University Press, 1999. Print.

Restuccia, Frances. *Joyce and the Law of the Father*. New Haven: Yale University Press, 1989. Print.

Rice, Thomas Jackson. "The Geometry of Meaning in *Dubliners*: A Euclidian Approach." *ReJoycing: New Readings of* Dubliners. Eds. Rosa M. Bolletieri Bosinelli and Harold F. Mosher Jr. Lexington: University Press of Kentucky, 1998. 41–52. Print.

Rickard, John. *Joyce's Book of Memory: The Mnemotechnic of* Ulysses. Durham: Duke University Press, 1999. Print.

Riquelme, John Paul. "Joyce's 'The Dead': The Dissolution of the Self and the Police." *ReJoycing: New Readings of* Dubliners. Eds. Rosa M. Bolletieri Bosinelli and Harold F. Mosher Jr. Lexington: University Press of Kentucky, 1998. 123–41. Print.

———. "'Preparatory to Anything Else': Joyce's Styles as Forms of Memory – The Case of 'Eumaeus.'" Ulysses *in Critical Perspective*. Eds. Michael Patrick

Gillespie and A. Nicholas Fargnoli. Gainesville: University Press of Florida, 2006. 9–34. Print.

Rubin, Jeffrey B. *The Good Life: Psychoanalytic Reflections on Love, Ethics, Creativity, and Spirituality*. Albany: State University of New York Press, 2004. Print.

Sanner, Kristin N. "Exchanging Letters and Silence: Moments of Empowerment in *Exiles*." *James Joyce Quarterly*. 39.2 (Winter 2002): 275–88. Print.

Schmidt, Gilya Gerda. *Martin Buber's Formative Years: From German Culture to Jewish Renewal, 1897–1909*. Tuscaloosa: University of Alabama Press, 1995. Print.

Schwaber, Paul. *The Cast of Characters: a Reading of* Ulysses. New Haven: Yale University Press, 1999. Print.

Shaffer, Brian W. "Kindred by Choice: Joyce's 'Exiles' and Goethe's 'Elective Affinities.'" *James Joyce Quarterly*. 26.2 (Winter 1989): 199–212. Print.

Shelton, Jan. *Joyce and the Narrative Structure of Incest.* Gainesville: University Press of Florida, 2006. Print.

Sicker, Philip. "Leopold's Travels: Swiftian Optics in Joyce's 'Cyclops.'" *Joyce Studies Annual 1995*. Ed. Thomas F. Staley. Austin: University of Texas Press, 1995. 59–78. Print.

Silberstein, Laurence J. *Martin Buber's Social and Religious Thought: Alienation and the Quest for Meaning*. New York: New York University Press, 1989. Print.

Simpson, J.A. and Weiner, E.S.C., eds. *Oxford English Dictionary, Second Edition*. New York: Clarendon Press, 1989. Print.

Singer, Irving. *The Nature of Love: The Modern World.* Chicago: University of Chicago Press, 2009. Print.

Thornton, Weldon. *The Antimodernism of Joyce's* Portrait of the Artist as a Young Man. Syracuse: Syracuse University Press, 1994. Print.

Utell, Janine. *James Joyce and the Revolt of Love: Marriage, Adultery, Desire*. New York: Palgrave Macmillan, 2010. Print.

Valente, Joseph. "Joyce's (Sexual) Choices: A Historical Overview." *Quare Joyce*. Ed. Joseph Valente. Ann Arbor: University of Michigan Press, 1998. 1–16. Print.

———. "Thrilled by His Touch: The Aestheticizing of Homosexual Panic in *A Portrait of the Artist as a Young Man*." *Quare Joyce*. Ed. Joseph Valente. Ann Arbor: University of Michigan Press, 1998. 47–75. Print.

Van Hulle, Dirk. "The Lost Word: Book IV." *How Joyce Wrote* Finnegans Wake*: A Chapter-by-Chapter Genetic Guide*. Eds. Luca Crispi and Sam Slote. Madison: University of Wisconsin Press, 2007. Print.

Vesala-Varttala, Tanja. *Sympathy and Joyce's* Dubliners*: Ethical Probing of Reading, Narrative, and Textuality*. Tampere, Finland: Tampere University Press, 1999. Print.

Wheatley-Lovoy, Cynthia D. "The Rebirth of Tragedy: Nietzsche and Narcissus in 'A Painful Case' and 'The Dead.'" *James Joyce Quarterly*. 33.2 (Winter 1996): 177–93. Print.

Williams, Trevor L. "No Cheer for 'the Gratefully Oppressed': Ideology in Joyce's *Dubliners*." *ReJoycing: New Readings of* Dubliners. Eds. Rosa M. Bolletieri Bosinelli and Harold F. Mosher Jr. Lexington: University Press of Kentucky, 1998. 87–109. Print.

Wright, David G. "The Secret Life of Leopold Bloom and Emily Sinico." *James Joyce Quarterly*. 37.1/2 (Winter 1999/2000). 99–112. Print.

Ziarek, Ewa. "Circe: Joyce's *Argumentum ad Feminam*." *James Joyce Quarterly*. 30.1 (Fall 1992). 51–68. Print.

Index

For Product Safety Concerns and Information please contact our EU representative GPSR@taylorandfrancis.com
Taylor & Francis Verlag GmbH, Kaufingerstraße 24, 80331 München, Germany

www.ingramcontent.com/pod-product-compliance
Lightning Source LLC
Chambersburg PA
CBHW071504110726
47908CB00003B/726

* 9 7 8 1 1 3 8 2 5 0 4 6 8 *